Queer Words, Queer Images

Queer Words, Queer Images

Communication and the Construction of Homosexuality

EDITED BY

R. Jeffrey Ringer

New York University Press
NEW YORK AND LONDON

NEW YORK UNIVERSITY PRESS
New York and London

Library of Congress Cataloging-in-Publication Data
Queer words, queer images : communication and the construction of
homosexuality / edited by R. Jeffrey Ringer.
p.   cm.
Includes bibliographical references and index.
ISBN 0-8147-7440-7 (cloth : alk. paper)—ISBN 0-8147-7441-5 (pbk. : alk. paper)
1. Homosexuality—United States.   2. Homosexuality in television—
United States.   3. Homosexuality in motion pictures.   4. Symbolism
in communication.   I. Ringer, R. Jeffrey.
HQ76.3.U5Q44   1994
306.76′6—dc20   93-30242
                              CIP

New York University Press books are printed on acid-free paper,
and their binding materials are chosen for strength and durability.

Manufactured in the United States of America

10   9   8   7   6   5   4   3   2

Contents

Acknowledgments

Many people have contributed to this project. At the beginning six associate editors (James Darsey, Joe DeVito, Karen A. Foss, Fred Jandt, Mercilee Jenkins, and Lynn Miller) read over 100 essays to identify the best and most appropriate for this volume. Each of these essays was anonymously reviewed by two associate editors. Together we selected fifteen of the essays that appear in this volume. I would like to thank them for the many hours they contributed as readers and for their advice that helped shape this volume.

After these essays were selected I invited a guest author to read each of the essays in a section and to comment upon them. These outstanding individuals (James Chesebro, Larry Gross, Lynn Miller, Dorothy Painter, and Mercilee Jenkins) are experts in their fields. Their essays have added tremendously to this volume by providing synthesis and direction.

I would like to thank several individuals from the Ohio State University. James Darsey served as a liaison while I was working in Denmark for one year. His department provided support for duplicating, mailing, and clerical help. We would like to thank department chair Joseph Foley, Betty Moeller, and Elizabeth Carlson for this assistance. I would also like to thank James Darsey for his comments and advice on the introduction.

In addition to the associate editors and guest authors, the remaining authors were extremely cooperative and understanding of this long process. Their patience has been greatly appreciated.

At St. Cloud State University, Donna Banks provided clerical assistance by typing and mailing letters. The Department of Speech Communication at St. Cloud under Chairs Chuck Vick and Judy Litterst were extremely supportive of me while I was working on this project. I appreciate all of the support I have received from the entire department. Financial assistance and support were provided by Dean Michael Connaughton of the College of Fine Arts and Humanities. Indeed, the entire university has been supportive.

At New York University Press, our editors Niko Pfund and Despina Papazoglou Gimbel have been tremendously supportive and understanding—particularly of missed deadlines. Their assistance has helped make this project a reality.

Finally, the Caucus on Gay and Lesbian Concerns of the Speech Communication Association deserves recognition. Their presence has given all of us the motivation to investigate these important issues that are often ignored by mainstream researchers. Their strength and devotion ensures that we will continue to explore and understand the communication in our lives.

R. JEFFREY RINGER, PH.D.
St. Cloud State University

Queer Words, Queer Images

Introduction

R. Jeffrey Ringer

The origin of this book dates back to 1981. At that time, the Caucus on Gay and Lesbian Concerns of the Speech Communication Association published an anthology of essays on gay male and lesbian communication entitled *Gayspeak: Gay Male and Lesbian Communication.* The central premise of that anthology was that the social reality human beings have created around the concept of homosexuality has made homosexuality an issue. In a departure from investigations that sought to explain aspects of sexual orientation, the responses to the behavior rather than the behavior itself became the legitimate subject of inquiry. Thus, the authors in *Gayspeak* chose to examine human responses to homosexuality from the viewpoint of the communication discipline. "Homosexuality," contended James Chesebro, the editor of *Gayspeak,* "is predominantly a communication problem, and . . . a humane understanding and resolution of this issue is to be found in established frameworks, methods, principles, and perspectives of the discipline of communication" (1981, xiii).

Gayspeak examined the languages of lesbians and gay men, communication patterns among lesbians in established relationships, the rhetoric of the gay rights and lesbian-feminist movements, images of gays and lesbians in the media and drama, the campaign efforts of pro- and antigay forces, as well as other communication related topics. These articles, reflecting the substance and diversity of the communication discipline, have been acknowledged as pioneering efforts in understanding gay and lesbian communication.

The current anthology is based on premises similar to those that motivated its predecessor. The Caucus on Gay and Lesbian Concerns continues to believe in the value of examining the language, nonverbal acts, and symbols of gay men and lesbians. Thus, *Queer Words, Queer Images: Communication and the Construction of Homosexuality* examines the rhetoric of gay politicians, the symbols and strategies used during the coming out process, the strategies used to resolve conflicts in gay and lesbian relationships, and the decision whether or not to come out in the classroom as these reflect the gay and lesbian experience, primarily in the United States, today.

The editor and authors also continue to believe in the importance of examining the ways in which heterosexuals conceive of and respond to homosexual behavior. Thus, this volume critically examines a court case that involves the use of a well-known symbol by a gay/lesbian group, portrayals of gays and lesbians in literature and in the media, and the "female athlete = lesbian" myth.

These concerns focus on what James Darsey (1981), in a contribution to *Gayspeak,* termed the idiographic aspects of gay male and lesbian communication, those aspects that provide insight into the unique patterns, usages, and strategies of the gay male and lesbian communities negotiating with each other and with the larger society, those aspects that would have the greatest importance to the emerging area of gay studies.

But to read these essays only in this light is to neglect a significant part of their value. In addition to their contribution to understanding homosexuals and homosexual behavior, these essays should enrich communication theory in general and should find an audience among those interested in what Darsey identified as their generic aspect. Research into the communication patterns and behaviors of gay and lesbian couples—who often assume different role relationships than members of heterosexual couples—will clearly provide rich information for the development of marital communication theory. Models developed from analysis of one gay man's political campaigns may be useful to other politicians and students of persuasion regardless of sexual orientation. Analysis of portrayals of lesbians and gay men in the media and literature help us develop theory and increase our understanding of the role that media play in all our lives. As the reader will see, most of the articles in this book not only inform us about gay and lesbian communication but inform us about human communication in general.

For each of the five sections in this collection, we have invited a distinguished author to comment on the articles in that section. These authors were asked to reflect upon the major issues identified in the articles in their section, to identify how the concepts and issues raised in these articles relate to communication theory in general, and to identify a research agenda for the area. These commentaries add their own unique perspective to the issues at hand as well as make the book more useful for the classroom. Students reading any section will be guided in their understanding of the material in that section by reading the accompanying commentary.

There are four goals for this book. The first is to provide current substantive research findings for those interested in viewing homosexuality from a communication perspective. The articles reflect five different areas of the communication discipline: gay and lesbian rhetoric; interpersonal communication among lesbians and gay men; portrayals of gay men and lesbians in language and text; portrayals of lesbians and gay men in the media; and a specific issue related to instructional communication—coming out in the classroom. The second goal is to identify how research into gay and lesbian behavior informs communication theory in general. The third is to provide a research agenda for the future. And the fourth is to provide a supplemental textbook for courses that desire to explore the issues raised by the human response to homosexuality.

It was with great pleasure that I was able to work with these authors to make this second volume a reality. I hope that it lives up to the tradition of the original volume by providing an outlet for much-needed research on gay and lesbian communication, encouraging more research, and providing a classroom tool for student exploration of these important issues.

Works Cited

Chesebro, James W. 1981. Introduction to *Gayspeak: Gay Male and Lesbian Communication,* edited by James W. Chesebro, ix–xvi. New York: Pilgrim Press.

Darsey, James. 1981. "'Gayspeak:' A Response." In *Gayspeak: Gay Male and Lesbian Communication,* edited by James Chesebro, 58–67. New York: Pilgrim Press.

PART ONE

Gay and Lesbian Rhetoric

1. The Logic of Folly in the Political Campaigns of Harvey Milk

Karen A. Foss

Harvey Milk did not enter politics until he was forty-three; he lost three of the four political offices he sought; and when finally elected, he served only eleven months in office. The political record of San Francisco's first openly gay supervisor, however, does not tell the whole story. In the course of four political campaigns, Milk moved from being an unknown outsider in virtually every way possible to a member of the Board of Supervisors, a position of considerable political power in San Francisco.

Milk's background offered little evidence that he would become successful in San Francisco politics or that he would become a symbol for gay rights.[1] He grew up in a suburb of New York City and kept his gay identity a secret through college and during a stint in the Navy. Dissatisfied with his chosen career as a high school teacher, Milk moved from job to job before becoming a financial analyst on Wall Street. At the same time, he began working on a friend's Broadway productions, which introduced him to the counterculture of the 1960s. When his partner took a job as stage manager for the San Francisco production of *Hair,* Milk moved with him to San Francisco, again taking a job as a financial analyst. He was fired for burning his BankAmericard during a protest against the Vietnam War, after which he returned to New York to again work in theater. Milk settled permanently in San Francisco in 1973, where he and his new partner, Scott Smith (who would become his campaign manager), opened a store called Castro Camera.

The failure of government to meet people's needs was the impetus for Milk's decision to enter San Francisco politics. Three separate incidents in the summer of 1973 infuriated him: the lack of honesty in government revealed by the Watergate scandal, a special tax charged him as a small-business owner, and a request by a teacher to borrow a projector from the camera store because her district could not afford one.[2] Milk decided he could make a difference in politics and announced his candidacy for the 1973 supervisorial race. He did surprisingly well for a newcomer to San Francisco politics, coming in tenth out of thirty candidates.[3]

Milk ran again for the Board of Supervisors in 1975; this time, he came in seventh after the six incumbents on the Board, all of whom were reelected.[4] George Moscone, the new mayor of San Francisco, appointed Milk to a seat on the Board of Permit Appeals.[5]

Milk announced his decision to run again for public office only two months after taking his seat on the Board of Permit appeals.[6] This time, his goal was the California Assembly; he sought the Democratic nomination for a seat in the Sixteenth District. Again, however, Milk was unsuccessful, losing to Art Agnos by a narrow margin.[7]

Milk was successful when he ran for supervisor for a third time, in 1977. Out of the seventeen candidates in the race, he won 30.5 percent of the votes cast.[8] Milk, however, served only eleven months of his term. On November 27, 1978, Milk and Mayor George Moscone were assassinated by Supervisor Dan White.[9] On the day of the killings, Moscone was to have announced his decision not to reappoint White to the Board of Supervisors, from which White recently had resigned.

On the surface, the campaign strategies that are evident in Milk's political campaigns appear to be the usual moves of a candidate who becomes increasingly astute about the political process; they suggest typical adaptations in terms of language, dress, and decorum to the political arena. Milk's name recognition alone, after conducting three campaigns in four years, undoubtedly contributed to his ultimate political victory. That Milk was gay, however, and ran for office at a time when the gay and lesbian community, even in San Francisco, was not a political force, created a rhetorical situation that was far from ordinary.

In this essay, I suggest that the logic of folly provides a means of explaining how Milk's political campaigns effectively addressed the particular circumstances he confronted as a gay man seeking political office. Milk used the dimensions of folly as an underlying logic to preserve and foster his relationship with the gay community while simultaneously appealing to traditional political audiences. This study of Milk's campaign rhetoric, then, offers a model useful for other gay and lesbian office seekers and may apply to other contexts in which gays and lesbians—and other outsider groups— seek positions of influence without abandoning or compromising their own identities.

In using the term folly in reference to Milk, I am not suggesting the casual meanings of the term—lacking good sense or refusing to accept reality—that are more likely than not to imbue contemporary definitions of folly. Instead, I refer to the notion of folly as defined and experienced in traditional societies. While fools of one sort or another have been part of virtually every culture, traditional folly was a distinct historical phenomenon in prerational societies: "when human societies were not yet ruled by bureaucracy, technology, and the sciences, when human minds were leavened with metaphysical notions and associative patterns of thought, when reality was experienced as a vast field of contingencies, structured mainly by fictitious and magical connections between cause and effect."[10]

In such a worldview, any kind of change or period of transition was experienced with a certain amount of trepidation and awe. Even the expected transitions of everyday life—the movement from one season to another, from the old to the new year, from life to death—were vulnerable times in which reality lost its usual structures and meanings. To cope with these times, traditional people invented rituals and ceremonies that functioned as rites of passage.[11] The fool was held in esteem because s/he could deal with the mysterious and especially difficult phase of transition. Neither male nor female, good nor evil, fools embodied and spoke for worlds that existed beyond reality. They reminded society of the power, energy, and magic of the cosmos, of "what could become of them if they would chance to abandon tradition and forsake the established norms and values of their society."[12]

While modernity has altered profoundly the nature of folly,[13] the essential dimensions of it can still function profitably as a critical framework for illuminating periods of transition. Among the central features of folly is its parasitic status—it is simultaneously outside of and in society. Folly flourishes in those moments that are outside the usual social order and thus is a phenomenon marked by marginality; yet folly is dependent on the very reality it calls into question. The effectiveness of the fool depends on the ability to hold a mirror up to the traditional social order, exaggerating its features and showing that reality as it is experienced could very well be different. The function of folly is to show the members of a society the borders of their worldview, and by bringing to consciousness taken-for-granted assumptions about what reality is, folly reinforces existing values, norms, and meanings of society.

The two techniques that are the special province of the fool are reversal and laughter. Reversal is the epitome of how folly functions since the fool's essential act is to invert the social order and thus suggest that the world may not be as it appears:

Folly would focus on the opposites of human existence, . . . [and] play an irreverent game with them: male fools would dress up and behave like women, female fools would act like men and assume male roles and responsibilities; they would change into animals or undifferentiated, crassly materialistic and rudely erotic monsters. Left would be changed into right, right into left, sacred into secular, secular into sacred. [14]

The technique of reversal permits a society to envision new alternatives and ways of doing and being. Ernesto Grassi's study of folly in the writings of the Italian humanists further underscores the importance of folly as a critical perspective. Grassi sees folly as embodying the fundamental human process, embedded in language, of making connections and seeing similarities; folly is "reality in the unveiling of its essence." [15] Donald Verene, in the preface to Grassi's work on folly, elaborates: "To see human affairs as folly is to have an ontological insight into what is possible in any situation; that is, to see all as folly is to realize that things are never what they seem." [16] Folly, then, is not a loss of contact with reality—a form of psychotic insanity—but the distinctive human capacity to imagine self in new situations and to deal with those situations effectively: "It is folly which allows the projection of . . . one's own desires, hopes, worries, expectations, fears . . . on the stage of life." [17]

Laughter is also the particular province of the fool, a feature that, like reversal, accomplishes important functions for a society beyond mere entertainment. When watching a fool "fool around" in terms of worldviews, meanings, values, and norms, laughter often seems to be "the only sensible response" to the performance: "the fool renders his audience speechless."[18] Under the guise of laughter, ideas that would be unsettling in other circumstances can be raised without anyone having to take them too seriously. Thus, folly provides a way by which to verbalize what has heretofore been unspeakable, and the fool can encourage dialogue about issues that previously were not available for discussion.[19]

Traditional folly, then, was serious business and bore little resemblance to the forms of comedy, humor, and wit that accompany modernity. In contrast to the contemporary tendency to use the word "fool" as only a derogatory label, the traditional fool held a position of considerable importance because of the capacity to respond ritually to a world that was seen as unpredictable, hazardous, and enchanted.

The description of traditional folly has many parallels to the situation in which Milk and the gay community generally found themselves in the early 1970s. San Francisco had become a haven for gays and lesbians, and the long-time residents of the city generally displayed a benign tolerance of the openness of the gay/lesbian community. At the same time, gays had not yet secured representatives in any of the leadership positions in the city; the record on gays and lesbians in politics in San Francisco looked no different from most cities in its reluctance to grant a formal voice to this community.[20] Furthermore, gays had been so continually harassed that they did not see themselves as a group with political power and were reluctant to publicly declare their collective support for any political candidate.[21]

In response to the existing political atmosphere, indirectness characterized gays' approach to politics. The leaders of the gay community urged gays to work to elect liberals who would be sympathetic to their demands once in office, and various gay political clubs were formed to work toward these ends. For all of these liberal friends, however, gays had not been appointed to any city commissions or achieved a comprehensive civil rights law that banned discrimination against gays.

The political world Milk sought to enter, then, was in direct opposition to the marginalized gay world. Political success was granted to those prepared to stay within a narrow range of expectations and behaviors. Typical politicians were straight family men who dressed appropriately in suits and ties; in their campaign rhetoric, their aim was to avoid offending as many segments of their audience as possible. In contrast, Milk was a hippie, which violated traditional values of the political realm about lifestyle and dress; in fact, hippies have been considered examples of contemporary fools in the premium they played on nonrational thoughts and feelings, rejection of rational structures, and a search for "emotionally gratifying enchantments."[22]

That Milk was gay heightened the similarities with images of fools because gays and lesbians, like traditional fools, play havoc with traditional gender roles. What the dominant society has considered "normal" in terms of intimate relationships, reproduction, and family directly is contradicted by the preferences and experiences of gays and lesbians. In fact, many have not considered gays to be human, and inhumanity is a feature frequently ascribed to the fool. In addition, the gay community is known for literally reversing traditional gender roles. Dressing "in drag," for example, flaunts a reversal of gender characteristics and makes problematic the intrinsic connection between sex and gender to which the dominant culture typically subscribes. The similarities between the position of gays and lesbians and fools has not been lost on the gay community. One of the earliest gay groups in the United States, the Mattachine Society, took its name from the Italian Matachinos, court jesters who, behind a mask, could speak the truth to otherwise intractable rulers.[23]

A large gap, then, existed between Milk and the attainment of political office, which he addressed by turning for tactics to folly. Using laughter, reversal, transcendence, and his insider/outsider status, Milk helped create a climate in which dialogue on issues became possible. He also provided a means to integrate the disparate voices of his various constituencies. In order to highlight the progression of his strategies, I will deal with each of Milk's four campaigns in turn.

The 1973 Campaign for Supervisor

In Milk's first campaign for supervisor, his antics demonstrate especially close parallels with the role of the fool. This is not surprising given the gap that existed between the gay reality and the political system in San Francisco. Among the most obvious manifestations of the presence of folly was Milk's total disregard for political authority and decorum. He wore blue jeans and refused to cut his long hair, pulling it back instead into a ponytail. He was also given to making outrageous statements that only confirmed the beliefs of many about him—that he was at best foolish and at worst crazy. Michael Wong, who later became a staunch Milk supporter, had such a reaction upon meeting Milk for the first time at a candidate's forum:

I had heard from the so-called gay leaders—Jim Foster and the Alice B. Toklas Gay Democratic Club—that this guy was a nut. I was very wary of even talking to him. But in the course of the conversation I was really impressed with the issues he brought up. . . . But halfway through this conversation, . . . Harvey told us that he thought . . . that some father who learned that he's homosexual will come out and shoot at him and he'll survive the shooting but that'll give him so much sympathetic publicity that he'll win on that. . . . And then I thought, Jim Foster was right—this guy is a nut.[24]

Milk's irreverence gained him considerable negative publicity, but Milk knew that even this kind of press kept his name before the voters: "Sticks and stones may break my bones, but just spell my name right."[25] His embodiment of folly made him visible to voters in ways that less outrageous approaches would not have done.

In addition to the irreverence he exhibited toward political decorum, Milk played up his marginalized role. As an outsider in virtually every way possible—gay, Jewish, a hippie, a newcomer to San Francisco and to politics—he portrayed himself as a symbol for all underrepresented and disenfranchised groups: "I stand for all those who feel that the government no longer understands the individual and no longer respects individual rights."[26] In a flier about the waste of taxpayer money, he focused on how he would serve as a representative of all disgruntled taxpayers because of his embodiment of that role: "I am an irate taxpayer. . . . I'm irate enough for all of us. . . . Give me your support and I'll fight for you. . . . I'll fight for you because I am you."[27] Milk capitalized on the marginality that is endemic to the fool's role to create identification with underrepresented groups in the city. His campaign slogan, "Milk Has Something for Everybody," proclaimed this desired identification.[28]

Milk's first campaign also revealed evidence of the technique of reversal, holding a mirror up to existing society and showing its alternate possibilities. Milk's portrayal of what was needed to make San Francisco a great city provided one example of this strategy in action. Milk envisioned a city that could be improved with less rather than more money:

San Francisco can start right now to become number one. . . . We can start overnight. We don't have to wait for budgets to be passed, surveys to be made, political wheelings and dealings . . . for it takes no money . . . it takes no compromising to give the people their rights . . . [and] it takes no money to respect the individual. It takes no political deal to give people freedom. It takes no survey to remove repression.[29]

Milk also used the technique of reversal to construct and present a vision of the city that directly contradicted that espoused by the Board of Supervisors. While the Board members advocated building more garages in downtown San Francisco, Milk argued that "private auto traffic in [the] downtown core area" be banned.[30] Rather than proposing complicated solutions for improving the city's rapid transit system, Milk argued for an amendment to the city charter to require city officials to ride Muni to work everyday: "It's the only way that the people of San Francisco will ever get better Muni service."[31] As a final example, Milk contrasted traditional images of the impersonal nature of city life with images of neighborhoods as places of connection and caring:

The American Dream starts with the neighborhoods. If we wish to rebuild our cities, we must first rebuild our neighborhoods. And to do that, we must understand that the quality of life is more important than the standard of living. To sit on the front steps—whether it's a veranda in a small town or a concrete stoop in a big city—and talk to our neighborhoods [*sic*] is infinitely more important than to huddle on the living room lounger and watch a make-believe world in not-quite living color.[32]

The outcome of Milk's "foolish" techniques during the 1973 campaign was dialogue, one of the possible results of a fool's performance. In the process of pointing out the range of choices that existed in terms of political candidates and their visions of San Francisco, Milk created an atmosphere in which dialogue among opposing factions was possible. He then cultivated opportunities in which that dialogue could culminate in action. One of his campaign leaflets, for example, listed Milk's position on thirteen city issues on the left-hand side of the page; on the right side, he described the present Board's stance on each issue. In the middle, complete with blank lines, was a column titled, "Write in Your Position."[33] Milk sought to encourage conversation among the disparate groups in San Francisco, even if that conversation meant his own position would not necessarily win out. He wanted the supervisors talking with the streetsweepers, the gays with the union workers, and police officers with small-business owners.

Another example of Milk's ability to facilitate the exchange of ideas where normally there would be none—a hallmark of the fool—occurred because of the treatment Milk received at a candidates' forum. Milk and another supervisorial hopeful, Alfred Siniora, called a joint press conference "to complain of shabby treatment" by the various city clubs that held candidates' nights, charging the clubs with encouraging their members to vote early in the evening before even hearing the lesser known candidates.[34] That Milk—a gay Jewish Democrat—and Siniora—an Arab Republican businessman—joined forces proved especially effective in generating talk about campaign procedures.

Ironically, this incident proved even more effective for Milk's purposes when Siniora reprinted one of Milk's campaign fliers, simply substituting his name for Milk's. Rather than berating his opponent as another candidate might have done, Milk used the incident to stage yet another performance and to generate even more dialogue. Milk called a second press conference at which he pointed out that if an Arab Republican could use his campaign literature, he must be doing a good job of bridging ideologies.[35]

In his first campaign, Milk handled his entrance into politics as an openly gay man in a manner that heightened the contrast between the world of which he was a part and the political world to which he aspired. His unusual campaign practices and dress made him laughable, but under the guise of laughter, he was able to introduce some possibilities that otherwise would not have been tolerated—foremost among them, the possibility of a gay politician. Milk also used the role of the fool to encourage questioning of the taken-for-granted political reality in San Francisco. In making use of the fool's technique of reversal, too, he encouraged dialogue among the opposing groups whose positions he highlighted in his campaign. Milk's tactics, which generally earned him amusement if not ridicule, allowed him to get his foot in the door of San Francisco politics while simultaneously maintaining identification with the marginalized gay community.

The 1975 Campaign for Supervisor

In his 1975 bid for supervisor, Milk continued to use the fool's technique of reversal to preserve his identification with the gay community and to reach new audiences that traditionally avoided alliances with marginalized groups. Whereas in his first campaign, he linked underrepresented groups and appealed to voters to see them as a collective source of power ignored by the political establishment, in his second campaign he sought out groups at opposing ends of the political spectrum and showed the similarities among them. This move created a strong awareness of the need for some kind of middle ground which, of course, Milk saw himself as providing.

Even his dress in the second campaign suggested a mediating stance between his initiation into politics with the 1973 campaign and his potential inclusion in it. Milk cut his hair and exchanged his jeans for three-piece suits that he bought second-hand from a dry cleaners.[36] His manner of accommodation—wearing second-hand suits rather than investing in an elaborate new wardrobe—maintained his fundamental identification with his hippie roots and did not signal a fundamental shift in values to the traditional establishment. He also swore off marijuana and bathhouses—not because he no longer believed in the lifestyle these activities represented, but because he believed he could make a difference in San Francisco if elected to political office: "I decided this [his political career] was all too important to have it wrecked because of smoking a joint or being in a raid at some bathhouse."[37] Pointing up opposites is very much in line with the functions of traditional folly. Where Milk deviated was in specifying a moderate ground—something usually left to the audience's imagination in a fool's performance.

The most prominent example of Milk addressing and bringing together disparate groups in order to provoke the possibility of new ways of seeing the political situation was reversal of the traditional images of gays and union members. Whereas unions typically are seen as effective at collective political activity and gays were viewed as nonpoliticized wimps, Milk was successful at organizing gays to boycott Coors beer in gay bars as part of a Teamsters' action against beer distributors who would not sign a union contract.[38] This success earned him the endorsement of several labor unions, despite the traditional disparity between gays and labor unions. At first the reaction among the rank and file was what might be expected: " 'Whaddaya mean you're thinkin' of endorsin' this Harvey Milk guy? For Chrissakes, I'm supposed to go back to work and tell the guys we endorsed some goddamn fruit for a supervisor.' "[39] But when Milk managed to do what the union had been unable to accomplish—implement an effective boycott—union leaders began to think differently about Milk's candidacy.

Milk's ability to offer a middle position between these opposing groups came in large part from his personal ability to talk the language of whatever audience he was with. A labor leader praised Milk this way: "A lot of our guys think gays are little leprechauns tip-toeing to florist shops, but Harvey can sit on a steel beam and talk to some ironworker who is a mean sonuvabitch and probably beats his wife when he has a few too many beers, but who would sit there and talk to Harvey like they knew each other for years."[40] In fact, union members were responsible for Milk's next campaign slogan. When Milk sought but failed to win the endorsement of the entire Labor Council, members of the fire fighters' union arrived at Castro Camera to cheer Milk up, with "Make Mine Milk" chalked on the backs of their rubber coats.[41] In contrast to his earlier slogan, "Milk Has Something for Everybody," this slogan was individualistic in tone and suggested Milk's ability to appeal to widely divergent groups, each in different ways. He presented himself as the candidate of choice of many groups and individuals, each with their own reasons for voting for him.

Milk's capacity to hold up for reflection both the reality of the political establishment and its marginalized opposite—the gay community—also was visible in his popularization of references to himself as the "unofficial mayor of Castro Street."[42] Milk, in fact, may have created this title for himself; but whether it was bestowed or created, it showed Milk's awareness of the need to maintain identification with both groups between which he mediated—gays and the political establishment.

As a member of the gay community—the unofficial dimension of his identity because of gays' marginalized status—Milk threw himself into efforts to improve the Castro, the primary gay neighborhood in San Francisco. He started the highly successful Castro Street Fair and resurrected and ran the Castro Village Association, an organization for merchants to deal with problems of the neighborhood.[43] At the same time, the very efforts he made on behalf of the Castro showed his organizational talents, sensibilities, and energy to the larger political community in a manner befitting the best of mayors. In this way, Milk managed an ongoing reversal of focus for both the gay and straight constituencies. He showed the establishment as the reverse of his Castro neighborhood, unable to function properly because of bureaucratic practices; at the same time, he offered the Castro as an example of effective political functioning.

By the second campaign, Milk's use of folly concentrated almost solely on the technique of reversal. He pointed out how groups that seemingly had nothing in common could indeed find areas of agreement. In highlighting the differences among these groups, Milk created an awareness of the need for a common rallying point and offered himself as the appropriate candidate to handle this role because of his understanding of all of the disparate positions. Although Milk did not win this election, George Moscone appointed him to the Board of Permit Appeals following the campaign, a sign of Milk's growing clout with established political forces.

The 1976 Assembly Campaign

Milk's decision, after only a few months on the Board of Permit Appeals, to run for the Democratic nomination for a seat in the California Assembly, appears unwise from the standpoint of traditional political analysis: he had been appointed to a position of some clout in the city but gave it up to run again for a political office that he might not win. The framework of folly, however, provides a different reading of this campaign. Fundamental to Milk's political vision was the election of representatives from marginalized groups. In his announcement of his bid for the Assembly, Milk stated: "I think representatives should be elected by the people—not appointed. . . . I think a representative should earn his or her seat. I don't think the seat should be awarded on the basis of service to the machine."[44] While referring to a political deal, struck over a year earlier, between the top political leaders in the Democratic party to run Art Agnos as the Democratic candidate, Milk's statement also reflected his own position as an appointee to the Board of Permit Appeals. In accepting a political appointment, Milk had allowed the political establishment to dictate the role he would play, not those whom he identified as his political base.

In addition, it offended Milk's sense of politics that a deal had been struck, so far in advance of the election, as to who the Democratic candidate would be. He chose to violate the political decorum expected in such situations by calling attention to the deal and proposing a deal of his own. Milk called those party officials who had decided on Agnos as the candidate and said that he would stay out of the race if he were backed by the Democratic party for supervisor in 1977.[45] In this situation, Milk brought to public awareness the existence of a behind-the-scenes political decision-making machine that was the real means by which candidates were chosen. Milk suggested, in his exposé of a political counter-reality, that he was outside the political machine and would keep the people's needs, not those of the machine, in mind.

While Milk began the campaign by presenting himself as outside the political establishment, he reversed the notion of insider/outsider as the campaign progressed by describing himself as the true insider to what mattered politically:

He's [Art Agnos] been an observer, not a participant, and has never really experienced the daily fight for survival that most of us have to face. I'm not being accusatory here—in some respects, I may be envious. I'm a small businessman and I'm well aware of the uncertainties of the economy, exactly what the "inflationary spiral" means when I'm forced to raise prices to my customers, and how taxes can eat into your earnings.[46]

Milk also reversed the meanings usually associated with being human. In this campaign, he suggested that he was fully human in contrast to the dehumanizing nature of the political machine, an image that also played off of the image of gays as not fully human. His campaign slogan was "Milk versus the Machine," and the contrast between humans and machines dominated his campaign literature: "The overriding issue is simply: do the people . . . that make up the Sixteenth Assembly District have the right of political self-determination—or, can the machine take that right away? Machines operate on oil and grease; they're dirty, dehumanizing, and too often unresponsive to any needs by those of the operators."[47]

In addition, Milk also made his business experience a major campaign theme to counter fears across the state that he was a gay radical. Thus, in another reversal, Milk essentially ran as a conservative candidate. The only two public officials who endorsed Milk were, in fact, State Senator Milton Marks, the only Republican legislator from San Francisco, and Quentin Kopp, the most conservative member of the San Francisco Board of Supervisors.[48]

During this campaign, too, Milk began to employ strategies of transcendence that are characteristic of folly—the ability to be simultaneously embedded in a social order and also able to visualize broader possibilities. In Milk's case, he spoke as a member of the gay community, but constructed a vision that allowed all groups to participate in and benefit from the enfranchisement of gays. Ironically, Milk's opponent, Art Agnos, was seemingly responsible for Milk's deliberate incorporation of transcendence into this campaign. After hearing Milk's pitch at numerous candidates' forums, Agnos is said to have suggested that Milk needed a more upbeat finish to his speeches.[49] Milk began to conclude his speeches with an appeal to hope with which all disenfranchised groups could identify. This became the standard closing (with minor variations in terms of town names) to his speeches:

And the young gay people in the Altoona, Pennsylvanias and the Richmond, Minnesotas who are coming out . . . : The only thing they have to look forward to is hope. And you have to give them hope. . . . Without hope, not only gays, but the blacks, the seniors, the handicapped . . . will give up. And if you help elect . . . more gay people, that gives a green light to all who feel disenfranchised, a green light to move forward. It means hope to a nation that has given up because if a gay person makes it, the doors are open to everyone.[50]

Milk's use of reversal in the Assembly campaign was more subtle and varied than in his previous campaigns. Whereas in the second campaign he had emphasized divisiveness in order to provoke discussion about a middle ground, during this campaign, he moved to a strategy of transcendence to solidify all of the positions he had constructed previously without abandoning his fundamental identification with gays.

The 1977 Campaign for Supervisor

In Milk's final campaign—his successful 1977 bid for supervisor—he continued to offer the juxtaposition of insider/outsider roles he had offered to voters in his previous campaign. The portrayal of himself as a true insider was even more fully pronounced, however, in that he emphasized what he had accomplished for San Francisco despite never having held office. Milk's personal notes on the campaign began with the question: "Since there is no incumbent in the district [5] it will be a race of 'Why me over the others?' " Milk's answer was that he functioned as an incumbent.[51] His campaign materials repeatedly listed his role in starting the Castro Street Fair, his community activities, and his willingness to speak out forcefully and consistently on the issues.[52]

At the same time that he presented himself as an insider, he also reinforced his independence from the political establishment, thus holding on to the position his fool's persona had established—that of a political maverick. He exaggerated his account of the consequences of his decision to run for Assembly in order to distinguish himself from the political status quo and to portray himself as its victim: "Harvey was appointed to the Board of Permit Appeals, the first gay person appointed to a city commission. Later he was fired for his political independence."[53] In fact, Milk knew in advance he would be dismissed from the Board by Mayor Moscone if he chose to run for the Assembly. Likewise, in describing his Navy experience, Milk made it sound as if he had been dishonorably discharged because he was gay: "Harvey Milk was a decorated deep-sea rescue diver during the Korean War. Then the Navy found out he was gay."[54] In actuality, Milk served out his term of enlistment without the Navy discovering his homosexuality. While exaggeration is a frequent campaign tactic, in Milk's case such embellishments served to demonstrate his willingness to be part of the political system while also maintaining his distance from it, a traditional stance for the fool.

Milk as Supervisor

Milk's election brought him full circle—from using laughter to verbalize the previously unspeakable proposition of a gay politician, to embodying that possibility once in office. Whereas in earlier campaigns he concentrated on getting various groups to start talking to and taking gays seriously, now he could simply urge gays to speak out for themselves: "I'm tired of the silence, so I'm going to talk about it. And I want you to talk about it."[55] For Milk, his election signalled possibilities for dialogue that had not previously been available: "If every Gay person were to come out only to his/her own family, friends, neighbors and fellow workers, within days the entire state would discover that we are not the stereotypes generally assumed."[56]

One of Milk's ways of "talking about it" was to speak out publicly, as an elected official, against Proposition 6. Shortly after his election, state senator John Briggs introduced a ballot initiative which, if successful, would have allowed school boards to fire teachers who practiced, advocated, or indicated an acceptance of homosexuality.[57] Milk stumped the state, debating Briggs and giving speeches about gay issues in order to make sure that accurate information about gays was available to the public. Milk genuinely believed that "talking about it is the beginning of understanding,"[58] so even the talk that occurred during the campaign over Proposition 6 encouraged him: it meant people were finally talking openly about gays and lesbians.

The importance of dialogue as an outcome of the fool's performance also characterized Milk's relationship with another new member of the Board of Supervisors—Dan White. The elections of Milk and White typified the diverse citizenry of San Francisco; White, an Irish Catholic police officer, represented the conservative, working class neighborhoods of the city, while Milk stood for a liberal and/or gay constituency. The two made several joint appearances on local talk shows, and Milk was optimistic about their working relationship on the Board of Supervisors: "I'm gonna sit next to him every day and let him know we're not all those bad things he thinks we are. . . . As the years pass, the guy can be educated. . . . Everyone can be reached."[59] As a supervisor Milk optimistically continued to carry forward those elements of folly that had characterized his campaigns.

Milk's Assassination

A discussion of Milk's adoption of the logic of folly would be incomplete without an attempt to understand his death in those terms. While assassination is, on the surface, incongruous with folly, there are elements of folly that hint at the possibilities of a tragic ending.

One way of explaining the ultimate demise of an individual functioning within the frame of folly is that it always is a partial way of seeing the world. Looking back at what Kenneth Burke calls a "happy time,"[60] we realize that folly deals with exaggerations and contrasts; thus, the frame is incapable of simultaneously encompassing all of the necessary motivations and features of a situation. Certain "over-emphases and under-emphases" result, in which "favorable factors are seen too favorably [and] unfavorable factors are neglected. While the thinker trains himself and his audience to balance on one tightrope, history is stretching a tightrope elsewhere."[61]

In Milk's case, his optimistic belief in the powers of reason and dialogue to win over Dan White may have been an example of an "over-emphasis" that kept Milk from seeing his relationship with White clearly. As the liberal and conservative anchor points on the Board of Supervisors, Milk and White disagreed fundamentally on many issues. Milk refused to consider the possibility that White could not be convinced by continued discussion and debate. He was caught up in the belief in the power of dialogue that is a function of folly.

The natural divisiveness that is inherent to folly, too, may help explain Milk's assassination. Perhaps the oppositions set in place by the mirroring of alternative realities cannot be completely overcome by laughter. The divisiveness of folly may not be resolved so much as it is covered up or ignored in favor of a happier attitude. Milk's efforts to unify gays and other disenfranchised groups may have caused him not to attend to the depth of the divisive undercurrent that continued to exist in San Francisco. White's act simply pointed out how profound that divisiveness still was.

A final possibility—and perhaps the most appropriate explanation—is found in the original reasons for folly's existence: to provide a means of coping with a hazardous, often unexplainable, and chaotic world. Milk's death may simply exemplify a period of transition when almost anything can happen. While folly is designed to ritualize and help us move through such times, it does not prevent the unexplainable from occurring. Interestingly, too, Milk himself had premonitions of his own violent death,[62] which is not without parallels with folly, since fools were considered by some to be seers with special abilities to "convey messages from beyond, from the yet unseen world."[63]

Conclusions

In this study of Harvey Milk's political campaigns, I suggest that his success can be explained in terms of the frame of folly. Faced with a difficult political challenge—moving from the marginalized status of a gay, unknown newcomer to a position of leadership in San Francisco—Milk used strategies grounded in folly to manage the transition between the two worlds.

Milk's approach to his political situation suggests that there may be a progression in terms of the use of folly as a rhetorical strategy. Milk's tactics changed over time as he closed the gap between gays as a neglected political audience and personal political power as a gay man. In his 1973 campaign, Milk did not single out his homosexuality as a campaign issue, but included it as one of many reasons for his disenfranchised status. At a time when the possibility of a gay office holder was unthinkable, Milk raised the issue under the guise of laughter and ridicule, with himself in the fool's role. While he had little chance of actually winning a supervisorial post, his outrageous tactics put his name before the voters and brought to public awareness the notion that a gay man could be elected to office. Milk's willingness to fully assume the fool's persona proved an extremely effective way to give voice to a silenced group: the public did not have to appear to take Milk seriously, yet they could not avoid thinking about the issues he raised. Milk also introduced the fool's strategy of reversal, mirroring back to San Franciscans another vision of the city: one in which revitalized neighborhoods and quality of life take precedence over traditional concerns of city bureaucrats with traffic, business, and parking. Thus, Milk juggled his two audiences—gays and the political establishment—identifying the specific concerns of each but also introducing each to the other. His ability to reinforce the individualistic features of a political audience while ultimately working to achieve unity among his diverse constituencies characterized all of Milk's campaigns.

When Milk ran a second time for supervisor—in 1975—he directed attention to a political middle ground by highlighting opposing groups and showing what they had in common. One of the functions folly serves is to identify the borders of a culture, which prompts an awareness of and appreciation for traditional norms and values. Similarly, Milk cultivated a moderate position for himself by showing that he had something to offer widely divergent groups. The oxymoron of the "unofficial mayor of Castro Street," invented in this campaign, captured his efforts to force together jarring opposites—to provoke dialogue among groups that usually saw themselves as having nothing to say to each other.

Milk's bid for the California Assembly saw him offer an even greater number of reversed images to his voters: he presented himself as a conservative small business owner concerned about the state's fiscal record, he showed himself to be a humane alternative to the political machine, and he labelled himself a political insider because he knew about day-to-day issues of survival. Milk's willingness to project a multifaceted image of himself as a potential officeholder increased the number of audiences to which he could appeal.

During this campaign, too, the fool's capacity to be outside of but in society simultaneously also emerged in Milk's strategy of transcendence. He introduced his "hope" speech during this campaign, in which he stated that if a gay man could win a political office, the process essentially was open to all disenfranchised groups. While maintaining his fundamental allegiance with his gay constituency, he effectively broadened his appeal to suggest benefits to all society from such a possibility.

Finally, by his third run for supervisor, and his fourth campaign in as many years, Milk projected himself as within the political establishment. He ran as if he were an incumbent, although he had never held office, citing his extensive record of political activity. At the same time, he did not divorce himself from the marginality of the gay community; he reinforced his image as a political maverick, ensuring those marginalized groups that had constituted his original audience that he would indeed retain the independence of an outsider while in office. When finally elected, he became a spokesperson for those marginalized groups that previously had not had a voice in the political system. Not content to serve as their representative, he also urged gays to speak for themselves in order to break down stereotypes. Milk thus essentially moved from a position of verbalizing an unspeakable issue to becoming a voice for that position in political office.

Milk's use of the strategies of laughter, reversal, simultaneous insider/ outsider, and transcendence effectively allowed him to court two different constituencies at once. Each of these techniques succeeds because it contains two levels of meaning that work in concert: laughter takes precedence over talk; reversal shows two paired worlds, each with alternative possibilities; the insider/outsider aspect of folly allows for competing vantage points to coexist; and transcendence depends on incorporating competing perspectives but rising above them all to see the whole picture. The fool's role thus allowed Milk to keep both the views of his gay followers in mind while creating the necessary identifications with the political establishment.

The adoption of the logic of folly, too, seems to have the benefit of catching and keeping one's audiences always off-guard. The role of the fool has a certain immunity, because of the difficulty of figuring out how best to respond to the fool's tactics. Those who mock a fool become foolish themselves, and any response has the possibility of backfiring.[64] Folly provides a certain amount of protection for a candidate wishing to get a start in an alien context—as politics was for gays and lesbians in the early 1970s— because the role is largely an untouchable one. The role allows the candidate a measure of control that is not possible with other roles that are dependent upon the proper performances by a supporting cast. The fool, while certainly dependent on an audience in crucial ways, does not wait for them to dictate a performance.

Of course, folly must be used well in order to succeed, and there undoubtedly are many for whom this tactic would be inappropriate. Milk happened to be a highly energetic, charismatic figure with a love of theatrics and nothing to lose—the perfect candidate for the fool's role. He also had the benefit of four campaigns in which to adjust his image of the fool to fit the changing circumstances. This role may not be an effective strategy in only a single run for office because it does not allow the candidate time to counter the early antics—designed to attract initial attention—with more serious efforts at reversal and transcendence. Folly, however, is a critical frame that deserves further attention, especially for use by marginalized groups who wish to enter a mainstream context.

Notes

1. All information about Milk's life, prior to his political career, is taken from Randy Shilts, *The Mayor of Castro Street: The Life and Times of Harvey Milk* (New York: St. Martin's Press, 1982). For an overview of Milk's life and career, see Karen A. Foss, "Harvey Milk: 'You Have to Give Them Hope,' " *Journal of the West* 27 (April 1988): 75–81.
2. Shilts, 71.
3. Ibid., 79.
4. Ibid., 107.
5. Ibid., 128.
6. "Milk Will Run—Loses Permit Board Seat," *San Francisco Chronicle*, March 10, 1976: 6.
7. Ron Moskowitz, "Harvey Milk Blames 2 Factors for Defeat," *San Francisco Chronicle*, June 10, 1976: 7.
8. "The Complete Election Results," *San Francisco Chronicle*, November 10, 1977: 4.
9. Dan White's resignation and subsequent efforts to be reappointed apparently triggered the assassinations. For information about the killings, see "Another Day of Death," *Time*, December 11, 1978: 24–26; "Mayor Was Hit 4 Times," *San Francisco Chronicle*, November 28, 1978: 1, 12; and Mike Weiss, *Double Play: The San Francisco City Hall Killings* (Reading, Mass.: Addison-Wesley, 1984). On May 21, 1979, White was convicted on two counts of voluntary manslaughter; he served less than five years of his sentence before being paroled. See Michael Weiss, "Trial and Error," *Rolling Stone* 12 (July 1979): 47–49; and Katy Butler and Randy Shilts, "Big S.F. Protests Against Dan White," *San Francisco Chronicle*, January 7, 1984: 2. The film *The Times of Harvey Milk*, produced by Richard Schmeichen and directed and co-produced by Robert Epstein (Cinecom International Films, 1986), also spends a great deal of time on the killings, White's trial, and the response of the gay community to his sentence. White committed suicide on October 21, 1985. See "S.F. Mayor's Killer Dies in His Garage," *San Francisco Chronicle*, October 22, 1985: 1.
10. Anton C. Zijderveld, *Reality in a Looking-Glass: Rationality through an Analysis of Traditional Folly* (Boston: Routledge & Kegan Paul, 1937), 1.

11. Arnold van Gennep, *The Rites of Passage,* trans. Monika B. Vizedom and Gabrielle L. Caffee (Chicago: University of Chicago Press, 1960), 44.
12. Zijderveld, 4.
13. Zijderveld argues that in modernity, folly has lost its impact and reason for existence: "It withered away because Rational Man could no longer acknowledge the existence and the relevance of contingency and spuriousness. . . . That is, life is no longer experienced in terms of transitional phases but instead structured in a uniform, predominantly bureaucratic manner" (ibid., 32).
14. Ibid., 1.
15. Ernesto Grassi and Maristella Lorch, *Folly and Insanity in Renaissance Literature* (Binghamton, N.Y.: Medieval and Renaissance Texts and Studies, 1986), 92.
16. Donald Phillip Verene, "Preface," ibid., 11.
17. Ibid., 89.
18. Zijderveld, 16–17.
19. Ibid., 26.
20. Shilts, 61.
21. As late as 1971, police arrested an average of 2,800 gay men a year on public sex charges in San Francisco, in contrast to only sixty-three such arrests during that year in New York City. These high numbers are attributed to Mayor Joseph Lawrence Alioto's desire to bring a Catholic cardinal's post to San Francisco, which he felt was unlikely as long as the city "allowed perverts to run wild." See Shilts, 62.
22. Zijderveld, 161.
23. Shilts, 26.
24. Michael Wong, interviewed by David Lamble in *Harvey Milk Remembered,* an audio documentary compiled and produced by David Lamble, San Francisco, 1979.
25. Shilts, 78. Ironically, when Milk finally won election to the Board of Supervisors, the *San Francisco Chronicle* misspelled his name, substituting an "N" for the "M." See Jerry Burns, "New S.F. District Supervisors—Six Incumbents are Elected," *San Francisco Chronicle,* November 9, 1977: 1.
26. "Shopowner Runs for Supervisor," *San Francisco Examiner,* July 27, 1973: 3.
27. "Harvey Milk: Harvey Comes Down On: The Waste of Taxpayers' Money," 1975, Harvey Milk Archives, San Francisco, California.
28. Shilts, 72.
29. Milk, "Address to the Joint International Longshoremen and Warehousemen's Union of San Francisco and to the Lafayette Club," September 10, 1973, 2, Harvey Milk Archives.
30. "Harvey Milk for Supervisor: 'Positions' Paper," 1973, Harvey Milk Archives.
31. "New Ploy: Make VIPs Ride Muni," *San Francisco Examiner,* September 28, 1973: 4.
32. Shilts, 353–54.
33. "Harvey Milk for Supervisor: 'Positions' Paper."

34. "S.F.'s Strange Alliance," September 22, 1973, *San Francisco Chronicle;* and "An Open Letter to the Mayor of San Francisco," September 22, 1973, Harvey Milk Archives.
35. Shilts, 78.
36. Ibid., 97.
37. Ibid., 80. Milk's decision to cut his hair and stop visiting the baths suggest symbols traditionally associated with rites of passage. To cut the hair "is to separate oneself from the previous world," while the presence of a taboo prohibiting sex is common when an individual "wishes to enter the sacred world" (van Gennep, 166 and 169). Obviously, I am not suggesting that there was anything beyond audience adaptation (in the case of Milk cutting his hair) and a desire to avoid arrest and therefore damage a potential political career (in Milk's decision to stop frequenting the baths). Nevertheless, the fact that these acts, which have such strong significance in many cultures, occurred simultaneously suggest that this was a pivotal point in Milk's decision to seriously seek a political career.
38. Shilts, 83.
39. Ibid., 95.
40. Ibid., 97–98.
41. Ibid., 98.
42. Ibid., 87.
43. Milk's revival of the Castro Village Association is described by Shilts, 89–90. His role in starting the Castro Street Fair is described in a campaign brochure. See "Street Fairs, Harvey Milk & You," 1977, Harvey Milk Archives.
44. Shilts, 134.
45. Ibid., 131.
46. "Milk Forum: My Concept of a Legislator," *Bay Area Reporter,* May 27, 1976.
47. "Statement of Harvey Milk: Candidate for the 16th Assembly District," March 9, 1976, Harvey Milk Archives.
48. Shilts, 144.
49. Ibid., 142–43.
50. Milk, "The Hope Speech," in Shilts, 363.
51. "The Campaign: General Notes," 1977, 1, Harvey Milk Archives.
52. Ibid., 1.
53. "The Day after Election Day Is Too Late to Find Out Where Your Candidate Stands on the Issues," 1977, Harvey Milk Archives.
54. Ibid.
55. Milk, "That's What America Is," in Shilts, 366.
56. Milk, *Coast to Coast Times,* June 13, 1978, Harvey Milk Archives.
57. For information about Milk's campaign against Proposition 6, see "Milk Forum: Gay Freedom Day Speech," *Bay Area Reporter,* July 6, 1978: 11; Stephen Hall, "Fiery Clash Over Prop. 6," *San Francisco Chronicle,* September 16, 1978: 7; and Eugene Robinson, "A Wild Debate—Briggs vs. Milk," *San Francisco Chronicle,* October 12, 1978: 6.

58. Lamble, *Harvey Milk Remembered.*
59. Shilts, 185.
60. Kenneth Burke, *Attitudes toward History,* 3d ed. (Berkeley: University of California Press, 1984), 40.
61. Ibid., 40.
62. For an overview of Milk's premonitions, see Randy Shilts, "Harvey Milk: His Forebodings of Death," *San Francisco Chronicle,* March 7, 1982: 4, 7–9. Milk's political will, tape-recorded a week after winning his supervisorial post and "to be played only in the event of my death by assassination," can be found in Shilts, 372–75.
63. Zijderveld, 26.
64. An example from Nixon's 1960 campaign demonstrates the difficulty of responding to the tactics of a fool. The morning after the first Nixon-Kennedy debate, the Kennedy campaign planted an elderly woman at the airport who rushed up to and embraced Nixon with the words, "Don't worry, son. Kennedy won last night, but you'll do better next time." There was no productive response to such a situation, and anything Nixon might have said probably would only have increased his own foolishness. See Gladwin Hill, *New York Times,* October 9, 1962; cited in Orrin Klapp, *Symbolic Leaders* (Chicago: Albine, 1964), 207.

2. On the Owning of Words: Reflections on *San Francisco Arts and Athletics vs. United States Olympic Committee*

Paul Siegel

On June 25, 1987, a 7–2 Supreme Court ruled that the United States Olympic Committee had not overstepped its authority in bringing suit against a nonprofit California corporation. The plaintiffs successfully invoked relevant provisions of the federal Amateur Sports Act of 1978, which gave USOC exclusive rights to use, among other things, the word "Olympics" for promotional purposes. At issue was the corporation's desire to sponsor an international amateur athletic competition under the rubric, "Gay Olympics" (*San Francisco Arts and Athletics vs. United States Olympic Committee* 1987).

The case was of interest not only to the litigants and to gay activists everywhere; it also raised some fundamental questions concerning the unavoidable but only recently recognized conflicts (Denicola 1982; Shaughnessy 1987; Tasker 1987) between trademark protection of words and the first amendment rights of those wishing to use such words for arguably political ends.

The purpose of this essay is to explore some of the contested values that emerge from a careful reading of the "Gay Olympics" case. After briefly reviewing the facts of the case and its adjudication, we will examine three contested issues arising from it. The first of these found the courts engaged in the process of "statutory construction," trying to decipher the meaning of a law from its own language. As we shall see, the grammatical ambiguities involved in the Amateur Sports Act, caused chiefly by the absence of a comma at a crucial juncture, carried enormous weight in the final outcome of the case.

The second controversy required the courts to assess the meaning of the label, "Gay Olympics." Was this a simple appropriation of USOC's protected service mark, or was a political element especially deserving of first amendment protection inherent in SFAA's choice of labels?

The final controversy concerns, in a real sense, the meaning of the "US" in "USOC." That is, did USOC function as a state agent? Only if the courts so found could SFAA even hope to raise the issue of selective enforcement: that USOC chose to sue SFAA, but not similarly offending groups using the "Olympics" service mark, presumably owing to USOC's squeamishness concerning gay-oriented labels.

A brief concluding section will offer some tentative comments about the ultimate significance of the Gay Olympics case both from the perspective of the gay rights movement and from the perspective of theoretical development in trademark and first amendment caselaw.

The Facts and Adjudication of the Case

San Francisco Arts and Athletics, Inc., is a nonprofit California corporation. After its incorporation in 1981, it began to promote the "Gay Olympic Games," planned as a nine day event in San Francisco. In late December 1981, however, the executive director of USOC wrote to SFAA, citing federal legislation granting USOC exclusive use of the word "Olympic" for promotional purposes. Initially, SFAA agreed to cease its use of "Olympic," but after consultation with legal counsel, they resumed such use a month later.

USOC then brought suit in federal district court, seeking a temporary restraining order and a preliminary injunction against SFAA, both of which were granted by the court (*International Olympics Committee vs. San Francisco Arts and Athletics* 1982), which was summarily upheld by the Circuit Court of Appeals. The case before the Supreme Court was in essence a replay of the 1982 litigation, with the appellate court this time having upheld the trial court's issuance of a permanent injunction against SFAA's use of the "Olympic" mark.

Thus it was that the "Gay Games" rather than the Gay Olympics were held in 1982 and quadrennially ever since.

Statutory Construction: The Case of the Missing Comma

Although the word trademark has already been used several times in this paper, the Gay Olympics case has not been referred to herein as a "trademark case." There is a reason for this linguistic caution; in essence, much of the statutory construction engaged in by the courts in this case was aimed at determining whether this was an ordinary trademark case, or whether the Amateur Sports Act's provisions went beyond those of trademark law.

Trademark law in the United States is found in the common law and in the Lanham Act of 1947 (15 USC 1051. et seq.). Section 1114 of the law makes clear that trademark infringements occur only when the infringing use is likely to cause confusion, or to deceive. One of the tasks before the courts adjudicating the Gay Olympics case was to determine whether the Amateur Sports Act contained prohibitions against the use of the word Olympics that were coextensive with the Lanham Act "likely to cause confusion" requirements, or if the 1978 law was more restrictive of speech. (Discussion of a corollary concern, whether more restrictive protections would be permissible under the First Amendment, is postponed to a later section.)

In order to understand the nature of the puzzle laid before the courts, it will be necessary to quote extensively from the language of the Amateur Sports Act.

The Act of 1978 provides in relevant part (section 380) that (a) Without the consent of the Corporation [the USOC], any person who uses for the purposes of trade, to induce the sale of any goods or services, or to promote any theatrical exhibition, athletic performance, or competition—

(4) the words "Olympic," "Olympiad," "Citius Altius Fortius," or any combination or simulation thereof *tending to cause confusion,* to cause mistake, to deceive, or to falsely suggest a connection with the Corporation or any Olympic activity;

shall be subject to suit in a civil action by the Corporation for the remedies provided in [the Lanham Act] (483 U.S. at 528; emphasis added).

Statutory construction here becomes grammatical analysis. What, specifically, does the highlighted phrase ("tending to cause confusion") modify? Does the phrase modify only the words beginning "or any combination or simulation thereof?" If so, the implication is that defendants using a "combination" or a "simulation" of words protected under the Act are liable for damages only if such simulations or combinations will tend to cause confusion, but that USOC could sue persons using the word "Olympic" itself (SFAA was such an entity) without having to prove a tendency to cause confusion. Did Congress *presume* that a use of the word Olympic itself would have a tendency to cause confusion, so no proof of such a tendency was necessary?[1] Attorneys for USOC contended that, if the "tending to cause confusion" language was supposed to modify not only the "or any combination or simulation thereof" phrase but also the word "Olympic," "a comma should have followed 'thereof' " (Brief for Respondents, 16).[2]

Predictably, SFAA and its *amici* had a differing interpretation of the excerpt from the Amateur Sports Act being scrutinized. Citing the 1985 edition of Webster's Standard American Style Manual for authority, one *amicus* brief argued that the clause, "tending to cause confusion, to cause mistake, to deceive, or to falsely suggest a connection with the Corporation or any Olympic activity"

probably modifies the predicate "words" at the beginning of subparagraph 4. This interpretation would mean that the use of the word "Olympic" is only prohibited when "tending to cause confusion. . . . " The punctuation is not consistent with interpreting the "tending" clause as restricting only the meaning of the last clause ("any combination or simulation thereof") in the series including the word "Olympic." If such a meaning were intended, the conjunction "or" should have been placed between the words "Olympiad" and "Citius Altius Fortius;" and a semicolon should have replaced the comma after "Citius Altius Fortius" (Brief of Amateur Athletic Union at 25–26).

A later section of this same brief allows that "the wording used by Congress is very complex and ambiguous" (24). Similarly, a brief filed by the AFL-CIO admits that "on a strictly linguistic level, both of the parties' interpretations are tenable" (7).

The federal district court, in any event, ruled that an unauthorized use even of the word "Olympic" itself must be found to have a tendency to cause confusion in order to be actionable. The court did find such a tendency, and thus ruled against SFAA. The appellate court had an easier time ruling against SFAA, in that the three-judge panel found no need to prove even a tendency to cause confusion (781 F. 2d at 736). And Justice Lewis Powell, writing for a 7–2 majority, held that the language and legislative history of the Act "demonstrates that Congress intended to provide the USOC with exclusive control of the use of the word 'Olympic' without regard to whether an authorized use of the word tends to cause confusion. . . . " (483 U.S. at 530). Justice Powell's decision thus created hundreds, perhaps thousands, of criminals nationwide, proprietors of everything from the Olympic Donut Shop to the Olympic BBQ to the Olympic Novelty Handwear Company (789 F. 2d at 2323).

Did Congress Overstep Its Bounds? Trademark and Free Speech

Having found against SFAA on the issue of statutory construction, the Supreme Court could not skirt the larger constitutional issues posed by the Gay Olympics case. For our purposes, the real clash of symbols begins here, as the Court and the litigants tried to assess the value of competing interests. The argument moves from the designative to the evaluative, as we no longer ask *"Did* Congress do this?" but rather *"May* Congress do this?"

Courts attempting to outline the First Amendment limitations on property rights granted in copyright and trademark are walking on relatively untrod ground. The notion that judicial enforcement of a writer's proprietary rights granted under copyright law might raise important First Amendment questions is a relatively new one to the law. As UCLA law professor Melville Nimmer recently explained, "There is a fundamental conflict or tension" between copyright and freedom of speech (Taylor 1985, 11). The cacophony of clashing values probably reached its high point in *Harper and Row vs. The Nation* (1985), in which the magazine quoted excerpts without permission from former President Ford's soon to be published memoirs, resulting in a 6–3 decision upholding Harper and Row's copyright.

So too in trademark law, the recognition that protection of trademarks or service marks may sometimes raise important First Amendment issues is a relatively new one. To be sure, the courts have probably never interpreted the trademark right as an absolute one. Yet the typical anti-trademark ruling is based not on constitutional grounds, but rather on a finding that the mark was not protectible in the first place (because it was not "distinctive" enough, or because it was "merely descriptive," or had become "generic").

The conflict between trademark protection and First Amendment interests manifested itself in the Gay Olympics case in two ways. First, SFAA argued that, even if Congress *did* intend to give USOC virtual monopoly over the promotional use of the word "Olympics" (without a prerequisite finding of a likelihood of, or "tendency towards" confusing the public), any legislation codifying such an intention would itself be unconstitutional. Alternatively, SFAA argued that, even if the scope of the Amateur Sports Act were not found unconstitutional as written, application of the Act to this particular litigant, whose speech had clear political overtones, would be constitutionally suspect.

This first argument was set forth in its most persuasive form by Judges Kozinski, Pregerson, and Norris, dissenting from the Court of Appeals' decision not to rehear the case *en banc:*

By passing the Act, Congress extracted a word from the English language and gave it to a private party to use in connection with any commercial endeavor or public event. This raises serious first amendment concerns. . . .

The word Olympic has a meaning unique within our language. It connotes open and intense competition among non-professional athletes, usually involving the best and most accomplished contestants. Thus, we have Special Olympics, Junior Olympics, Police Olympics, and Canine Olympics, normally involving competition among the best and finest within the denoted category. I have great difficulty with the idea that Congress can deny all of us that word, and the idea it embodies, in connection with all public endeavors. . . .

To say that the word Olympic is property begs the question. What appellants challenge is the power of Congress to privatize the word Olympic, rendering it unutterable by anyone else in connection with any product or public event, whether for profit or, as in this case, to promote a cause. . . .

If Congress has the power to grant a crown monopoly in the word Olympic, one wonders how many other words or concepts can be similarly enclosed, and the extent to which our public discourse can thereby be impoverished (789 F. 2d at 1320–23).

The Supreme Court majority rejected Kozinski's and his colleagues' reasoning, but found no need to rule on the issue of whether Congress *could* simply remove a word from the English language by privatizing it. Rather, Justice Powell found that the word "Olympic" is a special word, one whose commercial value "was the product of the USOC's own talents and energy, the end result of much time, effort and expense" (483 U.S. at 583; see also Brief for Respondents at 14; Brief for AFL-CIO at 25–26). And as USOC added on its own behalf, "it is the modern Olympic Games, and not some tale from ancient times, that petitioners consciously copied" (Brief for Respondents at 26).

Justice Powell borrowed and expanded this latter point, as he enumerated the differences between the ancient games and the modern ones:

The ancient Olympic Games lasted five days, whereas the modern Olympics last for 10 days. The ancient Games always took place in Olympia in southern Greece; the modern Olympic Games normally move from city to city every four years. . . . In ancient Greece there may have been a burning fire for religious sacrifice, since the Olympic Games were part of a religious festival. . . . The torch relay, however, was an innovation of the modern Olympic Committee. . . . There is no indication that the ancient Olympics included an "Olympic anthem" or were organized by an entity called an "Olympic Committee." The awards in ancient Greece were wreaths of wild olive, rather than the gold, silver and bronze medals presented at the modern Olympics (483 U.S. at 540–41, n. 18).

Since the Gay Olympics were designed to parallel the modern rather than the ancient Olympics (they would run for nine days, be held in different cities in later years, and include a torch relay, a parade, and an Olympic anthem, while the awards would be in the form of gold, silver, and bronze medals), Justice Powell had no difficulty in rejecting SFAA's claim that the group had "taken" from USOC only the trappings of a generic or merely descriptive mark.

Powell's reasoning is, in essence, to claim that the word "Olympic" had over the years since USOC's creation acquired what trademark lawyers call a "secondary meaning." In effect, the secondary meaning doctrine provides that even an unoriginal, nondistinctive mark (one thus not normally registrable) can be protected if the corporation seeking such protection can demonstrate that it had been using the mark in commerce for an appreciable period of time and that the public had come to associate the mark with its own company, to the exclusion of others (Brown and Denicola 1985, 508; Goldstein 1980, 322).

The elegant circularity of all this, of course, is that Powell is using the results of a Congressional action to support the initial constitutionality of that action. Since 1950, when the legislation creating the Committee was enacted, everyone but USOC has been legislatively prevented from using the term "Olympic" to promote athletic events. It is highly likely (though apparently no empirical evidence was presented at trial on the matter) that most Americans nowadays, upon seeing the word "Olympic," do indeed conjure up a mental image of the games conducted under the auspices of USOC. But that reality is clearly the result of the word having been, as Kozinski claimed, plucked from the dictionary and granted to one private entity. The question before the Court, which Powell does not satisfactorily answer, is whether that initial plucking was constitutional.

Seen in this light, it is also clear that the differences enumerated by Powell between the modern and the ancient Olympics are trivial ones indeed, not at all related to the mental image most of us conjure up in response to the one word stimulus, "Olympics." Our mental image is of athletic competition on an international scale, and is not dependent upon the number of days the competition runs, or the other kinds of contrasts Powell enumerated between the ancient and modern games. In essence, that which we conjure up in our minds constitutes precisely the kinds of "generic" qualities the word enjoyed prior to the creation of the modern games.

Moreover, even had the term "Olympic" acquired a secondary meaning, well-settled doctrine in trademark law tells us that a competing corporation may still use that same mark, as long as it is used in its "descriptive" sense. Thus, if SFAA's use of the Olympic label was intended to conjure up only that which the label always connoted generically (e.g., "the best athletes within a designated class"), that use might be protected as "fair use in description" (Kitch and Perlman 1982, 279).

First Amendment arguments against the Amateur Sports Act were not limited to the assertion that Congress had no right to privatize an ordinary dictionary word such as "Olympic." A second line of argument posited that even if Congress might have such a right in the abstract, surely the Act is unconstitutional as applied to a group such as SFAA, whose use of the word has clear political overtones. Again, the most powerful articulation of this viewpoint appears in the dissent from the appellate court's decision not to rehear the case *en banc:*

> In organizing the Gay Olympic Games, the SFAA sought to create a more realistic image of homosexual men and women in all societies and to provide more alternatives for homosexual men and women to move into the mainstreams of their respective societies. . . . The word Olympic was no doubt chosen to foster a wholesome, normal image of homosexuals. Denying SFAA use of the word thwarts that purpose. To say that the SFAA could have named its event "The Best and Most Accomplished Amateur Gay Athletes Competition" no more answers the first amendment concerns here than to suggest that Robert Paul Cohen could have worn a jacket saying "I Strongly Resent the Draft" [instead of "Fuck the Draft"]. . . . (789 F. 2d at 1321)

From USOC's perspective, the "Gay Olympics" did not constitute protected political speech, but a purely commercial enterprise:

> Petitioners did not seek to discuss the Olympic Games. They did not seek to criticize the Olympic Games. What they sought to do was promote their own product, using the goodwill associated with USOC's protected name. . . . Petitioners had no more First Amendment right to market the "Gay Olympics" than they would "Gay Coca-Cola," or "Gay Kodak" cameras, or "Gay Ivory Soap" (Brief for Petitioners at 34).

Justice Powell's majority opinion gave only terse treatment to the expressive speech argument; moreover, his ruling in favor of USOC on this point seems dependent upon his earlier holding that the Olympic label had developed a protectible secondary meaning. Powell concluded, with little explanation, that "the mere fact that the SFAA claims an expressive, as opposed to a purely commercial, purpose does not give it a First Amendment right to appropriate to itself the harvest of those who have sown" (483 U.S. at 541).

There are two conflicting ironies underlying the pro-USOC resolution of the political speech issue. First, we have to recognize that, in order to make its political point effectively, SFAA *had to* make their games very similar to USOC's own Olympics. Just as a parodist must appropriate that which is necessary in order to "conjure up the original" in the minds of the audience (Kitch and Perlman 1982, 705–7), so too SFAA had to closely mimic the "real" Olympics in order to make their political statement—that lesbians and gay males strive for excellence too (and especially with respect to gay males, that they are not "sissies" uninterested in athletic pursuits). The more clearly SFAA made its political message, the more "likelihood of confusion" it would create between its games and USOC's games, and that confusion would be a cogent argument against SFAA's legal position even in a typical trademark infringement case.

The uncovering of a second irony concerning the expressive speech argument requires reference to one of the points raised by USOC's brief. After rebutting SFAA's assertion that it had been singled out for legal action because of its sexual orientation, USOC attorneys felt compelled to add that even if their clients *had* been guilty of such seemingly discriminatory conduct, "there is ample authority holding that . . . trademark holders may enjoin uses reasonably judged likely to affect the designation's value . . . " (40, n. 56). In other words, USOC would not be attacking SFAA because of USOC's antipathy toward the latter's sexual orientation, but rather in dispassionate response to the feared antipathy on the part of others (including potential donors).

Even eschewing the argument that the Court has rejected such "discrimination by proxy" in numerous contexts (see, for example, *Palmore vs. Sidoti,* 1984, holding that predicted societal antipathy cannot become an argument against interracial adoption), this reasoning cuts both ways. Whereas USOC's argument seems to be that the more despised lesbian and gay males are to mainstream America, the more damaging *their* use of the Olympic label might be, the opposite conclusion can just as easily be defended. After all, if lesbians and gay males are so despised, a casual observer seeing an ad for the "Gay Olympics" would be very unlikely to assume that USOC had anything to do with the sponsorship of the event.

Justice Powell's majority opinion is thus intellectually unsatisfying with respect to the political speech question. He simply subsumed the free speech interest to the property claim, but nowhere explained why the latter should outweigh the former.

The Question of State Action: How Much "US" Is in "USOC"?

Whether USOC's suit against SFAA constituted "state's action" was a crucial issue affecting the Court's ultimate decision, for if the Court had so held, it would have to at least address the issue of "selective enforcement."

Since only the government can, by definition, "discriminate" in the legal sense (in this case, violating the equal protection component of the fifth amendment's due process clause), a failure to find state's action means that USOC may quite properly seek an injunction against the Gay Olympics, while permitting or encouraging the Special Olympics, the Police Olympics, even the Canine Olympics.

In traditional constitutional analysis, there are two means of finding "state's action." The first is to demonstrate that the agent involved *is*, in fact, a government actor (483 U.S. at 542; Lockhart, Kamisar, and Choper 1981, 1047). Justice Powell rejected the assertion that USOC is such an actor. "The fact that Congress granted it a corporate charter does not render the USOC a government agent," Powell pointed out. Moreover, even the fact that the Amateur Sports Act specifically permits USOC to seek Congressional funding is not dispositive: "The government may subsidize private entities," Powell wrote, "without assuming constitutional responsibility for their actions" (483 U.S. at 544).

Justice William Brennan's dissenting opinion (joined by Justice Marshall, and in which Justices O'Connor and Blackmun concurred with respect to the equal protection analysis) admonished Powell for failing to recognize the fact that not just financial support, but an overall "symbiotic relationship" between USOC and the U.S. government, require a finding of state's action (483 U.S. at 556). As Brennan reminded us,

In the eye of the public, both national and international, the connection between the decisions of the United States government and those of the USOC is profound. The President of the United States has served as the Honorary President of the USOC. The national flag flies both literally and figuratively over the central product of the USOC, the United States Olympic team. The connection is not lost on the athletes; who can imagine an Olympic hopeful postponing a lucrative professional career with the explanation, "I cannot pass up this chance to represent the United States *Olympic Committee*." . . . It would certainly be irony amounting to grave injustice if to finance the team that is to represent the virtues of our political system, the USOC were free to employ government created economic leverage to prohibit political speech. (483 U.S. at 557–58)

The second possible way of establishing state's action, in the absence of a close interdependence between the agent and the government itself, is to find nonetheless that the agent performs some functions that have been traditionally the exclusive prerogative of the government (483 U.S. at 548; Lockhart, Kamisar, and Choper 1981, 1051–52).

On this point, Justice Powell observed correctly that "neither the conduct nor the coordination of amateur sports has been a traditionally governmental function," (483 U.S. at 545), while Justice Brennan claimed that the majority failed to take into account "the extraordinary representational responsibility that Congress has placed on the USOC" (483 U.S. at 550). Brennan continued:

> The athletes the USOC select are viewed not as a group of individuals who coincidentally are from the United States, but as a team of athletes that represents our Nation. . . .
>
> Every aspect of the Olympic pageant, from the procession of athletes costumed in national uniform, to the raising of national flags and the playing of national anthems at the medal ceremony, to the official tally of medals won by each national team, reinforces the national significance of Olympic participation. (483 U.S. at 551)

Justice Powell's rejoinder cleverly accuses Brennan of proving a bit too much:

> Absent the additional element of governmental control, this representational function can hardly be called traditionally governmental. All sorts of private organizations send "national representatives" to participate in world competitions. Although many are of interest only to a select group, others, like the Davis Cup competition, the America's Cup, and the Miss Universe Pageant, are widely viewed as involving representation of our country (483 U.S. at 545, n. 27).

Brennan in turn chides Powell for misunderstanding the unique representational role played by USOC. "At stake are significant national interests that stem not only from pageantry," Brennan asserted, "but from politics" (483 U.S. at 551). Brennan went on to remind us of the events leading up to the U.S. boycott of the Moscow games in 1980, in protest of the Soviet invasion of Afghanistan. The President threatened legal action and funding cuts to USOC if it did not comply. The fact that the President used the State of the Union address itself to outline his concerns is further indication of the unique role played by USOC, Brennan maintained.

For Powell, the very fact that President Carter could only *threaten* fund cuts and legal action is of some importance. Carter knew he did not have the authority to simply forbid USOC to participate in the games. All he could use was "the power of persuasion" (483 U.S. at 546, n. 27).

While Brennan let the argument end here, he could have suggested that the state's action issue is not resolvable simply by taking note of how directly or indirectly President Carter would have needed to act against USOC to obtain his desired results. Rather, the argument should focus on *why* the President would feel so strongly about those results in the first place. Surely Carter would not have attempted to make political points by boycotting the Miss Universe Pageant, even if it were scheduled to be held in Moscow in 1980. Clearly, Brennan was right when he argued that American prestige is on the line in a unique way when the United States Olympic team competes. There is, in short, a great deal of the "US" in "USOC."

In that only four Justices reached this conclusion, however, SFAA did not have the chance to have the high court rule on its allegations of antigay, discriminatory enforcement of the Amateur Sports Act.

Conclusion

The Gay Olympics case was looked to with much interest not only by gay activists but also by those seeking some definitive words concerning the natural tension between trademark protection of words and first amendment protection for political expression.

Concerning the latter group of court watchers, it can only be said that Justice Powell's majority opinion was unsatisfying, in that it adroitly skirted most of the more interesting issues posed by the case. We do not learn, for example, whether Congress has the right to simply remove a word from the dictionary and grant exclusive control of that word for promotional purposes to a private entity. Although the facts of the Gay Olympics case seemed to cry out for a ruling on this matter, Powell chose to rule more narrowly, hanging his opinion on what may or may not be a convenient fiction—the assertion that USOC has performed a "creative" role over the last few decades, and that it is this creative energy, rather than Congressional fiat, that makes them the owners of the "Olympic" label.

Those who watched the Gay Olympics case closely out of concern for the present and future status of the gay rights movement also walked away unsatisfied. This is not for the obvious reason that the gay litigants were unsuccessful. Rather, it is because the narrow posture adopted by the majority did not even permit the raising of the most salient issue for this group—that is, were the gay litigants victims of a discriminatory action?

The issue was not addressed in any definitive way in Powell's opinion, in that he fails to find any state's action on the part of USOC.

From the perspective of gay advocates, the narrowness of the Court's ruling will have to be its own silver lining. The attorneys for USOC were no doubt correct when they asserted that, despite the Court's final results, gay groups would still be wholly free to comment upon the Olympics, to criticize the Olympics, even to compare their own athletic competition to the Olympics. They would only be prohibited from *calling* their competition the "Gay Olympics."

San Francisco Arts and Athletics vs. USOC will likely not provide the galvanizing force of the *Hardwick* sodomy decision, nor does it indicate that gays' first amendment rights are in jeopardy. It will probably be remembered as a case in which the Court chose *not* to offer a new pronouncement on the law of trademark, free speech, or equal protection.

Notes

1. It is also worth noting, of course, that the burden of proving that an offending use of a protected mark may have a "tendency" to cause confusion, arguably a requirement of the Act, is still a lesser burden of proof than that required by the Lanham trademark law, which speaks instead of infringements "likely" to cause confusion or deception.
2. Throughout the text of this essay, reference will be made to the briefs filed by the respondent, the appellant, as well as by various *amic*. All such briefs were filed by the litigants in front of the United States Supreme Court in *San Francisco Arts and Athletics vs. United States Olympic Committee* 1987. They will not be listed separately in the Works Cited section.

Works Cited

Bowers vs. Hardwick, 478 U.S. 186 (1986).

Brown, Ralph, and Robert Denicola. 1985. *Cases on copyright, unfair competition, and other topics bearing on the protection of literary, musical, and artistic works.* Mineola, N.Y.: Foundation Press.

Denicola, Robert. 1982. "Trademarks as speech: constitutional implications of the emerging rationales for the protection of trade symbols." *Wisconsin Law Review* (1982): 158–207.

Goldstein, Paul. 1980. *Copyright, patent, trademark and related state doctrines.* Mineola, N.Y.: Foundation Press.

Harper and Row vs. The Nation, 105 S. Ct. 2218 (1985).

International Olympics Committee vs. San Francisco Arts and Athletics. 1982. 219 USPQ 982.

Kitch, Edmund, and Harvey Perlman. 1982. *Legal Regulation of the Competitive Process.* Mineola, N.Y.: Foundation Press.

Lockhart, William, Yale Kamisar, and Jesse Choper. 1981. *The American Constitution.* St. Paul, Minn.: West Publishing Company.

New York Times vs. Sullivan, 376 U.S. 254 (1964).

Palmore vs. Sidoti, 466 U.S. 429 (1984).

San Francisco Arts and Athletics vs. United States Olympic Committee, 789 F. 2d 733, as modified, 789 F. 2d 1319 (1986), affirmed, 483 U.S. 522 (1987).

Shaughnessy, Robert. 1987. "Trademark parody: a fair use and first amendment analysis." *The Trademark Reporter* 77: 177–215.

Tasker, Tyrone. 1987. "Parody or satire as a defense to trademark infringement." *The Trademark Reporter* 77: 216–47.

Taylor, Stuart. 1985. "Conflict over copyright." *New York Times,* 21 May: 11.

3. Die Non: Gay Liberation and the Rhetoric of Pure Tolerance

James Darsey

> We see not our signs: there is no more any prophet: neither is there among us any that knoweth how long.
>
> —Psalms 74:9

> Prudence operates on life in the same manner as rules on composition: it produces vigilance rather than elevation, rather prevents loss than procures advantage; and often escapes miscarriages, but seldom reaches either power or honor. . . . Prudence keeps life safe, but does not often make it happy.
>
> —Samuel Johnson
> The Idler, No. 57

Our word "radical" shares its origins with the word "radish"; both are concerned with roots and are often bitter. Radicalism is defined by its concern with the political roots of a society, its fundamental laws, its foundational principles, its most sacred covenants. It is common for radicals to claim to be the true keepers of the faith; they oppose their society using its own most noble expressions and aspirations.[1] Their rhetorical posture generally follows Aristotle's dictum that wrongs committed in the name of the state are properly appealed to the court of higher law for redress; there is in radical rhetoric a consistent denigration of the idea that political and economic power is necessarily connected to righteousness.[2] It is possible to take a cynical view of Aristotle's advice and to see in it no more than the exercise of those resources that best serve the case, but it is equally plausible to see an inviolable and uncompromisable moral claim in the higher law, especially as Aristotle solemnly asserts in another place: "For there really is, as every one to some extent divines, a natural justice and injustice that is binding on all men, even on those who have no association or covenant with each other."[3]

Within a philosophy of natural or divine law, all of the arrangements of humankind are subject to evaluation by criteria that cannot be abrogated by considerations of political expedience or majority will. "Because it functions as an absolute standard for testing positive law," writes Kathleen Jamieson, "natural law is the obvious rhetorical appeal to be employed when confronting tyranny or injustice."[4] At the same time, as Jamieson goes on to recognize, the potency of the appeal is "tied to the audience's ability to believe that a knowable moral norm correctly articulated by the rhetor inheres in all men."[5] Natural law most effectively warrants the argument "when the audience is willing, because of utility or commonality of belief structure, to grant that the posited law or right may function as an unchallenged first premise."[6] In other words, an effective appeal to natural law requires a community of belief; it requires the presence of a religion, literally a bond, that gives a society coherence, that religious conception without which Ortega said no society can exist.

But the postmodern world is characterized precisely by the absence of such bonds; deconstruction has replaced exegesis.[7] It is the acceptance of the partiality of the world that marks the residue of nineteenth-century liberalism in twentieth-century thought, a profound and unfettered individualism.[8] The consequences for argument are great. In contrast to the moral stance described by Jamieson and manifested in radicalism, Irving Horowitz describes the rhetorical possibilities in pluralism: "The more one emphasizes the fragmentation of the world, the more one must insist on the pragmatic values of men, the less can an argument be made for action as good in itself," he writes.[9] What Horowitz describes is the antithesis of radicalism. It is the stance of the compromiser, not one who would insist on the integrity of first principles. Yet Aristotle's bold appeal to natural law notwithstanding, it is also the model stance of the rhetorician. It is recommended to those who seek changes in the world as "reasonable" and thus efficacious.

Idealists from Plato to Richard Weaver have condemned such a rhetorical stance as morally corrupt, and their condemnation has been largely identified with conservative philosophies. Modern American liberals, on the other hand, have tended to embrace the noncoercive character of pluralism as salutary and enlightened; recall the negative reaction of so many liberals to the tactics, not the aims, of student and black protest in the 1960s. Students, in particular, were condemned for their untempered "idealism."

I want to argue, though, that liberals have been too hasty in declaring notions of natural law, in whatever form, to be moribund, too eager to consign them to an intellectual museum as disembodied relics of a dark age past. Liberal reformers have created a grievous rhetorical handicap for themselves in allowing conservative radicals exclusive claim on the supernal, the fundamental, the roots of society. To follow the horticultural metaphor suggested by the etymology of radical, modern liberals are left to do only pruning, snipping, and other topiary alterations while conservative ideologues are left to control the health and destiny of the plant.

Nowhere can this be more readily seen than in the case of the gay liberation movement in the United States. Among American social movements, the gay liberation movement has a strong claim to being the most thoroughly postmodern, not just in its chronological placement, but in its sanguine acknowledgment of the partiality of the world, the death of God, and the decay of natural law. Gay liberationists have good reason historically for viewing the order associated with religious community as an instrument of their oppression, but if a social movement concedes, even embraces, the absence of divine order rather than claiming to be the embodiment of that order, what resources are available for persuasion? By looking at the society in which gay liberation found its voice and at the strategies gay liberationists adopted in opposing the established repositories of the law we identified as oppressive, I think we can see the inherent weakness in a mode of argument so democratic that it refuses to impose a point of view on its audience.

Tolerance and the Secular Society

Early in the twentieth century, thinkers as diverse as Max Weber and John Dewey began to see in modern societies a tendency toward differentiation, specialization, and increasing bureaucratization. Both Dewey and Weber made their observations in the context of discussions of social change, and Weber's conclusion that society, in this process of diffusion and participation, becomes "demystified" is particularly revealing for our purposes. A world where there is no center, where there is no division between the center and the periphery, is a world without the mystery and separation necessary to the sacred, and where there is no externalization of truth, there is no principle that commands assent except self-interest, and there is thus no community.[10]

Jürgen Habermas, following both Weber and Dewey, extends the analysis of the demystification or rationalization of society to the "scientization of politics," finding that "rationalizing tendencies" come both from above and from below. From below, there is a demand for some compensatory value to replace that meaning and order that are lost in modern society. Typically, the succedaneum is economic, as this is the value that characterizes capitalist societies. From above, there is a recognition that the mythologies— "the public religion, the customary rituals, the justifying metaphysics, the unquestionable tradition"—must be converted to a more negotiable form; they must become secularized.[11]

Dostoevsky, in *The Brothers Karamozov*, presents us with the potentialities of a world where God is absent. "When there is no God, everything is permitted," is Ivan's refrain. If there is no God, no absolute truth, there is no law, no ordonnance, no basis for prohibition; the consequences are at once liberating and terrifying. At first glance, it may seem that the absence of moral claims on either side is no more static than are moral claims in competition, but the critical difference lies in the fact that the absence of moral claims forecloses the possibility of moral debate completely. Moral claims at a point of stasis presume a tension that may be broken or resolved; secular argument is flaccid and inert.

Negotiation, as opposed to the proclamation of prophecy, is the form of secular debate. Secular debate reflects the economic values of its time by assuming the form of the so-called "rational exchange model" or "game theory."[12] Unlike the absolutisms of moral argument, all positions in rational economic argument are bargainable; the old ethic of exclusion and prohibition is replaced by tolerance. As Robert Paul Wolff has written:

Tolerance in a society of competing interest groups is precisely the ungrudging acknowledgment of the right of opposed interests to exist and be pursued. The economic conception of tolerance goes quite naturally with the view of human action as motivated by interests rather than principles or norms. It is much easier to accept a compromise between competing interests—particularly when they are expressible in terms of a numerical scale like money—than between opposed principles which purport to be objectively valid. [13]

In the transition from what was in a profound sense, a religious society, a society that had a sense of transcendental authorship and purpose, to a society based on pluralistic tolerance, we in the United States have changed from a society based on authority to a society based on economics; in Robert Bellah's phrase, we have broken the sacred covenant. [14] For this we have sought to substitute a utilitarian calculus; reason is no longer the faculty by which the truth is apprehended as it was for Thomas Paine, but the rules for calculating the advantages and disadvantages of particular strategies; [15] in Robert Wolff's phrase, "the voices of reason" in the contemporary world are arrayed "against the passion of intolerant faith." [16] Reason, in the modern view, makes no moral demands, for such demands are in themselves discredited. Reason offers some evidence of resources convertible to economic terms in exchange for privilege; it does not demand rights. In this world, there are no prophets; only madmen talk to God.

Gay Rights vs. Natural Right

It is in the world as described by Weber and those who have followed him that the movement for homophile liberation in America first made its appearance. Only since 1948 has there been a sustained effort on behalf of gay and lesbian rights in the United States. [17] Sociologist Edward Sagarin has puzzled over the failure of homophile-rights activists to organize before this time and offers as part of his explanation that homosexuals, having internalized much of society's hatred of them, did not believe themselves worthy of rights. [18] Sagarin's statement suggests the presence of an ideology puissant enough to secure the denigration of the self. As long as such an ideology could be effectively maintained, it is reasonable to believe that it would preclude any possibilities of organization on behalf of gay rights. Before homosexuals could organize for rights, there had to be a significant dereliction of this ideology by its three most redoubtable proponents.

"In the past, three great institutions had joined to label homosexual behavior unacceptable: the law, the church, and the medical profession. The law regarded homosexual activity as criminal, the church as immoral, and the medical profession as perverse, if not psychopathic." [19] This statement, from Howard Brown's posthumously published book *Familiar Faces, Hidden Lives,* is representative in its view of the sources of homosexual oppression.[20] The church, medical science, and the law are viewed by gay and lesbian activists as three parts of a mutually reinforcing system of social control. Religion and science, with their shared assumptions about the objectivity of the world and the ability to know it in absolute terms, have tended to treat the world they reveal as external to human kind, something separate, sacred; science profanes the temple by exposing its innermost chambers and by using the forces of nature to its own ends, but it cannot alter the basic substance; it cannot make human beings and nature co-equal.[21] Both religion and science find normative implications in the worlds they reveal, and both have used the law to enforce these norms in human society; or considered another way, the law has used both religion and science as justification for its strictures. In the interplay among religion, science, and law, we find the collocation "the laws of nature and of nature's God." As evidenced in the statement by Brown and countless others like it, gay men and lesbians in America share a profound understanding of their status as violators of this monolithic law.

Liberation through Tolerance

If gay men and lesbians could not command the recognition of God-given rights, there was at least hope that, in the absence of God, certain rights might be granted. Although Dennis Altman, like many who write on the homophile movement in America, finds the genesis of gay liberation at a much later point in time than I do here, what he says about the character of the movement is revealing: "Because gay liberation opposes so many of the basic assumptions around which society is organized, because it repudiates both the expectations of the straight world and the guilts and hostilities that these have produced in the gay, it could only emerge amidst conditions of flux and considerable uncertainty about traditional moral values. . . . "[22] The aftermath of World War II saw the efflorescence of uncertainties that had been germinating since the turn of the century, and it was in this atmosphere of confused permissiveness that homophile liberation organizations were at last able to take root.[23]

The two World Wars and the Great Depression had focused America's attention for a time on our common devils, granting us the illusion of community, but as soon as the devils were vanquished and we had the opportunity to look again to ourselves, we discovered that we had no common God. William Lee Miller provides a chiaroscuro of the tensions by tracing the development of religious "neo-orthodoxy" in the period between the world wars. Neo-orthodoxy was an attempt to restore a sacred code in the void left by "liberal Protestantism," which Miller characterizes as "'tolerant' and inclined to deprecate creedal-doctrinal distinctions; . . . 'democratic' and humanistic in ethics and strongly inclined to reduce religion to ethics; . . . optimistic and progressive, taking a sanguine view of man and society: in all this it fits very well into American ideas."[24] But neo-orthodoxy had contradictions of its own, suffered an infection of liberal pluralism, and was itself reduced to rules of etiquette, a truly civil religion, charming but impotent.[25]

The ethic of tolerance, however, was more than an ethic of default; tolerance was seen as a positive good. In 1962, Arthur M. Schlesinger, Jr., looked upon the American landscape and eulogized a twentieth-century view of freedom that had long shed itself of its nineteenth-century companion, moral absolutism: "Freedom implies humility, not absolutism; it implies not the tyranny of the one but the tolerance of the many. Against the monolithic world, the American intellectual tradition affirms the pluralistic world. Against the world of coercion, it affirms the world of choice."[26]

Freedom, the god-term of the American revolution, Wendell Phillips's abolitionist rhetoric, and Eugene Debs's labor agitation here has a strange harmonic; its tone is no longer colored by the counterpoint of "duty," "right," and "judgment." Edwin Schur provides an incisive characterization of the modern view of freedom when he writes, "Unless one subscribes to some thoroughgoing conception of natural law, it would seem that the realities of life in a culturally (and morally) pluralistic world should cause one to be extremely cautious about implying a basis for moral certitude."[27] Schur pinpoints exactly the missing element of the new freedom; liberty is no longer a right endowed by nature, but a permission.

In an atmosphere of permissiveness, Alfred Kinsey's *Sexual Behavior and the Human Male* was merely another symptom of the "scientization" and "demystification" of the world and the rationalization of sexual mores, not a causal factor of moral crisis as Sagarin insinuates.[28] The first so-called "Kinsey report" and the almost simultaneous genesis of homophile liberation groups were both made possible, not only by the evanescence of sacred prohibitions, but by the active encouragement of a new enlightenment.

As a part of this enlightenment, the 1948 Kinsey report represented an important shift in the focus of science where sexual mores were concerned. Left to support the weight of an otiose moral code, the medical and social sciences found themselves divided; deprived of a common faith, they were left with nothing but their own profession of impartiality and objectivity as a guide. Recognizing that "whatever beneficent results medicine might promise, by the mid-twentieth century it had in fact branded homosexual men and women with a mark of inferiority no less corrosive of their self-respect than that of sin and criminality," John D'Emilio goes on to make the following observation:

Yet to a certain extent physicians also subverted the earlier approaches. Once homosexual behavior entered the realm of science, it became subject to careful investigation. No matter how solid the consensus that homosexuality was a disease, the accumulation of empirical evidence could inspire dissenting theories, whereas Christian teachings rested on the immutable words of the Bible. Unlike moralists and law enforcement officials, doctors had a vested interest in naming, describing, and classifying the "unmentionable vice" in all its forms. . . . The medical model introduced a dynamic element into discussions of same-sex eroticism that could serve the interests of reformers.[29]

In the postwar period, science found itself incapable of enforcing proscriptions in the name of nature and of nature's God that religion was unwilling to make. The diminuendo of God's "Thou shalt not . . . " following the Second World War represents a very real change for sexual mores in general and for homosexuals in particular; the dereliction of natural law allowed for a new ethic of permissiveness. It is in this sense of permission that homophile liberation is best understood.

Deprived of the authority of religion and science, the law stood exposed as a very fragile creation. Grant Gilmore, in the 1974 Yale Law School Storrs Lectures on Jurisprudence, argued that American law over the first half of this century suffered the loss of the nineteenth-century ideal of one true law in the Platonic sense, eternal and unchanging, and yielded to a pluralistic legal realism. Gilmore describes the law, not as holy writ, but as something "designed to insure that our institutions adjust to change, which is inevitable, in a continuing process which will be orderly, gradual, and, to the extent that such a thing is possible in human affairs, rational. The function of the lawyer is to preserve a skeptical relativism in a society hell-bent for absolutes. When we become too sure of our premises, we necessarily fail in what we are supposed to be doing."[30] Like latter-day Hobbesians, legal realists assume no law behind the law; the law is not something that is found, but something that is, in Gilmore's word, "designed." Consequently, Gilmore finds a great increase in statutory law in the twentieth century, for there is no conception of an unwritten law that governs those cases not explicitly redacted.[31]

When the sacred is demystified it is reduced to the pedestrian; when Toto drew back the curtain and revealed the Wizard, we discovered that he was really just a displaced Kansan, a man like ourselves against whom our demands could be boldly pressed. The vulnerability of the law and its power, stripped of any countervailing claims, to provide the sanction of legality, if not righteousness, was not lost on homosexuals. One of the most important products of the movement toward legal realism is the Model Penal Code of the American Law Institute. Reflecting the best impulses in twentieth-century pluralism, the Model Penal Code, among its other provisions, decriminalized homosexual behavior between consenting adults. From the time of its publication in 1955, the Model Penal Code provided an opportunity for a movement, heretofore purely defensive, to take the offensive by opening up laws to criticism based on twentieth-century notions of the reasonable, a criticism that could never have impugned the sacred. The *Mattachine Review* hailed the Model Penal Code and Britain's "Wolfenden Report," most notorious for its recommendations concerning the decriminalization of homosexual acts between consenting adults, as evidence that "responsible bodies in both countries are willing to wrestle with the difficult problem of trying to make accumulated legal sanctions just and fair on reasonable grounds."[32]

Later law-reform arguments continue to reflect this realist, demystified idea of the law. In extensive coverage of recommendations of the New York Bar Association's special committee on homosexual law reform in 1971, the New York *Mattachine Times* published the following comment on New York's consensual sodomy law:

Criminal or civil law has no right to legislate morality (Ecclesiastical sin) when there is no valid social purpose (protection). Repeal will avoid court tests. The law is based solely on religious-biblical taboos. Historically homosexuality was only an ecclesiastical sin introduced into British Common Law (later U.S.) from Henry VIII's divorce from Roman Catholicism to prove his political power versus the church. The wording in most states is "Crime against nature" which exposes the origin of the laws. Catholic church caused reinstatement of the law after elimination in 1964 revision of N.Y. penal code[.] Original biblical taboos intended to promote population of a small persecuted minority sect. (Judaism) Arguments are no longer valid (if ever). Over-population threatens destruction. Birth control and abortion are legal so state cannot argue sodomy law is necessary to enforce procreation.[33]

In this argument, religion and the state, ecclesiastical law and civil law, are clearly separated. Religious prohibition is insufficient to warrant legal proscription. Legal proscription can be justified only by reasonable arguments, that is, those arguments that measure the advantages of the law (protection, adequate population) against realities of the current situation (court tests, overpopulation, the presence of birth control, and abortion).

At the same time that it provided new rhetorical opportunities, the publication of the Model Penal Code also served to circumscribe the range of homophile rights argument. From the publication of the code in 1955 to the present, the rhetoric of homophile liberation has been narrowly legalistic and heavy with appeals for tolerance under the law.[34] The name of the largest and most long-lived gay newspaper, *The Advocate,* reflects this tendency, as do samples of gay rhetoric. Early issues of the *Mattachine Review* published not only draft No. 4 of the American Law Institute's Penal Code in 1956, but also an outline of Great Britain's "Wolfenden Report" in 1957.[35] In 1971, New York's *Mattachine Times* published a complete text of the proposed revisions in the New York State penal code regarding homosexuality.[36] Chicago's *Gaylife* featured two regular columns by attorneys, one of which was "Law and Us," in addition to news items on legal developments. Even publications that are primarily vehicles for advertising and soft pornography reflect legalistic concerns in their editorial content.[37] Other evidence of the legal obsession of gay rights activism includes the existence of groups like the National Gay Rights Advocates, "a nonprofit, public interest law firm involved in litigation to advance the civil rights of lesbians and gay men through the country." The NGRA heads its newsletter with the motto "Defending Our Rights . . . Creating New Law."[38]

That a group largely defined in legal terms should be concerned with legal issues is not surprising, but the posture taken by gay activists before the law is revealing. A March 1977 editorial in *The Advocate* illustrates the gay community's reaction to the exposure of widespread domestic spying by the FBI. The editorial denounces the activities as "assaults on our most basic civil liberties," "illegal," and as "a violation of First Amendment rights." The editorial urged its readers to "demand effective legislation to regulate and curtail political intelligence on American citizens" and to write for their files under the provisions of the Freedom of Information Act.[39] The editorial is typical of gay rights discourse in its focus on the legality of the FBI's activity rather than on its justice, in its recognition of the law as the source of rights, and in its advocacy of a solution that is within the law.[40]

The rhetorical posture assumed in this and other gay protests reflects an acceptance of what Stuart Scheingold has termed "the myth of rights": "The myth of rights rests on a faith in the political efficacy and ethical sufficiency of law as a principle of government."[41] Ronald Dworkin relates this belief in the ethical sufficiency of the law to the overall intellectual climate we have traced by labeling it "legal positivism," the understanding "that individuals have legal rights only insofar as these have been created by explicit political decisions or explicit social practice."[42] Consistent with this outlook, gay rights activists have repeatedly waged our most important and visible battles in the legislative or judicial arenas, attempting to change our status through changes in the law and its interpretation. In subscribing to a positivistic conception of the law, gays and lesbians reflect the tendencies toward scientization and demystification discussed by Weber, Dewey, and Habermas rather than the natural rights philosophies of the American radical tradition. The distance between gay rights activists and our radical forbearers is perhaps best illustrated in one of the most visible and celebrated battles waged by the gay rights movement to date.

In 1977, the Metropolitan Commission for Dade County Florida set the stage for what became a nationwide battle over gay rights when it passed an ordinance banning discrimination in employment and housing based on affectional or sexual preference. Save Our Children, led by singer and evangelical Christian Anita Bryant, quickly gathered 66,000 signatures on a petition to force a referendum on the measure. The ensuing contest, which garnered enormous attention in the national media, including a cover story in *Newsweek*,[43] drew international attention to the discrepancies between activities in Miami and President Carter's human rights policies,[44] extended itself to such far-flung locales as St. Paul, Minnesota, Eugene, Oregon, Seattle, Washington, and California,[45] made a significant impact on the sales of Florida citrus products, still looms large in the considerations of gay rights activists, and reveals something significant about the rhetorical style of gay rights protest in the United States.

In an interview in *Christopher Street,* Ethan Geto, the New York–based political strategist who was recruited to run the campaign for the Dade County Coalition for the Humanistic Rights of Gays, disclosed his fundamental strategies. Geto makes clear that, based on results of polls done for his organization, he planned to capitalize on a distinction made by residents of Dade County between their disapproval of homosexuals and homosexual acts and their basic sympathy toward the issue of human rights. Geto describes his campaign this way:

I decided to run an affirmative, positive, aggressive campaign on human rights— the Constitution, the Declaration of Independence, the Bill of Rights. I waved the flag and talked patriotically about America and what America is all about, the basic guiding principles of this country, etc. And then I went into scare stuff too. Topics about taking away people's rights and asking where does dictatorship start. Stating dictatorship starts by taking away the rights of the most vulnerable minority and if that works, they keep going. They start to take away everybody's rights.[46]

Accompanying the Geto interview are reproductions of ads from both sides of the campaign, including one from the Geto camp that carries the headline: "Don't Let Them Chip Away at the Constitution." Superficially, the rhetoric of the Constitution, the Declaration of Independence, and the Bill of Rights indicates a direct link between gay rights activists and the American revolutionaries, but closer examination reveals two widely divergent vocabularies. In Geto's discourse, there is no suggestion of any grounding for the Constitution. Unlike the revolutionary Whigs who later wrote the Constitution, Geto makes no claims to rights exclusive of charters or governmental agreements. Geto's discourse exhibits an inconclusiveness as to the source of rights: "No matter what you thought about homosexuals, they are American citizens—they deserve basic human rights," he argues.[47] Do homosexuals deserve rights as American citizens or as human beings? In campaigning for the gay rights ordinance in the first place, gays subscribed to the idea that rights have their provenance in the state, that they are a grant of the legislature, and Geto here acknowledges that assumption in recognizing that rights can be legislatively taken away. But the ad, which begins with an appeal to the Constitution, concludes by urging the reader to "Vote against Repeal of Human Rights." The oxymoron is left unresolved.

The rhetorical posture described by Geto reveals a faith in the Constitution and the legal process; it is incapable of appealing to the "world court" or any higher court, or of making any claims on the body politic to which that body has not obligated itself; in keeping with the outlook of pluralistic tolerance, gays and lesbians have renounced all claim on the empyrean.[48] Barry Brummett accurately captures the flavor of the pro-gay rhetoric emanating from Miami in claiming that it "specifically opposed" its "standard of rights" to the "standard of morality" raised by Anita Bryant and her followers. Pro-gay rhetoric, in Brummett's analysis, assumed a perspective that "requires a pluralistic, decentralized society, and it features tolerance rather than control;"[49] it emphasizes individual freedom instead of duty.

In fleeing the temple, gays and lesbians have left our opponents in uncontested occupancy. It is the antigay rights forces who have been able to exercise the implacable power of righteous anger in such slogans as "Gay rights are wrong." In Miami, Anita Bryant and her forces exercised an exclusive claim on the vocabulary of moral commitment. It was Bryant who sought to establish charismatic authority: "This is not my battle, it's God's battle."[50] It was Bryant who crusaded on behalf of righteousness: "God says there are some things that are evil and some things that are good. That's simple enough for even a child to understand. Certain things are right; other things are wrong. But they are right or wrong because God says so. We are right when we do God's will; we are wrong when we do not."[51] It was Bryant who rejected the power of legal reformulation in opposition to God's law.[52] Ronald Fischli's criticism of Bryant's misology is correct in its characterization, but Fischli's own pluralist preference for "reasoned and flexible dialogue," "self-criticism," and "the democratic process" neglects the power of Bryant's implacable absolutism, the coercive power of absolute duty.[53] If there was a rhetoric imitative of the American radical tradition in Miami, it was the rhetoric of Anita Bryant, not that of gay rights activists.

In contrast to the position taken by the fundamentalist right, most mainline churches have taken a position that reinforces the distinction between church and state, the sacred and the civil law, on which gays have built their case for rights. Many sects and denominations have continued to hold homosexual acts to be sinful while simultaneously welcoming nonpracticing homosexuals as members and endorsing gay rights legislation.[54] The logic of this position derives from two separate sources: (1) The rejection of the idea that homosexuality is defined by acts that represent perverse choices on the part of the actor,[55] and (2) the acceptance of pluralism as a necessary part of our form of government and the consequent incompatibility of governing by the absolute laws of the church. This distinction has enabled proponents of gay rights to solicit the support of the church in the narrow sphere of civil justice without challenging its authority in the area of sacred law. The case of Wisconsin's "gay rights bill" is illustrative.

In 1981 Wisconsin became the first state in the country to enact legislation banning discrimination in employment, housing, and public accommodations based on sexual orientation. The bill was signed into law by Governor Lee Dreyfus in early 1982. In debate over AB70, State Representative David Clarenbach, author and primary sponsor of the bill, clearly defined the argumentative field: "Members of the Assembly, Assembly Bill 70 is not a question of morality. It's a question of civil rights. The question before us today is not whether homosexuality is admirable. It's a question of whether discrimination is tolerable."[56] Clarenbach, like Geto in the Miami campaign, reflects the peculiar notion that the state can somehow grant human rights when he notes, "The state of Wisconsin needs to grant homosexuals, as we have granted all other minority groups, protection to realize basic human rights and live life with dignity."[57] Clarenbach clearly divorces the question of tolerance from that of approval and thus defines the respective and exclusive domains of civil and moral law with regard to the proposed legislation; his careful distinctions allow the church to proclaim, "Render unto Caesar that which is Caesar's."

Generally, Wisconsin churches responded in kind. The Most Reverend Rembert G. Weakland, O.S.B., Roman Catholic Archbishop of Milwaukee, expressed the opinion of his church as follows: "You will recall that the National Conference of Catholic Bishops spoke to this issue in 1976. There has been no change in the Catholic position concerning homosexual activity, which has always been considered as morally wrong; on the other hand, it has also been consistent with Catholic teaching that homosexuals should not be deprived of their basic human rights."[58] Marjorie S. Matthews, Bishop of the United Methodist Church, Wisconsin Area, drew from a 1980 statement of Social Principles of the United Methodist Church in framing her support for AB70: "We insist that all persons are entitled to have their human and civil rights ensured, though we do not condone the practice of homosexuality and consider this practice incompatible with Christian teaching."[59] Robert S. Wilch, Bishop of the Wisconsin-Upper Michigan Synod of the Lutheran Church in America, provided a similar quotation from a statement on human sexuality adopted by his church in 1970.[60]

These responses are representative of the positions taken by a large number of churches in Wisconsin during the debate over AB70.[61] Because the question was strictly framed, the Church as a body was able to grant its benison to AB70 without diminishing Church authority in the moral realm. In fact, through its assent, the Church reaffirmed its moral authority by reserving the right to decline jurisdiction on a civil question. The success of this position is indicated in the statement issued by Governor Dreyfus explaining his decision to sign the bill. In the first paragraph, Dreyfus testifies to the power of the church and tacitly bows to its decision: "AB70 prohibits discrimination in employment, housing and public accommodations based on sexual orientation. This bill has a controversial history and my office has been under heavy pressure to veto it. It also, however, has the support of a wide ranging group of religious leadership, including leadership of the Roman Catholic Church, several Lutheran synods and the Jewish community."[62]

Later in the same statement, Dreyfus "firmly states that this restriction on discriminatory actions or decisions does not imply approval or encouragement [of homosexuality]."[63] The separation of the moral and legal and the retention of church power in the former is further testified to by the fact that the same Wisconsin state legislature that passed the nation's first statewide gay rights ordinance had, by 1982, repeatedly failed to pass a so-called "consenting adults bill," a bill that would have decriminalized sexual acts then proscribed by sodomy statutes. A critical difference between the two bills was that the Roman Catholic church in Wisconsin saw the latter as a moral, not a civil, question and withheld its support.[64] This resulted in the peculiar condition, as Clarenbach noted in an interview, in which "it's illegal to perform homosexual sex acts in Wisconsin yet you are protected by law against discrimination if you are a homosexual."[65]

The arguments surrounding AB70 can be fairly characterized by the fact that they center on the legal arena, either the courts or the legislature, and rather than radically confronting society on its own god-terms, homosexuals and their supporters prefer to define the legal arena very narrowly, avoiding confrontation on fundamentals. By emphasizing diversity and individuality, the gay rights argument attempts to mitigate the coercive force of duty. Without clashing over questions concerning the validity of certain sacred truths, gays and lesbians have simply asked to be excluded from their purview. It is a passive conception of liberty,[66] one that reveals its weaknesses when its opponents charge that it is merely libertinism.

The rhetoric of gay rights does not challenge the *polis*, singular, because it does not recognize the root that is necessary to ground the *polis*. Instead, gay rights rhetoric is almost apolitical in that it addresses the multitude as a mass of individuals, not as a political unity; its appeal is not to *de cive* but to man the maker of his own destiny; it is a rhetoric of disengagement. David Clarenbach, accounting for the success of Wisconsin's gay rights bill, emphasizes the individual, the private, not common positive valuation; he emphasizes the reluctance to enforce value:

There is a sector of the gay lifestyle which would be rather unacceptable to mainstream Wisconsinites. Yet, even in those small Midwestern towns that you think of in Norman Rockwell paintings, there is an overriding commitment to the principle of live and let live, love and let love. I don't think it's a conscious commitment to gay rights as such. I think most people in this country can't relate to, can't conceive of a homosexual. . . . But I think there's a real commitment to the principle that individuals have a right to sexual privacy.[67]

In all of this, the rhetoric of gay rights establishes itself, not as a rhetoric of judgment, but as a rhetoric of nonjudgment. The historic emphasis of gay rights rhetoric on difference and diversity is antithetical to the tendency to define, to order, to discipline, to regiment. There is no potential for radical commitment in such a discourse, for there is no clear locus for commitment, no compelling principle.[68]

The Best Little Boys (and Girls) in the World: The Questionable Virtues of Moderation

Just as we found an earlier paradox in the fact that sacred law in its immutability has generally been intended to preserve the status quo yet lends itself so well to radical reform, so we also find that desacralized law, because it is mutable, counsels obeisance while it is in force and moderation in its reform. As Locke so well understood:

This Doctrine of a Power in the People of providing for their safety a-new by a new Legislative, when their Legislators have acted contrary to their trust, by invading their Property, is the best fence against Rebellion, and the probablest means to hinder it. For Rebellion being an Opposition, not to Persons, but Authority, which is founded only in the Constitutions and Laws of the Government; those, whoever they be, who by force break through, and by force justifie their violation of them are truly and properly *Rebels.*[69]

Stuart Scheingold has noted the ambiguity in a legalist ideology that is both "rooted in a moral vision of a political society dedicated to maximizing individual freedom," and an instrumental promise of "a stable political order and a reliable structure of authority," but he has already provided the key to the legalist resolution of the conflict: "The law game provides an answer for every question and at the same times cuts the debate off short of first principles. As such, it contributes to and reinforces tendencies in the system toward rather modest ethical aspirations."[70] In other words, when there is a conflict between principle and process, a legalistic view of the world counsels adherence to process. This has been the overwhelming tendency in the rhetoric of gay rights.

In August 1965, Richard Conger, the editor of *One,* expressed the opinion that "the homophile is a worthy part of society and that as such he must merit and be accorded the same position and respect, the same Constitutional guarantees, as any other citizen." He went on to admonish homophiles: "But let it not be forgotten that he must merit and earn this freedom and this respect. Homophiles who play fast and loose with honesty and fair-dealing need not look for One's sympathy in their misconduct. In this broad and general sense One stands very much on the side of society as a whole."[71] Conger's gratuitous ethical profession is a thinly veiled disavowal of civil disobedience, perhaps the symptom of an immature and politically insecure reform movement. Yet two years after the so-called Stonewall rebellion of 1969 and the emergence of militant gay liberation, the editors of *The Advocate* were "encouraged" by the "strong evidence that between the hard conservatives and the intolerant radicals, young Gays are finding the middle ground productive."[72] The following year, the editors of the New York *Mattachine Times* scolded the leadership of the Gay Activist's Alliance for their "indecorous behavior," and their "disruptive and childish tactics." Mattachine's editors called for "discretion" in formulating protest strategies.[73]

If the older Mattachine groups were the only organizations to hold this view, it could be dismissed as marginal, but the attitude is not restricted to a time or to an organization. Lee Goodman, writing in the *GPU News* (Milwaukee) following the Miami defeat, counseled a "politics of patience":

Where the system has worked (and worked well), it has done so precisely to the extent that the constituencies, minorities, and pressure groups have acted with full and deliberated cognizance of the limitations and tensions which are internal to the political order. Good intentions, while often necessary, have seldom been sufficient; calculation, understanding, and rational assessment of means, ends, and costs are the payoff factors.[74]

At the beginning of this essay, we reviewed arguments to the effect that money becomes the primary source of value in a desacralized world; it also becomes the measure of rationality. We could not ask for a better example than Goodman's economic justification for moderate tactics. The emphasis on rationality and calculation suggests an implicit faith in the mechanical integrity of process, an exchange model of social reform; it is the process above all else that must be respected, for the denial of absolute truth has obviated the possibility that any given content could challenge the supremacy of the reasonable. Like Goodman, Michael Edwards also exalts process in his condemnation of certain militant tactics as symbolic, not of gay pride, but of "gay arrogance." Edwards charged that gay pride, "in its exuberance," often forgets the societal obligation to act "within reason."[75]

Amber Hollibaugh, though she would not agree with Goodman or Edwards on what should be done tactically, tends to confirm that their position is representative of what has been done. "The gay community too often doesn't resist," she writes, "and doesn't respect the gay people who do. Sometimes we are our own worst censors."[76] For Hollibaugh, the fight against the Briggs initiative in California in 1977 was the first gay rights campaign in the United States that did not subscribe to the assumptions of mainstream liberalism.[77]

The lesson Hollibaugh finds in gay rage did not take. In the summer of 1989, a year after the first Gay and Lesbian Pride March in Dubuque, Iowa, an event that provoked angry reaction garnering national attention and a regional response by lesbians and gays, the marchers returned to Dubuque in great numbers. There they were given a handout on "Non-Violence Guidelines" to which they were asked to give their assent. Among the provisos: "1. Our attitude will be one of openness and respect for all people we encounter. 2. We will not engage in physical violence, even in the face of hostility. 3. We will seek to express our feelings of anger, frustration, and pain without verbally abusing any individual." The lessons are the lessons of sublimation and control. In 1985, at a Chicago rally prior to the city council's consideration of a gay rights ordinance that had been in committee for thirteen years, those gathered sang a song popular at gay rights rallies, with a beginning and ending refrain of, "We are a gentle angry people, and we are singing, singing for our lives."[78] Here, with the emphasis on gentleness and song as a response to threat, we see a quality of gay protest that Nietzsche would have scorned as a variety of New Testament meekness.

John Reid's autobiographical work, though not ostensibly about gay politics, nonetheless captures much of the attitude behind it; that attitude is neatly summed up in the book's title, *The Best Little Boy in the World.*[79] Gay liberation plays by the rules, respects its elders, and never uses dirty words. As one of Ethan Mordden's characters notes: "Don't you realize that no one in America cares whether or not you're quietly homosexual? It's the gay stuff they hate, that's all. This public flogging of their feelings. You think the men upstairs are going to allow this filth to hector them indefinitely?"[80] Those who would claim that gay liberation is somehow radical or revolutionary are left making fatuous statements like, "Women's, gay and now men's liberation are embarked on a revolution that is so unlike our traditional concept of revolution that we tend not to recognize it for what it is."[81]

Perhaps it is a form of romanticized self-flattery to imagine ourselves in bright red clothes storming the barricades, but for whatever reason, the myth of the gay revolution persists, even when, as with the opening line of the controversial book, *After the Ball,* by Marshall Kirk and Hunter Madsen, it is only summoned as a measure of our folly and a call for renewed moderation. Kirk and Madsen, whose work received widespread notice in the mainstream as well as gay media, including a full-page review in *Time* magazine, may not be, as they claim they are not, homophobic—indeed, their obsession with the sanitary suggests that, in a world as dirty as ours, their phobias have a much wider reach than a simple fear of homosexuality—but the authors focus their prominently featured Harvard-bred puritanism on the sordidness of gay life. The following assessment, found near the end of the book, is interesting for the way in which the metaphors of cleanliness cross into the literal:

After the Ball has now detailed a comprehensive public-relations campaign that should go a long way toward sanitizing our very unsanitary image. But we can't hide forever beneath a coat of whitewash; we have to step out from behind the facade eventually, and unless we've made some real changes by the time we do, people will see that we're still the same old queers. Straights hate gays not just for what their myths and lies *say* we are, but also for what we *really* are; all the squeaky-clean media propaganda in the world won't sustain a positive image in the long run unless we start scrubbing to make ourselves a little squeakier and cleaner in reality. And as it happens, our noses (and other parts) are far from clean. In one major respect, America's homohaters have, like the proverbial blind pig, rooted up the truffle of truth; the gay lifestyle—not our sexuality, but our *lifestyle*—is the pits.[82]

The process of sanitizing, of cleaning, involves elimination—of dirt, of unhealthy elements, of the undesirable. In its most extreme form, it is a form of execution. We "kill germs." Hitler's purifying move involved the extermination of Jewish "lice" and "vermin," and it is in another bit of linguistic slippage that the insidious side of Kirk and Madsen's pogrom is fully revealed. When Kirk and Madsen write of gay pride marches tending "to degenerate before the TV cameras into ghastly freak shows, courtesy of newsmen seeking 'human interest material' and gender benders who think the mental health of uptight straight viewers is improved by visual shock therapy," the infinitive makes the verb form of "degenerate" unmistakable, but the reference to "gender benders" as the causal agent, coupled with other references to "flaming freaks," "screamers, stompers, gender-benders, sadomasochists, and pederasts" inevitably suggests the noun. As the reach of the sterilization expands, as "cocky mustachioed leathermen, drag queens, and bull dykes" are made to disappear in favor of public representatives who are "wholesome and admirable by straight standards, . . . completely unexceptional in appearance; in a word . . . indistinguishable from the straights we'd like to reach," a certain irony emerges in the suggestion that Kirk and Madsen provide an alternative to "gay suicide."[83]

The antiseptic campaign proposed by Kirk and Madsen to change America's views regarding homosexuality forthrightly takes as its model advertising, a discourse celebrated as "practical," "sensible," scientifically grounded, "completely unobjectionable," "hitched" to "pre-existing standards of law and justice," "expedient," and narrowly positivistic.[84] Not only does this set of descriptors represent a rather limited view of advertising, as the recent flap over Benetton ads and controversies surrounding campaigns of the past reveal, it also represents an idealized version of the

scientized, demystified, rationalized discourse of postmodern capitalist societies identified by Weber, Dewey, and Habermas, even to the economic
reductionism described earlier. "[I]n civil rights as in all other matters,"
aver the authors, "money talks."[85] If more evidence were needed of the
lack of transcendent value behind the Kirk and Madsen campaign, its
employment of primitive ends-justifies-means reasoning should provide
that evidence.[86]

If Kirk and Madsen were lonely eccentrics, isolated curmudgeons wag-
ing their rearguard war against decadence, they would not be worth our
attention, but I want to argue that they are, to the contrary, only the most
fulsomely articulated representatives of a tendency evident in U.S. gay
politics and rhetoric throughout its history and largely characteristic of it. It
is telling that even critics of *After the Ball* do not contest its fundamental
valorization of our society's present values, expressed as "Gay people
should behave like (better than) straight people" as measured by the
values professed by straight people. Instead, what those with visible and
established soapboxes, like Dave Walter, writing in *The Advocate,* choose
to argue is that gay people do, in fact, generally meet these standards. "It
is not true," Walter declared, "that gays are as irresponsible as Kirk and
Madsen suggest; the book's section about how gays misbehave simply does
not apply to the majority of gay people."[87] There is no suggestion in
Walter's dissent that there is anything less than perfect harmony between
him and Kirk and Madsen on the big questions of what constitutes responsibility and proper behavior, and there would seem to be little doubt that the
tactics of an organization like Act-Up, to name a group remonstrated by
Kirk and Madsen, or, even worse, Queer Nation, would be as alien and
offensive to Walter as they would be to our aspiring Madison Avenue–style
propagandists.

Despite the current visibility of groups like Act-Up and Queer Nation,
the evidence suggests that Messrs. Kirk, Madsen, and Walter reflect the
sentiments of the majority of gay American men and probably many lesbians
as well. In a 1977 letter to the editor of the Philadelphia *Gay News,* the
Lesbian Rights Committee of Delaware County decried the "radical lesbian/
feminist group committed to action," Dyketactics as having "the kind of
reputation that most self-respecting gay women's groups would risk their
necks to avoid getting. They have held numerous demonstrations during
their short existence, and each time they are held they fail to gain much, if
any support for us. If anything, they make the rest of us look like total

fools; an image that I do not think the gay women's groups enjoy very much!"[88] In a 1984 article in the New York *Native* entitled "The New Respectability," Philip Bockman was apparently ironic in identifying the urge toward respectability as "new." "Renewed," perhaps, maybe "recrudescent" or "resurgent," but Bockman really seems to suggest its constancy in gay history as he sadly remembers "the advice of some of my friends who had stood many rows behind me in the Stonewall Riot, on the fringes of the crowd. 'You want too much, you expect too much. If you ever want to get anywhere, you mustn't behave like this. You must try to be respectable.' "[89]

Our moderation stems from our fear of losing the rewards of good behavior. Activist Danny Sotomayor, characterized by the Chicago *Reader* as "the Angriest Queer," cast out now even from Act-Up, "the shock brigade of gay activism," embodies the rhetorical stance of the radical when he insists: "This isn't a popularity contest, you know. I really don't care whether people like me, or whether they approve of my style or my methods. The question is whether I'm right and whether we're making progress. Because if we are, then fuck 'em."[90] But the disregard of civility evidenced by Sotomayer and by groups like Act-Up often results in media coverage that is "nominal, and in some cases offensive."[91] Even PBS would not broadcast a documentary of an Act-Up "action" in St. Patrick's Cathedral in New York City, the action protesting John Cardinal O'Connor's opposition to condom distribution programs and gay rights. The documentary, network officials feared, was too controversial.

For our complicity with the rules, on the other hand, gays have been given the benediction of the liberal press. In 1976, an article in *Newsweek* appraised the progress gay rights had made since the Stonewall rebellion in 1969. The authors wrote:

At the outset of their drive for equal treatment, militant homosexuals alienated many people with their tactics of vivid confrontation. They mounted elaborate and boisterous demonstrations, led by blatantly effeminate men and masculine women, sometimes featuring obscene banners and deliberately provocative displays such as a giant phallus on a float.

Eventually, just as the civil-rights and women's movements evolved from confrontation to more sophisticated bargaining, the militant homosexuals learned the merits of lobbying and legal stratagems.[92]

"Bargaining" is praised as a sophisticated stratagem; the legislature and the courts are touted as the proper locus of appeal; alienation and confrontation are dismissed as puerile. Writing less than a year before the eruption in Miami, the authors of this article confidently promised the rewards of good behavior: "On balance, the prospect is that the activists will continue gradually to win more and more of the civil rights that have been denied to homosexuals in the past, and with these gains perhaps an increasing degree of public tolerance."[93]

The promise is of some indefinite set of benefits to be granted at some indeterminate future time. The insubstantiality of the package is readily revealed in confrontations like that with Anita Bryant's "Save Our Children." But the problem is more than terminal vagueness; the preferred considerations are counterfeit; they have no content.

Tolerance is a specious attainment; it has nothing to pose against the declaratory stance of the opposition. It is always supplicant, consisting as it does of the good will of the powerful. Tolerance, as Thomas Paine well understood, is no substitute for rights: "Toleration is not the *opposite* of Intolerance, but is the *counterfeit* of it. Both are despotisms. The one assumes to itself the right of withholding Liberty of Conscience, and the other of granting it."[94] At its best, tolerance provides, in Christopher Isherwood's phrase, "annihilation by blandness." At its worst, tolerance "serves the cause of oppression."[95] Tolerance too easily becomes senescent and indiscriminate; ultimately, its impartiality can be extended to include even prevailing intolerance and suppression.[96]

A society that has abdicated its ability to determine the right is a society that must allow the Nazis to march through the Jewish community of Skokie, Illinois. A society that has forfeited any idea of a truth to which it is responsible is a society that resolves its contests in the coliseum. It is no accident that the New Christian Right has turned to the referendum as its primary tool against gay rights.[97] Marcuse writes of this symptom of twentieth-century turpitude: "This pure tolerance of sense and nonsense is justified by the democratic argument that nobody, neither group nor individual, is in possession of the truth and capable of defining what is right and wrong, good and bad. Therefore, all contesting opinions must be submitted to 'the people' for its deliberation and choice."[98] It is a peculiarly inconsistent strategy in its implication that the majority can create or at least validate sovereign right, and it is the greatest of ironies that today, the fundamentalist Christians, who loudly equate homosexuality with the decadence of Rome, sit in the stands while the "Romans" battle the lions. The society that reduces moral issues to sport is genuinely decadent.

The battle over gay rights is seen as an ongoing process. Gay rights activists tend to maintain a liberal idea of progress, viewing defeats like that in Miami as temporary setbacks. At least in this respect, the process tends to validate their conception; no decision is absolute; each decision is only a measure of the popular will at a particular point in time. Certainly there is nothing to prevent homophile activists from raising these issues again—except inertia and the ability of tolerance to tolerate intolerance. Radicals, although they may not always be immediately successful, at least have a justification for their continuing insistence on reform; society must make its practice conform to what is right. In a reasonable and tolerant world, what right have gay activists to continue to trouble the populace with their wishes? What ground exists for appealing the decision of today? Not justice. And what moral duty does the population have to respond?

Notes

1. For an overview of the social-scientific idea of radicalism, see Egon Bittner, "Radicalism," in *International Encyclopedia of the Social Sciences,* ed. David L. Sills (Macmillan and Free Press, 1968), 13: 294–300.
2. Aristotle, *Rhetorica,* trans. W. Rhys Roberts, in *The Basic Works of Aristotle,* ed. Richard McKeon (New York: Random House, 1941), 1375a25–1375b7. See also *Politica,* trans. Benjamin Jowett, in *Basic Works,* 1324b27, where Aristotle writes: "Unlawful it certainly is to rule without regard to justice, for there may be might where there is not right."
3. Ibid., 1373b6.
4. Kathleen M. Jamieson, "Natural Law as Warrant," *Philosophy and Rhetoric* 236. David Lyons, in his article "Utility and Rights," states: "Moral rights are not merely independent of social recognition and enforcement but also provide grounds for appraising law and other social institutions. If social arrangements violate moral rights, they can be criticized accordingly" (in *Theories of Rights,* ed. Jeremy Waldron [Oxford: Oxford University Press, 1974], 114; emphases Lyons's).
5. Ibid.
6. Ibid., 242, n. 7.
7. See Charles Newman, *The Post-Modern Aura: The Act of Fiction in an Age of Inflation* (Evanston, IL: Northwestern University Press, 1985); Michael Harrington, *The Politics at God's Funeral: The Spiritual Crisis of Western Civilization* (New York: Viking-Penguin, 1985); T. J. Clark, "Clement

Greenberg's Theory of Art," in *The Politics of Interpretation*, ed. W. J. T. Mitchell (Chicago: University of Chicago Press, 1983), 203–20.

8. Irving Louis Horowitz, "The Pluralistic Bases of Modern American Liberalism," in *Ideology and Utopia in the United States 1956–1976* (Oxford: Oxford-University Press, 1977), 169. On the evolution of twentieth-century liberalism from its nineteenth-century roots, see Robert Paul Wolff, "Beyond Tolerance," in Robert Paul Wolff, Barrington Moore, Jr., and Herbert Marcuse, *A Critique of Pure Tolerance* (Boston: Beacon Press, 1969), 5–52. Wolff argues that the individualist emphasis in nineteenth-century liberalism could not be maintained in harmony with absolutist tendencies, and in the twentieth century, it is the individualist emphasis which is regnant. See also Ronald Dworkin, *Taking Rights Seriously* (Cambridge, Mass.: Harvard University Press, 1977), esp. vii–xiii, passim. Dworkin finds contemporary American legal theory to be a product of two parts of liberalism, the positivistic and the utilitarian; its structure leaves it open for criticism both for excessive rationalism and permissiveness from both the right and the left.

9. Horowitz, 169.

10. Peter L. Berger and Thomas Luckmann develop the idea of externalization of reality and its role in society in *The Social Construction of Reality: A Treatise in the Sociology of Knowledge* (Garden City, N.Y.: Doubleday-Anchor, 1967). Robert Wolff makes the telling remark that "the very essence of social constraint is that one feels it as objective, external, unavoidable, and hence genuinely a limit beyond which one's desires may not extend" (34).

11. See particularly Habermas, *Toward a Rational Society: Student Protest, Science, and Politics*, trans. Jeremy J. Shapiro (Boston: Beacon Press, 1970), passim, esp. 68, 98; *Legitimation Crisis*, trans. Thomas McCarthy (Boston: Beacon Press, 1975), passim.

12. For critical discussions of game theory and rational exchange models of conflict, see Thomas M. Steinfatt and Gerald R. Miller, "Communication in Game Theoretic Models of Conflict," in *Perspectives on Communication in Social Conflict*, ed. Gerald R. Miller and Herbert W. Simons (Englewood Cliffs, N.J.: Prentice-Hall, 1974), 14–75. Steinfatt and Miller note that "game Theory recognized all types of bases of conflict, but concentrates on rational features of the conflict situation; i.e., on rational self-interests pursued by the conflicting parties through their choices of alternative courses of action with different potential payoffs for the parties" (16). See also Fred E. Jandt, "Communication and the Simulation of Social Conflict," in Miller and Simons, 76–89; Herbert Simons's review essay, "Changing Notions About Social Movements," *Quarterly Journal of Speech* 62 (1976): 425–30; finally, see my review of Charles Tilly's *From Mobilization to Revolution*, *Quarterly Journal of Speech* 68 (1982): 102–4.

13. Wolff, 21.

14. Robert Bellah, *The Broken Covenant: American Civil Religion in Time of Trial* (New York: Seabury Press, 1975); see also "The Stone Which the Modern

70   *James Darsey*

Builders Rejected," in *Interpreting the Prophetic Tradition: The Goldensen Lectures, 1955–1966,* ed. Harry M. Orlinsky (Cincinnati: Hebrew Union College Press; New York: Ktav, 1969).
15. Almost all discussion of rights today centers around attitudes toward utilitarianism. See the readings in Waldron, for example; also H. L. A. Hart, "Between Utility and Rights" and Richard Wollheim, "John Stuart Mill and Isaiah Berlin: The Ends of Life and the Preliminaries of Morality," both in *The Idea of Freedom: Essays in Honour of Isaiah Berlin,* ed. Alan Ryan (Oxford: Oxford University Press, 1979); and Dworkin.
16. Wolff, 20.
17. Homosexual gathering places and social societies have a much longer history in America, but were quite distinct in composition and purpose from modern rights organizations. See Edward Sagarin, *Structure and Ideology in an Association of Deviants,* unpublished Ph.D. dissertation, New York University, 1966, 36–38; Jonathan Katz, *Gay American History: Lesbians and Gay Men in the U.S.A.* (New York: Thomas Y. Crowell, 1976), esp. 385–93, 407; John Lauritsen and David Thorstad, *The Early Homosexual Rights Movement (1864–1935)* (New York: Times Change Press, 1974), esp. 36, 71. Other sources that provide historical information on gay rights organizations in the United States include John D'Emilio, *Sexual Politics, Sexual Communities: The Making of a Homosexual Minority in the United States, 1940–1970* (Chicago: University of Chicago Press, 1983); Toby Marotta, *The Politics of Homosexuality* (Boston: Houghton Mifflin, 1981); Dennis Altman, *Homosexual: Oppression and Liberation* (New York: Avon, 1973).
18. Edward Sagarin, *Odd Man In: Societies of Deviance in America* (Chicago: Quadrangle Books, 1969), 80–81.
19. Howard Brown, *Familiar Faces, Hidden Lives: The Story of Homosexual Men in America Today* (New York: Harcourt Brace Jovanovich, 1976), 201–2.
20. See similar statements in Katz, 7; introduction to Martin P. Levine, ed., *Gay Men: The Sociology of Male Homosexuality* (New York: Harper and Row, 1979), 2–3; Bruce Voeller, "Society and the Gay Movement," in *Homosexual Behavior: A Modern Reappraisal,* ed. Judd Marmor (New York: Basic Books, 1980), 238. D'Emilio explores the attitudes of the church, medical science, and the law toward homosexuality in a helpful overview, 13–19.
21. Kenneth Burke, like Malinowski, often focuses on the essential differences among magic, science, and religion, but the repeated grouping of the three suggests their essential kinship, and Burke occasionally explicitly acknowledges this as when he writes, "Magic, religion, and science are alike in that they foster a body of thought concerning the nature of the universe and man's relation to it" (*Counter-Statement* [Berkeley: University of California Press, 1968], 163). In Burke's statement, we find a common objective in magic, religion, and science —that of defining man's relationship to a universe that is not man. See also Bronislaw Malinowski, *Magic, Science, and Religion* (Garden City, N.Y.: Doubleday-Anchor, 1954). On the demystifying tendencies in sci-

ence, Burke notes: "There is, in science, a tendency to substitute for ritual, routine. To this extent, there is an antipoetic ingredient in science" (*The Philosophy of Literary Form: Studies in Symbolic Action,* 3d ed., revised [Berkeley: University of California Press, 1973], 130). Thomas Lessl has illuminated the rhetoric of science as a rhetoric of religion focusing on Carl Sagan: Thomas M. Lessl, "Science and the Sacred Cosmos: The Ideological Rhetoric of Carl Sagan," *Quarterly Journal of Speech* 71 (1985): 175–87.

22. Dennis Altman, *Homosexual: Oppression and Liberation* (New York: Avon, 1973), 185; on Altman's view of the genesis of gay liberation as opposed to the homophile movement, see 152ff. For a view that stresses the continuities between the so-called "homophile liberation movement" and the later "gay liberation movement," see D'Emilio.

23. Martin S. Weinberg and Colin J. Williams find a reevaluation of sexual mores after the Second World War to be a major factor in the formation of the homophile liberation movement in America, *Male Homosexuals: Their Problems and Adaptations* (New York: Oxford University Press, 1974). John D'Emilio traces the disruptive influences of the war and of new patterns of living following the war.

24. William Lee Miller, "The Rise of Neo-Orthodoxy," in Arthur M. Schlesinger, Jr., and Morton White, eds., *Paths of American Thought* (Boston: Houghton Mifflin, Sentry, 1970).

25. For this analysis and use of the term "civil religion," see John Murray Cuddihy, *No Offense: Civil Religion and Protestant Taste* (New York: Seabury Press, 1978).

26. Arthur M. Schlesinger, Jr., "The One against the Many," reprinted in Schlesinger and White, 538.

27. Edwin M. Schur, "The Sociologist Comments," in *Victimless Crimes: Two Sides of a Controversy,* ed. Edwin M. Schur and Hugo Adam Bedau (Englewood Cliffs, N.J.: Prentice-Hall, 1974), 118.

28. Sagarin, *Odd Man In,* 82–84.

29. D'Emilio, 18.

30. Grant Gilmore, *The Ages of American Law* (New Haven, Conn.: Yale University Press), 110, *passim.*

31. Ibid., 95f.

32. "Changing Public Opinion," *Mattachine Review* 3 (November 1957), 2.

33. "How Far We Have Come," *Mattachine Times* (October–November, 1971),1.

34. For a quantitative corroboration of this claim, see James Darsey, "From 'Commies' and 'Queers' to 'Gay Is Good,'" in *Gayspeak: Gay Male and Lesbian Communication,* ed. James Chesebro, 224–47 (New York: Pilgrim Press, 1981); James Darsey, "From 'Gay is Good' to the Scourge of AIDS: The Evolution of Gay Liberation Rhetoric, 1977–1990," *Communication Studies* 42, no. 1: 43–66.

35. *Mattachine Review,* September 1956, November 1957.

36. *Mattachine Times,* October–November 1971.

37. See for example, *California Scene* (Summer 1975), esp. "Editorial," 2, and David Johns, "Penal Code Reform and Other Bills," 17.
38. *NGRA,* National Gay Rights Advocates Newsletter (Spring 1988).
39. "A Call for Action," *The Advocate* (March 9, 1977).
40. For other examples, see "Your Right to Be Different!" *New York Mattachine Newsletter* (January 1960), 3; "Calling Shots," *Mattachine Review* 7 (November 1961), 2; *Mattachine Review* 9 (September 1963), 2, 10, 12, 13; "AB 489: Two-Way Winner," *The Advocate* (June 4, 1975), 26.
41. Stuart A. Scheingold, *The Politics of Rights: Lawyers, Public Policy and Political Change* (New Haven, Conn.: Yale University Press, 1974), 17.
42. Dworkin, xii.
43. "Battle over Gay Rights: Anita Bryant vs. The Homosexuals," *Newsweek,* June 6, 1977, 16–26. See also "The Gaycott Turns Ugly: Homosexual Militants are Tormenting Foe Anita Bryant," *Time,* November 21, 1977, 33.
44. See for example the advertisement, "What's Going On in America?" sponsored by the Stichting Vrije Relatierechten Foundation (Foundation for Free Human Partnership), which appeared in *Time,* January 9, 1978, 73. The advertisement was signed by Simone de Beauvoir, Sir John Gielgud, Günter Grass, Bernard Haitink, Jean-Paul Sartre, and Jean-Francois Revel, among others. At home it was Marxist gay groups that mounted a similar criticism. For example, see *Red Flag, Newspaper of the Red Flag Union,* July 1977.
45. "Voting against Gay Rights: A Backlash against Growing Tolerance," *Time,* May 22, 1978, 21–22.
46. Charles Ortleb, interview with Ethan Geto, *Christopher Street,* August 1977, 27. Evidence from other sources corroborates the idea that Americans are willing to make a distinction between moral evaluation and civil rights. "How Gay is Gay?" *Time,* April 23, 1979, 72–76.
47. Ethan Geto, in "Miami Post-Mortem: Lessons From Losing: Four Perspectives of Dade County," *The Advocate,* August 24, 1977, 7.
48. Geto says of the Miami campaign, "We used our ads to ask voters to consider what America is all about, that it's about the majority respecting the rights of minorities; about the right to be different; that rights are not rewards to be distributed to people we like, but the birthright of every American" (*The Advocate,* August 24, 1977), 7–8.
49. Barry Brummett, "A Pentadic Analysis of Ideologies in Two Gay Rights Controversies," *Central States Speech Journal* 30 (1979): 253, 255, *passim.* See also Ronald Fischli, "Anita Bryant's Stand against 'Militant Homosexuality': Religious Fundamentalism and the Democratic Process," *Central States Speech Journal* 30 (1979): 263, *passim.* Both of these essays are reprinted in Chesebro.
50. Richard Steele, with Tony Fuller, "God's Crusader," *Newsweek,* June 6, 1977, 20.
51. Anita Bryant, *The Anita Bryant Story: The Survival of Our Nation's Families and the Threat of Militant Homosexuality* (Old Tappan, N.J.: Fleming H. Revell Co., 1977), 37–38, quoted in Fishcli, 267.

52. See Steele; Fischli, esp. 270.

53. Fischli, 270.

54. For some representative views, see "Homosexuality as Sin," *Time,* June 5, 1978, 53.

55. The question of whether or not homosexuality is a choice has been a significant argument for gay rights advocates and their opponents from the beginning. At stake is the question of whether or not gays are a legitimate minority like blacks and women or simply antisocial and irresponsible criminals like murderers and rapists. The most significant treatment of the question is Alan P. Bell, Martin S. Weinberg, and Sue Kiefer Hamersmith, *Sexual Preference: Its Development in Men and Women,* an official publication of the Kinsey Institute for Sex Research (Bloomington: Indiana University Press, 1981). On the significance of the argument, see Carol Warren, "Homosexuality and Stigma," in Marmor, 137f. See also Berger and Luckmann, 165, on the paradox in the position of the right on this issue.

56. I am grateful to Representative Clarenbach and to Dan Curd of his staff for supplying me with much of the material concerning AB70, including the transcript of the Assembly debate (October 23, 1981) from which this quotation was taken.

57. Ibid.

58. Letter to the Reverend John Murtaugh, March 2, 1981.

59. Letter to members of the Wisconsin State Legislature, April, 3, 1981.

60. Letter to members of the Wisconsin State Legislature, April 1, 1981.

61. See also letter to members of the Wisconsin State Legislature from the Right Reverend William C. Wantland, Episcopal Bishop of Eau Claire, March 19, 1981; letter to members of the Wisconsin State Legislature from Ralph P. Ley, Conference President, Wisconsin Conference of the United Church of Christ, April 1981; letter to members of the Wisconsin State Assembly from Vernon E. Anderson, President, The American Lutheran Church, Northern Wisconsin District, September 18, 1981. Some denominations expressed a liberal theology in addition to liberal politics. See letter to members of the Wisconsin State Legislature from Charles T. Gaskell, Bishop, Episcopal Diocese of Milwaukee. Inevitably, there were also some dissenters who threatened that free and legal acceptance of the homosexual lifestyle would rend the fabric of society. See letter to "Each Member of the Wisconsin State Assembly" from Richard E. Pritchard, Pastor, Heritage Church, Madison, Wisconsin, October 26, 1981. See also Seward Hiltner, "Homosexuality and the Churches," in Marmor, 219–31.

62. Statement from Governor Lee Sherman Dreyfus to Representative David Clarenbach concerning AB70.

63. Ibid. See similar remarks by Clarenbach in Carol Stroebel, "Nuns in the Gallery: The Church, David Clarenbach, and Wisconsin's Gay Rights Bill," *New York Native,* March 15–28, 1982, 15.

64. Stroebel, 15.

65. Ibid.

66. For some germane remarks on "liberty" as a "feminization of power," see Michael Calvin McGee, "The Origins of 'Liberty': A Feminization of Power," *Communication Monographs* 47 (1980): 23–45.
67. Stroebel, 16.
68. Guy Hocquenghem's analysis of the antipolitical nature of homosexuality as "desire" rather than "revolution," a desire which is, in fact, directionless, is relevant here: *Homosexual Desire*, trans. Daniella Dangoor (London: Allison and Busby, 1978), 120–25, 104. A recurrent theme in the rhetoric of gay liberation is the search for direction, and it is no accident that the movement achieves its greatest clarity of vision during crises perpetrated from without. In this sense, the movement has tended to be quite reactionary.
69. John Locke, *Two Treatises of Government*, ed. Peter Laslett (New York: New American Library, 1963), 464.
70. Scheingold, 59, 57.
71. Richard Conger, "Editorial," *One*, August 1965.
72. "Movement's New Hope," New York *Mattachine Times*, September 29–October 12, 1981, 22.
73. Charles Mountain [pseud.], "Discretion: An Editorial," New York *Mattachine Times*, February–March 1972.
74. Lee Goodman, "The Politics of Patience," *GPU News*, October 1977, 12–13.
75. Michael Edwards, "Gay Pride or Gay Arrogance?" Chicago *Gaylife*, June 23, 1978, 11.
76. Amber Hollibaugh, "Right to Rebel," in *Homosexuality: Power and Politics*, Gay Left Collective, ed. (London: Allison and Busby, 1980), 214.
77. Ibid., 212–13. In addition to Hollibaugh, the theme that runs throughout Marotta's analysis of gay politics is the prevalence of moderate goals and tactics. See also Barry D. Adam, "A Social History of Gay Politics," in Levine, 285–300. Adam, like Hollibaugh, is critical of what he terms the "assimilationist formula," but he too finds it to be the predominant approach of gay rights activists. See also the provisions of the 1972 Gay Rights Platform adopted at the meeting of NACHO in San Francisco that year as reprinted in Laud Humphreys, *Out of the Closets: Sociology of Homosexual Liberation* (Englewood Cliffs, N.J.: Prentice-Hall, 1972), 165–66. Morris Kight provided direction for the platform when he explicitly termed it "a civil rights plank, not a revolutionary document," quoted in Humphreys, 165. See also "New Directions," *Gay*, March 12, 1973, 3. A 1967 newsletter from Mattachine Midwest provided a summary of attitudes held by the editorial staff which included the ideas that "homosexuals must establish good rapport with parents, the opposite sex, and the world at large"; that "homosexuals are not special characters and have no special rights"; that "minority groups must make sacrifices to gain equal rights (to which all are entitled)"; that "no one had the right to 'carry on' indiscreetly or compulsively"; and that "homosexuals should not have to apologize except when they infringe (their homosexuality infringes) on the rights of others" (*Mattachine Midwest Newsletter* 11 [July 1967]: 1). When a gay rights bill was

being debated in the city council in 1985, Chicago gays were encouraged to engage in " 'quiet' lobbying efforts" on behalf of the proposed ordinance. See Tracy Baim, "Aldermen call for 'quiet' lobby efforts on City Council rights bill at Action forum," Chicago *Gaylife,* February 7, 1985, 1.

78. "Gentle Angry People," by Holly Near with new lyrics by P. Walowitz.

79. John Reid, *The Best Little Boy in the World* (New York: G. P. Putnam, 1973). The introduction of biographical writing at this point is of more than casual significance. Much of gay and lesbian writing is autobiographical, indicating an inward focus of attention on the individual. This is consistent with claims we have made about the existential, atomic focus of twentieth-century society. It is also consistent with the importance of consciousness raising to sexual liberation groups. Yet it is difficult to see how consciousness raising is necessarily either "radical" or "revolutionary," even propaedeutically. The new left's equation of the personal with the political seems a willful confusion of the nature of the political; consciousness raising is primarily therapeutic, and a trip to one's therapist can hardly be considered a revolutionary act. For prominent samples of gay and lesbian autobiographical material, see Nancy Adair and Casey Adair, eds., *Word is Out: Stories of Some of Our Lives* (San Francisco and New York: New Glide Publications and Delacorte Press, 1978); Alan Ebert, ed., *The Homosexuals* (New York: Macmillan, 1977); Arnie Kantrowitz, *Under the Rainbow: Growing Up Gay* (New York: William Morrow, 1977); Merle Miller, *On Being Different: What It Means to Be a Homosexual* (New York: Random House, 1971); and David Kopay and Perry Deane Young, *The David Kopay Story* (New York: Arbor House, 1977). On consciousness raising, see James W. Chesebro, John F. Cragan, and Patricia McCullough, "The Small Group Techniques of the Radical-Revolutionary: A Synthetic Study of Consciousness Raising," *Speech Monographs* 40 (1973): 136–46; A Gay Male Group, "Notes on Gay Male Consciousness-Raising," in *Out of the Closets: Voices of Gay Liberation,* ed. Carla Jay and Allen Young, 293–301 (New York: Pyramid, 1974); and Marotta, 100–133. John Shiers provides an illuminating perspective on consciousness raising versus *praxis* in "Two Steps Forward, One Step Back," in Gay Left Collective, 140–56.

80. Ethan Mordden, *Buddies* (New York: St. Martin's Press, 1986), 129.

81. Altman, 224.

82. Marshall Kirk and Hunter Madsen, *After the Ball: How America Will Conquer Its Fear and Hatred of Gays in the '90s* (New York: Doubleday, 1989), 275–76.

83. Ibid., 183, xxvi.

84. Ibid., xxvi, xxvi, 161, 207, 187, 276. Kirk and Madsen are fond of psychological jargon. They describe the workings of their campaign in terms of "desensitization," "conversion," "Associative Conditioning," and "Direct Emotional Modeling. (See 154–55 for an example.) One can only assume that the spirit of B. F. Skinner was still strong at Harvard when these lads were in school there. Not only do their descriptions of psychological processes sound unreflectively Skinnerian, but so does their emphasis on behavior and its modification. See

357, the ten "misbehaviors" in Chapter 1, *passim.* Finally, their naive view of the immutability of scientific logic reflects a staggering ignorance of recent work in epistemology, the philosophy of science, and the nature of rationality. Consider especially their definitions of "facts" and "logic" (341).

85. Ibid., 76; see also 204.

86. For a particularly unabashed example of this, consider the following: "It makes no difference that the ads are lies; not to us, because we're using them to ethically good effect, to counter negative stereotypes that are every bit as much lies, and far more wicked ones; not to bigots, because the ads will have their effect on them whether they believe them or not" (154). Unfortunately, Kirk and Madsen provide no basis for determining "ethically good effect." This quotation also reveals again a mechanistic faith in the operation of scientific psychology: bigots will be influenced by the ads whether they believe them or not.

87. Dave Walter, "After What Ball?" *The Advocate,* September 12, 1989, 23.

88. Philadelphia *Gay News,* April 1977, 22.

89. Philip Bockman, "The New Respectability," New York *Native,* September 24–October 7, 1984, 51.

90. Joseph Crump, "The Angriest Queer," Chicago *Reader,* August 17, 1990, 20.

91. Members of Act-Up/Seattle, "The Sweet Smell of Support," Seattle *Gay News,* March 30, 1990, 16.

92. Jerrold K. Footlick with Susan Agrest, "Gays and the Law," *Newsweek,* October 25, 1976, 101.

93. Ibid., 103.

94. Thomas Paine, *The Rights of Man,* ed. Eric Foner (New York: Penguin American Library, 1984), 85.

95. Marcuse, "Repressive Tolerance," in Wolff et al., 81. See also Leo Strauss, *Natural Right and History* (Chicago: University of Chicago Press, 1953), 5f.

96. Marcuse, 83, 88, 98, *passim.*

97. See Jan Carl Park, "Referendum Campaigns vs. Gay Rights," in Chesebro, 286–90.

98. Marcuse, 94.

4. Reflections on Gay and Lesbian Rhetoric

James W. Chesebro

Over a decade has passed since *Gayspeak: Gay Male and Lesbian Communication* was published.[1] The decade has been decisive. *Queer Words, Queer Images: Communication and the Construction of Homosexuality* was designed to respond to the changes that have occurred during the last decade.

Gayspeak was conceived in the late 1970s. Accordingly, *Gayspeak* responded to a sociosexual culture and critical era dramatically unlike the norms and mores that govern the 1990s. In 1981, the rhetorical analyses included in *Gayspeak* presumed—quite unconsciously—that gay liberation was only one of several "typical" movements that could appropriately be assessed within the parameters of the modern era, that institutional change from within was to be expected, that a single and cohesive audience in the form of the "American public" existed, that rhetorical strategies and the media employed to transmit these strategies—as the available means of persuasion—could be understood as "ideologically pure," and that liberal ideals constituted an appropriate set of topoi for securing a shift in audience attitudes and measuring persuasive effectiveness. All of these presumptions—which functioned as assumptions in *Gayspeak*—have now become issues within the discipline of communication.

In this commentary, it is appropriate to identify explicitly the shifts that have occurred since 1980, and then to provide a placement of the three rhetorical analyses that define the "Gay and Lesbian Rhetoric" section of *Queer Words, Queer Images* within this context. The placement suggests that some of the rhetorical analyses contained in *Queer Words, Queer Images* contribute to our understanding of the post-1980 era, while others are more aptly viewed as updating the rhetorical system presumed in *Gayspeak.*

Of the several changes which might be identified, three specific shifts since 1980 constitute significant benchmarks for comparing and distinguishing *Gayspeak* and *Queer Words, Queer Images.* These changes include (1) the emergence of AIDS as a deadly epidemic in 1981, often identified as a "gay disease"; (2) the emergence of postmodern rhetorical theory and criticism that has challenged traditional and basic concepts in the discipline of communication such as the meaning of the term audience; and (3) the recognition, provided predominantly by feminist scholars, that rhetorical strategies and the media employed to transmit these strategies are ideological in origin and use.

AIDS as a Political Variable Defining the Rhetorical Situation of Gay Male and Lesbian Discourse

While cast in different ways, a basic premise of rhetorical theory holds that conditions and audiences affect communication choices and outcomes. As Burke has stated the case, "If there is any slogan that should reign among critical precepts, it is that 'circumstances alter occasions.' "[2] In Bitzer's conception, "It is the situation which calls the discourse into existence."[3]

In 1980, gay male and lesbian discourse was perceived as culminating in a new definition of homosexuality. As Darsey observed in 1981:

Despite the tremendous complexity involved in the discourse of a social movement over a quarter century, what is clear from this analysis is that people in the United States, by and large, now hold different beliefs about homosexuality than they did twenty-five years ago. . . . In 1969 a Harris poll revealed that 63 percent of Americans considered homosexuality harmful to the American way of life. Yet, in 1977 Yankelovich, Skelley, and White reported that 56 percent of those polled said they would vote for legislation guaranteeing the civil rights of homosexuals.[4]

Darsey concluded that the phrase "Gay is good" aptly reflected this new orientation toward homosexuality which "is not the result of a search for knowledge; it is the creation of knowledge through the evolution of discourse."[5]

Yet a dramatic reverse began to manifest itself in the 1980s and into the 1990s. Since the early 1980s, when AIDS was first identified and often linked to homosexual behavior, Gallup has reported a significant decline in the percentage of people who think "homosexual relations between consenting adults should be legal" and a corresponding increase in the number of people who think "homosexual relations between consenting adults should be illegal":[6]

Trends in Attitudes toward Homosexual Relations

Year	Legal	Illegal	No Opinion
1977	43%	43%	14%
1982	45%	39%	16%
1985	44%	47%	9%
1986	33%	54%	13%
1987	33%	55%	12%
1991	36%	54%	10%

In October 1991, the Gallup Poll specifically reported that "Americans have grown less accepting of homosexuals. Three in five (61 percent) feel the tolerance of gay life in the 1960s and 1970s was a 'bad thing for our society.' Only 36 percent of adults today believe homosexual relations between consenting adults should be legal, a figure comparable to 1986 (33 percent), when it declined from the 43–45 percent level recorded between 1977 and 1985."[7]

The critical factor affecting this reversal was the discovery of the HIV virus and AIDS and the attribution of these pathogenic factors to a social grouping, homosexuals. The Gallup Poll captures this perceived causal link by way of an example: " 'They were just beginning to get some of their rights and come out of their closet with their sexual habits, and then AIDS hit the scene,' says the thirty-nine year old Cape Cod father, whose baby boom age group is more tolerant of gays than those over forty-five (41 percent vs. 26 percent). The youngest, baby bust age group is most tolerant of all: 45 percent support legalization of gay relations."[8] Similarly, a 1991 New York Times/CBS News Poll found that "only 39 percent said they have a lot or some sympathy for 'people who get AIDS from homosexual activity,' about the same as the 36 percent who expressed such sentiment in 1988."[9] Finally, it should be noted that many common AIDS educational programs apparently make people less tolerate of those with AIDS. Researchers at Georgia Tech have found that workers who attended AIDS educational programs "less than two hours long were significantly less tolerant of people with AIDS than were workers who had received other forms of education, or none at all."[10] In all, AIDS has altered how people respond to homosexuality, decisively altering the measured progress and quest for liberation that characterized the outcome of the discourse of gay males and lesbians in the 1960s and 1970s.

AIDS had clearly become a decisive political issue by 1986, and it has continued to function as a rationale for dramatic reversals for gay male and lesbian civil, legal, and social rights. A case study illustrates some of the issues.[11] In May 1992, Colorado for Family Values, a group formed to "stop gay activists before they trample on freedoms," gathered 65,000 valid signatures to place on the November 1992 ballot a proposal to "bar any civil rights measures intended specifically to protect homosexuals, lesbians or bisexuals" and to "void existing laws in Denver, Boulder and Aspen that ban anti-gay bias in housing, employment, and health and welfare services." The initiative won support of University of Colorado football Coach William McCartney, who has called homosexuality "an abomination of almighty God," identified gay male and lesbian civil rights as protections that "force you and me to give our state's legal blessing to aberrant homosexual behavior and life styles," and described the AIDS epidemic as the "self-created miseries of pleasure-addicted gays."

In all, since 1981, AIDS has become a critical factor in altering political trends. It has functioned as a rationale for political oppression, isolated gay males from the mainstream of society, and provided a foundation for reversing the civil, legal, and social rights secured by gay males and lesbians in the 1960s and 1970s. It has ultimately altered dramatically any claims that might have been made about the continuity of progress toward the establishment of gay male and lesbian rights.

The AIDS epidemic functions as a benchmark when offering a synoptic placement of the first three essays in Part One of *Queer Words, Queer Images.*

Paul Siegel's "On the Owning of Words: Reflections on *San Francisco Arts and Athletics vs. United States Olympic Committee*" and Karen A. Foss's "The Logic of Folly in the Political Campaigns of Harvey Milk" are most appropriately perceived as pre-AIDS analyses, constrained by symbolic orientations of the 1970s, and are probably not to be understood as rhetorical events that have had the power to overcome the impact of the negative association between homosexuality and the AIDS epidemic. And it should be noted that both authors are careful to restrict their analyses to the immediate arena in which these rhetorical events occurred.

Siegel discusses only the legal implications of the June 1987 Supreme Court decision, holding that the decision "will likely not provide [the gay rights movement] the galvanizing force" of earlier decisions and does not "indicate that gays' first amendment rights are in jeopardy"; he is optimistic in believing that the "narrowness of the Court's ruling will have to be its own silver lining" and ultimately casts the decision as possessing legal implications for freedom of speech cases rather than functioning as a critical legal and civil case for gay male and lesbian rights. Of the *San Francisco Arts and Athletics vs. United States Olympic Committee* decision, Siegel concludes: "It will probably be remembered as a case in which the Court chose *not* to offer a major new pronouncement on the law of trademark, free speech, or equal protection."

Foss is likewise particularly cautious in identifying any long-term consequences for the kind of political campaign tactics represented in the case of Harvey Milk. As Foss notes, "The description of traditional folly has many parallels to the situation in which Milk and the gay community generally found themselves in the early 1970s." Additionally, in an era in which the AIDS epidemic might easily intensify any negative claim about gay males and lesbians, Foss reports that she is using the terms *folly* and *fool* in a "traditional" sense when folly "was serious business and bore little resemblance to the forms of comedy, humor, and wit that accompany modernity" or in the "contemporary" sense with its "tendency to use the word 'fool' as only a derogatory label." At the same time, given the social atmosphere created by the AIDS epidemic, one may wish to qualify Foss's claim that "this study of Milk's campaign rhetoric, then, offers a model useful for other gay and lesbian office seekers and may apply to other contexts in which gays and lesbians—and other outside groups—seek positions of influence without abandoning or compromising their own identities."

In sharp contrast to the mainstreaming symbolic orientation presumed by Siegel and Foss, James Darsey, in his essay "Die Non: Gay Liberation and the Rhetoric of Pure Tolerance," writes: "A world where there is no center, where there is no division between the center and the periphery, is a world without the mystery and separation necessary to the sacred, and where there is no externalization of truth, there is no principle that commands assent except self-interest, and there is thus no community." Dismissing a world of "morality," for "only madmen talk to God," and the significance of Supreme Court decisions and political campaigns designed to attract, Darsey maintains that economic power provides the most meaningful indication of privilege: "Reason offers some evidence of resources convertible to economic terms in exchange for privilege; it does not demand rights." Employing a larger time frame, Darsey maintains that "the Second World War represents a very real change for sexual mores in general and for homosexuals in particular; the dereliction of natural law allowed for a new ethic of permissiveness. It is in this sense of permission that homophile liberation is best understood." Indeed, rather than respond to specific legal and political institutions, the rhetoric of tolerance described by Darsey "is almost apolitical in that it addresses the multitude as a mass of individuals, not as a political unity; its appeal is not to *de cive* but to man the maker of his own destiny; it is a rhetoric of disengagement"; for Darsey holds that "the historic emphasis of gay rights rhetoric on difference and diversity is antithetical to the tendency to define, to order, to discipline, to regiment." He concludes, "There is no potential for radical commitment in such a discourse, for there is no clear locus for commitment, no compelling principle."

In the context of the AIDS epidemic, Darsey's analysis deserves special attention. Certainly, the positive orientation found in Darsey's *Gayspeak* essay—with the attention it devoted to increasingly positive opinion polls in the 1970s and the belief in the potential rhetorical power of "Gay is good"—is missing in his *Queer Words, Queer Images* article. Indeed, the AIDS epidemic appears to have altered profoundly how Darsey would conceive and view the rhetoric of a social movement. In the spring of 1991, Darsey reported:

Over the course of the next two years [since 1981], as death tolls rose and the multifarious forms of the disease were identified as having a common provenance, AIDS became the obsessive concern of gay rights activists, coloring all activity concerning the welfare of gay men and lesbians in the United States. AIDS presented the gay community with not only a public health crisis, but crises in the social, legal, and psychological spheres as well. AIDS catalyzed a shift in the rhetoric of the gay movement.[12]

In this 1991 essay, Darsey's conclusions were complex. He held that AIDS has not diminished the need to formulate demands of society: "From

1977 to 1990, as the emerging prominence of work-determination-strength appeals suggests, there is little of the old hesitation among gays in asserting that better and more equitable treatment is deserved from society."[13] At the same time, Darsey maintained that AIDS may have created profound questions regarding the role, if any, of the homosexual within the moral scheme of the larger sociopolitical system:

In recent years gays may have come to feel better about themselves as individuals than they did in the 1950s, but it appears that this may be tied to their ability to eschew stereotypes in their own lives and to emulate the surrounding straight culture; it appears that there remain very real reservations about homosexuality in general precisely in the degree that it fails to share the values of the larger society. . . .

Perhaps this is the fundamental question for any movement for social reform, the question of how to define success. How much do *we* become like *them* in order to enjoy the fruits of what they call success, and how much do *we* make *them* acknowledge that there are alternatives that must be respected?[14]

At the outset of this essay, I suggested that the rhetorical system governing *Gayspeak* is profoundly different than the rhetorical system that has emerged since the devastation of the AIDS epidemic. AIDS has altered the rhetoric of gay liberation in ways that could not have been predicted in 1980, and it has generated a discourse that advocates a structural separation of gay males and lesbians from the morality of the larger sociopolitical system, a separation that creates a historical discontinuity between the rhetorical acts of the 1970s and the rhetorical acts of the 1980s through the 1990s. Of the essays included in this section of *Queer Words, Queer Images,* the first two essays are best understood as reflecting the rhetoric of gay liberation in the 1970s, while the third recognizes, identifies, and captures the rhetoric of gay males and lesbians as it has emerged since 1981.

The Emergence of Postmodern Rhetorical Theory and Criticism

Since the publication of *Gayspeak* in 1981, changes within the discipline of communication, and particularly among rhetorical critics, have also occurred. Of these changes, postmodern rhetorical theory and criticism, developed in the mid-1960s in Western Europe, has perhaps offered the most thorough challenge to traditional American rhetorical theory and criticism. Indeed, Karen A. Foss—along with her coeditors Sonja Foss and Robert Trapp—have surveyed the "different perspectives on rhetoric" that have dominated the twentieth-century "contemporary" rhetorical "period," and they devote over one-third of their attention to postmodern rhetoricians such as Ernesto Grassi, Michel Foucault, and Jürgen Habermas.[15] "Such an emphasis," Bernard L. Brock, Robert L. Scott, and I have maintained, "reflects, rather than distorts, the emerging and growing attention that has been devoted to postmodern critics in the discipline of communication by both rhetorical critics and social scientists."[16]

All of the precepts of postmodern rhetoric have by no means been accepted by contemporary American rhetoricians, but certain postmodern principles are sufficiently compelling to warrant serious attention. This commentary does not provide me with the space to detail the origins of these principles, to compare and contrast modern and postmodern theory and criticism, or to identify the potential implications for contemporary American rhetorical theory and criticism. However, I do want to draw attention to one postmodern principle: *Every rhetorical analysis inherently conveys multiple and contradictory meanings.*[17] The principle presumes that we exist within a multicultural environment in which different sociocultural groups—be they ethnic, racial, religious, socioeconomic, or gender-based—have constructed diverse symbolic systems which affect how discourse is perceived, understood, and evaluated. In this sense, the intent of the author may provide little indication of how discourse is apprehended by the multiple audiences that will come into contact with a rhetorical act. In terms of rhetorical theory and criticism, this postmodern principle advises that the effects or consequences of any rhetorical act should be examined in terms of several audiences rather than one homogeneous audience.

The postmodern emphasis upon multiple audiences provides a useful base for providing yet another synoptic placement of the first three essays in Part One.

Siegel's and Foss's essays are most appropriately perceived as single-audience orientations, constrained by a symbolic orientation some have identified as liberal,[18] and accordingly should not be treated as universal analyses of the rhetorical events they examine.

Implicitly arguing that institutional participation is significant, Siegel focuses upon the degree to which the first amendment rights of gay males and lesbians have and have not been extended by the Supreme Court's

June 1987 *San Francisco Arts and Athletics vs. United States Olympic Committee* decision. Additionally, Siegel's conclusions are noteworthy. He concludes that the decision "will probably be remembered as a case in which the Court chose *not* to offer a new pronouncement on the law of trademark, free speech, or equal protection" and that the decision does not "indicate that gays' first amendment rights are in jeopardy." One might well imagine that conservative and reactionary political commentators would offer alternative views to Siegel's conclusions, beginning with the proposition that the decision justly and appropriately precluded gay males and lesbians from using the Olympic label.

Likewise, Foss implicitly maintains that institutional participation is likely to make a difference for gay males and lesbians, and she specifically maintains that "Milk's campaign rhetoric" offers "a model useful for other gay and lesbian office seekers." Foss is equally convinced that her characterization of Milk as a fool employing the rhetorical strategies that can be clustered under the label of folly will be understood in the "traditional" sense in which her analysis is intended. Yet the postmodern notion of diverse audience readings of such characterizations would at least allow for the possibility that the terms fool and folly can be read by antigay and lesbian advocates as negative, if not a partial rationalization for the killing of Milk.

In sharp contrast to the single-audience orientation presumed by Siegel and Foss, in his essay, Darsey directly examines the emergence of diverse audiences, audiences which he believes lack a unifying morality, which therefore makes liberation through tolerance the most meaningful rhetorical strategy. Darsey's conclusion bears repetition:

The battle over gay rights is seen as an ongoing process. Gay rights activists tend to maintain a liberal idea of progress, viewing defeats like that in Miami as temporary setbacks. At least in this respect, the process tends to validate their conception; no decision is absolute; each decision is only a measure of the popular will at a particular point in time. Certainly there is nothing to prevent homophile activists from raising these issues again—except inertia and the ability of tolerance to tolerate intolerance. Radicals, although they may not always be immediately successful, at least have a justification for their continuing insistence on reform; society must make its practice conform to what is right. In a reasonable and tolerant world, what right have gay activists to continue to trouble the populace with their wishes? What ground exists for appealing the decision of today? Not justice. And what moral duty does the population have to respond?

Rhetorical Strategies as Ideology

Since the publication of *Gayspeak* in 1981, some rhetorical critics have increasingly asked whether or not rhetorical criticism itself must always and necessarily be a reflection of the ideology of the rhetorical critic.[19] Other rhetorical critics have asked whether or not rhetorical strategies themselves are ideologically neutral tools that can be used for either good or evil and can therefore be used in support of any number of rhetorical and political positions. Christine Oravec, for example, has suggested that the autobiography, as a rhetorical form, may possess a gender-based "ideological quality" that "inscribes in its very form the ideology of the self-made man; the strong, autonomous leader; the self-interested investor; the search of the secular soul for ultimate reward and fulfillment."[20]

This concern for rhetorical form as ideology constitutes an important feature of any rhetorical critic's analysis. The discovery of a dominant, if not governing, rhetorical form suggests the existence of a sociopolitical program, even if that program is unconsciously advocated. Similarly, the discovery of a dominant or governing rhetorical form implies that the rhetorical critic assess the viability of the sociopolitical program sought by a rhetor.

In this commentary, I lack the space to suggest how rhetorical forms and strategies might be systematically linked to political positions.[21] Moreover, my intent at this juncture is only to highlight the findings and consequences of the choices made by the rhetorical critics in Part One. In this regard, I am convinced that the objects of study of each of these rhetorical critics and the rhetorical form they have discovered reflect potential ideological directions for how the discourse of gay males and lesbians should be formulated. The issues can be aptly summarized in a series of questions raised by the three essays we have been examining: Can gay males and lesbians realize their objectives through concerted legal efforts? Can gay males and lesbians realize their objectives through concerted political campaigns? Can gay males and lesbians realize their objectives outside of the moral scheme of the larger sociopolitical system?

There are no easy answers to these questions, for the questions themselves conceal more than they reveal. It remains unclear, for example, if gay males and lesbians can be treated as a cohesive social unit. Even if one assumes that gay males and lesbians function as a single and cohesive unit, it remains unclear if one or many objectives govern the lifestyle concerns of gay males and lesbians. And assuming that a governing objective or set of objectives can be discovered and agreed upon, it remains unclear what set of rhetorical strategies can be employed that will reflect the objective or objectives sought.

Conclusion

The first three essays in Part One constitute extremely important points of departures for resolving critical issues regarding the proper nature and character of gay male and lesbian discourse during the 1990s. Rather than viewing them as definitive, the essays offer tremendous potential as heuristic theories positing potential directions for rhetorical action. Moreover, rather than selecting among these options, all three perspectives may ultimately shape the discourse of gay males and lesbians. And it may be beneficial to add yet another set of critical essays as probes that increase the range of options available. In any event, the rhetorical criticisms contained within this section demonstrate that any analysis of gay male and lesbian discourse will constitute a response to existing sociocultural conditions, provide guidelines for which audience or audiences to attend to, and will ultimately suggest an ideological direction for gay males and lesbians. In these senses, reading rhetorical criticism is a serious business that requires our full concentration, for rhetorical criticism constitutes a rhetorical act, and we need to consciously assent or dissent with the renderings provided by rhetorical critics.

Notes

1. James Chesebro, ed., *Gayspeak: Gay Male and Lesbian Communication* (New York: Pilgrim Press, 1981).
2. Kenneth Burke, *The Philosophy of Literary Form: Studies in Symbolic Action,* 3d ed. (Berkeley: University of California Press, 1973), 23.
3. Lloyd F. Bitzer, "The Rhetorical Situation," *Philosophy and Rhetoric* 1 (January 1968): 2.
4. James Darsey, "From 'Commies' to 'Queers' to 'Gay is Good,' " in Chesebro, *Gayspeak,* 246.
5. Ibid., 247.
6. "Sex in America," *The Gallup Poll Monthly,* 313, October 1991, 62.
7. Ibid.

8. Ibid.

9. Michael R. Kagay, "Poll Finds AIDS Causes Single People to Alter Behavior," *New York Times,* June 18, 1991, C3.

10. "AIDS Talks in Study Hurt More Than Help," *New York Times,* May 28, 1991, C2.

11. "Colorado to Vote on Barring Gay-Rights Laws," *New York Times,* May 24, 1992, A31.

12. James Darsey, "From 'Gay is Good' to the Scourge of AIDS: The Evolution of Gay Liberation Rhetoric, 1977–1990," *Communication Studies* 42: 43–66, esp. 55.

13. Ibid., 58.

14. Ibid., 60.

15. Sonja K. Foss, Karen A. Foss, and Robert Trapp, *Contemporary Perspectives on Rhetoric* (Prospect Heights, Ill.: Waveland, 1985).

16. Bernard L. Brock, Robert L. Scott, and James W. Chesebro, "The Postmodern Perspective," in *Methods of Rhetorical Criticism: A Twentieth-Century Perspective,* 3d ed. (Detroit: Wayne State University Press, 1990), 430.

17. For details regarding postmodern theory and criticism, see ibid., 428–500.

18. See, e.g., Bernard Lee Brock, *A Definition of Four Political Positions and a Description of Their Rhetorical Characteristics* (Ph.D. dissertation, Northwestern University, 1965). Brock maintains (21–25) that liberals extend societal trends by using existing institutional systems.

19. See, e.g., Philip Wander, "The Ideological Turn in Rhetorical Criticism," *Central States Speech Journal* 34 (Spring 1983): 1–18.

20. Christine Oravec, "The Ideological Significance of Discursive Form: A Response to Solomon and Perkins," *Communication Studies* 42 (Winter 1991): 383–91, esp. 384.

21. In another essay, I have suggested how strategies can be systematically associated with specific value orientations, motivations, and political positions; see Chesebro, "Communication, Values, and Popular Television Series—A Seventeen Year Assessment," *Communication Quarterly* 39 (Summer 1991): 197–225; see esp. Table 5 and the related discussion, 214–19.

PART TWO

Portrayals of Gay Men and Lesbians in the Media

5. Guilt by Association: Homosexuality and AIDS on Prime-Time Television

Emile C. Netzhammer and Scott A. Shamp

With great regularity, controversial social issues become conventionalized and are mainstreamed into television news, television movies, soap operas, and prime-time television series. In 1985, with the death of Rock Hudson, media coverage of Acquired Immune Deficiency Syndrome (AIDS), a medical condition that had already claimed fifteen thousand lives (Centers for Disease Control 1985), increased significantly. Also in 1985, NBC accorded AIDS "the ultimate status of a social problem" by airing *An Early Frost,* a made-for-TV movie about an AIDS patient (Colby and Cook 1989, 42). Eventually, in the 1987 and 1988 seasons, AIDS was assimilated into the plots of several prime-time television series.

Colby and Cook maintain that the media, especially television, "played a critical role in the social construction of the AIDS epidemic" (1989, 2). Television news reports, documentaries, and movies that deal with AIDS help to shape the way the American public thinks about AIDS and people with AIDS (PWAs). The treatment of AIDS in prime-time series also shapes public thought. In fact, evidence suggests that viewers' parasocial interaction with characters in entertainment programming gives prime-time series special power to influence people's perceptions of AIDS and those who have it (Cathcart 1986, 207).

However, the constraints imposed on prime-time, episodic television influence the way these programs deal with AIDS. First, the fact that regular characters must be around for next week's episode usually prevents central characters from becoming infected with a disease that will probably kill them. Second, the economic necessity that forces television series to appeal to the largest possible audience discourages writers from violating societal norms. AIDS is a sensitive issue because it is associated with other social concerns, such as drug use and sexuality. Third, prime-time series fall into particular genres, and treatments of AIDS must be fitted to those genres. Finally, an AIDS storyline cannot violate the textual codes that already exist in a particular program. The audience comes to an episode with certain expectations, and the story cannot betray those expectations (Allen 1987, 151). Therefore, the treatment of AIDS in prime-time dramas or situation comedies is shaped by a complex system of constraints.

This article examines the way in which eight regularly scheduled prime-time television series handled AIDS issues. The programs are *Designing Women, The Equalizer, Houston Knights, Leg Work, Midnight Caller, Mr. Belvedere, 21 Jump Street,* and *A Year in the Life.* Although they approach AIDS from a number of different directions, these television series foster a particular understanding of the disease, the epidemic, and the infected. The episodes promote a unified ideology concerning AIDS. Although several important themes run through the presentations of AIDS in these programs, this article concentrates on the ways episodic television has cast AIDS as a universal problem perpetrated by gays. Altman notes that "the fact that the first reported cases were exclusively among homosexual men was to affect the whole future conceptualization of AIDS" (1986, 33). The media perpetuated this association by framing AIDS as a gay disease, particularly during the period when the disease was being defined for the public (Colby and Cook 1989, 39).

These prime-time series strengthened the understanding of AIDS as gay-related by explicitly and implicitly connecting homosexuality and AIDS. In half of the programs, the PWA is a gay or bisexual man, making an explicit connection between AIDS and homosexuality. However, even when the PWA is not homosexual and the method of transmission is not through homosexual activity, related plots, situations, and humor make an implicit connection between homosexuality and the disease.

This article analyzes the patterns in the various programs' treatments of AIDS. Specifically, it focuses on the rhetorical impact of the programs that tie AIDS to a particular lifestyle as opposed to particular behaviors. The first section examines the impact of programs that explicitly connect homosexuality and AIDS. The second section explores the implicit connections made in all of the programs between homosexuality and AIDS.

AIDS and Homosexuality: Explicit Connections

AIDS has affected gay and bisexual men in disproportionate numbers. They currently comprise around 60 percent of all AIDS cases in the United States. It is not unreasonable, then, to expect that a television series that raises AIDS as an issue would also raise homosexuality as a related issue. Four television programs used in this study deal explicitly with homosexuality and AIDS by including a gay or bisexual character with an HIV-related illness as central to the story. In *Designing Women* and *21 Jump Street,* the PWAs around whom the stories revolve are gay; in *Midnight Caller* the character is bisexual and has transmitted the virus to both women and men. Finally, *Leg Work* contains both bisexual and homosexual characters. [1]

These programs displayed certain patterns in their portrayals of AIDS and people with AIDS. In these programs, the gay PWA is a catalyst that causes the regular characters, all heterosexual, to examine how complicated life has become due to AIDS. In addition, the structure and dialogue used in these shows promote the belief that AIDS is caused by people with a particular lifestyle—homosexuals. These two patterns work closely in tandem to communicate a unified viewpoint common to all four programs: AIDS is a crisis affecting everyone for which gays are responsible.

AIDS, of course, has complicated the lives of both homosexuals and heterosexuals. It has made the already complex social issues surrounding sexual activity even more onerous. New issues must be confronted in both long-term and casual relationships. However, the manner in which these series connect homosexuality to AIDS subtly promotes the view that gays have complicated life for everyone else.

In *Leg Work,* for example, Claire McCaren, a detective, has been hired by Steve Amati, a gay PWA, to do contact tracing. Steve wants to find a former bisexual partner so he can tell the partner to get tested for HIV. The secondary plot involves Claire's search for "Mr. Right," whom she apparently finds in Ben. However, the case forces Claire to rethink her relationship. In a conversation with Willy, a female colleague, Claire complains: "I like him. I like him a lot. [But] It's all clouded over with my work, the case I'm working on." Later, Claire says, "It's devastating. It's [AIDS] an unavoidable part of our lives now." Willy responds, "And I hate it. It's too complicated."

Leg Work also suggests the culpability of gays in the spread of AIDS in the way past sexual encounters and the related issue of promiscuity are presented. Both Willy and Steve have extensive sexual histories. But their sexual histories are discussed very differently. Willy's sexual promiscuity places her at risk for contracting AIDS. Steve's promiscuity is discussed in the context that he may be spreading AIDS, a strategy that implicitly blames gays for AIDS and the complications it has introduced into modern life.

Claire's first scenes with Willy and with Steve demonstrate this point quite well. In the first scene, Willy wants to know how Claire's date went the night before. Her response is that "times sure have changed." She follows a comment about Willy's "wild" past by saying, "I think that there's even a lot today that you wouldn't do." This exchange illustrates two points. First, it makes explicit the changes in sexual behavior imposed by the AIDS epidemic. More subtly, though, it demonstrates a fundamental difference in the way heterosexual promiscuity and homosexual promiscuity are dealt with. Claire makes no judgment about Willy's past sexual exploits. They are an accepted fact.

The contrast with the treatment of homosexual promiscuity is striking. When Steve hires Claire to find his ex-lover, he tells her, "Stuart and I have been together for four years now. But before I met him, *obviously,* I spent time with other men" (emphasis added). "Obviously," as used in this context, is clearly a loaded term. In the same scene, Steve tells Claire, "I was in love with this man, and I never even knew his name." Steve's statement elicits judgment from the viewer, while Willy's evokes compassion. Steve's promiscuity makes him culpable for the spread of AIDS; Willy's has made her susceptible to it.

Leg Work explores a universal concern: the impact of the AIDS epidemic on relationships. However, the episode discusses how AIDS has changed only heterosexual relationships, even though the stimulus for these discussions is an encounter with a gay man. The appearance of these discussions and plot devices subtly makes gays culpable for the spread of AIDS.

Leg Work demonstrates that AIDS is a problem affecting everyone, but it implicitly blames gays. This argument is evident in the other programs as well. Like *Leg Work, Midnight Caller* subtly encourages the perception that gays are guilty of spreading AIDS. Both shows involve the search for a man who is infecting people with HIV. In *Midnight Caller,* Mike Barnes, a bisexual PWA, has physically and emotionally complicated the life of Tina Cassidy by infecting her with the virus and getting her pregnant. This is another contact tracing story in which Jack Killian, a former police officer with a radio show, tracks down the man who infected Tina, Jack's ex-girlfriend, with the AIDS virus. Her intentions are noble: Tina wants to notify Mike that he is infected, and she wants to include him in the decision whether to abort the pregnancy, even though "it goes against everything I believe." At the end of his search for Mike, Jack finds a vindictive man who plans to bring down as many people as he can.

The impact of *Midnight Caller* is somewhat different than *Leg Work* in that it clearly demonstrates the impact the AIDS epidemic has had on the gay community. Arguably, the change was due to a series of protests by gay and AIDS action groups against NBC and the producers of the show. The producers modified the program in response to these protests (O'Connor 1988, A22; Farber 1988, A24). Jack's search takes him to the bars, where he learns about AIDS's impact on the gay community. A bartender Jack meets tells him, "We '86' irresponsible cruisers like Mike Barnes. We've had too many friends die." He also meets Mike's ex-lover who explains how HIV has affected his life.

Even though the program shows some gay men in a positive light, *Midnight Caller* focuses on an unscrupulous, bisexual man. Mike Barnes is identified as a "killer" who is deliberately infecting people by having promiscuous sex. He is the source of HIV disease. In the world of *Midnight Caller* he is "patient zero." The similarities between Mike and Gaetan Dugas, the patient zero of *60 Minutes, Time* magazine, and *And the Band Played On,* are striking. None of the other HIV-infected characters question whether they got it from Mike—an assumption both the characters and the writers make. Blame for the spread of HIV is placed unquestionably on Mike Barnes and, therefore, gay and bisexual men. By making him bisexual, the threat to heterosexuals is made even more real. In the program, Mike's bisexuality is the bridge through which the virus enters the heterosexual community. Using a pregnant woman in the episode also stresses that AIDS can be passed to innocent children, further emphasizing the danger to heterosexuals posed by same-sex promiscuity.

Midnight Caller and *Leg Work* approach the subject of AIDS through similar plot devices resulting in a similar rhetorical stance, that AIDS is a disease gays have unleashed on society. The plots that run through *21 Jump Street* and *Designing Women* achieve a similar rhetorical impact with different plot devices. They focus on AIDS's impact on the traditional family unit. The blame put on the gay community, while present, is less pronounced than in *Leg Work* and *Midnight Caller*.

As in the dramas discussed above, the regular characters in *21 Jump Street* are confronted with AIDS in the line of duty. Officer Tom Hanson is assigned to guard Harley, a teenage hemophiliac who has contracted AIDS. A surprise ending, however, makes it clear that Hanson and the viewers have been deceived. Harley tells Hanson, "There are only three ways to get AIDS: blood transfusions, needles and . . . [dramatic pause] . . . Well, I don't use needles, and I've never had a blood transfusion." Harley then says, "Dad is the Anita Bryant of the hardware business," making the point that his father was ashamed of Harley's homosexual activity, so he lied.

Hanson's life is complicated by his involvement with Harley and by extension AIDS and, ultimately, homosexuality. Even something as simple as drinking milk becomes problematic. (Hanson's refusal to take a sip of Harley's milk becomes a running source of tension.) Harley's mother is also a key figure in several scenes, when she discusses how AIDS has had an impact on her life. In other scenes, parents protest in an attempt to keep Harley out of school, tying AIDS to the protection of *all* children and making it a threat to the traditional family unit.

Homosexual culpability for AIDS comes in a subtler way. Because the viewer is not informed that Harley is homosexual until the end, the implicit blaming of gays is not as pronounced. Hiding Harley's sexual orientation, though, intensifies the inseparability of homosexuality and AIDS by accepting the logic of religious fundamentalists—unspeakable acts have brought forth this disease.

Designing Women, as in most situation comedies, has two plots running simultaneously. In one plot Kendall, a twenty-four-year-old colleague, asks the women to plan his funeral because he is dying of AIDS. In the second plot, Mary Jo Shively, a regular character, attends a PTA meeting where she must defend the distribution of condoms in the school. Several times, she voices her frustration at having to deal with this issue and defend "condoms for teenagers." Condom distribution, while certainly critical, is discussed as a means of protecting our children, not as a way to stop the

spread of AIDS. Once again, for heterosexuals, the issue is one of susceptibility to a disease that comes from somewhere else.

In *Designing Women,* the connection between AIDS, homosexuality, and
promiscuity is made by an unsympathetic character. This character, Ima
Jean, confronts Kendall with the familiar line, "If you boys weren't doin'
what you're doin'. . . . " The program explicitly works to undercut this
stereotype by giving such lines to a bigoted character, but the connection
is made nonetheless. To be sure, the episode portrays Kendall as very
sweet, well adjusted and very sympathetic—a laudable portrayal of a gay
man. Still, it juxtaposes the susceptibility of heterosexuals (condoms in
schools) with a gay man dying from an AIDS-related illness. The ideology
of "heterosexual problem, homosexual culpability" is once again
strengthened.

Although they present gay men dying from AIDS-related illnesses, each
of these four programs strongly maintains a narrow "heterosexual perspective." These programs encourage the perception that gays are to blame for
AIDS and that, by spreading AIDS, gay men are ruining the lives of
everyone else.

The four episodes establish a telling dichotomy in the way they deal with
heterosexuality and homosexuality. Heterosexuals must curb their sexual
activity because it puts them at risk for contracting HIV. Homosexuals
must curb their sexual activity because it will transmit HIV. By taking such
a perspective, the blame for the more complicated existence of heterosexuals is implicitly put on gays.

AIDS and Implicit Connections to Homosexuality

A number of programs in this study present characters in prime-time series
who contract (or possibly contract) HIV in ways other than by engaging in
sex with a gay or bisexual man. *Mr. Belvedere* devotes an episode to a
hemophiliac child who has contracted HIV through a blood transfusion. In
Houston Knights, one of the stars receives an "inconclusive" positive result
on an "AIDS test," and in the last few minutes of the program the viewer
is told a blood transfusion might have given the character AIDS. A child in
The Equalizer contracts AIDS in the womb from his heroin-addicted

mother. In each case, the character who is or may be HIV infected is free from what Rosenberg calls the perception of volition—the notion that they are somehow guilty victims who contributed to their contraction of the disease (1988, 18).

The distinction between guilty and innocent victims is important, because sympathy is garnered for those who have been infected through no fault of their own. As noted above, gay characters have been shown as culpable for AIDS, making them guilty victims. In only one program is the viewer presented with the possibility that a case of AIDS is the result of heterosexual transmission. In *A Year in the Life,* a character with a detailed heterosexual history discloses that he has AIDS, but the method of transmission is explicitly left vague when he states, "I guess I slept with the wrong person."

The programs have the potential to avoid the issues of homosexuality by not using gay characters in connection with AIDS. Gilman noted that a primary problem in dealing with AIDS has been the tendency to dismiss it as a disease of "the other"—people on another continent, people who use drugs, or people of a different sexual orientation (1988, 1–6). This false sense of immunity is a prime factor in many people's decisions to avoid preventive behaviors. By presenting HIV-infected characters who are not gay or bisexual, these programs have the potential to undermine the conceptualization of AIDS as a gay disease. Unfortunately, this potential has not been realized. Even though the PWA does not contract the virus from a gay man, homosexuality is introduced in most of the programs. (*The Equalizer* is the one exception.) The programs make what appears to be an obligatory observation that AIDS is not a gay disease, but then proceed to connect AIDS and homosexuality in a number of ways. Oblique references, typically in the form of gay jokes or denigration of homosexuality, make an important comment on the relationship between homosexuality and AIDS. Television has exploited gays frequently in the name of comedy (two notable examples are *Soap* and *Three's Company*). However, in a program dealing with AIDS, such ridicule takes on new meaning. The use of such humor further strengthens the connection to homosexuality. Gay jokes in a program in which the person with AIDS is gay, while not tasteful, are not unexpected. However, when gay jokes surface in a program where homosexuality is not involved, the humor suggests that homosexuality and AIDS are inseparable.

Two situation comedies, *Designing Women* and *Mr. Belvedere,* have aired AIDS episodes. As mentioned earlier, the AIDS episode of *Designing Women* includes a gay man with AIDS. Although the program makes use of gay humor in other episodes, the AIDS episode avoids gay jokes completely. In contrast, although the person with AIDS in the *Mr. Belvedere* episode is not gay, the episode uses gay humor in a subordinate plot. In the episode, the Owen family must learn to deal with the AIDS diagnosis of a friend of Wesley, the youngest son. The episode opens with George, the father, discovering that his oldest son, Kevin, is sewing a dress. Kevin then asks his father to check on his muffins. George gets a worried look on his face and says, "We never did have that little man-to-man talk, did we?" Kevin explains that he is taking home economics at school for the easy "A." George looks relieved. However, each time Kevin does something in connection with the home economics class, such as cooking dinner or winding yarn, his father looks at him askance. George's concern about his son's masculinity is a running source of humor.

In a class pageant where students are portraying presidents, the boy playing James Buchanan makes the following speech: "I am James Buchanan, the fifteenth president of the United States. I was the first president to receive a telegraphic message via underwater cable. I never married. [He looks distressed.] But I'm sure I dated." While such humor stemming from the fear of being labeled gay is familiar, in a program dealing with AIDS it helps to convince the viewer that homosexuality and AIDS are so intertwined as to be inseparable.

Other programs do the same thing. *21 Jump Street* uses gay jokes throughout its AIDS episode. The captain asks Officer Hanson to take on the assignment of protecting a teenager with AIDS:

Captain: I have an assignment and it's a tough one.
Hanson: I'm not going to have to wear a dress again, am I? Last time I did some mook from homicide sent me a dozen roses.
Captain: How much do you know about AIDS?
Hanson: Not much. I never thanked him for the roses.

In a separate plot, another male undercover cop tries to get a date with a woman.

Woman: I'm tired of dating a guy and then finding out that he has a whole other life.
Cop: Me too!

Woman: [Stops walking and turns to look at him]
Cop: I mean dating a girl!

The same undercover cop is the butt of another gay joke when his old girlfriend returns after a long absence and finds the flowers he has placed on a table in preparation for a date with his new girlfriend. Looking at the flowers, she asks, "You haven't turned into a flip, have you?"

In *Midnight Caller,* Jack Killian is looking for the bisexual man who infected an ex-girlfriend. He enters a bar and is stopped by a woman:

Woman: You can eat quiche in my bed anytime!
Jack: I'm looking for a guy.
Woman: Aren't we all.

Jack explains that he is not looking for a guy in the romantic sense, but rather he is trying to locate a specific person.

In each of these examples, questioning a man's sexuality becomes the source of humor. The joke or implication provides a vehicle through which a character's masculinity can be challenged for comic purposes and then reaffirmed. In *Mr. Belvedere,* George uses a joke to show he does not approve of his son's behavior and, if necessary, will straighten Kevin out with a "man-to-man talk." Kevin shows that his masculinity is beyond reproach because he is only in home economics for the easy grade—well within masculine norms. The elementary school child's discomfort in playing an unmarried president is followed by his assertion that the president he is portraying had relationships with females. What is especially disconcerting about this humor is that it establishes the masculinity of the main characters by ridiculing alternative lifestyles.

Using humor to reaffirm a character's sexual orientation by ridiculing alternative orientations has dangerous implications in the context of a program about AIDS. The references and allusions to homosexuality strengthen its association with AIDS. Instead of encouraging a way of thinking about AIDS as independent of homosexuality, *Mr. Belvedere* introduces the issue through comic references to sexual orientation.

The overt connection between AIDS and homosexuality in the joke about wearing a dress in the *21 Jump Street* episode has more serious implications. For Hanson, AIDS is synonymous with homosexuality; one need worry about the disease only if planning to reciprocate another man's advances. This is an honest enough scene—after all, most PWAs in 1988 in this country were gay. The captain then tells Hanson that Harley is a hemophiliac who contracted HIV from a blood transfusion. The writers set the stage to erode the connection between homosexuality and AIDS that Hanson has made. Hanson has the potential to learn that AIDS is more than a gay disease. Near the end of the program, however, Hanson discovers that Harley is not a hemophiliac; he is gay after all. The automatic connection that Hanson originally makes between homosexuality and AIDS, a connection he and the viewer are encouraged to question, proves to be accurate. Far from forcing Hanson to rethink the association, his initial and dangerous understanding of AIDS is reaffirmed. And in the process, the viewer learns that homosexuality is so deviant that it must be hidden.

An AIDS episode of *Houston Knights* makes similar use of gays and gay humor. A marginal character, who plays no role in the plot and is gay by stereotype, is introduced into the story. LaFiamo and Lundy are mistaken for gangsters and locked in a small-town jail. Sharing the cell with them is a bleached blond who wears a white T-shirt and tight jeans and is well built. This character sits on the edge of his cot, leering at LaFiamo. LaFiamo tells Lundy to have a seat, but Lundy looks at the cellmate, shakes his head, and says, "I think I'll stand." Lundy deliberately keeps his distance from the cellmate. Soon, an officer comes for Lundy. He turns back to tell LaFiamo in an almost joking, campy tone to "be careful, big boy." Lundy tells the Sheriff he has to get back to LaFiamo "before his cellmate makes him nervous." The manner in which the main characters act around and talk about this character creates suspicion and feeds hostility toward him and gays in general. Lundy, and to a lesser extent LaFiamo (an important point later), are apprehensive about being in the same room with a gay person.

After the jail scene, the "gay" character does not appear again, but Lundy and LaFiamo refer to him in a telling exchange. In the episode's main plot, a mob informant is hiding in the town under the federal witness protection program. Lundy and LaFiamo suspect this, and Lundy thinks they should investigate further. LaFiamo tells Lundy that looking into this man's past would be a violation of his privacy. In a revealing nonsequitor, Lundy says that if LaFiamo had, in the past, been locked in a cell "with an amorous car thief, you would have invaded his privacy real fast." LaFiamo attributes this to "getting mellow," but Lundy replies, "What you're getting is strange." The assertion that one of the "good guys" in the show would mistreat a person simply because that person was gay is disturbing (although certainly not out of context in such an urban cowboy context). This exchange strengthens the connection between homosexuality and AIDS because LaFiamo has taken an HIV antibodies test, and the viewer has seen him coming to grips with the possibility that he has AIDS.

The connotation of the word "strange" is also important. LaFiamo's new-found sensitivity to gay rights leads Lundy to question LaFiamo's sexual orientation. The show not only seems to be suggesting that being gay gives you AIDS but that having AIDS can make you gay. Homosexuality and AIDS are made almost synonymous.

In the following exchange, LaFiamo laments the indignities he has suffered as a policeman and then reveals to Lundy that he has taken an AIDS test:

LaFiamo: Man, all they do is dump on us. Since I've been on the force, I've been bitten by junkies, scratched by whores, puked on, spit on, bled on. I even had a transvestite put a knitting needle through my hand.
Lundy: Guess we all have—except maybe the knitting needle part.
LaFiamo: My doctor wanted me to take an AIDS test.
Lundy: Might not be a bad idea, you've been with a lot of gals.
LaFiamo: I know as much about safe sex as you do.
Lundy: Sorry man, bad joke.
LaFiamo: It's not sex—it's blood. I had a blood transfusion a couple of years ago that was supposed to save my life—now it turns out that transfusion might end up killing me.

Although no explicit link between HIV transmission and the actions of the transvestite (generally linked with homosexuality) is made, the mention of AIDS and transvestism so close together reinforces AIDS as a gay issue. In addition to their relationship in semiotic space, the proximity between "AIDS," "transvestite," and "blood transfusion" can be empirically supported by the fact that the term "transvestite," linked by many with homosexuality, and the program's first and only use of the term "AIDS" are separated by only twenty-four words, while the distance between the mention of the blood transfusion, the potential method of transmission, and AIDS is forty words.

In the programs where homosexual transmission is not an element of the plot, humor and ridicule are used to assert the heterosexuality and masculinity of male characters. These programs have the potential to erode the conception of AIDS as a gay disease by using characters who contract HIV through means other than homosexual activity. But they don't. Although different types of people are afflicted with AIDS, the programs do not resist the temptation to use gay humor, gay characters, and gay behaviors in telling the story of AIDS. These programs argue that AIDS and homosexuality are related.

Conclusions

AIDS originally was conceptualized as a gay disease because the first AIDS cases were exclusively gay men (Altman, 33). This forged a strong link between AIDS and homosexuality in the public's understanding of the disease. Though understandable, the connection between homosexuality and AIDS has serious implications for the effectiveness of AIDS prevention as well as the acceptance of homosexuality.

Associating homosexuality with AIDS creates and reinforces a specific way of knowing AIDS: as a gay disease. Although consistent with early patterns of HIV-infection, this view of AIDS is at odds with the changing demographics of the AIDS epidemic. As the spread of AIDS in the gay community decreases and transmission in other sectors of the population increases, the validity of such a view is growing tenuous.

In addition, understanding AIDS as an exclusively gay disease creates certain dangers. Such an understanding provides a false sense of insulation for individuals whose behaviors might be placing them at risk. Framing AIDS as a gay disease reduces its salience for others who are at risk, and such framing could inhibit preventive behaviors.

Understanding AIDS as a gay disease is also dangerous because it further stigmatizes gays. Before AIDS, hatred and mistreatment of gays were based on a perceived threat to cultural or religious norms. The consistent implication that gays are responsible for AIDS furnishes new reasons to discriminate against gays and gives new power to antigay movements. Hatred and mistreatment are motivated by a new rationale: homosexuality no longer just threatens norms, it threatens lives. Identification of AIDS in this way encourages a nonproductive and negative focus on gays, not the disease, as "the problem." Goldberg illustrates a common misconception concerning the role of the media in AIDS education (1987, 5–6). A self-proclaimed mission of television has been to provide AIDS education.

The prime-time television programs in this study participate in this informational mission—they say how people get AIDS and how they might keep from getting it. Goldberg's positive assessment of television's role in the AIDS crisis is based on the medium's performance in providing factual information. But providing the medical facts about AIDS is only the first step in truly educating the public about AIDS. To serve a positive role in the AIDS crisis, television must respond to the special needs of its audience. Providing the information that will prevent viewers from becoming infected with the virus is certainly important, but television must help the viewer to understand the sociological impact of the AIDS epidemic and see it as a personal issue. Since as many as 1.5 million people in the U.S. might be HIV infected, the average prime-time viewer is increasingly likely to know someone who has AIDS. The public needs guidance in how to deal with this fact.

In a very real sense, the social policies concerning AIDS are dependent upon the beliefs and attitudes of the viewing public. The viewers' tax dollars will provide funds for research and the astronomical health care costs connected with AIDS. As parents, these viewers determine how children with AIDS are treated in schools. As workers, these viewers determine whether people with AIDS can return to work. As employers, they will decide how to protect the interests of their employees who have AIDS. General responses to AIDS are determined by how those in front of the television set think about the disease.

How is television preparing society for what lies just ahead? By consistently connecting homosexuality and AIDS, television is doing society a disservice. The incessant linking of AIDS with homosexuality, especially in programs with gay PWAs, is achieved in ways that make gays culpable for the AIDS epidemic. Television is giving medical facts, but it must break away from the increasingly inappropriate stereotypical conceptualizations of AIDS that vilify gays and legitimate homophobia.

Perhaps because of the conventions of entertainment programming, television is concerned primarily with AIDS and the heterosexual majority. In this worldview, gays are the closest equivalent to a villain in this health crisis. Through its explicit and implicit connections between AIDS and male homosexuals, the television programs never directly attribute the problems of AIDS to homosexuality—but they offer smoking guns aplenty. Gratuitously injecting homosexuality into all discussion of AIDS—even when the specific case being discussed does not involve same-sex sexual transmission—imputes blame. The perception of guilt has stigmatized the gay community.

This study has examined programs aired in 1987 and 1988. Four years later, AIDS is still making its way into prime-time programming, with some shows going to great lengths to break the connection between AIDS and homosexuality. In 1989, *Midnight Caller* aired a sequel to its AIDS episode in which Tina finally succumbs to the disease. After consultation with AIDS activists and gay leaders, any hint of gay culpability was excised from the script. In 1991, *Beverly Hills 90210* discussed AIDS in the context of a women's first heterosexual sexual experience, and a *Doogie Howser, M.D.* episode centered on discrimination against PWAs. Neither show mentioned homosexuality. *L.A. Law* closed its 1992 season with a case involving AIDS and health insurance. The episode did not focus on how the central character got HIV.

Other programs continue to link AIDS and homosexuality. An episode of the *Hogan Family* that aired on World AIDS Day presented a sensitive portrayal of a PWA, but included a subplot in which a boy's sexual orientation is questioned because he is taking a home economics course. (The program is strikingly similar to the *Mr. Belvedere* episode.) A 1992 *Equal Justice* episode dealt with the criminal prosecution of a PWA for infecting someone. This episode stresses culpability and includes gay references similar to the ones discussed in this study: a character is harassed for taking tango lessons because "real men don't dance." Finally, a 1991 episode of *Doctor Doctor* opened its AIDS episode with the lead male wearing a set of fake breasts, while the script utilized tired gay stereotypes and referred to gays as "fairies." This show epitomizes television's inability or unwillingness to consider AIDS independent of homosexuality.

Television teaches about AIDS. Each television program repeats the standard information paraphrased from the wording of government tracts. The recitations, which revolve around "bodily fluids," "safe sex," and "condoms," have taken on the significance of other cultural incantations such as the Lord's Prayer and the Pledge of Allegiance: we have become so habituated to the language that the words mean less than the act of saying them. Education must go well beyond this. Entertainment television, with its stereotypical portrayal of AIDS, is doing little to help. Understanding AIDS as a "gay disease" is easy and comfortable. But if television is to play a proactive role in helping society cope with AIDS, it must explore new ways of framing the AIDS epidemic. The media must break the old, counterproductive connections and find new ways to humanize the disease.

Notes

1. When writing about AIDS, appropriate use of terminology is crucial. In this paper, we have adopted the terminology utilized by the various programs. This requires a word of caution. With the exception of *Midnight Caller,* which uses the term "HIV positive," all the programs use the term "AIDS" to refer to any manifestation of HIV disease. In a small number of cases the term "AIDS virus" is used as well, but generally any individual infected with the Human Immunodeficiency Virus is said to have AIDS.

Works Cited

Allen, Robert C. 1987. "The Guiding Light: Soap Opera as Economic Product and Cultural Document." In *Television: The Critical View,* edited by Horace Newcomb, 141–63. New York: Oxford University Press.

Altman, Dennis. 1986. *AIDS in the Mind of America.* Garden City, N.J.: Anchor.

Cathcart, Robert. 1986. "New Soap Opera Friends." In *Intermedia: Interpersonal Communication in a Media World,* edited by Gary Gumpert and Robert Cathcart, 207–18. New York: Oxford University Press.

Centers For Disease Control. 1985. *Morbidity and Mortality Weekly Report,* 31 December.

Colby, David C., and Timothy E. Cook. 1989. "The Mass Mediated Epidemic: AIDS and Television News." Paper presented at International Communication Association Convention, San Francisco.

Farber, Stephen. 1988. "AIDS Groups Protest Series Episode." *New York Times,* 8 December: A24.

Gilman, Sander. 1988. *Disease and Representation: Images of Illness from Madness to AIDS.* Ithaca, N.Y.: Cornell University Press.

Goldberg, Marshall. 1987. "TV Has Done More to Contain AIDS than Any Single Factor." *TV Guide,* 28 November, 5, 6.

O'Connor, John J. 1988. "A Caller Episode on AIDS." *New York Times,* 13 December: A22.

Rosenberg, Charles E. 1988. "Disease and Social Order in America: Perceptions and Expectations." In *AIDS: The Burdens of History,* edited by Elizabeth Fee and Daniel M. Fox, 12–32. Berkeley: University of California Press.

6. Whose Desire? Lesbian (Non)Sexuality and Television's Perpetuation of Hetero/Sexism

Darlene M. Hantzis and Valerie Lehr

Contemporary feminist theorists argue that the dual assumption of innate heterosexuality and innate desire to mother has restricted women's lives and masked social constructs as biological imperatives. Adrienne Rich frames her discussion of "compulsory heterosexuality" with Alice Rossi's prior observation of the ways in which heterosexuality and mothering are conventionally understood to be central to women's identity: "Biologically, men have only one innate orientation—a sexual one that draws them to women—while women have two innate orientations, sexual toward men and reproductive toward their young" (Rich, 26). Rich asserts that unless the compulsory nature of heterosexuality is revealed, women's sexual options will be regulated toward relationships with men. The unmasking of compulsory heterosexuality disrupts maternalism as well, challenging the social devaluing of the labor of mothering, which depends on understanding mothering as the expression of an innate tendency.

The social mechanisms that construct compulsory heterosexuality manifest self-perpetuating patriarchal structures, which seek to contain women's desire. Shari Zeck identifies the containment of women's desire as the mediation of a threat to patriarchy: "It is certainly within the interests of the patriarchy to keep women from examining their . . . relationships to other women, for the greatest threat to male dominance lies precisely in women redefining their own relationships to each other without regard to their patriarchal obligations to men and the institutions of marriage and the family" (Zeck, 143). Chris Straayer echoes Zeck, noting that "acknowledgement of the female-initiated active sexuality and sexualized activity of lesbians has the potential to reopen a space in which straight women as well as lesbians can exercise self-determined pleasure" (Straayer, 50). Examinations of the social forces that construct compulsory heterosexuality, while simultaneously masking that construction, potentially disrupt the apparatus of hetero/sexist oppression.

In this text, we examine television as a social force that participates in constructing and affirming the patriarchal reality that restricts the definition and expression of women's desire. Zeck notes, "We must also acknowledge the ways in which . . . televisual conventions move toward a containment of the threat female bonding poses to existing institutions" (Zeck, 143). Our examination focuses on *Heartbeat,* a prime-time television dramatic series. The context and characters of *Heartbeat* position it as particularly revelatory of the issues considered in this paper. The series is set in a women-run medical clinic, Women's Medical Arts. Also, and of primary interest here, *Heartbeat* features a continuing and central character who is lesbian—Marilyn.

The critical context of *Heartbeat* includes questions about the minimal presence of lesbian and gay characters on television and, consequentially, the significance of a central lesbian character on television.

Lesbians and Gay Characters on Popular Television

Lesbian and gay characters appear typically, when they appear at all, as "featured" characters in television programs, generally written as unbalanced individuals—often good suspects in some crime (e.g., *Police Woman, Kojak, Hunter*). A movement toward more positive depictions of women and minorities on television has led to a few differences in the portrayal of lesbian and gay characters. Although still functioning primarily as featured characters, more positive depictions of lesbian and gay characters are appearing; a few gay characters have appeared in continuing or repeated, though not central, roles.

Recent popular programs that have featured more positively viewed gay characters in single episodes include *Dear John, Cheers,* and *Designing Women. Golden Girls* and *Designing Women* have each featured a lesbian character in single episodes. Typically, the featured gay and lesbian characters develop an attraction to a lead character; the storyline follows the heterosexual character's dilemma as s/he attempts to resolve this "difficult" situation. *Designing Women* employed different devices. In one episode, a gay colleague dying of AIDS is introduced; the story confronts the issues surrounding AIDS. Another episode introduces a former beauty contest acquaintance of Suzanne's who has come out of the closet; the story line revolves around Suzanne's realization of and response to her friend's revelation. Regardless of the particular treatments of the lesbian and gay characters, many of the programs were shown despite threats by sponsors and viewers to withdraw support in protest of the storylines.

Fewer depictions of continuing featured lesbian and gay characters appear on television. *Hill Street Blues* featured the repeated character of a gay male prostitute-turned-snitch, who was eventually killed. More recently, *Hooperman* (like *Hill Street Blues,* a Steven Bochco creation/production) featured two continuing gay characters—a middle-aged Black drag queen and a young Italian cop. *Hooperman* was cancelled midway through its first season. The cast of *Thirtysomething* included a gay character—an artist and friend of one of the lead characters. Several unidentified gay characters appear in single episodes as his friends and associates. Although an episode during the 1989–90 season depicted the beginning of a sexual relationship between the gay character and a second featured gay character, that story was not revisited until a year later when we learn that no relationship had developed and one is again suggested. The producers of *Hooperman* and *Thirtysomething* report negative responses from viewers and sponsors to the presence of the gay characters. Several sponsors withdrew advertising from *Thirtysomething;* negative reaction failed to keep the episode from airing but it was removed from the roster of summer reruns. While several factors determine the success or failure of any single episode of a series, the explicit presence of gay or lesbian characters appears to generate negative reception.

Discussions of the consequences of the "new" presence of lesbian and gay television characters must admit that lesbian and gay characters are still virtually absent. This merits scrutiny. Certainly the numbers indicate that television fails to mirror the "real" proportion of gays and lesbians in the population. Information from the Alliance of Gay and Lesbian Artists, which tracks appearances of gay and lesbian characters on television, indicates minimal presence and a clear tendency to portray gay rather than lesbian characters.[1] The increases in the numbers of lesbian and gay characters on television may also be misleading. Both AGLA and the Gay Media Task Force recognize that the increase in the number of gay characters appearing on television results in part from television's attention to AIDS.[2]

Our examination of the construction of the character of Marilyn suggests complex consequences of depicting lesbian characters. Specifically, our analysis suggests that "positive" lesbian characters may function to perpetuate hetero/sexism. The construction of Marilyn as lesbian without any integration of her life *as a lesbian* into the program combines with the fact that she is situated within a strongly heterosexual and maternalistic context to recuperate the disruptive potential of the character.

Context of Heartbeat

The fact-based clinic in *Heartbeat* was founded by three women frustrated with a male-dominated medical establishment.[3] The premiere episode explains that medical school roommates Eve Rossi and Joanne Haleran decided to form their own practice after being denied surgical and teaching positions, respectively.[4] In a later episode, the founding story is retold to include Marilyn. The clinic employs three female doctors (Joanne and Corey, ob/gyn specialists, and Eve, a surgeon) and three male doctors (Leo, a pediatrician, Stan or Nathan, a psychiatrist, and Paul, an infertility specialist). Marilyn works as a physician's assistant and office manager; Alice and Liz are clerical staff.

During an argument in the premiere over hiring Leo, Eve reminds Joanne that the clinic is to enable them to control their lives and address traditionally marginalized women's health concerns: "It works because we practice medicine differently; we set everything up our way."[5] The differences that Eve asserts exist in their medical practice provide new options. However, in the context of the assertion of difference, conspicuous absences appear in the program. With the exception of the one single woman (who is both wealthy and a friend of Eve's) who seeks in-vitro, nontraditional couples are not among the patients.[6] No real attention to teaching or self-help programming is given nor is any demystification of processes attempted. Although pro-bono work is discussed, the only depicted pro-bono case is treating an extremely rare pregnancy that will guarantee great notoriety for Eve and Corey.[7] In this environment, it is difficult to argue convincingly that a different medical practice has been constructed. The critique of the authenticity of the "difference" in the medical practice echoes the critique of the authenticity of the representation of Marilyn as lesbian.

The fact of a women-run women's clinic suggests that acceptable roles for women are changing. However, just as only minimal differences appear in the medicine practiced by the women, only minimal changes appear in the roles permitted to women. Although the women characters explicitly function in previously denied roles, they are constrained by patriarchal conceptions of appropriate behavior, especially in the arena of personal interactions. The scripting of the women maintains the dominant discourse of patriarchy and contains change. We argue that *Heartbeat* constructs a patriarchal female sexuality, which is most clearly illustrated in the character of Marilyn. Each of the women characters is constituted in part within a patriarchal denial of her desire. Their enactment of nontraditional roles places the femininity of the women doctors at risk. To reduce this risk, *Heartbeat* continually locates the doctors in hetero-typical relational situations. The heterosexual women agonize over the relative success of their roles as objects of desire for men. Joanne is seen as abnormal because she cannot successfully integrate her relationship with Leo into her working life; Eve moves through a series of superficial relationships, which Nathan explains as the result of her inability to commit; Corey, the only married doctor, fights the good fight to preserve her family while pursuing her career and suffers a nervous breakdown. It is clear that the status-value of the heterosexual women doctors is tied to their ability to attract and hold male attention. Their continually proven attractiveness and participation as objects of male desire mediates the potential threat to patriarchy represented by their roles as doctors and restores their femininity. Marilyn's lesbianism also threatens the patriarchy. The threat represented by Marilyn is also strategically mediated. One strategy locates Marilyn as an object of male desire when an accountant "falls" for her.[8]

The need to depict women as objects of male desire emerges not only from enactment of nontraditional roles but because the women are involved in close relationships with each other. Zeck comments that "the dearth of serious representations of female friendships on television is evidence of the potential for such representations to disrupt televisual codes and genres and perhaps of the disruptive potential of such relationships in the real world as well" (Zeck, 135). The threat represented by women together is usually sufficiently addressed by heterosexual signification. Women spend large percentages of time discussing men and declare their preference for male attention.[9] In *Heartbeat*, the heterosexual women discuss men frequently and the womens' friendships are seen as secondary to fulfilling their roles as objects of male desire. While Joanne prepares to meet Leo at "his place" for dinner (and sex), Corey attempts to engage her in an intimate conversation. However, in the midst of Corey's serious discussion of her concerns about her son, Joanne interrupts with "Well, that's as good as he's going to get," and leaves.[10] Marilyn displays the acceptable privileging of male attention when she stands-up her lover (Patti) in order to comfort Paul over an after-work drink.[11]

Heterosexual female competition also devalues women's friendships. In particular, Joanne and Eve are placed in a recurring competition over Leo, involving petty insults and internal power plays.

The decidedly nonfeminist message articulated by *Heartbeat* supports the patriarchy; it allows women to occupy nontraditional jobs (although not without pain) and the presence of a lesbian, as long as the women continue to enact patriarchal conceptions of femininity.

Marilyn and the Denial of Women's Desire

Fundamental to Marilyn's enactment of patriarchal conceptions of femininity is the absence of female desire. Although Marilyn is shown to be involved in a continuing relationship, the relationship is wholly asexual. Marilyn never expresses sexual desire or passion. Marilyn's absent desire, in particular, perpetuates the heterosexist notion that women are unable to define their desire. Heterosexual women have access to desire through men who define and contain that desire; lesbianism, which offers a site of female desire, is controlled in *Heartbeat* when it is rendered as nonsexuality. Heterosexual characters constantly discuss their sexual relationships; Marilyn never discusses her relationship and *no one asks her about her relationship*. Patti is not a continuing character and is positioned outside the story in the few episodes in which she appears. Straayer comments on the absence-presence tension in the depiction of lesbians: "when one searches for lesbian exchange . . . one finds a constant flux between competing forces to suggest and deny it" (Straayer, 54).

The absence of desire effectively removes all signs that Marilyn is lesbian. She twice states that she is lesbian, but her character is never permitted to *perform* as a lesbian. The absence of a performance of lesbianism is not simply the absence of any representation of lesbian sex, but the absence of any representation of lesbianism as a factor of Marilyn's identity. The invisibility of Marilyn's lesbianism not only allows *Heartbeat* to avoid any substantial portrayal of an experience outlawed by the dominant patriarchal discourse, but to obscure homophobia. Although lesbianism is acknowledged, "the *condition* of lesbianism within culture" is not (Straayer, 56). Amazingly, no story involves a confrontation about Marilyn. No continuing characters or guest characters react negatively to the fact that Marilyn is lesbian when that fact is known; the accountant who pursues Marilyn happily becomes a friend when he is told about Patti.[12]

The absence of representations of homophobia protects the patriarchal discourse from the challenge that the recognition of heterosexism/sexism issues. In *Heartbeat* the social construction of heterosexuality remains, effectively, masked. Thus, rather than celebrating the absence of homophobic reactions to Marilyn, we suggest that the invisibility of her lesbianism supports patriarchal values by removing the need to confront the homophobia and heterosexism/sexism that visible lesbianism signifies.

Although we may wish for the level of acceptance of lesbians and gays portrayed in *Heartbeat,* it is clear that the portrayal of lesbian life free of external conflict obscures the internal conflict and pressures put on lesbian relationships.

Two episodes of *Heartbeat* feature Marilyn's daughter Allison's marriage and potentially confront difficulties experienced by lesbians. The episodes provide an opportunity to display problems lesbian mothers confront in a heterosexist society that defines "real women" as heterosexual *and* mothers and views "lesbian mother" as nonsensical and dangerous.

The program fails to confront the connections between compulsory heterosexuality and compulsory mothering, choosing instead to examine the question solely in terms of Marilyn as an individual. This is clearly revealed when Marilyn tells Allison that she married because she wanted children. During their first talk after a four-year silence, Allison explains: "It's not that you're a lesbian. That's not what bothers me." Rather, her anger emerges from feelings of abandonment, jealousy, and confusion.[13]

The scripts deny Marilyn any recognition of homophobia as a factor in her relationship with Allison. Marilyn reviews her life in personal terms with no attention to social/political realities. She asks, "What were my options? Stay in a marriage that was false? To live a lie? To sneak around and deceive your father? Because once he knew, he wanted no part of me." Viewed in this way, Marilyn's choices are determined by the relationship in which she happens to find herself; no recourse through political action is considered. The absence of a politicized view of the personal in *Heartbeat* again masks homophobia and reinforces hetero/sexism. When Allison expresses concern that she may one day "find out like I'm like you," Marilyn assures Allison that her heterosexuality is evidenced in her obvious love for her future husband. Marilyn does not question (or even suggest) the compulsory nature of heterosexuality; she reasserts the authenticity of love rather than situating it as a socially constructed and controlled experience. Female sexuality is muted later when Allison asks Marilyn, "How did you know [that you were lesbian]?" and Marilyn responds, "It was in my heart. That is the truth, Allison. It wasn't . . . [pause] . . . just physical." It is important that lesbianism not be defined solely in terms of physical sexual practices. However, because Marilyn is *never* shown in a sexual situation, the words further remove her from desire.

The show's tacit endorsement of public restrictions on physical/sexual contact between lesbians and on public acknowledgment of lesbianism reinforces hetero/sexism, renders lesbian reality invisible, and may contribute to the dangers faced by lesbians who are unwilling to deny the significance of their lesbian relationships. When a patient asks Marilyn if she is married and she replies, "Once upon a time. But that's a different story," she is being technically honest, but she is also denying her sexuality and her lover.[14] For a lesbian viewer, such denial may be painfully familiar and realistic. For many viewers, however, Marilyn's response may make it easier to accept her and to indict lesbians who discuss their relationships.

Suzanne Pharr suggests that heterosexual feminists have often dealt with lesbianism by seeing it as a private issue: "By making it just a bedroom issue (without an attendant homophobia) then people feel free to argue that sex should be private and therefore lesbians can and should keep our sex lives private" (28).

The privatization of Marilyn and Patti's sex life in *Heartbeat* employs more complexity. As noted earlier, sex in *Heartbeat* is not wholly defined as private. Heterosexual couples are shown in various sexual encounters in both public and private spaces; Marilyn and Patti are not. Their infrequent touches are gestures of concern and caretaking and are not reciprocal. We see Marilyn and Patti in their home, but we never see their bedroom (although we see several heterosexuals' bedrooms). Still, in *Heartbeat,* a bedroom is not a requirement for sexual encounters. Joanne and Leo make love on the living room and kitchen floors and in the office. Marilyn and Patti do not make love.

This disparity in sexual display perpetuates heterosexism: "It is acceptable, then, for heterosexuals to be affectionate in public, to talk about their families and social lives, to be open about their social networks and activities, etc., but if homosexuals do, then they say that we are flaunting our deviance. We are endangering ourselves, our families and friends, and the organizations that employ us" (Pharr, 29).

Every episode of *Heartbeat* affirms this difference, as heterosexual sexuality occurs without prohibitions of space or time. Not only does this display normalize and endorse heterosexuality, but, by situating Marilyn alongside heterosexual display, *Heartbeat* requires viewers interested in seeing a lesbian to engage in celebrations of heterosexuality.

The consequences of the particular portrayal of Marilyn for *Heartbeat* are many. Marilyn allows *Heartbeat* to claim the innovative presence of a lesbian character without confronting any of the challenges faced or issued by lesbians. Marilyn is a lesbian in name only and is singularly unable to articulate the challenges faced or issued by lesbians. Marilyn is virtually indistinguishable from the other women characters. Her similarity is oddly indicated when Joanne receives the surprise birthday gift of a male stripper from the nurses at the hospital and Marilyn visibly enjoys watching the stripper *as much as* the other women.[15] The technique of erasing the difference signified by lesbians is employed in *Golden Girls* and *Designing Women*. Moritz comments, "When two of the Golden Girls meet their first real life lesbian . . . [,] she is not someone who is different as much as she is someone who is the same" (17). *Designing Women*'s Suzanne resolves her "trouble" with her lesbian friend by stating, "Ya' know we're really just alike." This erasure also circumvents the charge that lesbians are "man-hating dykes" and protects the show from the charge of being "anti-male" (Marilyn likes men!).

The characterization of Marilyn is particularly insidious not only because she is portrayed as nonsexual and the same but because her sexual desire is replaced with maternalism. *Heartbeat* affirms the patriarchal value of mothering to further counter the threat issued by women doctors and lesbianism.

Maternalism

The portrayal of Marilyn as lacking desire grounds her emergent role as an ultimate "Mother." *Heartbeat* articulates an endorsement of maternalism through the scripting of each of the characters, but especially through the character of Marilyn, whose expression of maternalism exceeds that of any other character.

The fact that Marilyn is a mother contributes to her image as "Mother," but in significantly less important ways than do other characteristics. At least in part, this is because her relationship with her daughter has been virtually nonexistent since she came out. Her age and role within the relational dynamics of the clinic also help construct Marilyn as "Mother." She is older than her partners and her lover. She assists Paul with in-vitro fertilization and artificial insemination. Marilyn has no office of her own. She is available to everyone.

Perhaps most importantly, Marilyn is consistently scripted as caretaking, conciliatory, and nonconfrontational. Her physical contact with others is limited and, when present, restricted to gestures of concern. This limitation contradicts her general depiction as physically demonstrative and must be read in the context of her lesbianism. We see Marilyn touch a married patient to reduce her anxiety during in-vitro.[16] Other than this episode, which is prior to the episode that explicitly identifies Marilyn as lesbian, we do not see Marilyn in physical contact with any patients, even those who are experiencing emotional distress. Marilyn is allowed to engage in physical, nonsexual contact with a lesbian friend who is in the hospital dying from cancer (not incidentally, the script reveals that the women have never been lovers).[17] It is remarkable that, although Marilyn is specifically designated as the "caretaker," she is restricted to verbal gestures of reassurance and encouragement in her interactions with patients and colleagues.

The restrictions on physical gestures echo the restrictions on Marilyn's contact with Patti. Simultaneously, they may indicate a reality of lesbian's lives that needs to be challenged, not reflected in a normative manner—that touching other women is controlled by lesbians who feel vulnerable to charges of sexual seduction. The show's denial of physical contact in Marilyn's life allows the writers and producers to reassure viewers that lesbians are able and willing to perform the (unrewarded) caretaking traditionally played by women, while reassuring them that lesbians will not try to seduce every woman with whom they come into contact. The societal tendency to see lesbians as inclined to behave like stereotypical men (i.e., as sexual predators) is challenged only by stripping Marilyn of any desire or affection.

Marilyn's caretaking extends everywhere: she helps Corey when she is in distress, restores Paul's confidence when he doubts himself, encourages Joanne when she feels insecure, reassures Patti when she feels unimportant, and helps a friend face death. The distress that Marilyn is called upon to remedy often results from tensions in intra-office and personal relationships. Marilyn, the conciliator, bridges disagreements and restores harmony.

Marilyn remains nonconfrontational and nonassertive. At the daily staff conferences, Marilyn speaks infrequently and without the same authority as the other founding members or staff doctors. Indeed, an episode on midwifery clearly establishes the minimal authority of Marilyn's voice in clinic policy and decision making. The need to defend a midwife's practice divides the clinic staff; Marilyn fails to persuade anyone to vote with her to support the midwife. In the end, Marilyn warns that she will have *her* midwife's certification in six months and will practice "somewhere." She does not demand her right as a founding partner to take space for herself. Marilyn's moves toward conciliation are especially significant in the midwife episode, as Joanne and Eve question their "commitment" to women and change when they find themselves failing to support the midwife. Marilyn's healing discourse forecloses the critique.

Maternalism is valorized as the only appropriate expression of female sexuality, particularly through the portrayal of Marilyn. Indeed, the maternalism inscribed throughout *Heartbeat* works to contain all the women in patriarchy. They each express a desire to have children and admit that a lasting relationship with a man is necessary to childbearing. Marilyn tells her daughter that she married because she wanted children. Eve will not become pregnant outside of the context of a committed relationship with a man.[18] When Joanne becomes pregnant, she and Leo plan to make their relationship "more legitimate."[19] Corey, mother of three, attempts to adopt an abandoned child and persuades her husband not to have a vasectomy.[20]

The particular circumstances of the lives of these women further instruct that it may be possible to satisfy the desire for a child without wholly enacting traditional conceptions of femininity, but it is not likely. The episodes dealing with Allison's marriage suggest that Marilyn's lesbianism cost her her relationship with her daughter, which is reestablished only when Allison is an explicitly heterosexual adult. Eve laments her lack of children and worries about the "ticking of her biological clock." Joanne's pregnancy results in a miscarriage.[21] The multiple demands on Corey (doctor-wife-mother) cause her to have a nervous breakdown.[22]

Conclusion

Given the fact that so few lesbian and gay characters appear on television, it could be argued that *any* portrayals of lesbians and gays that are not clearly negative should be valued. The movement away from television's depiction of lesbians and gays as murderers, molesters, psychotics, or exaggerated stereotypes may be seen as positive in the struggle for acceptance of lesbians and gays by the popular culture media. However, because "positive" depictions of lesbians and gays usually constitute them as not significantly different from "positive" heterosexuals, a "positive" lesbian or gay character is one who is nonthreatening to heterosexuals—that is, nonsexual.[23]

We reject the notion that *any* positive portrayal of lesbian and gay characters merits celebration and argue that many "positive" portrayals serve as mechanisms to perpetuate hetero/sexism even as they appear to display the "good will" of various producers, directors, and writers toward lesbian and gay issues.

While we recognize the multiplicity of experiences lived by lesbians and gays and resist essentializing lesbian and gay identity, we assert that lesbians and gays share the need to survive a world that abhors their desire and views their sexuality as dangerous. As evidenced in the analysis of the character of Marilyn, the new "positive" portrayals of lesbians create no substantial difference in television's portrayal of sexuality or human relationships and fail to depict lesbian experience or issue any challenge to homophobia and hetero/sexism.

Popular television endorses a patriarchal concept of heterosexuality, grounded in a misogynistic denial of women's desire, which produces sexism and heterosexism simultaneously. The character of Marilyn illustrates the denial of women's desire more clearly than heterosexual female characters who act in expected and predictable ways—lacking a desire of their own and responding to male desire.

Situating the fact that Marilyn is lesbian as incidental in the pattern of her daily life denies her sexuality and constructs a lesbian character who is singularly unable to function as an avenue by which to present the experiences of lesbians. Rather, Marilyn embodies the ideal patriarchal image of Woman.

These observations generate an argument that television is unwilling to represent women's desire because it is unwilling to threaten heterosexuality and the heterosexist male role of definer and center of female relationships. Until television is prepared to threaten heterosexism/sexism, lesbian and heterosexual women and gay characters will continue to be limited and denied.

In spite of the manipulations that virtually erase Marilyn's lesbianism, *Heartbeat* was cancelled after one season. Given the caveats about determining the causes of the failure of a television series, it is significant that the pre-release responses to *Heartbeat* expressed negative reactions to the as-yet-unseen central lesbian character and that during the run of the show producers released to the press their intentions to reduce Marilyn's role.

The analysis of Marilyn and *Heartbeat* suggests avenues for future research. Questions about audience response to lesbian and gay characters on television need to be asked. In the case of *Heartbeat,* we may argue that support among a heterosexual audience and among a lesbian and gay audience was equally lessened by the scripting of Marilyn. For homophobic/heterosexist viewers, the mere presence of Marilyn might have been enough to restrict viewership. Viewership among lesbians and gays, and particularly lesbians, might have been determined by the show's hetero/sexist denial of Marilyn's desire and the denial of the desire of all of the women characters. An audience-based analysis would benefit from a comparison of response to *Heartbeat* and *Cagney and Lacey.* Perhaps a character such as Chris Cagney, from *Cagney and Lacey*—which, as D'Acci documents, clearly had a lesbian following—draws more lesbian viewers than a character like Marilyn because Cagney was seen to enact desire. This enactment locates her outside of the norms of society, even if the site of her desire remained within acceptable boundaries. Research that examines and articulates the construction of sexuality and human relationships on television is also necessary. Popular culture discourse functions as a powerful perpetuation of dominant power structures, most particularly hetero/sexism.

As our analysis of Marilyn indicates, hetero/sexism depends on a particular construction of sexuality that denies women's desire. Patriarchal sexuality ultimately limits women's lives and restricts the development of lesbian, gay, and heterosexual relationships.

A greater understanding of the consequences of hetero/sexist sexuality on the quality of human relationships may lead to a more critical-consuming audience willing to compel alternate constructions of sexuality from popular culture media and in our society.

Notes

1. The AGLA reports the number of gay and lesbian characters appearing in Movies of the Week and in miniseries, and also on television series in both recurring and single-episode roles. The statistics for 1986 reveal the minimal numbers of gay and lesbian characters and a clear preference for gay characters: six men and one woman in Movies of the Week or miniseries, four men and no women as recurring characters in television series, and fifteen men and six women in single episodes of television series. For a review of the presence of lesbian images on prime-time television, see Moritz.

2. Interestingly, of the lesbian and gay characters noted earlier, only one appears in an AIDS related story (*Designing Women*).

3. *Heartbeat* was inspired by the Santa Monica Women's Clinic, founded by Dr. Karen Blanchard, who served as consultant to the show and as the model for the character of Dr. Joanne Haleran.

4. Premiere episode, teleplay by Sara Davidson, directed by Harry Winer. (The episodes were untitled. We have assigned them the titles used in these notes.)

5. Considering the ostensibly feminist pose of *Heartbeat*, it is important to note that Joanne complains that they have interviewed at least twenty-five women pediatricians and have not found one to be comparable to the male candidate, whom she is advocating.

6. "Single Woman In-Vitro" episode, teleplay by Frederick Rappaport and Douglas Steinberg, directed by Robert Becker.

7. "Pro-Bono" episode, teleplay by William A. Schwartz, Frederick Rappaport, and Douglas Steinberg, directed by Bill Duke.

8. "Accountant" episode, teleplay by Doris Silverton, directed by Helaine Head.

9. D'Acci discusses attempts to ameliorate the threat represented by the close relationship between Cagney and Lacey; Hantzis and Fuoss discuss the response in *Designing Women*.

10. Premiere episode.
11. "Abandoned Baby" episode, teleplay by Jean Vallely, directed by Dale White.
12. "Accountant" episode.
13. "Allison's Wedding, III" episode, teleplay by Dan Wakefield, directed by Gene Reynolds.
14. "Con Artist" episode, teleplay by Julie Sayres, directed by Glenn Arner.
15. "Joanne's Birthday" episode, teleplay by Robert Harders, directed by Robert Becker.
16. Premiere episode.
17. "Claire" episode, teleplay by Frederick Rappaport and Douglas Steinberg, directed by Gregory Rose.
18. "Single Woman In-Vitro" episode.
19. "Claire" episode.
20. "Abandoned Baby" episode.
21. "Claire" episode.
22. "Corey's Nervous Breakdown" episode, teleplay by Robert Harders, directed by Nancy Malone.
23. Although the previously mentioned episodes of *Dear John, Cheers,* and *Golden Girls* feature gay and lesbian characters experiencing attraction, their attraction is for heterosexual characters with whom no sexual relationship is possible. These depictions may also serve to reinforce heterosexual suspicions that lesbians and gays continually attempt to seduce heterosexuals.

Works Cited

D'Acci, Julie. 1987. "The Case of Cagney and Lacey." In *Boxed In: Women and Television,* edited by Helen Baehr and Gillian Dyer, 203–26. New York: Pandora Press.

Davidson, Sara. 1988–89. Creator, *Heartbeat.* Aaron Spelling Productions, Inc.

Hantzis, Darlene M., and Kirk Fuoss. 1989. "Designing a Feminist Laughter on Television: *Designing Women* and *Roseanne.*" Paper presented at the Speech Communication Association Convention. San Francisco.

Moritz, Marguerite J. 1987. "Coming Out Stories: The Creation of Lesbian Images on Prime Time TV." Paper presented at the Speech Communication Association Convention. Boston.

Pharr, Suzanne. 1988. *Homophobia: A Weapon of Sexism.* Inverness, Calif.: Chardon Press.

Rich, Adrienne. 1986. "Compulsory Heterosexuality and Lesbian Existence." In *Blood, Bread, and Poetry: Selected Prose 1979–1985.* London: Virago Press.

Straayer, Chris. 1990. "The Hypothetical Lesbian Heroine." *Jump Cut* 35: 50–57.

Zeck, Shari. 1989. "Female Bonding in *Cagney and Lacey.*" *Journal of Popular Culture* 23: 143–54.

7. Old Strategies for New Texts: How American Television Is Creating and Treating Lesbian Characters

Marguerite J. Moritz

In response to the Women's Liberation Movement, Hollywood in the 1970s began producing what came to be called New Women's films. *Alice Doesn't Live Here Anymore* (1975), *Julia* (1977), *An Unmarried Woman* (1977), and *Starting Over* (1979) are among the most popular of that genre, which is generally characterized by its focus on women seeking new definitions of themselves and their personal relationships. Those movies and many more like them have been the center of several important discussions among feminist critics who have demonstrated the many ways in which the visual and narrative codes of cinema have often worked to restore female characters to their "proper place," often within the traditional family structure.

These film strategies have direct application to the portrayal of women on American television. Prime-time television programming, like Hollywood cinema, can be considered "the limiting case, the ideal-type," so pervasive that it serves as a "model for modes of production and modes of representation" all over the world (Kuhn 1982, 21). Just as dominant cinema relies on fictional characters playing out their roles in a narrative context, so too does American television find its entertainment value in storytelling. The similarities and connections between film and television are also clear from an institutional standpoint: indeed, many Hollywood studios now routinely produce television programming while aspiring Hollywood filmmakers often begin their careers in television. And most significantly, these industries share a long and well-documented history of being white, male, heterosexual, and capitalistic both in terms of what they produce and how they produce it (Kuhn 1982, 25).

Just as feminist film critics have demonstrated that the post-Liberation women created by Hollywood are often not so liberated after all, this essay will show that lesbian characters created for prime-time American television may offer viewers little more than new texts created with old strategies in mind.

Recuperation and Ambiguity in Hollywood Cinema

Early Hollywood cinema in its classic era of big studio and big star films provided several stories in which strong women characters defy convention, only to be brought to the brink of ruin by their bold behavior. Before the closing credits, however, they are rescued from their shaky precipice and repositioned in a more socially acceptable space. *Mildred Pierce* (1945), a melodramatic murder mystery starring Joan Crawford, offers perhaps the most analyzed example of how this kind of recuperation plays out.

The main character, in the person of Crawford, is possessed of traits not typically associated with her wife-mother-homemaker status. She is ambitious, aggressive, determined, and decisive. When her unemployed husband fails to provide sufficiently for her and her daughters, she asserts herself, proceeding to banish him from their home and to accomplish what he apparently cannot. Within a short time the uneducated but savvy Mildred builds up a booming restaurant business. But then success begins to take its toll. Mildred's personal life starts to unravel. Her youngest daughter succumbs to a tragic illness. Her oldest daughter is defiant and deceitful. And when it looks as though Mildred herself will be revealed as a murderer, the real culprit is uncovered and a devastated Mildred is taken back by her husband, presumably ready to retreat from her role in the outside world.

Mildred's take-over of the place of the father has brought about the collapse of all social and moral order in her world. . . . In the face of impending chaos and confusion the patriarchal order is called upon to reassert itself and take the Law back into its own hands, divesting women completely of any power they may have gained while the patriarchal order was temporarily impaired. This involves establishing the truth without a doubt, restoring "normal" sexual relationships and reconstituting the family unit, in spite of the pain and suffering which such repressive action must cause. (Cook 1978, 75)

The outcome presented in *Mildred Pierce* is seen by many feminist critics as prototypical of classical Hollywood films portraying strong female characters. "Often narrative closure itself seems to necessitate the resolution of problems and ambiguities brought up by the desire of women characters to go to work, to be sexual beings, or both. The end of the story becomes the solution of that story when the woman is returned to her 'proper' place, i.e., with her husband, at home" (Walker 1982, 167). While other narrative closures for these kinds of stories do exist, they run a narrow range. Kuhn suggests that recuperation is inevitable and is accomplished "thematically in a limited number of ways: a woman character may be restored to the family by falling in love, by 'getting her man,' by getting married, or otherwise accepting a 'normative' female role. If not, she may be directly punished for her narrative and social transgression by exclusion, outlawing or even death" (Kuhn 1982, 34).

Given that they were prompted by the women's rights movement and directed toward a more liberated female audience, it might be expected that the New Women's films of the 1970s would deal differently with narrative closure. But like history, Hollywood has a way of repeating itself. *Klute* (1971), starring Jane Fonda as prostitute Bree Daniels, is one of the first of this genre and, like *Mildred Pierce,* one of the most analyzed. At the time of its release, some feminists hailed the film for its gripping portrayal of a strong woman by a politically active star. "*Klute* became a focus of critical attention because of the questions it raised about audience pleasure. It immediately attracted feminist approval for the powerful image of Jane Fonda's Bree Daniels. She seemed to be, at last, a positive Hollywood heroine, an 'independent' woman for other women to identify with" (Lovell and Frith 1981, 15). But many other feminist writers developed a far different reading of the film. Gledhill argues that precisely because of its contemporariness, this film text is more able to mask its real message. For her, the Bree Daniels role is simply an updated version of the evil woman created in 1940s film noir.

The film is trying to articulate, within the ambience of the thriller, a modern version of the independent woman, conceived of as the sexually liberated, unattached, hip woman and without mentioning feminism or women's liberation arguably trying to cash in on these concerns to enhance the modernity of the type. . . .

I would argue that *Klute's* production of the stereotype is no different in its ultimate effect, and that the film operates in a profoundly anti-feminist way, perhaps even more so than the '40s thrillers from which it derives. (Gledhill 1978, 114)

Not all of Hollywood's efforts to woo the New Women's audience relied on the restoration of male dominance. In fact, one of the marks of these films is their use of textual ambiguity. *Julia* is a case in point. The film is an account of writer Lillian Hellman (played by Jane Fonda) and her revolutionary friend Julia (Vanessa Redgrave). The film clearly raises a question as to whether the two women had a romantic sexual relationship, yet deliberately avoids answering it. "While most reviewers agree that the relationship portrayed between the women is central to the film . . . there are almost as many opinions as there are reviews concerning the precise nature of that relationship" (Kuhn 1982, 38). In *An Unmarried Woman* and *Alice Doesn't Live Here Anymore,* ambiguity itself becomes a form of resolution. By making the future of the female protagonist unclear, these texts provide a way in which the narrative can simultaneously appeal to audiences that want to see patriarchy challenged and those that expect to see it restored.

It would be problematic for a cinematic institution whose products are directed at a politically heterogeneous audience overtly to take up positions which might alienate certain sections of that audience. Films whose address sustains a degree of polysemy—which open up rather than restrict potential readings, in other words—may appeal to a relatively broad-based audience. Openness permits readings to be made which accord more or less with spectators' prior stances on feminist issues. *Julia* illustrates the point quite well: while lesbians may be free to read the film as an affirmation of lesbianism, such a reading—just as it is not ruled out—is by no means privileged by the text. (Kuhn 1982, 139)

If strong female characters have typically been dealt with through recuperation or ambiguity by cinema in earlier decades, are the same strategies finding their way into American television portrayals today? The question is of particular interest when it is raised about stories with lesbian characters because these scripts might be seen as network television's most progressive efforts.

Homosexuality and American Television

During most of its history, American television effectively banned the portrayal of homosexuals. The three major networks were never legally bound to do so, but claimed instead that they were governed by what they termed matters of public taste. "In the '50s, they couldn't use the word pregnant when Lucy was expecting a baby [on *I Love Lucy*]," explains Dianna Borri, NBC's manager of standards and practices in Chicago (quoted in Moritz 1989, 13). The networks contend that they reflect societal trends rather than set them. Therefore, as homosexuality has become more socially acceptable, so have gay characters.

It was only in 1973 that American television offered its first fictional portrayal of homosexuality with the made-for-TV movie *That Certain Summer,* starring Hal Holbrook as a gay father coming out to his son (Henry 1987, 43). A few other shows with homosexual themes followed, but that abruptly changed in 1980 when a more conservative national mood gave rise to the Moral Majority's campaign against television shows with too much sex and violence. ABC and CBS canceled their plans for four separate productions with gay themes and NBC revamped its *Love, Sidney* sitcom to virtually eliminate any reference to the main character's homosexuality (Moritz 1989, 14).

By the second half of the 1980s, network attitudes appeared to be shifting once again, this time toward a more liberal approach to both language and story themes. The emergence of AIDS, the relatively marginalized position of broadcast television brought on by increasing cable penetration and home video ownership, the demonstrated commercial viability of gay-themed material in other mass media, and the appeal of emerging social issues in general as a backdrop for broadcast productions all contributed to the creation of a climate in which homosexuality was once again permitted to emerge on American television. Lesbian characters, always a rarity in the past, were no longer invisible.

Starting in the mid-1980s, lesbian characters and story lines began their fictional coming out, the result at least in part of a changing institutional context in which what was once taboo had become potentially viable and sellable. *Golden Girls, Kate and Allie, L.A. Law, Hill Street Blues, Moonlighting, Hunter,* and *Hotel*—some of the most popular shows on TV—all have had episodes (since 1985) with lesbian parts. *My Two Loves,* an *ABC Monday Night Movie,* explored in uncommonly explicit visual detail two women involved in a love affair. In addition, ABC introduced a series in the spring of 1988 that featured prime time's first regular cast member with a lesbian identity: *Heartbeat,* an hour long drama about a women's medical clinic, presented actress Gail Strickland as Marilyn McGrath. Her role as an older woman, a nurse-practitioner, a mother, and a lesbian no doubt gave her considerable demographic appeal. After its initial six-episode spring run, ABC renewed the show and put it on its fall 1988 schedule. It was canceled later that season because of consistently weak ratings.

Of course the fact that lesbians are now being portrayed may simply reflect the industry's current attempt to give a contemporary look to its standard fare of sitcoms, cop shows, and nighttime soaps. In fact, if these portrayals do nothing more than extend negative stereotypes about women in general and about lesbians in particular, then they are neither indicators of pro-social programming nor of progressive politics at the networks. It is with that in mind that we look at how five recent prime-time American television shows construct and frame lesbian characters. They are *Heartbeat* (two episodes), *Hunter, Hotel,* and *Golden Girls.* These episodes were selected because the lesbian characters in them are central rather than peripheral to the structure of the narrative.

Recuperation and Narrative Closure

The most striking case of recuperation to bring about narrative closure is seen in "From San Francisco with Love," an episode of the detective show *Hunter* in which the macho Los Angeles cop for whom the show is named tries to unravel the murders of a millionaire and his son. As the story unfolds, Hunter goes to the scene of the first murder in San Francisco and meets Sgt. Valerie Foster, who originally investigated the case. She is more than cooperative, sharing not only her police files with him, but her bed as well. She claims to be eager to help break the case and introduces Hunter to the millionaire's cool, cunning, very young widow. But Sgt. Foster is really trying to throw Hunter off the track. She is also plotting to murder the millionaire's son and in fact, we see her calmly shoot him in the head, her way of eliminating his claim to his father's fortune.

Why is Sgt. Foster doing all this? Because she is the lesbian lover of the millionaire's widow and together they plan on getting away with murder and an $80 million fortune. Eventually Hunter uncovers the fact that the cop and the widow are actually lovers, but he still can't prove that they are murderers. Hunter now prepares a plan in which he plays on the women's basic distrust of each other. The plan works, and the widow turns the cop in. But the cop has herself covered. She produces a tape recording she secretly made the night the women planned the killings. Both women are therefore implicated, both are caught, and both are guilty. The recuperation in this denouement is both unambiguous and complete. The women lovers prove to be their own undoing. They have, in fact, been cunning enough to get away with murder, but their deceitfulness and lack of trust is so total that they are doomed to fail in any venture that requires mutual reliance. Thus they have transgressed by being lesbians, murderers, and disloyal lovers. They obviously are beyond restoration to a "normative" female role. For these actions, they must and will be removed from society and properly punished.

This episode of *Hunter* was considered to portray lesbians so negatively that it drew a protest from the Alliance of Gay and Lesbian Artists (AGLA), an activist group based in Los Angeles that has been working to improve the image of homosexuals on television. "The network realized why [we protested] and afterwards came to us and asked us to submit scripts [that would be acceptable]," AGLA member Jill Blacher says (Moritz 1989, 11).

The episode of *Hotel,* an hour-long drama about the people who work in a luxury San Francisco hostelry, takes a far different approach to its narrative closure, but the recuperation of its lesbian subjects is no less complete. Here the sexual involvement of hotel coworkers Carol Bowman and Joanne Lambert comes out only after Joanne tragically dies in a car crash. Carol is left not only to grieve her lost mate but also to deal with Joanne's father, who comes from the East Coast to take home his daughter's body and her personal effects. The father has no idea that his daughter has been living with a female lover, but he finds out when a hotel attendant brings him a package from his daughter's employee locker that is addressed to him. The package contains a videotape that he watches from his suite.

Joanne (on videotape): Happy birthday, Dad. My gift to you this year is a heart-to-heart talk, at least my half of it. I know it's never been easy between us. . . . I know you never meant to be so stern, so unapproachable. . . . [Carol and I have] been together for six years now, Dad. Like they say, I guess it must be love.

Enraged, the father now storms into the office of the hotel's top executive, Mr. McDermott, and accuses Carol Bowman of corrupting his daughter.

Lambert: My daughter was always a good girl. Unfortunately, she and I were not very close. At home, she was rather shy, quiet. I always felt she was too easily led, influenced by others. One of her friends, a member of your staff, took advantage of Joanne, corrupted her. . . . Whatever our problems might have been at home, my daughter was not abnormal. She dated a great deal. She was not interested in other women.

McDermott: Why are you telling me this?

Lambert: Good Lord, man, isn't it obvious? This Bowman woman works with the public every single day representing you and your hotel.

McDermott: What do you want me to do? Fire her?

Lambert: You certainly aren't going to leave her in a position of being able to prey on other unsuspecting young women.

Given Mr. Lambert's distinct disapproval, Carol Bowman decides that he can have everything; she will be satisfied with her memories. In the final scene, we see Carol and Mr. Lambert packing up Joanne's things. The opening shot has the camera positioned high above them, shooting down, which both diminishes their presence and suggests that the deceased lover, Joanne, may be looking on from above. When Mr. Lambert finds a doll that he gave his daughter at age five, he begins to cry and Carol comes to his side to comfort him.

Lambert: Maybe you're right. Maybe memories are the most important things. I was always a better talker than a listener. . . . Maybe it's time I started listening a little.

Carol: What do you mean?

Lambert: You're the only one who can help me fill in all the blanks. Keep what's important to you. . . . Just do me a favor. Just take me through them, tell me what they meant . . . and maybe I can understand who Joanne grew up to be while I wasn't looking.

They embrace and the camera begins a long, slow pullout, again from the perspective of Joanne, looking on from above.

This narrative closure is ambiguous in that it does offer a degree of hope and acceptance for the lesbian lover. The irate father does after all admit that he wants and needs to know about his daughter's life, and that he will rely on her lover to give him that very personal information. Even though the daughter and her lover both are granted a measure of acceptance, that happens only after their relationship has been irrevocably terminated. The daughter is recuperated by virtue of her ultimate exclusion, and her lover is restored only now that she no longer is in the illicit relationship. In other words, the terms of their acceptance are based on their separation by death.

In two episodes of *Heartbeat* with lesbian themes, recuperation is achieved not through punishment or death but through the reaffirmation of patriarchy as it plays out in the lives of the other characters in the show. The fifth and sixth episodes, the final two programs of the show's first season, were aired on two consecutive nights during the critical May ratings sweeps. The narrative involves four separate story lines, each one tracking a problematic relationship in which medical staff members are embroiled. One follows an impotent doctor and his impatient fiancée, a second involves the resident psychiatrist's efforts to deal with his life after his marriage falls apart, and the third deals with a jealous romance between two doctors on the staff. The lesbian story centers on nurse-practitioner Marilyn McGrath and her unresolved relationship with her daughter Allison. Allison is coming back to California to be married in the home of her father, which her mother had left a decade earlier after revealing her lesbian identity. She makes it clear that she does not want her mother's lover, Patti, to attend the wedding, that she does not accept her mother's life-style, and that she is embarrassed by it.

Allison: Dad and Elaine [his new wife] would be more comfortable if you sat in the front row but didn't walk down the aisle.
Marilyn: I see. Is that what you want?
Allison: I want things to go smoothly.
Marilyn: So do I. Patti and I will do anything we can to help.
Allison: I don't want there to be any tension. I don't think it would be a good idea for you to bring her. I'm sure she's a lovely person but a lot of my friends don't know about you.

Marilyn agrees to her daughter's request, but later feels guilty and upset. ("She doesn't want you to come to her wedding and I agreed," she confesses to lover Patti. "I don't want to go without you. I want to be with my partner.") Her lover, however, assures her that she has done the right thing.

It is Patti who urges Marilyn to make amends with her daughter ("It's your daughter and it's the biggest piece of unfinished business in your life. You've got to try to get through to her. Go and see her.") Marilyn indeed does go back to the family home she once left and has a painful exchange with Allison.

Allison: It's not that you're a lesbian. That's not what bothers me. It's, why did you marry Dad? Why did you have me?
Marilyn: I thought I could make a life with your father. I wasn't in love, but I liked him and I wanted children. And I decided I could keep those different feelings buried deep within me.
Allison: But you left me.
Marilyn: I didn't have a choice. It was the hardest thing I ever did, but believe me it would have been more devastating for you if I had stayed.

After Marilyn assures Allison that she will not turn out to be a lesbian too, the mother and daughter cry, embrace, and apparently patch up their differences. Patti is allowed to go to the wedding, and it is here that all four story lines are resolved.

The scene opens with a shot of Marilyn and Patti seated next to each other in the front row, as the organist plays "Here Comes the Bride." After the ceremony, the story turns to the still-impotent doctor and his increasingly uninterested fiancée as they line up at the buffet table. When she strikes up a conversation with another man, the impotent doctor asserts his proprietary rights and tells the man to "take a hike." At this, the fiancée stalks out, but the doctor catches up with her in the bedroom where she has left her coat. They quarrel. She slaps him. He grabs her, kisses her, throws her down on the bed and begins making passionate love to her, his potency obviously restored. Thus ends one story line.

Next, we see the two doctors who have been having a difficult time with their newly established relationship. She has accused him of being secretly involved with Eve, the sexy blond breast-implant surgeon at the clinic. Only now, as they dance cheek to cheek at the reception, does she accept his pledge of love and loyalty. He kisses her fingers, she strokes his hair, they smile lovingly and embrace. Thus ends the second story line.

The third narrative concludes with the psychiatrist waiting for his car to be brought around by the attendant so he can leave the reception. The seductive Eve appears, makes sarcastic note of his depression, and strikes a very responsive chord.

Eve: What's the matter Stan? No one to dance with?
Stan (the psychiatrist): I don't feel much like dancing.
Eve: Wedding's a little painful, huh?
Stan: You really like to kick 'em when their down, don't you?
Eve: You call this down? No, you've got a lot more room to drop.
Stan (looking angry): This must be your way of showing affection, right?

The camera cuts to a close up of Eve looking at Stan alluringly. Then we see him grab her, wrap his arms around her, and kiss her. At that moment, the attendant drives up with Stan's car. Stan opens the door and pushes Eve inside.

Stan: Get in.
Eve: So doctor, where are we going?
Stan: You'll know when we get there.

Show credits start to roll as he screeches out of the driveway, apparently off to a place where they can continue what they've started.

The narrative closure in *Heartbeat* is accomplished through the restoration of the patriarchal system not just once, but four separate times, beginning with the ceremony most symbolic of patriarchy: the wedding. In direct succession we see the three heterosexual couples who have shared the narrative's focus with the homosexual couple. In each case, the resolution of their problems revolves around an overtly sexual exchange in which the men exert their virility and dominance over the women in their lives. The impotent doctor rekindles his manhood by confronting another suitor, calling his girlfriend a "slut," and having a sexual response to getting slapped in the face. The ever-collected and rational psychiatrist finally lets loose, getting physical and assertive with a colleague whom he treats like a young thing he's picked up at a party. Even Leo, the gentle pediatrician, makes it clear he is in charge as he tells his jealous mate on the dance floor, "If you're looking for a fight, baby, you ain't gonna find it here."

While the heterosexual couples find resolution in romance, passion, and drama, the lesbian couple is depicted as utterly prim and proper, completely self-contained and unobtrusive. The narrative closure of *Heartbeat* clearly shows that what does not happen to the lesbian couple is more important than what does.

The script is open-ended or ambiguous to the extent that the lesbian couple, after a considerable struggle, has achieved a victory. But even though they have obtained permission to come to the wedding, this narrative closure does not permit them to participate in the event. Marilyn has one line of dialogue ("I think I'm going to cry"). She and Patti are seen in one shot as the processional starts and in a second shot as the ceremony opens; then they become invisible. While the heterosexual couples exhibit an outpouring of desire as the wedding reception plays out, the lesbians are politely kept from our view, never intruding on the show's vision of what it is to be a couple or to be in a romantic relationship. They agree to accept a limited place, not walking down the aisle, apparently not dancing, eating, or mingling with anyone but nicely tucked back in the closet, out of view from the rest of the guests and from the audience as well. The overall effect is to reaffirm the patriarchal order and to tell the audience that what really counts goes on in the heterosexual world, the arena of passion, desire, and drama.

It is interesting and perhaps not simply coincidental that the one situation comedy in the group of television shows under discussion is the one show in which the narrative closure does not rely on punishment, death, or exclusion to bring about narrative closure. *Golden Girls* is a half-hour sitcom that regularly features four women characters, three friends in late middle age and one of their mothers who is in her eighties. All four women live together in an upscale Miami home. This particular episode opens with Dorothy telling her elderly mother that she's expecting a visit from her college friend Jean. The crusty old mother, one of the more knowledgeable of this group, immediately recalls Jean as a lesbian, astonishing Dorothy.

Dorothy: How did you know?
Mother: A mother knows.

Now Dorothy and her mother have to decide whether to tell Rose and Blanche, the other women in the house, about Jean's sexual identity. When Jean arrives Dorothy and her mother take up the topic with her.

Dorothy: I wanted to make sure it was okay with you before I told them.
Jean: . . . If you think they can handle it, I prefer to tell them.

At this moment, Rose walks in with a tray of her special "clown sundaes," which she makes with raisin eyes and chocolate chip noses. The gesture epitomizes Rose's lack of sophistication and general inability to grasp what is going on around her and prompts Jean to deliver this aside to Dorothy.

Jean: It'll just be our little secret.

As the show unfolds, Jean finds herself increasingly drawn to the kind-hearted Rose. They both grew up on farms, and both like sad movies and staying up late playing card games. Eventually, Jean tells Dorothy that she thinks she has fallen in love with Rose. Dorothy passes on the information to her mother and together they reveal the story to Blanche. Now only Rose is unaware that Jean is a lesbian and that Jean is in love with her. When Jean tries to tell her how she is feeling ("I'm quite fond of you"), Rose finally begins to suspect something.

In the final scene, Jean asks to speak with Rose alone and she explains some of what she has been going through. Since her longtime lover died last year, Jean says, she has been in mourning.

Jean: I thought I could never care for anyone again, until I met you.
Rose: Well I have to admit I don't understand these kinds of feelings. But if I did understand, if I were—you know—like you, I think I'd be very flattered and proud that you thought of me that way.

As the two women put their arms around each other, the crotchety old mother enters and they hasten to explain lest she get the wrong impression. But she is still one step ahead of them.

Jean: This isn't what it looks like.
Mother: I know, I was listening at the door.
Rose: Why were you listening at the door?
Mother: Because I'm not tall enough to see through the window.

The camera cuts to Dorothy and Blanche, who have obviously been listening in at an open window all along. They give a sheepish wave, in effect admitting their intense curiosity over the Jean and Rose affair, and bring the show to its conclusion.

This narrative closure exhibits little need for recuperating the lesbian character. Jean will go back home and go on with her life and her lifestyle and will be better off knowing that she is once again willing to take risks and to engage with people. Thanks to Rose, she now realizes she can have feelings for women other than her deceased lover. Rose will also carry on with her life but will be enriched and enlightened by her experience with Jean. This is a story ending where differences are allowed to exist. The message to the audience is that a lesbian and a straight woman can have a friendship and can accept each other without finding fault or choosing sides.

Throughout the show, however, the subject matter is never treated seriously. Instead, lesbianism is represented as outside the experience of these women, something they don't even know about. One of them confuses lesbians with Lebanese people, saying they can't be so bad because Danny Thomas is one. Another says she may not know what a lesbian is but she could look it up in a dictionary. Only the tough old mother, who often speaks of connections with the Cosa Nostra in her native Sicily, knows about women like that. Since the topic is never treated seriously, it cannot pose a serious threat and therefore does not require any serious redress. Like the rest of the show, the ending is permitted to be basically light-hearted and humorous.

Recuperation and Cinematic Structures

One of the chief contributions of feminist film scholars to cinema studies is their work on textual analysis. This approach attempts to uncover the ways in which cinema specifically creates meanings through its visual as well as its spoken story. The analysis therefore looks not just at character and plot but also at lighting, camera framing and movement, editing, and other aspects of the visual to see how it operates in conjunction with character and plot to create specific cinematic meaning. Textual analysis is pertinent in television studies because television has adopted many of its codes directly from Hollywood cinema. It is pertinent here since in both film and television texts, at least some aspects of recuperation and ambiguity are carried out visually, not simply in accomplishing closure, but in structuring and positioning the lesbian characters throughout the narrative. Feminist film theory asks how women are *not* represented in a script; it also asks how women are represented visually, what fixed images of women are appealed to, and how those images operate interactively in the story line and in the visual structuring (Kuhn 1988, 81). We now look at these same five television programs with these questions in mind, examining specifically how television treats lesbian characters with respect to three significant areas of depiction: sexuality, personal rights, and publicity or public disclosure.

Sexuality

With the exception of the conspiring murderers in *Hunter,* none of these lesbian characters is permitted to be sexual or even romantic. The contrast between the lesbian lovers and their straight counterparts in *Heartbeat* is stark. The lesbian couple never even approaches getting physical, but the male-female couples are frequently shown in close-up passionately embracing, kissing, and alluding to their love-making plans. In one instance a couple is shown undressed in the bed where the guests have left their coats at an afternoon wedding reception. At the same time, in the entire two-hour course of the show, the lesbian lovers are limited to one medium shot in which they share a limp, passionless embrace. That comes at a moment when they are reassuring each other that their problems will work out. Thus when they embrace, rather than being sexual with each other, they really are consoling each other. In the final scene there is a close-up of their hands touching, one woman's hand resting on top of the other's. Again, the context of the story makes it clear that this also is not a sexual moment. It is a tender moment and a reassuring gesture, but sexual it is not.

In *Hotel,* to cite another example, the lesbians are never shown to-gether. The script uses a videotape as a device through which to bring the dead lover on camera. It could have used that same device to show the women together. Similarly, it could have used flashback to accomplish the same purpose. But it did not. The only shot of the lesbians together is in the still photos that remain in the apartment they shared and even here there is not a hint of sexuality or romance. We see close ups of very innocent "vacation" pictures; the two women might just as easily be com-panions and friends as lovers and partners for the previous six years. One photo shows the two women bicycling with two men, as heterosexual a depiction as possible given the story line.

In *Golden Girls,* recuperation is carried out in the looks, dress, and demeanor of the lesbian character. First, the lesbian part is played by Lois Nettleton, a well-known and respected actress. She is feminine, quiet, soft, and soft-spoken. She wears pretty dresses and high heels. Like the Carol Bowman character in *Hotel,* like Marilyn and Patti in *Heartbeat,* she is depicted visually as distinctly feminine. This kind of visual rendering combines with narrative story lines that produce characters who basically are desexualized.

The exception are the lesbian killers in *Hunter*. These characters are clearly not drawn in the timid fashion used with the other lesbians. They are at the opposite end of both the visual and the emotional spectrum. These women are obviously sexual. They dress in sophisticated, revealing clothes. ("The way she's dressed," says Hunter's partner of Sgt. Foster, "she's got herself a date.") Of all the lesbian characters under discussion, these two are the only ones who are shown expressing their sexual passion for each other. The following exchange, for example, takes place as we see a close-up of the two women, facing each other, their bodies touching as Casey runs her hand slowly down Valerie's cheek, throat, and low-cut blouse.

Casey: It's cold out, Val.
Valerie: When do I get my mink?
Casey: As soon as the dust clears. But you will look better in sable.

They have been given narrative permission to be sexual because they are evil and willing to use their sexuality to achieve evil ends. The young widow, after all, ensnared the millionaire into marriage, not for his love, but for his money. Her lover, Sgt. Foster, slept with Hunter to see what he would reveal about his investigation ("She thought I was going to be one of those after-sex talkers," Hunter tells his partner.) The connection seems clear: if they are sexual then they also must be vicious, greedy, deceitful, cunning, and deadly—direct inheritors of the film noir genre.

Personal Rights

In both *Heartbeat* and *Hotel* the lesbian characters discover that they have limited personal rights and go on to accept that limitation without challenge. Marilyn, for example, agrees to her daughter's demand that lover Patti stay away from the wedding. When she confesses that to her lover, Patti not only shows no anger or resentment but tells Marilyn that she should agree to whatever her daughter wants so as to seize this "golden moment."

At another point in the show, Marilyn recounts what happened when she revealed her sexual identity to her husband several years earlier. He effectively banished her from their home and demanded that she give up any claim on custody of their daughter. She agreed because she felt she had little choice.

And now, years later, Marilyn is still agreeing and feeling as though she has little choice. Not once does she insist on having the same rights as her ex-husband, who is bringing his new mate to the wedding without hesitation. Indeed, Marilyn's demeanor throughout conveys her sense of responsibility for having caused heartache in the life of her daughter. While she is continually agonizing over what she did in the past and what she should do to make things better in the present, it is the daughter who is given the right to be angry and enraged. If the daughter is mature enough to marry, one might argue that she is mature enough to accept her mother's choices. Yet her mother never makes that demand. Even though Marilyn admits that she is "terrified" to do it, we see her returning to her ex-husband's home to find her daughter and once again apologize for being who she is. Marilyn is positioned as the person who is at fault, a position she never takes issue with. Her daughter is positioned as the person who was injured or wronged and that gives her every right to vent her considerable anger both publicly and privately.

A similar kind of inequity of rights plays out in *Hotel,* only now it is the parent who is given the right to be angry and enraged and the lesbian daughter and her lover who must seek forgiveness for their transgression.

First we see, via videotape, the deceased daughter trying to explain to her father who she is and how she lives her life. It is an explanation she could never bring herself to make in person. As in *Heartbeat,* it is the lesbian whose appearance conveys nervousness and guilt, positions that carry over to the main character in the show, her lover, Carol Bowman.

This character emerges as a person without power or knowledge. We see her proceed through a series of steps, all attempts at discovering the real limitations of her world, her situation, herself. Her first step is to seek advice and emotional support from a friend and co-worker. The "tell me what to do, Julie" scene sets the stage for her encounters with the three individuals who really can determine her future and describe her personal rights. Carol goes to three men in succession to find out her fate. First, she meets with her boss, Mr. McDermott, to ask if her job is in jeopardy now that he knows about her sexual relationship with Joanne.

Carol: Will this affect my job? I know people can be, well, oversensitive about . . . [pause] . . . things.

McDermott: You should know by now: the only thing Miss Frances and I are sensitive about is the way our guests are treated.

Next Carol goes to her dead lover's father and briefly puts up her one fight. She tells Mr. Lambert that his daughter never got up the courage to actually mail him that videotape because she was afraid of his rejection. She accuses him of rarely phoning, never visiting, and now wanting to stake his claim on a daughter he barely knew.

Carol: You think you can just sail in here and pick up the pieces. Well some of those pieces belong to me and you can't have them. . . . I'm going to fight you on this.
Lambert: Don't do it, Miss Bowman. I will use the courts. I will use publicity, whatever it takes, and you will regret it. I swear you will.

Finally, she consults with a lawyer, but his advice in not encouraging.

Lawyer: It's not what you or Mr. Lambert wants, but what state law dictates. In the absence of a will, Joanne's family becomes her sole heir. . . . Realistically, the most you could hope for is some sort of nuisance settlement, you know, to make you go away.
Carol: But it's not fair.
Lawyer: But it is the law. You know my advice to you is to ask yourself whether a court fight would be worth it. The time, the money, and [he gives her a knowing look] the public exposure.

It is only after these three men have spoken that Carol knows what she can and cannot do, what her rights are. Her lack of power and control over her own fate is reiterated three times over. Even though she is a lesbian she is a character very much living in and dominated by a man's world. And this she is neither willing to challenge nor to fight. Rather than expressing anger at her lack of legal standing, she acquiesces. She not only agrees to give up any claim to her small, personal treasures, she helps the man who is determined to take them away from her. And when he experiences the grief that she has been dealing with all along, it is she who unhesitatingly comforts him, her subservience to him emphasized all the more by her kneeling at his feet.

Public Disclosure

The idea of public disclosure appears in the scripts of all five shows. In *Hunter,* the killer cop assures her lover that the worst that can happen to them is a little bad publicity. In *Hotel,* the father threatens to use publicity to win his case and the lawyer cautions that a court fight might not be worth the "public exposure." In *Heartbeat,* the daughter won't allow her mother's lesbian lover at her wedding because she wants things to go smoothly and because some of her friends don't know about her mother's sexual identity. The idea of keeping the lesbian character's sexual identity secret comes up in *Golden Girls* as well. And indeed, the decision is made to keep that identity private, even though the character says she prefers to be open about who she is.

Implicit in each of these constructions is the idea that public disclosure is likely to result in public scorn. This has interesting parallels in *I Passed for White,* a Hollywood film in which a light-skinned black woman tries to keep her identity hidden in an effort to win social approval or at least to avoid social rejection. Why, if being homosexual is acceptable, is it necessary for any of these characters to keep their identities secret? Obviously, the implied message in all these scripts suggests that it is not socially acceptable to be a lesbian, that caution is always advised in revealing these matters. Just as the lesbian characters show little heart for fighting for their personal rights, they show little inclination to reveal their personal identities. That message is revealed as much in how they look as in what they actually do. In *Hotel,* when her lawyer suggests she consider the public exposure, the camera cuts to a close-up of Carol to show her horrified countenance.

Conclusion

We began this examination by asking whether the same strategies that have been used in constructing strong women characters in both early and later Hollywood films are being used today by American television in its recent introduction of lesbian characters to prime-time television. Our examination makes it clear that the answer is yes. Except for *Hunter,* in which recuperation is total, these scripts employ a certain amount of ambiguity in that lesbian characters are permitted some degree of victory in their own personal battles. But in almost every instance, that victory is balanced by other messages, both in the text and in the visual content of the shows, that suggest these characters have a long way to go before achieving equal status with their heterosexual counterparts.

When we ask a question that has become central to feminist film criticism—how are these characters not depicted?—several interesting answers emerge. They are not depicted as sexual or passionate, even when they are labeled as lovers in the script. They are not depicted as angry, even though their circumstances suggest they have many reasons to be so. They are not shown as independent or assertive, particularly when it comes to securing their own personal rights. They are not shown making demands but rather are seen continually agreeing to the demands of others.

When we ask how are they depicted visually, the other part of the equation falls into place. In dress and manner both, they are shown to be feminine but not sexy, never daring. Any kind of physical exchange with a female partner is either omitted altogether or drawn in the most timid way (a hand resting atop another hand, a sweet but sexless hug). Close-ups of their faces often reveal an agonizing look, a repeated suggestion that their sexuality has caused others problems and for this they must take the blame and suffer the consequences.

These are not scripts that argue for the rights, legal or otherwise, of homosexuals. They are, instead, productions designed to attract mass audiences who will have varying degrees of willingness to accept any lesbian depictions in the first place. Just as Hollywood producers have been careful to incorporate a degree of polysemy into their cinematic texts, so too are American television producers careful to avoid alienating audience members by producing scripts that might be construed as too strident. While it may be argued that these scripts are by design relatively unconcerned with gay rights and more concerned with ratings, it is also true that once-taboo subjects in both cinema and television have gained acceptance only gradually. This may not be the first choice of feminists and lesbians, but it is a first step in working toward at least a small measure of social change.

This article was originally presented at the International Colloquium cosponsored by the editors of Media, Culture and Society and the Central Polytechnic of London, October 1988. The author wishes to thank the sponsors of that conference and Willard D. Rowland, Jr., Dean of the University of Colorado School of Journalism and Mass Communication, for the opportunity to participate.

Works Cited

Cook, Pam. 1978. "Duplicity in *Mildred Pierce.*" In *Women and Film Noir,* edited by E. Ann Kaplan, 68–82. London: British Film Institute.

Gledhill, Christine. 1978. *"Klute:* Part 2: Feminism and *Klute.*" In *Women and Film Noir,* edited by E. Ann Kaplan, 112–28. London: British Film Institute.

Henry, William. 1987. "That Certain Subject." *Channels* (April): 43–45.

Kaplan, E. Ann. 1982. *Women and Film.* New York and London: Methuen.

Kuhn, Annette. 1982. *Women's Pictures: Feminism and Cinema.* London: Routledge and Kegan Paul.

Lovell, Terry, and Simon Frith. 1981. "How Do You Get Pleasure? Another Look at *Klute." Screen Education* 39: 15–24.

Moritz, Marguerite. 1989. "Coming Out Stories: The Creation of Lesbian Images on Prime Time TV." *Journal of Communication Inquiry* 13, no. 2 (Summer).

Walker, Janet. 1982. "Feminist Critical Practice: Female Discourse in *Mildred Pierce.*" In *Film Readers: Feminist Film Criticism,* 164–72. Evanston, Ill.: Northwestern University Press.

8. What Is Wrong with This Picture? Lesbian Women and Gay Men on Television

Larry Gross

The Medium and the Message

The mass media provide the chief common ground among the different groups that make up a heterogeneous national and international community. Never before have all classes and groups (as well as ages) shared so much of the same culture and the same perspectives while having so little to do with their creation. In a society that spans a continent, in a cosmopolitan culture which spans much of the globe, the mass media provide the broadest common background of assumptions about what things are, how they work (or should work), and why. Television in particular has achieved a scope unequaled by any other medium in modern society.

Representation in the mediated "reality" of our mass culture is in itself power; certainly it is the case that nonrepresentation maintains the powerless status of groups that do not possess significant material or political power bases. Those who are at the bottom of the various power hierarchies will be kept in their place in part through their relative invisibility; this is a form of symbolic annihilation. When groups or perspectives do attain visibility, the manner of that representation will itself reflect the biases and interests of those elites who define the public agenda. And these elites are mostly white, mostly middle-aged, mostly male, mostly middle- and upper-middle class, and (at least in public) entirely heterosexual.

Mainstream film and television are nearly always presented as transparent mediators of reality that can and do show us how people and places look, how institutions operate; in short, the way it is. These depictions of the way things are, and why, are personified through dramatic plots and characterizations that take us behind the scenes to the otherwise inaccessible back stages of individual motivation, organizational performance, and subcultural life.

Normal adult viewers, to be sure, are aware of the fictiveness of media drama: no one calls the police when a character on TV is shot. But we may still wonder how often and to what extent viewers suspend their disbelief in the persuasive realism of the fictional worlds of television and film drama. Even the most sophisticated among us can find many components of our "knowledge" of the real world that derive wholly or in part from fictional representations.

Finally, the contributions of the mass media are likely to be especially powerful in cultivating images of groups and phenomena about which there is little firsthand opportunity for learning, particularly when such images are not contradicted by other established beliefs and ideologies. By definition, portrayals of minority groups and "deviants" will be relatively distant from the real lives of a large majority of viewers (cf. Gross 1988). Thus, in the case of lesbian women and gay men we might reasonably expect that the media play a major role in shaping the images held by society, including in many cases by gay people ourselves. As an important case in point, the media played a major role in magnifying the tragedy of AIDS.

AIDS and the Sexual Counter-Revolution

In the late 1970s America was confronted with the specter of the epidemic spread of a seemingly incurable disease contracted through sexual contact: genital herpes. The media were quick to point out that the causes of the epidemic were to be found in the so-called sexual revolution: "Health officials say that genital herpes became a growing problem only during the mid-1970s, after sexual codes had loosened in American society" (*New York Times Magazine,* February 21, 1982, 94). Despite all the attention it received, the panic was short-lived and the fear of herpes did not ring down the curtain on the sexual revolution. Perhaps the extent of the "epidemic" was exaggerated, or perhaps herpes, while incurable at present, wasn't a sufficient deterrent to play the role it was assigned as the chief weapon of the emerging sexual counter-revolution of the 1980s. But the stage was set for the arrival of a much more potent and deadly threat: AIDS.

AIDS provided mainstream society and the media with a double-edged opportunity and challenge: here was the truly frightening specter of a deadly disease that could be associated with sexual permissiveness, but it was showing up among a group that the media have consistently defined as being outside the mainstream.

The first accounts of AIDS in the media emphasized its apparent link to gay men's sexuality (there were also at that time two other outsider "risk groups," IV–drug users and Haitians, and the first "innocent victims," hemophiliacs). The first story on AIDS aired by NBC News began with Tom Brokaw framing the issue in a fashion that remained constant in much subsequent coverage: "Scientists at the National Centers for Disease Control in Atlanta today released the results of a study that shows that the lifestyle of some male homosexuals has triggered an epidemic of a rare form of cancer" (June 17, 1982).

By 1983 nearly all mass media attention to gay men was in the context of AIDS-related stories, and because this coverage seems to have exhausted the news media's limited interest in gay people, lesbians became even less visible than before (if possible). Already treated as an important medical topic, AIDS moved up to the status of "front page" news after Rock Hudson emerged as the most famous person with AIDS.[1] At present AIDS stories appear daily in print and broadcast news—often with little or no new or important content—and the public image of gay men has been inescapably linked with the specter of plague (in the context of television drama, Netzhammer and Shamp adroitly illustrate the subtle and not-so-subtle ways homosexuality and AIDS are linked rhetorically, this volume, chapter 5).

Media coverage of AIDS is very likely to reinforce hostility to gays among those so predisposed—there is abundant evidence of growing anti-gay violence in many parts of the country (Gross, Aurand, and Addessa 1988; Comstock 1991)—and to further the sense of distance from a strange and deviant "subculture."

Ironically, these very homophobic attitudes may prevent audiences from understanding and absorbing media information about the nature of AIDS and the ways in which it is transmitted. Studies are beginning to suggest "that anti-gay attitudes foster exaggerated beliefs about AIDS transmission and prevent accurate information in the media from being accepted by substantial proportions of the population" (Stipp and Kerr 1989). As Netz-hammer and Shamp argue, "Framing AIDS as a 'gay disease' reduces its salience for others who are at risk, and such framing could inhibit preventive behaviors."

A further irony is provided by the finding of Reardon and Richardson that gay men at risk for AIDS often reject media warnings concerning high-risk behaviors because they see such reports as exaggerated and intentionally biased against gays (1991).

A heritage of homophobia can thus be seen as a threat to the reception of accurate information about AIDS by both gay and straight audiences; the former because they have come to distrust the motives and thus the honesty of the media, the latter because their prejudices permit them to maintain a dangerous sense of distance and a false sense of security. Netzhammer and Shamp correctly note that "providing the medical facts about AIDS is only a first step in truly educating the public about AIDS." The responsibilities of the media as they face the threats presented by AIDS must, therefore, begin with an attack on the homophobic attitudes and pervasive heterosexism that may well be the most serious impediments to the educational efforts now recognized as the most critical line of defense.

It would be misleading to focus primarily on news and documentary programming if we wish to understand television's role in helping or hindering the fight against AIDS. For most Americans television drama is a far more potent teacher, and thus we must ask how television drama has dealt with AIDS and gay men: which stories have been chosen and which stories have been ignored?

Victims and Villains

As with many other minorities gay people have almost always seen themselves reflected in the media in one of two roles: as victim (of ridicule or violence, or both) or as villain (Gross 1989). AIDS stories have featured both of these stereotypes. Victims, as in the family-centered dramas *An Early Frost* (NBC, 1985) and *Our Sons* (ABC, 1991), are objects of pity, and when treated well by the authors they end by being tearfully reconciled with their families.

Programs that are less family-centered, such as the ones discussed by Netzhammer and Shamp, are more likely to show us the AIDS carrier as villain, threatening the health of innocent victims. An egregious example of the villain scenario occurred on the episode of the NBC series *Midnight Caller* in December 1988, which Netzhammer and Shamp analyze. The story focussed on Mike Barnes, a bisexual man who knows he is infected with HIV but continues to be sexually promiscuous. The hero of the series, a San Francisco radio talk-show host, learns that his former lover (a woman) has tested HIV + after an affair with the man, and he uses his radio show to track the man down. In the original version the woman kills the bisexual man at the end, but after protests from AIDS groups who saw the script, he is saved by the hero, and some conciliatory additions were made to the script. These include a brief scene in a gay bar that "carefully lets the bartender emphasize that 'Mike Barnes is an exception, an aberrant' in sexually active circles" (O'Connor 1988).[2]

The other concession was more interesting. As John O'Connor of the *New York Times* put it, "One of the most sympathetic characters turns out to be Ross Parker, Barnes' abandoned lover, who is dying of AIDS. 'It's nice just to talk to somebody. I don't get a lot of company these days,' " he says to the hero, who visits him while hunting for Barnes. O'Connor ends his review with the thought that "perhaps a future episode can focus primarily on a character like Ross, a decent person with AIDS who finds himself abandoned by friends, family and society" (O'Connor 1988). Here O'Connor unwittingly touches upon a truly important point: the AIDS stories that television has assiduously avoided. But these are not the stories of pathetic abandonment that O'Connor urged on programmers.

The Greatest Stories Never Told

There are some truly dramatic and important AIDS stories that we never see enacted or even reflected glancingly in TV drama, but they aren't stories of villainous AIDS carriers or abandoned victims who may finally be accepted back into the arms of their families. These are stories of how the gay community responded to an unparalleled health crisis with an unprecedented grassroots movement of social service and medical organizing; of sex and public health education; of research-backed militant agitation for reforms in the testing and approval of drugs; of coalition building with other marginalized groups suffering from disproportionate AIDS risk; and pushing the issue of health care and health insurance onto the national agenda.

The consistent feature of all TV dramatic programming on AIDS (and most news, public affairs, and documentary programming as well) has been to focus on individual people suffering from AIDS and, if the angle of vision is widened at all, it will then include (straight) family members and possibly a lover (as long as they barely touch) and perhaps one or two friends (more likely to be straight than gay). What is wrong with this picture?

What's wrong is that it not only leaves out all of the important—and dramatic—achievements of the gay community noted above, but that it falsely suggests that gay people with AIDS are alone and abandoned, unless and until they are taken back into the bosom of their family. Even the best of the TV AIDS stories fall into this pattern.

An episode of *L.A. Law* (May 16, 1991) includes a gay lawyer dying of AIDS who sues his health insurance company to obtain payment for an experimental drug that might prolong his life (he wins, with the assistance of *L.A. Law* regular Victor Sifuentes). The ailing lawyer is shown as a strong and principled person who is willing to fight for his rights, and for the rights of others in his situation. But viewers of the program would never know—from this episode, or from any other prime-time TV drama— about the significant efforts and dramatic achievements of the militant organization Act Up in forcing the medical establishment, the FDA, and drug companies to deal more equitably and openly with patients. It has been widely acknowledged by medical scientists, such as Anthony Fauci of the National Institutes of Health, that Act Up has wrought substantial changes in the way the medical community relates to the populations it serves. These successes were not brought about by lone individuals, however courageous and eloquent, and thus the *L.A. Law* episode, for all its good intentions, continues the tradition of isolating the gay person as a lone victim.[3]

For Whom the Heart Beats

In 1972, just a few years after Stonewall, network television's first (relatively) sympathetic portrait of a gay man appeared on the ABC made-for-

TV movie *That Certain Summer,* in which two gay men actually were shown touching (on the shoulder), and none of the gay characters had to die at the end of the story.[4] This "breakthrough" was something of a false spring, however, as it did not herald the blooming of a hundred (or even a dozen) gay and lesbian characters. True, gay and lesbian characters did begin to appear from time to time for one-shot appearances on network series, and in 1978 ABC produced *A Question Of Love,* a TV movie based on a real lesbian mother's child custody case (the women never kiss, but one is shown tenderly drying her lover's hair).

The slight increase in gay (and less often lesbian) visibility in the mid-seventies was quickly seized upon by the political right as sign of media capitulation to what in the eighties came to be called "special interests." The apocalyptic tone of their jeremiads is well represented in a nationally syndicated column by Nicholas Von Hoffman, who noted that the "old-style Chinese have the Year of the Tiger and the Year of the Pig," but the "new-style Americans are having the Year of the Fag" (April 11, 1976). Von Hoffman charted the decline of the American character as beginning with a "presentable gay" in the *Doonesbury* comic strip and "from there it was but a hop, skip and a jump to television where the flits are swarming this year." Hoffman plaintively asks, "Is a new stereotype being born? Is network television about to kill off the bitchy, old-time outrageous fruit and replace him with a new type homo?" Among the horrors he foresaw were *"The Six Million Dollar Queer* or *The Bionic Fruit."*

But although the right wing attacked the networks for what they considered to be overly favorable attention to gay people, gay people were in fact usually portrayed in news and dramatic media in ways that served to reinforce rather than challenge the prevailing images.[5] Rather than *The Six Million Dollar Fruit,* television viewers were treated to gay characters who tended to be so subtle as to be readily misunderstood by the innocent (as in the case of Sidney in *Love, Sidney,* whose homosexuality seemed to consist entirely of crying at old Greta Garbo movies and having a photo of his dead lover on the mantelpiece), or confused about their sexuality and never seen in an ongoing romantic relationship (as in the case of Stephen Carrington in *Dynasty,* whose lovers had an unfortunate tendency of getting killed).

Kathleen Montgomery observed the efforts of the organized gay movement to improve the ways network programmers handle gay characters and themes. In particular she describes the writing and production of a made-for-TV network movie that had a gay-related theme, and involved consultation with representatives of gay organizations. And the result?

> [T]hroughout the process all the decisions affecting the portrayal of gay life were influenced by the constraints which commercial television as a mass medium imposes upon the creation of its content. The fundamental goal of garnering the largest possible audience necessitated that (a) the program be placed in a familiar and successful television genre—the crime-drama; (b) the story focus upon the heterosexual male lead character and his reactions to the gay characters rather than upon the homosexual characters themselves; and (c) the film avoid any overt display of affection which might be offensive to certain segments of the audience. These requirements served as a filter through which the issue of homosexuality was processed, resulting in a televised picture of gay life designed to be acceptable to the gay community and still palatable to a mass audience. (1981)

Acceptability to the gay community, in this case, means that the movie was not an attack on our character and a denial of our basic humanity; it could not be mistaken for an expression of our values or perspectives. But of course they weren't aiming at us, either; they were merely trying to avoid arguing with us afterwards.

As Hantzis and Lehr (this volume, chapter 6) and Moritz (this volume, chapter 7) document, the pattern established in the seventies continued through the eighties and into the nineties: occasional one-time appearances by gay or lesbian characters on series, with the story line largely focused on the responses of the heterosexual regular characters (episodes of *Golden Girls, Dear John,* and *Designing Women,* among others). Although they have appeared from time to time on daytime soaps or cable channels,[6] continuing lesbian or gay characters on network series are still nearly nonexistent. Interestingly, two of the series that have included continuing gay characters (both on ABC)—*Hooperman* and *Heartbeat*—did not survive very long. But while they lasted, they did provide a glimpse of how network television construes "positive" characterizations of gay people.

No Sex Please, We're Lesbians

The papers by Hantzis and Lehr and by Moritz both focus centrally on the depiction of the lesbian physicians' aide Marilyn McGrath on *Heartbeat,* played by Gail Strickland, and they agree that behind the superficial feminism of the program beats a familiar patriarchal heart.

Hantzis and Lehr unmask the sexism lurking behind the feminist front of *Heartbeat* and raise the important question of whether portrayals intended to be "positive" within television's terms are in fact constructing images of lesbians and gays that are "nonthreatening to heterosexuals" through the erasure of lesbian and gay sexuality. Moritz's analysis of *Heartbeat* supports this conclusion with examples of lesbian characters on other series: "with the exception of the conspiring [lesbian] murderers in *Hunter,* none of the these lesbian characters is permitted to be sexual or even romantic." As both analyses demonstrate, although *Heartbeat* often presents detailed accounts and images of the heterosexual characters' romantic and sexual involvements, the lesbian character has a lover who is rarely shown, and they are never permitted to express desire or passion. The desexualization of Marilyn McGrath thoroughly demonstrated in these papers did not, however, deflect the wrath of Reverend Donald Wildmon's American Family Association, whose massive campaign against the program may have contributed to its cancellation after one season.

In this context we should not be surprised at the furor aroused in February 1991 when two female attorneys on NBC's *L.A. Law* engaged in the first lesbian kiss on network television. Predictably, Rev. Wildmon geared up his fundamentalist letter-writing battalions to "brow-beat the networks and advertisers into censoring such acts by threatening them with product boycotts" (Enrico 1991), and equally predictably, NBC began hedging its bets: " 'We were not attempting to create a lesbian character in that episode,' said NBC spokeswoman Sue Binford. 'It was much more of an attempt to add texture to C. J.'s character. It was a minor part of the overall story line' " (ibid.).

Yet this minor texture added to the character of C. J. Lamb continued to attract attention from right-wing media watchdogs, lesbian and gay media viewers and activists, and the "infotainment" industry. Actress Amanda Donohue, who plays the apparently bisexual C. J. Lamb, tirelessly appeared on shows ranging from *Today* to *Entertainment Tonight* to *Arsenio Hall* to discuss her controversial character. Although she declined to identify C. J. Lamb as a lesbian, she also refused to distance herself from the role; and while she made a point of saying she "had many gay friends," at least we were spared an account of her boyfriend's response to the "kiss." In the last few episodes of the season the recipient of the famous kiss,

Abby Perkins (played by Michele Green), seemed eager to push things even further, only to have C. J. hold back and declare that Abby wasn't really ready. Viewers would have to wait to find out if network television is ready to permit two women to express sexual desire for each other.

Where Do We Go from Here?

By now we have sufficient documentation of the simple fact that Hollywood is not interested in depicting the reality of lesbian and gay lives. Although, as Vito Russo noted in the second edition of his pioneering study *The Celluloid Closet*, "homosexuality is no longer in the closet either on or off screen" (1987, 248), it is also true that "mainstream cinema is incapable of giving to members of any minority the kind of films that truly touch their lives and experiences. . . . Mainstream films about homosexuality are not for gays. They address themselves exclusively to the majority" (ibid, 322, 325). This is even more true of network television, which is more constrained by public pressure and advertiser timidity. The resulting images range from old-fashioned victims and villains (see discussions of *Midnight Caller* and *Hunter* by Netzhammer and Shamp and Moritz), to well-meaning approaches that plead for tolerance by representing gays as no different from heterosexuals, a "liberal" strategy that dictates complete asexuality.

What should be the agenda for lesbian and gay research on the mass media? Although it is obviously essential to continually monitor the mass media's presentation of lesbian and gay characters and to decode their "hidden" meanings, as researchers and as activists we face challenges beyond surveillance and analysis.

We know something about the ways in which the networks have dealt with external pressure from gay groups. Kathleen Montgomery (1981, 1989) shed some light on this territory in her analysis of the efforts of advocacy groups to influence television programming, and Moritz (1989) extended this analysis in a more recent study of how network television dealt with lesbian characters in the late 1980s. When Montgomery conducted her study of advocacy groups in the late 1970s, gay pressure on the networks was exercised primarily by the National Gay Task Force (now the National Gay and Lesbian Task Force), then located in New York, and by one man (psychologist Newton Deiter) in Los Angeles operating under the impressive title of the Gay Media Task Force. By the time Moritz spoke to network executives and gay activists in the late 1980s, there was an Alliance of Gay and Lesbian Artists' Media Watch Committee. In addition, the current scene includes increasingly active and effective New York and Los Angeles branches of the Gay and Lesbian Alliance against Defamation (GLAAD), which issue reports and alerts encouraging lesbian and gay responses—both positive and negative—to counter the campaigns organized by the right. In other words, the stage is set for an updated study of the battlefield on which the current struggle over lesbian and gay images is being fought.

Beyond the responses to outside pressure groups, we need studies of the backstage workings of the Hollywood dream (and nightmare) factories that manufacture the images absorbed by millions around the world. The factory image is not inappropriate: we need to be aware that most of what shows up on the screen is dictated by industrial processes of "mass production" rather than the imagination of individual artists. The decisions about whether two gay *thirtysomething* men will be allowed to touch each other, or whether C. J. and Abby will ever go beyond that famous first kiss, will be debated and resolved at the highest levels, but many of the images of gay people that we encounter are determined at much "lower" levels. This is often true of the familiar and infuriating characterizations that lurk in the background of the media landscape. As Turow has shown, "stereotypes are vehicles for getting work done quickly, efficiently, and with a lower risk of individual failure," because they capitalize on "what the audience can buy instantaneously" (Turow 1984, 169, 174).

Although there is a small body of research on the inner workings of the media (e.g., Gitlin 1983; Turow 1984), there has yet to be an account of the lesbian and gay component of the film and television industry. It will not be an easy task, however, to explore beneath the surface. As the "outing" controversies have revealed to any who might not have known already, Hollywood is rife with closeted gay and lesbian executives, producers, directors, writers, and actors who have assiduously avoided becoming part of the solution, and have thus become part of the problem (cf. Gross 1991).

Hollywood is where a gay director makes anti-homosexual films so that he can continue to work with the big boys. Hollywood is where gay screenwriters churn out offensive teenage sex comedies and do it well because there isn't anything they don't know about pretending to be straight. Hollywood is where a lesbian rock singer arrives at the American Music Awards on the arm of a gay superstar. Hollywood is where Joan Rivers obligingly asks gay actors how many girlfriends they have and proceeds to tell fag jokes. (Russo 1987, 322–23)

Clearly, these aren't conditions conducive to candid confessions and illuminating interviews, but that should not prevent researchers from trying to chart this largely unexplored territory. One promising approach is historical research, using the abundant archival resources of USC, UCLA, and the Academy of Motion Pictures Arts and Sciences Library, among others. A fine example of what can be done with such documentary data is George Custen's account of Hollywood's reconstruction of Cole Porter's life in *Night and Day* (1992).

Finally, in addition to studies of the people and the institutions responsible for producing the images of lesbian and gay people that are absorbed by millions in this country and beyond, we need more studies of how actual audience members, gay as well as nongay, interpret and respond to these messages. It is by now a commonplace of fashionable postmodern theory to argue that audiences are not "cultural dupes" who passively absorb and parrot the messages of the mass media (cf. Fiske 1987), but we have little direct evidence of how images of lesbians and gays are responded to. I happen to believe that the optimistic assumption that audiences routinely engage in "oppositional readings" which shield them from the hegemonic impact of "dominant codes" has not been supported by very much empirical research, or even common sense. Simply put, if audiences are being all that resistant, why don't we see signs of actual resistance?

In the case of lesbian and gay characterizations in the mass media, there is even less reason to assume that "general" audiences would be moved to adopt oppositional decodings, but this is an empirical question worth asking. In the case of lesbian and gay audiences we have even less research evidence available, but these are questions well worth pursuing. Among those who have investigated the responses of female spectators of film and television (cf. Pribram 1988), Chris Straayer (1985) and Elizabeth Ellsworth (1986) have specifically focused on the readings of the film *Personal Best* by lesbian viewers. The challenge of understanding the responses of lesbian and gay viewers to network television and to other media as well— MTV, independent lesbian and gay film, pornography—should provide more than enough terra incognita to tempt adventurous explorers.

Notes

1. Ronald Milavsky, then Vice President of NBC, described the coverage of AIDS.

   The most striking thing . . . is the low level of reporting until Rock Hudson's illness and the rather continuous high level after that. AIDS did, after all, have a focal event, like the Tylenol poisonings, the death, after thousands of others, of a famous person who most people did not think of as being homosexual. Rock Hudson's illness, death, and his admission that he was indeed dying of AIDS was a very unusual combination that was big news and stimulated the public's interest. From July to December 1985, NBC broadcast over 200 stories on AIDS—three times as many as during the entire 1980 to 1984 period. The other news media reacted similarly. (Milavsky 1988)

   Note the implication that it was the low level of public interest which was responsible for the lesser amount of coverage before Rock Hudson.
2. The inclusion of such brief scenes, or the addition of brief disclaimers at the beginning or the end of a program or movie, are familiar "concessions" wrung by protestors from producers of bigoted dramas. There is little reason to believe that these effectively counteract the primary messages of the programs, nor any evidence that many people even read the fine print of crawling disclaimers.
3. This isolation is heightened by a scene in which the gay lawyer stumbles into the private wedding ceremony of Sifuentes and lawyer Grace Van Owen and is asked to stay as a witness; his disease ravaged face is dramatically contrasted with those of the joyfully united couple and the jocular judge who marries them.
4. It is worth noting, however, that the main character, a gay father who comes out to his son, says that if he were given a choice he would not choose to be homosexual.
5. In a response to an inquiry about their policy regarding homosexual characters, an ABC official wrote, "We want to assure you that the portrayal of homosexuals on television will not be a very common occurrence but when depicted and appropriate to a particular story line or plot, such characterizations in ABC programs will be governed by standards of good taste" (Dan Rustin to Leland Mellott, April 1, 1977).
6. Soap opera queers included a lesbian psychologist who was briefly included among *All My Children* and a gay man who came out on *As The World Turns* and then left to take care of his lover who was dying of AIDS off camera. The longest continuing gay characters were the seemingly straight Cliff and the hyper-camp (but sympathetic) Donald on Showtime's *Brothers,* now in syndication.

Works Cited

Comstock, Gary. 1991. *Violence Against Lesbians and Gay Men.* New York: Columbia University Press.

Custen, George. 1992. *Biographical Movies: How Hollywood Constructed Public History.* New Brunswick, N.J.: Rutgers University Press.

Ellsworth, Elizabeth. 1986. "Illicit Pleasures: Feminist Spectators and *Personal Best." Wide Angle* 8:2, 45–56.

Enrico, Dottie. 1991. "The media fallout from 'lesbian kiss': Advertisers on LA Law caught in the middle." *San Francisco Chronicle,* 5 March, E1.

Fiske, John. 1987. *Television Culture.* New York: Routledge.

Gitlin, Todd. 1983. *Inside Prime Time.* New York: Pantheon.

Gross, Larry. 1988. "The ethics of (mis)representation." In *Image Ethics: The Moral Rights of Subjects In Photography, Film and Television,* edited by L. Gross et al., 188–202. New York: Oxford University Press.

———. 1989. "Out of the Mainstream: Sexual Minorities and the Mass Media." In *Remote Control: Television, Audiences, and Cultural Power,* edited by Ellen Seiter, et al., 130–49. New York: Routledge.

———. 1991. "The Contested Closet: The Ethics and Politics of Outing." *Critical Studies in Mass Communication,* 352–88.

Gross, Larry, Steven Aurand, and Rita Addessa. 1988. *Violence and Discrimination against Lesbian and Gay People in Philadelphia and the Commonwealth of Pennsylvania.* Philadelphia: Philadelphia Lesbian and Gay Task Force.

Milavsky, Ron. 1988. "AIDS and the Media." Paper presented at the Annual Meeting of the American Psychological Association, Atlanta, 15 August.

Montgomery, Kathleen. 1981. "Gay activists and the networks." *Journal of Communication* 31:3, 49–57.

———. 1989. *Target: Prime Time.* New York: Oxford University Press.

Moritz, Marguerite. 1989. "American television discovers gay women: The changing context of programming decisions at the networks." *Journal of Communication Inquiry* 13:2, 62–78.

O'Connor, John. 1988. "Debated Episode on AIDS." *New York Times,* 13 December, C22.

Pribram, Dierdre, ed. 1988. *Female Spectators: Looking at Film and Television.* London: Verso.

Reardon, Kathleen, and J. Richardson. 1991. "The important role of mass media in the diffusion of accurate information about AIDS." *Journal of Homosexuality,* 63–76.

Ross, Chuck. 1989. "Gay Stays on 'thirtysomething.'" *San Francisco Chronicle,* 18 November, C9.

Russo, Vito. 1987. *The Celluloid Closet: Homosexuality in the Movies.* 2d Edition. New York: Harper and Row.

Stipp, Horst, and Dennis Kerr. 1989. "Determinants of public opinion about AIDS." *Public Opinion Quarterly* 53, 98–106.

Straayer, Chris. 1985. *"Personal Best:* A lesbian feminist audience analysis." *Jump Cut* 29, 40–44.

Turow, Joseph. 1984. *Media Industries: The Production of News and Entertainment.* New York: Longman.

PART THREE

Portrayals of Gay Men and Lesbians in Language and Text

9. A Portrait of the Adolescent as a Young Gay: The Politics of Male Homosexuality in Young Adult Fiction

Kirk Fuoss

Numerous scholars comment on the importance of books in the lives of gays and lesbians. Barbara Gittings, for example, contends that "most gays, it seems, at some point have gone to books in an effort to understand about being gay."[1] Similarly, Mark Lilly writes, "I started to realize that it was genuinely the case that heterosexual readers did not know what it was like, for example, for a young student to stand in her/his university library surrounded by books in almost every one of which homosexuality was either represented as poisonous or ignored altogether."[2] I share Gitting's and Lilly's sentiments concerning the importance of books by and about gays and lesbians. Intersecting with this belief is another—namely, that adults do not have a corner on the market with regard to concern about sexual orientation. Unfortunately, however, as Rose Robertson has noted, "Most of the literature on homosexuality in the past has assumed that the difficulties associated with this orientation are the prerogative of adulthood. But the experience of all counseling and supportive agencies has been that questions of sexual orientation in fact begin in adolescence."[3] The publica tion in 1986 of *One Teenager in Ten,* a collection of personal narratives by gay and lesbian adolescents, corroborates Robertson's claim.[4]

Given the importance of books in the lives of gays and lesbians and given that issues of gender preference emerge during adolescence, we would be well advised to study the resources libraries offer young readers concerning homosexuality. This essay attempts to do just that with regard to a specific group of texts—namely young adult (YA) problem-realism fiction representing male homosexuality.[5] After reviewing the major features of YA problem-realism novels, four political strategies related to the representation of male homosexuality in YA novels are explored. The final section reflects on the question, who/what is responsible for the shaping of homosexual characters in YA problem-realism novels?

Before proceeding with this agenda, two preliminary concerns warrant consideration. First, what constitutes the political, and how do YA texts depicting male homosexuality participate in the political? Second, even if these texts do participate in the political, why analyze them in terms of this dimension rather than another—say, their artistry or sensitivity?

For purposes of this investigation, "politics" refers to the struggle among competing interests for the power to define, establish, and maintain a norm. Politics, as defined, includes (among others) sexual and textual politics, encompassing both attempts to bolster and attempts to resist the hegemonic might of status quo norms. Young adult novels addressing male homosexuality are political on at least two levels, content and circulation/ reception. These novels are political at the level of content to the extent that they position male homosexuality within a normative spectrum marking acceptable and deviant forms of same-sex love, acceptable and deviant forms of familial organization, and acceptable and deviant forms of interacting with those who transgress these norms. These novels are political at the level of their circulation/reception to the extent that their value and movement within the symbolic economy depends upon the norms by which they are appraised. After all, the question "Is this novel good?" makes little sense apart from the questions that contextualize this evaluative endeavor—namely, good for whom, and good at doing what?

Why focus on the political dimensions of these novels rather than some other dimension such as their artistry or sensitivity? Because to focus on some other dimension of these novels does not result in an apolitical, objective, and disinterested reading but only in a reading that denies or effaces its political grounding. If, for example, I suggest that I will bracket off the political and focus exclusively on the aesthetic dimension of these texts, the assumption underlying this suggestion is that this is indeed a possibility, and this assumption itself marks a particular textual politics, a textual politics that has increasingly been called into question by contemporary literary theory. Similarly, to suggest that I will deal with the sensitivity rather than politics of the representations offered by these novels effaces the political grounding on which any appraisal of sensitivity rests. After all, I can not determine whether the novels offer a sensitive representation of a homosexual, until I engage the more fundamental and thoroughly political questions: What is a "homosexual"? What constitutes a "representation of" a homosexual?[6] What makes a representation of a homosexual sensitive? And, finally, sensitive for whom? To a religious fundamentalist, a representation of a homosexual that includes tar and feathering, confinement, eternal damnation, or death from AIDS might very well be viewed as sensitive. Like beauty, sensitivity, it seems, is in the eye of the beholder. Thus, I focus my reading on the political dimensions of these novels for two reasons: first, because the novels are themselves thoroughly political, and second, because, although it is possible to efface the political nature of one's reading of these texts, it is not possible to read these texts apolitically.

Background

Texts belonging to the problem-realism genre typically differ from other YA texts in their choice of characters, in their use of colloquial language (including profanity and ungrammatical constructions), in their overt discussion of sex, and in their privileging of tragic and ironic modes over romantic and comic modes. The typical protagonist in a problem-realism novel is an anxiety ridden and alienated adolescent facing some sort of problem-situation. The protagonist confronting the problem usually narrates his/her own story, bestowing on the narrative a decidedly confessional tone. The conclusions of problem-realism novels, moreover, usually suggest that the protagonist is only beginning to come to terms with the problem and that a difficult period of adjustment and/or recovery still lies ahead.[7]

While it is difficult to identify the first problem-realism text, no such difficulty arises in identifying the first problem-realism text to include a "homosexual incident." John Donovan's *I'll Get There, It Better Be Worth the Trip,* published in 1969, caused too much stir to go unnoticed. Reviewing the book for *Atlantic Monthly,* Martha Bacon wrote: "The book is craftsmanlike and competent. But its purpose and execution pose a number of questions. The loss of innocence is an adult's subject. . . . The language of children is inadequate to it, and the application of grammar school jargon to corruption and passion is neither natural nor comforting."[8] A radically different review of the novel appeared in *Commonweal:* "This is a beautifully written, poignant depiction of how Davey absorbs his [homosexual] experience and begins to grow toward manhood. It could only be found objectionable by the most narrow-minded of little old librarians from Iowa."[9]

Once Donovan broke the silence, other authors of YA fiction quickly followed suit, with two novels—Isabelle Holland's *The Man without a Face* and Lynn Hall's *Sticks and Stones*—published in 1972. According to *The Bookfinder,* the years between 1969 and 1987 witnessed the publication of thirteen problem-realism texts that deal with male homosexuality. Eight of these thirteen books remain in print.[10]

The Politics of Male Homosexuality in YA Fiction

That fictional texts written for children and young adults are political is well established. In *Catching Them Young,* Bob Dixon notes, "Anyone interested in how ideas—political ideas in the broadest and most important sense—are fostered and grow up in a society cannot afford to neglect what children read."[11] Similarly, in "Sexuality in Books for Children," Barbara Wersba writes, "What we're talking about is political. We're talking about the control of one group of people by another group of people: namely, children by adults."[12]

This section identifies four recurrent political strategies related to the representation of male homosexuality in YA fiction. Three of these strategies—presence/absence, containment, and unhappy endings—operate at the level of textual representations; one strategy—transcendence—operates at the level of reviewers' responses to these textual representations.

While it appears obvious that there are signifying presences in a text, it is perhaps less obvious that there are signifying absences as well. What a text means depends not only on what the text says, but also on what the text does not say. For example, when a picture book depicts only caucasians in its illustrations, the absence of minorities in the worldview projected by the text necessarily figures as a component in that text's meaning. Similarly, when YA novels include as characters only heterosexuals, the absence of gays necessarily figures as a component in the meaning of these texts. "Any view of reality in children's literature," writes Anne McLeod, "is refracted through adult attitudes toward children and society, with the result that these stories are often as suggestive for what they leave out as for what they include."[13]

The absence of homosexuality in YA fiction prior to 1969 assisted the dominant heterosexual culture in its drive toward "ex-nomination,"[14] its drive to unname itself. The motive underlying ex-nomination is the naturalization of what is culturally specific. When the operation of unnaming is successful, cultural constructs appear not as constructs, but as part-and-parcel of "the nature of things." Heterosexual culture does not like to conceive of itself as "heterosexual culture," preferring instead to conceive of itself as "culture." As long as YA fiction persisted in relegating homosexuality to the status of absence, it also persisted in perpetuating the myth that heterosexuality is the natural sexuality.

The political implications of presences and absences do not disappear with the emergence of YA novels containing homosexual incidents or self-identified homosexual characters. On the contrary, these new developments merely result in the shifting of the question from "Is male homosexuality present in the text?" to "How is male homosexuality presented in the text?" Two general answers can be posited to the latter question. First, physical acts of male homosexuality (including kissing, hugging, and holding hands) are more often than not presented as occurring off-stage and out of sight. Second, homosexuals are more often than not presented as characters in someone else's story than narrators of their own life stories.

To illustrate the first of these points, let's examine the moment in John Donovan's *I'll Get There, It Better Be Worth the Trip* when homosexuality would seem to be most present, the moment referred to by the jacket blurb as "an unforeseen moment of open sexuality."

I take Fred [the narrator's dog] out for his finals. When I come back, Mother tells me that she has just hung up, that Douglas is a wonderful boy, that Mrs. Altschuler thinks I'm a wonderful boy, and that Douglas and I are going to have a wonderful day together. He is going to stay over Saturday night, Mother tells me.

Chapter Twenty-one

My mother does not come home until very late on Saturday, so she is still snoozing when Altschuler [Douglas] leaves on Sunday morning. It is the strangest, weirdest goodbye I ever had to say to anybody—somebody I saw every day last week, including Saturday, and will see every day this week. We horse around over some fried eggs I make and talk about Miss Stuart and stuff like that, but I have a new way of looking at Altschuler because of what we did together last night. Don't get me wrong, I'm not ashamed. There was nothing wrong about it, I keep telling myself.[15]

This passage demonstrates the way in which Donovan's novel undoes any tidy determination regarding the presence/absence of homosexuality. The placement of "it"—of "what [they] did together last night"—in the cusp between two chapters makes not so much for an "unforeseen moment of open sexuality" as an unseen moment of unknown sexuality. Isabelle Holland employs a similar strategy in *The Man without a Face:*

I could feel his heart pounding, and then I realized it was mine. I couldn't stop shaking; in fact, I started to tremble violently. It was like everything—the water, the sun, the hours, the play, the work, the whole summer came together. The golden cocoon had broken open and was spilling a shower of gold.

Even so, I didn't know what was happening to me until it had happened.

When I woke up I was alone and in the bed rather than on it which was the way I had gone to sleep.[16]

Holland's novel, like Donovan's, grants physical expressions of homosexual love all the presence of an ellipsis.

This absencing of overt physical expression of same-sex desire is especially disconcerting when two additional factors are considered: first, to the extent that heterosexual intercourse is treated with less probity, this absencing does not reflect a general prohibition against representing acts of sexual expression in YA texts, but a much more specific prohibition against representing acts of homosexual expression in YA texts; second, while it is apparently not acceptable to represent acts of homosexual expression in YA novels, there appears to exist no prohibition against depicting acts of homophobic violence. Sandra Scoppettone's *Trying Hard to Hear You,* for example, remains circumspect with regard to acts of physical endearment between Jeff and Phil (the narrator, Carmilla, does not even see, but only hears about, their exchange of a kiss behind a bush), but shows no such restraint in reporting the details of an act of homophobic violence:

There was Jeff, lying on his back, a gag in his mouth, in his underwear. He was spread-eagled and his wrists and ankles were tied to some posts that had been pounded deep into the sand.

Phil smashed through the circle and Eben and Harlan grabbed him, pinning his arms behind him.

"You want the same queer?"

"Let me go. Let me go," he shouted.

Eben smacked him across the mouth and told him to shut up.[17]

I do not wish to suggest that Scoppettone's portrayal of this incident is sympathetic to the homophobic attackers; it is not. I do, however, wish to suggest that when acts of homophobic violence are fair game for an author's representation but physical expressions of same-sex desire are not, then a particular sexual-textual politics is being operationalized.

A second generalization regarding the way homosexuality and homosexual characters are presented in YA novels centers on the distinction between being a character in someone else's narrative and being the narrator of your own life story. Homosexual characters, like their heterosexual counterparts, may be presented as articulating subjects narrating their own life story or as articulated components in the discourse of an other. Of the thirteen YA texts in question, only two—Aidan Chamber's *Dance on My Grave* (1982) and Frank Mosca's *All-American Boys* (1983)—are narrated in the first person by a character who is unambiguously gay. In actuality, only one and one half of the thirteen texts meet this requirement, for in the case of *Dance on My Grave,* the narration is divided between a young gay (Hal) and the social worker assigned to his case (Ms. Atkins). If the past twenty years have led to an increase in the number of YA texts that include homosexual "ingredients," this increase is not as much a cause for optimism as one might initially have imagined. Although homosexuality may not be silenced in or absenced from YA texts to the extent that it was prior to 1969, the texts published since then nevertheless exhibit a sustained resistance to the articulation, by a gay narrator, of his own story. The implication seems to be that while it's one thing to permit talk about homosexuality, it is quite another matter to permit a homosexual to talk.

A second political strategy, containment, acquires its potency by maintaining a distinction between doing and being, between action and identity. The politics of containment result in the representation of homosexuality as a discrete, isolatable behavior that need not be assimilated as an enduring aspect of identity. As long as homosexuality remains an exteriorized behavior rather an interiorized dimension of self-identity, it is still manageable, controllable, reversible. For those who fear homosexuality, the salient feature of the politics of containment is that homosexuality—defined as a behavior—always takes the form of an observable act. Because the act is observable, it can also be policed.

The politics of containment plays a role in four of the YA texts considered in this paper: John Donovan's *I'll Get There, It Better Be Worth the Trip* (1969), Isabelle Holland's *The Man without a Face* (1972), Carolyn Meyer's *The Center: From a Troubled Past to a New Life* (1979), and Emily Hanlon's *The Wing and the Flame* (1980). In each of these novels, the adolescent protagonist experiences a homosexual "incident." Moreover, in each of these novels, the incident's cause is ultimately attributed not to a desire that has been acted upon, but to an external and transitory exigence. In Donovan's *I'll Get There, It Better Be Worth the Trip,* for example, the homosexual incident is depicted as occurring spontaneously as a result of the incredible loneliness felt by the boys: Davey's grandmother has just died and he's been forced to move to New York City to live with his alcoholic mother, and Doug's best friend has recently died of leukemia. Similarly, in Isabelle Holland's *The Man without a Face,* fourteen-year-old Charles Norstadt engages in a homosexual incident with a middle aged tutor (Justin McLeod) he has hired to help him get into a New England prep school. The two spend the night together immediately following Charles's traumatic discovery that his pet cat has been killed by his sister's boyfriend and that the cause of his father's death was alcoholism. Describing their homosexual encounter of the previous evening, Justin McLeod reassures Charles: "There's nothing about it to worry you. You reacted to a lot of strain—and shock—in a normal fashion. At your age, anything could trigger it. . . . It has something to do with me, sure. But nothing of any lasting significance. It could have been anyone—boy or girl. It could have been when you were asleep."[18] Emily Hanlon's *The Wing and the Flame* also involves the politics of containment. In this novel, the other-worldly nature of the Indian burial cave in which the two boys find themselves alone precipitates the homosexual experience. In each of these novels, the homosexuality presumably belongs only in the characters' pasts, not in their futures.

A third political strategy centers on the way in which these novels conclude. In the case of the thirteen YA texts under consideration, it is important to ask not only how the novel ends, but also what personal trajectory the "sexually suspect" characters follow during the course of the novel, and what their condition is at the end of the novel.

The thirteen problem-realism texts considered include a total of twenty-one characters who either question their sexuality, engage in a homosexual act, or are professedly homosexual or bisexual. Each of these characters follows a trajectory of sexual identity, beginning with their sexual identity at the opening of the novel and ending with their sexual identity at the close of the novel. Of the twenty-one "sexually suspect" characters, only eleven are self-identified as gay when their novels conclude. Of the remaining ten characters, one is bisexual, three are not gay, five are probably not gay though some question remains, and the sexuality of one of the characters remains truly ambiguous. It is interesting to note that this instance of true ambiguity appears to be the result of pressure exerted by the publisher on the author to change her ending. Lynn Hall, the author of *Sticks and Stones,* writes:

I wanted Tom and Ward to love each other, to live happily ever after, and that was the way I ended it. But the publishers would not let me do this. In their words, this would be showing a homosexual relationship as a happy ending and this might be dangerous to young people teetering on the brink. One editor wanted me to kill Tom in a car accident! At least I held out for a friendship at the end, one which might or might not develop into something more, depending on the reader's imagination.[19]

While Lynn Hall does not have Tom die at the conclusion of her novel, other novelists more freely bestow death on characters whose sexuality does not follow the straight and narrow path of heterosexuality. Of the twenty-one sexually suspect characters, five are dead by the time the novels conclude. At first glance, these deaths do not appear to possess any particular statistical significance, especially given the popularity of deaths in the conclusion of problem-realism novels in general. Upon closer examination, however, these deaths are inordinately concentrated among those characters who are either unambiguously gay or bisexual. While these characters—the unambiguously gay or bisexual—account for just over 50 percent of the twenty-one sexually suspect characters, 80 percent of the deaths are concentrated in this population. One of these characters dies in a motorcycle accident; another dies in a car accident; a third commits suicide because of his homosexuality; and a fourth character dies of AIDS. While in the case of the two accidents, no direct cause-effect relationship between homosexuality and death is explicitly posited, in the case of the suicide and the person with AIDS, the connection between death and homosexuality is explicitly maintained. The acceptance of a gay lifestyle by a character in a YA novel seems to be something of a metaphorical equivalent of the appearance of a cough for a character in a soap opera: both tend to function as warning signals, indicating the heightened propensity for the character's being written out of the script vis-à-vis death.

The fourth political strategy—transcendence—operates at the level of reviewers' responses to these representations. Transcendence occurs when a reviewer recognizes the homosexual content of the work but then relegates this content to a peripheral position, emphasizing—usually with much vigor—that the novel is "really about" something else. The *Publisher's Weekly* review of Donovan's *I'll Get There, It Better Be Worth the Trip* exemplifies this move:

Here is a remarkable book. . . . Don't be put off when you hear—and you will hear—that it is a story about homosexuality, because it isn't. Among the many incidents which the author describes with much insight and compassion, incidents to illustrate the boy's loneliness and his attempts to overcome it, is an incident with homosexual ingredients. But it is only one of many which add up to a perceptive, funny, touching story.[20]

Judy Blume's review of Lynn Hall's *Sticks and Stones* is strikingly similar. She writes: "Some will say this is a book about homosexuality. It isn't. What it is about is far more important; injustice through the power of gossip."[21] Likewise, of Carolyn Meyer's *The Center: From a Troubled Past to a New Life* (1979), the *Kirkus Review* wrote: "Only skirting the homosexual incident of the past, the real subject is what the center can do for a kid."[22]

I am not necessarily claiming that these reviewers are incorrect in their assessment of what these novels are "really about." What I am claiming is that when YA texts include homosexuality as a dimension of their content, the reviewers exhibit a pronounced tendency to vigorously downplay this dimension. The implication seems to be that as far as authors of YA fiction are concerned, it's okay to talk about homosexuality as long as what you are "really talking about" is something else.

The Power to Shape Gay Characters

YA novels that address homosexuality are embedded in a complex network of power relations, including, among other agents of power, authors, readers, editors, reviewers, and library acquisition staffs. A clearer conception of the nature of this network of power relations can perhaps be achieved by focusing on a very specific manifestation of power—namely, the power to shape fictional characters. Who/what possesses this power?

The first and most obvious answer to this question is that the author, of course, is the agent of power responsible for the shaping of a character. Undoubtedly, the author figures largely in this process; however, the nature of the power relations in which these texts are embedded is such that the author is at once in and out of control. As soon as an author decides that he/she will address a particular audience of actual readers, for example, he/she is no longer the sole shaper of characters. From this point on, the characters' shape is determined not only by the author's desires, but also by the exigencies associated with addressing a particular audience of readers.

In the case of the YA texts under consideration, the target audience consists primarily of adolescents. Adolescents are not exactly children, nor are they exactly adults. Rather, they are exactly neither and both of these things. The child-adult ambiguity associated with adolescent audiences constrains the author's free shaping of characters, resulting in symptomatic ambiguities related to the presence-absence of homosexual characters and experiences in these texts. To the extent that the adolescent readers are adults, it is permissible to treat homosexuality frankly; to the extent that the adolescent readers are children, it is necessary to treat homosexuality with probity. The adolescent audience slips into the crack between childhood and adulthood, and, as a result, the author's depiction of homosexual characters takes on a corresponding duality of presence and absence. The homosexual character, both present in and absenced from the novel, functions as a sort of ghost in the machine, a gay poltergeist whose role is central to the novel but whose actions are more often than not marginalized and ghettoized, occurring off-stage and out of sight.

In addition to authors and audiences, the genre in which the author chooses to write also possesses the power to shape characters. Characters in a tragedy, for example, are in some measure predetermined by their appearance within a tragic text. Similarly, homosexual characters appearing in the problem-realism genre are in some measure predetermined by the very nature of the genre in which they operate.

One of the generic factors of problem-realism that influences the depiction of homosexual characters centers on space constraints. "These texts," note Nilsen and Donelson, "tend to be condensed. With less space in which to develop characters, authors are forced to develop characters as efficiently as possible. One way to be efficient is to use stereotypes."[23] While the potential for stereotyping gays is not unique to YA texts, the space constraints operating in this genre make these texts particularly vulnerable to stereotyping.

The temptation to stereotype homosexual characters in problem-realism novels stems not only from limitations on the length of the novel due to the attention span of the readers but perhaps more importantly from the very nature of "realism" itself. In *Languages of Art*, Nelson Goodman writes: "Just here, I think, lies the touchstone of realism: not in quantity of information but in how easily it issues. And this depends upon how stereotyped the mode of representation is, upon how commonplace the labels and their uses have become."[24] What Goodman suggests is that we perceive texts whose way of seeing the world diverges the least from our own as most realistic. If, indeed, this is the case, then it would appear that novelists who desire to work within the problem-realism genre and who hope to correct stereotypes are working at cross purposes.

It is, I believe, no coincidence that the YA novel I find most worthy of praise—Aidan Chambers's *Dance on My Grave*—also departs most significantly from the norms of problem-realism. Novels adhering to the problem-realism formula are rooted in the assumption that if a topic is earnestly and realistically explored, then the reader will necessarily achieve a more complete understanding of it. *Dance on My Grave,* however, makes this very assumption the topic it explores. At one point in the novel, the self-identified gay narrator notes:

I was going to write pages more about those seven weeks. I wanted you to understand what we were like together. What Barry was like. Like to me: how I saw him, knew him, thought of him.

But this morning I got up and read everything I have written so far, and particularly what I wrote yesterday (all the Bits in Part Three up to this one) and I knew straightaway: it can't be done. The words are not right. They just are not right. They won't say what I want them to say. They tell lies. They hide the truth. I read the words and I can feel—feel—what they should be saying and they aren't. . . . What is written doesn't ever tell enough.[25]

Desire, the narrator argues, not only precedes but also exceeds language. The recognition in *Dance on My Grave* of this relationship between language and desire represents a marked departure from the implicit assumption of the other YA novels considered in this study. The other novels assume language's ability to adequately explain a desire that they (at least implicitly) define as a problem, and, more often than not, this desire is not so much explained as explained away. *Dance on My Grave,* however, alters the equation in such a way that the problem is not the desire itself but the inability of language to adequately capture and communicate that desire. In so altering the equation, the desire—or at least its inexplicability—is paradoxically explained.

The power to shape characters—one of the fundamental manifestations of power in a fictional text—does not issue from a single source, but from a variety of sources. Because YA texts dealing with homosexuality are embedded in a complex network of power relations, no single agent of power is exclusively responsible for the deployment of strategies of presence/absence, containment, endings, or transcendence. Instead, these strategies should be interpreted as bearing the imprint of the entire field of power relations. The power giving rise to these strategies issues from multiple sources, and, accordingly, the strategies often acquire a polyvalent force. The rhetoric of transcendence, for example, functions at one and the same time as a slap in the face (who wants to be transcended? who wants to be marginalized?) and a helping hand (in many instances, it is only by virtue of the reviewers' downplaying the "controversial" subject of homosexuality that the books make their way past conservative library acquisition staffs).

In closing, we need to remind ourselves constantly that complacency in the face of oppression is not a neutral attitude. There is no happy, complacent medium: failure to actively resist oppression—whether that oppression appears in the courtroom, the classroom, the workplace, or the library—amounts to the active perpetuation of that oppression. As Barbara Gittings has noted, "The literature on homosexuality is so crucial in shaping the images we and others have of ourselves, that distorted images must not be allowed to continue."[26]

Notes

1. Barbara Gittings, "Combatting the Lies in the Library," in *The Gay Academic,* ed. Louie Crew (Palm Springs, Cal.: ETC Publications, 1978), 107.
2. Mark Lilly, "Introduction: Straight Talk," in *Lesbian and Gay Writing: An Anthology of Critical Essays,* ed. Mark Lilly (Philadelphia: Temple University Press, 1990), 1.
3. Rose Robertson, "Young Gays," in *The Theory and Practice of Homosexuality,* ed. John Hart and Diane Richardson (Boston: Routledge and Kegan Paul, 1981), 170.
4. Ann Heron, ed., *One Teenager in Ten* (New York: Warner Books, 1986).
5. The decision to focus exclusively on male homosexuality results neither from a belief that the representation of lesbianism in YA fiction is less important than the representation of male homosexuality, nor from a belief that the representation of lesbianism in YA fiction is less political than the representation of male homosexuality, nor from an absence of YA novels depicting lesbianism. At least eight YA novels address lesbianism: Nancy Gordon, *Nancy on My Mind* (New York: Farrar, Straus, & Giroux, 1982); Deborah Hantzig, *Hey, Dollface* (New York: William Morrow, 1978); Elizabeth Levy, *Come Out Smiling* (New York: Delacorte Press, 1981); Nicholasa Mohr, *In Nueva York* (New York: Dial, 1977); Judith St. George, *Call Me Margo* (New York: G. P. Putman, 1981); Gertrude Samuels, *Run Shelley, Run* (New York: Thomas W. Crowell, 1974); Sandra Scoppettone, *Happy Endings Are All Alike* (New York: Harper and Row, 1978); and Stephanie Tolen, *The Last of Eden* (New York: Frederick Wave, 1980). The decision to focus exclusively on male homosexuality emerges from my assumption that differences exist between gay male and lesbian populations and that societal perceptions of, attitudes toward, and responses to the two populations differ. In short, the politics of male homosexuality and the politics of lesbianism represent two related but distinct objects of investigation.
6. Obviously, the way one defines "homosexuality" in large measure determines which novels will be deemed representations of it. In deciding which novels to consider, I followed the lead of *The Bookfinder,* a multivolume bibliography of young adult literature that includes the subject heading "male homosexuality."

I followed the lead of this reference guide not because the depictions of homosexuality in the novels it cites conform to my experience as a homosexual or my definition of "homosexuality," but because the very designation of certain novels as "about" male homosexuality is itself a part of the politics I wish to explore.

7. Aileen Pace Nilsen and Kenneth L. Donelson, *Literature for Today's Young Adult* (Glenview, Ill.: Scott, Foresman, 1985), 81–84; Sheila Egoff, *Thursday's Child* (Chicago: American Library Association, 1981), 66–77.

8. Martha Bacon, "Tantrums and Unicorns," *Atlantic Monthly* 224 (December 1969): 150.

9. Review of *I'll Get There, It Better Be Worth the Trip*, by John Donovan, *Commonweal*, May 23, 1969: 300.

10. Those still in print include Gary Barger, *What Happened to Mr. Forster* (New York: Clarion, 1981); Aidan Chambers, *Dance on My Grave* (New York: Harper and Row, 1982); John Donovan, *I'll Get There, It Better Be Worth the Trip* (New York: Harper and Row, 1969); B. A. Ecker, *Independence Day* (New York: Avon, 1983); Isabelle Holland, *The Man without a Face* (New York: J. B. Lippincott, 1972); M. E. Kerr, *Night Kites* (New York: Harper and Row, 1986); Frank Mosca, *All-American Boys* (New York: Alyson, 1983); and Sandra Scoppettone, *Trying Hard to Hear You* (New York: Harper and Row, 1974). Those no longer in print include Corrine Gerson, *Passing Through* (New York: Dial, 1978); Lynn Hall, *Sticks and Stones* (Chicago: Follett, 1972); Emily Hanlon, *The Wing and the Flame* (New York: Bradbury, 1980); Carolyn Meyers, *The Center: From a Troubled Past to a New Life* (New York: Atheneum, 1979); Eleanor Rachel Spence, *A Candle for St. Anthony* (New York: Oxford University Press, 1979).

11. Bob Dixon, *Catching Them Young* (New York: Pluto Press, 1978), xv.

12. Barbara Wersba, "Sexuality in Books for Children," in *Issues in Children's Book Selection*, ed. Lillian Gerhardt (New York: R. R. Bowker, 1973), 171.

13. Anne Scott McLeod, *A Moral Tale* (Hamden, Conn.: Archon Books, 1975), 10.

14. Roland Barthes, *Mythologies*, trans. Annette Lavers (New York: Hill and Wang, 1986), 138.

15. Donovan, 124–25.

16. Holland, 148–49.

17. Scoppettone, 180.

18. Holland, 149.

19. Lynn Hall, quoted in Frances Hankel and John Cunningham, "Can Young Gays Find Happiness in YA Books?" in *Young Adult Literature*, ed. Millicent Lenz and Ramona M. Mahood (Chicago: American Library Association, 1980), 211.

20. Review of *I'll Get There, It Better Be Worth the Trip*, by John Donovan, *Publisher's Weekly*, March 17, 1969: 51.

21. Judy Blume, review of *Sticks and Stones*, by Lynn Hall, *New York Times Book Review*, May 28, 1972: 8.

22. Review of *The Center: From a Troubled Past to a New Life,* by Carolyn Meyers, *Kirkus Review,* September 15, 1979: 1072.
23. Nilsen and Donelson, 85.
24. Nelson Goodman, *Languages of Art* (Indianapolis: Hacket, 1976), 38.
25. Chambers, 163–64.
26. Gittings, 108.

10. Self as Other: The Politics of Identity in the Works of Edmund White

Nicholas F. Radel

Though Edmund White's work does not always make explicit the political dimensions of gay identity, his novels *Nocturnes for the King of Naples* (1980a), *A Boy's Own Story* (1982), and *The Beautiful Room Is Empty* (1988) all contain gay characters who fail to achieve a coherent sense of self, and the failure can be attributed to the politics of sexual and gender difference. Gay identity is the explicit subject of many of White's works, and White cannot escape the problematics of gay identity in a culture that openly and tacitly assents to the naturalness of heterosexuality. Nor can he avoid the necessary revelation of his subject as bound to the discourses of power and control that Michel Foucault (1978) argues accompany the attempt to define sex and sexuality in the West at present. The sexual difference that several of White's novels celebrate—the author's interest in the gay man as a distinct type of individual, separate from the mainstream—signals a potentially or, as the French feminist Monique Wittig would say, necessarily political relationship, for Wittig insists on the essentially political nature of difference itself: "The fundamental difference, any fundamental difference (including sexual difference) between categories of individuals, any difference constituting concepts of opposition, is a difference belonging to a political, economic, ideological order" (1979, 115).

White's novels demonstrate the conflicting cultural impulses and ideological imperatives that undermine gay identity and, ultimately, gay community. They reveal the ways socially and culturally imposed restraints on gay freedoms necessarily deny gay subjectivity and isolate in gay men an idea of a homosexual self as Other that they themselves conceive as being separate from their apparently essential selves. And because this unique division of self from self contributes to or even creates gay men's roles as marginal outsiders, we cannot conceive it as a politically neutral fact of personality or individual psychology. In fact, we might view White's novels as part of the historical apparatus for revealing a gay subject as it responds to political pressure from the culture at large. Far from being mere aesthetic products, these novels about gay life both confirm and interrogate their historical milieu and its construction of sexual orientation as gender difference.

As Foucault and others have suggested, the gay man and lesbian have been given distinct identities only within the last two hundred years by a culture eager to proscribe and encapsulate their potential subversive power. Foucault suggests that the notion of homosexual identity did not take shape before the eighteenth and nineteenth centuries. Until that time, homosexual behavior existed, but there was no such thing, he says, as a homosexual person. Homosexuality came to exist only when the "homosexual became a personage, a past, a case history, and a childhood, in addition to being a type of life . . . a certain quality of sexual sensibility, a certain way of inverting the masculine and feminine in oneself." "The sodomite," he writes, "had been a temporary aberration; the homosexual was now a species" (1978, 43).[1] The emergence of such a particular subspecies engendered new possibilities for social control of gay behavior, and Foucault insists that the discourse of sexuality, the discourse that defines the homosexual as a separate species, is a discourse of power.

   The history of response to homosexuality provides a degree of empirical validity to Foucault's philosophic statement, for it confirms the sense in which specific behaviors have been defined by cultural institutions in ways that victimize and render powerless those who practice the behaviors. Any number of commentators on the history of homosexuality have testified to the early and continuing association of homosexual behavior with foreign influence; they have also noted the conflation of sodomy with witchcraft and heresy in the early church, which insured that homosexual acts would be seen as sinful and unorthodox. As is commonly known, the English word "buggery"—for a long time the preferred popular term that referred to a homosexual act—derives from the French *bougre*. This word, a corruption of the Latin *bulgaris,* refers not to homosexuals but to the heretical sect of Bogomiles in Bulgaria (Karlen 1980, 88). Though the persecutions of the early church were no less painful or destructive than later ones, Arno Karlen argues that the view of the church might, notwithstanding, be seen best as evidence of an encompassing sexual restrictiveness. Homosexuality was one sin among many, and it was not condemned primarily because it was conceived of as unusually abnormal or unnatural (Karlen 1980, 85; see Szasz 1970, 163–64).

But the construction of the homosexual as a unique personality and as a member of a particular subculture effectively brought him, his community, and his behavior into dialectical relationship with the larger community, confirming his distinction from and his inability to achieve synthesis with that community. The conversion that Foucault describes is part and parcel of what the psychoanalyst Thomas Szasz sees as the "ideological conversion from theology to science" that occurs during the eighteenth and nineteenth centuries (Szasz 1970, 160). As the ordering structures of theology lose their potency and the homosexual is described and defined by the scientific community, control is not lessened, only constituted anew. When the homosexual is invested with a personality, that personality can be seen as diseased and in need of correction. As Szasz points out, the result is that physicians confuse disease as a biological condition with disease as a social role, thereby establishing "themselves as agents of social control" (167). The coercive force of science, then, deprives the homosexual of his ability to change, to alter his behavior, or even to accept responsibility for freely choosing his sin. The physician ensures that the homosexual is a diseased victim, and the metaphor of illness clarifies his need for help and his dependence on others for that help. By defining the homosexual as ill, society can see itself as healthy; and in direct proportion to the gay community's assertion of itself as a self-serving entity, society can view itself as ill and take all necessary steps to regain its health.

From a Marxist point of view, sociologist Dennis Altman describes even the emergence of a self-defining gay community in the 1960s and 1970s as part of a larger pattern of social control. The development of this community, Altman believes, ensures that homosexuals can be co-opted as consumer forces in a capitalist society ("State"). More to the point, the development of this community, which seems posited on the idea of a distinct homosexual identity and culture, precludes the possibility of seeing homosexual behavior as a natural dimension of all human sexuality (Altman 1982, 184).

But even as it is important to see that, historically, the fabrication of the homosexual in the modern period has been an act of coercive power on every front, it is necessary to understand—if only partially—some of the ways that power has been culturally embodied. Though fundamentally at odds with Foucault's thought and method, Sartre's theory of the Other has nevertheless provided an explicit foundation for some feminist discussion of identity as a political issue, and this discussion clearly pertains to contemporary gay experience. Because it provides a way to see the politics of individual identity and the psychological configuration of gender difference rather than only the politics of history and culture, existentialist thought can clarify the ideological maneuvering that has gone into the creation of the individual gay man and help reveal the extent to which White's evocation of the homosexual self as Other occurs within a particular cultural context.[2]

Existentialism has, of course, been closely associated with the modern gay movement ever since Sartre's celebrated canonization of Genet, and Simone de Beauvoir's existentialist feminism has provided one of the formative statements of the modern feminist movement.[3] In adapting Sartre's formulation of the Other as the object that the authentic or authenticating self must be conscious of to exist, de Beauvoir argued that in a patriarchal society woman is cast in the role of object that is different from or the negative of man as positive norm: she is "defined and differentiated with reference to man and not he with reference to her; she is the incidental, the inessential as opposed to the essential. He is the Subject, he is the Absolute—she is the Other" (1964, xvi).

Both Sartre's and de Beauvoir's work insist on the need for the Subject self to seek transcendent freedom by triumphing over other Subject selves' attempts to objectify it. It is not surprising, then, that the concept of woman as Other has become part of the ideology of feminist liberation. But we need be especially concerned with those feminist theories that build upon de Beauvoir's remarks about women's collusion with men in allowing themselves to be defined as Other. These suggest that difference—as a sexual and political reality—cannot be (or has not so far been) constituted as an act of independence. For various reasons, de Beauvoir suggests, women have been unable until quite recently to identify themselves as Subjects or they have been seduced by the advantages of remaining protected objects. Meredith Tax describes this collusion as being necessitated by the recognition of power. For her, women have "to be tuned in to the nuances of social behavior so that they can please those whom it is essential to please" (quoted in Donovan 1985, 136). One result is a type of schizophrenia in which women divorce their minds from their objectified bodies; that is, they attempt to maintain a sense of self by reserving an essential core identity separate from the part of the self that men perceive as Other.

Mary Daly defines this process as spooking, frightening women into accepting limited, male-identified versions of themselves that keep them in thrall to the power men exercise (1978, 317–18). As does Tax, Daly implies that a divided self results in which one part is male and one part is victimized woman. Ultimately, woman is transformed into an outsider without the power to embrace that role for her own purposes. Any success or esteem she achieves can be enjoyed only through woman's identifying herself as a man. Paradoxically, then, women remain outsiders in a relative sense, for they remain part of the patriarchal ideological system in which the self—any self—can be conceived only in opposition to other selves. Even to break the bond through deliberate political dissent or unique biological awareness is to identify oneself in relation to the dominant absolute subjects that men represent.

These brief remarks on philosophy and history clarify an explicit politics of exclusion that guides the establishment of identity in groups outside the mainstream, and they reveal the ways in which the coercive power to define someone as Other necessarily precludes the Other's ability to define himself or herself. They also serve as prologue to several questions about White's work. First, as explorations of gay people's lives, what do these novels reveal about the political dimensions of gay identity? Second, to what extent can White's novels be defined as political documents in the search for gay identity? And finally, how do these novels contribute to— and not merely reflect—an awareness of gay men's status in American culture? Though I cannot answer all these questions fully, I hope at least to make a few introductory remarks.

Rather than explore White's work chronologically, it will perhaps be best to look first at the two later novels, *A Boy's Own Story* (1982) and *The Beautiful Room Is Empty* (1988). These works depend to a greater degree than does *Nocturnes for the King of Naples* (1980a) on traditional conventions of the novel, and their explicit theme is the growth and maturation of a young gay man. These novels were also written after White's nonfiction travelogue *States of Desire* (1980b), a highly subjective account of White's travels in gay America in the 1970s. Though in the epilogue White confesses to the limitations of his work (which largely excludes lesbians, black men, and rural and working-class gays), he also says that writing the book "radicalized" him. "In analyzing the behavior of individuals or groups," he writes, "I'm inclined to seek sociological rather than psychological causes. Of those causes, economic ones seem to me the most powerful, though they seldom come unclothed by ideology" (1980b, 335). White here admits to a newly politicized understanding of behavior, and we can clearly see his more radical vision at play in the later novels.

Perhaps more acutely than any other contemporary novel about gay male experience, *A Boy's Own Story* explores the social and cultural pressures that shape and misshape its nameless narrator hero. Behind its ironic title lies the wholesome world of the Victorian periodical *Boy's Own Magazine,*[4] and White seems concerned in this work to expose the distance between two worlds of boyhood expressed in these titles. The novel details the teenage years of a boy as he discovers and explores his gayness. In large part, the novel reveals the narrator's attempts to understand what it means to be a homosexual and his misguided attempts to change his orientation. To examine the problem of the narrator's identity, however, we might move immediately to the end of the novel.

In the final moments of the work, the narrator tries to justify his part in the betrayal of his teacher, Mr. Beattie. Beattie, a jazz musician, has come to teach at the all-male prep school that the narrator attends in an effort to avert his homosexuality through increased contact with masculine figures. The narrator, who has become friendly with Beattie through his badly behaved friend Chuck, decides to report the teacher for receiving a shipment of marijuana. He is alert to and bemused by the irony that he, of all people, should take it upon himself to defend public morality and the integrity of the school, and his self-awareness alerts us to a certain defensiveness. What he does not make explicit, however, is the probability that his animosity toward the teacher conceals desire for him. His plan for betraying Beattie is first to have sex with him and then to turn him in. His ostensible reason is, as he says, that Beattie "wouldn't be able to discredit me by saying I was a practicing homosexual since we would have practiced homosexuality together. He'd be powerless" (1982, 213).

The narrator's action brings into focus two conflicting desires, the desire for sexual fulfillment and the desire not to be a homosexual: "Sometimes I think I seduced and betrayed Mr. Beattie because neither one action nor the other alone but the complete cycle allowed me to have sex with a man and then to disown him and it; this sequence was the ideal formulation of my impossible desire to love a man but not be a homosexual" (218). In a clearly despicable action, White's narrator enacts the central tension of the entire book, for the young man has been encouraged from the beginning to identify his homosexuality as an alien desire and to find a real self in the world his father represents, the world of sexual privilege and power. The narrator, like all men, constitutes the homosexual as Other in his effort to legitimize the structures of privilege that empower him, and trouble results because the homosexual Other is himself.

White's novel makes clear the self-division that attends the cultural fabrication of the homosexual as an alien Other; it makes clear that the figure conceived of as the homosexual is unnatural and that even gay men conceive it as being so. Several times before his betrayal of Beattie, the narrator articulates a distinction between loving men and being a homosexual that makes perspicuous his confused attempts to reconcile a cultural norm with his own awareness of self. But the distinction and its importance become even more evident when we compare the sordid sexuality of the narrator's encounter with Beattie to the earliest evocation of gay sexuality in the novel. In the opening chapter, the narrator conceives a passion for and has sex with Kevin, the son of a friend of the family. The action is richly erotic—or as erotic as adolescent sex can be—and seemingly healthy and natural to the narrator, even though he knows his friend is not gay. Kevin's heterosexuality creates a profound irony, however, since his homoerotic actions do not label and define him as homosexual, and that fact alone empowers him. This distinction is not incidental, for it validates Foucault's understanding of sexual identity as an agency of power.

As the narrator's relationship with Kevin develops, the ironies inherent in it become increasingly clear. The narrator fears revealing himself, and when the revelation does come, it is not his sexual activity that reveals him but some mysterious action known only to Kevin and his younger brother Peter. Somehow, these two fully heterosexual boys find him out, and the narrator knows they have because they make fun of him and mock him. And the effect, as theorists of the Other have recognized, is to render the victim powerless and to label him unnatural. The narrator tells us that "each night Kevin [still] came to my bed, though now I no longer elaborated daydreams of running away with him. I was a little bit afraid of him; now that he knew I was a sissy, he could make fun of me whenever he chose to" (32). The narrator learns that to be a sissy, a homosexual, is to have no power in his society. It is the first (and not the last) time in this novel and its sequel that White dramatizes the objectifying gaze of the heterosexual man as he looks at his homosexual counterpart. But the power of the objectifying gaze lies not simply in its condemnation of alternate behavior, for, as we have seen, the behavior is shared. Its power derives, rather, from the heterosexual man's power to define the desire of another as not like his own, as abnormal.

To the extent that the nameless narrator is denied power and excluded from so-called normal society, *A Boy's Own Story* makes clear that he cannot take advantage of the entitlements of heterosexual male privilege. Legitimate society in the novel is exclusive, founded on power and manipulation. The point is made over and over, at first by Kevin's treatment of the narrator and then by each portrait drawn of a heterosexual male. Every incident in the novel, every attempt by the narrator to indulge or to disguise his homosexuality, suggests a ploy for affection, sympathy, or entitlement that must necessarily involve concealing truth and suppressing the homosexual Other within:

It was men, not women, who struck me as foreign and desirable and I disguised myself as a child or a man or whatever was necessary in order to enter their hushed, hieratic company, my disguise so perfect I never stopped to question my identity. Nor did I want to study the face beneath my mask, lest it turn out to have the pursed lips, dead pallor and shaped eyebrows by which one can always recognize the Homosexual. (169–70)

For the young narrator, the homosexual is an alien Other that must be suppressed if he is to become one with the men he so ardently desires.

Rather than merely revealing the difficulties of coming out in a heterosexist society, then, *A Boy's Own Story* reveals a world of power relationships—and hence of politics—that define and limit homosexual desire. The peculiar dialectics of heterosexual male power are clearly pointed to in the portrait of the narrator's father, who is described as a man who "so often ascribed cunning to other men . . . that he approached them as enemies to whom he must extend an ambiguous hand, one that when not offering a cold greeting could contract into a fist" (172). The novel reveals that these power relationships are translated into ideological and cultural imperatives that define the narrator against his will and contrary to his own experience of himself. The narrator himself seems to imply as much when he says that his father did not like his "nature," that is, "the fact that I was drawn to art rather than business, to people rather than things, to men rather than to women, to my mother rather than to him, books rather than sports, sentiments not responsibilities, love not money" (172). In short, the novel reveals the persistent objectification of the narrator that becomes a means of cultural control.

None of these considerations, however, obscures the sense revealed in the novel that the strongest power of oppression lies within the victim himself. *A Boy's Own Story* makes acute the uncomfortable feeling that its gay narrator most effectively victimizes himself because he has embraced the privileged power to objectify. As I have implied, the narrator's interest in Beattie, an apparent heterosexual, is not simple sexual interest. Like his father, the narrator is partially interested in power. Betraying Beattie allows him to act out a sexual fantasy first made sensible for him when he reads the poetry of Rimbaud and Verlaine: it is the fantasy of being the "harsh young lord" rather than the "obliging youth" (152). He apparently acquires this fantasy from his father, for he connects it with his father's sexual exploitation of a female employee.

Little in the novel, then, implies that even if the narrator has learned to be critical of the culture of his father, the culture that condemns him, he will be able to resist its fundamental modes of control and self-identification through the objectification of others. If his acquisition of power can be said, on one level, to allow the narrator to exercise a certain rage against the heterosexual Beattie's power to discredit him, it nevertheless on a more profound level, allows him to betray himself, to repudiate his own homosexuality. The power to manipulate and to exploit others—a power the narrator learns from and associates with his father—ultimately gives him the power to deny the homosexual Other that society has created and that he has internalized. Unfortunately, the narrator objectifies and displaces his homosexual yearnings onto Beattie, who thus becomes his unintended victim.

This is not to condemn the narrator, for he is too young to know to resist the forces that entrap him and Beattie; and the sense of the narrator's victimization is central to the ending of *A Boy's Own Story*. White carefully avoids closing his novel tidily or giving the impression that it is progressing to a climax in which the narrator learns something about himself that allows him to change or grow. Instead, the work ends indeterminately with the narrator's simple and stunning recognition of the forces that lead him to betray Beattie. White's failure to suggest the possibility of growth underlines the perception that the narrator's actions are determined in the conflict of cultural forces that surround him. It further underscores the sense that these actions preclude genuine growth or self-determination. The final words of the novel become richly ironic: "I who had so little power—whose triumphs had all been the minor victories of children and women, that is, merely verbal victories of irony and attitude—I had at last drunk deep from the adult fountain of sex. I wiped my mouth with the back of an adult hand, smiled and walked up to the dining hall humming a little tune" (218). This vision of adulthood and adult sexuality is terrifying. In the narrator's smug disregard for women and children, we detect an irony that reveals an equally smug disregard for the homosexual lurking inside that the narrator believes he has banished in favor of adult power. The narrator has not, of course, banished the homosexual; he has simply ensured that the figure will not become subversive or disruptive.

The Beautiful Room Is Empty, White's sequel to *A Boy's Own Story,* takes its title from one of Kafka's letters alluding to the unfortunate inability of two people (or perhaps two psyches) to inhabit a single space. The title of the novel, then, provides a clue that White will pursue the theme of the division of self from Other that informs the earlier work. *The Beautiful Room* follows White's narrator into his years at college and on beyond into the 1960s. Though the narrator remains nameless, one of his lovers calls him Bunny, and this affectionate nickname seems to imply a potential for identity never quite realized. Unlike the earlier novel, which emphasized the ideological imperatives that directed the narrator's private experience, this work explores the way society explicitly marginalizes the homosexual by manipulating metaphors of disease and crime. Here White portrays him as outsider: *The Beautiful Room* suggests that to be gay is necessarily to remain outside the boundaries of respectable society. It is clear, though, that the narrator's exile is forced, and the identity he establishes as an outsider is not his own but one imposed on him. The crime of being homosexual revealed in this work does not evoke the criminality Genet embraced as a subversive gesture (though it sometimes is that and is attractive to the narrator because it is); rather, the so-called crime proves to be no more than a normative definition of homosexuality that ostracizes gay men and divides them from themselves.

The fundamental tension of *The Beautiful Room* arises out of the narrator's inability to reconcile two conflicting parts of his personality: the sensitive, intelligent scholar-writer and the homosexual self he believes to be diseased. Although the narrator revels in his homosexuality in so far as it promises freedom from "the world of mild suburban couples, [with] his and her necks equally thick and creased, their white hair similarly cropped" (1988, 149), he nevertheless despises homosexuals and internalizes society's view of them as ill: "Homosexuality did not constitute a society, just a malady, although unlike other maladies it was a shameful one—a venereal disease" (149).

The evocation of a world in which homosexuality is seen as a sickness, of course, sums up the dominant attitude toward it throughout America in the sixties, and the novel makes clear that whether such thinking is a matter of historical record or accident, it serves distinct political purposes. First, it keeps gay men from accepting their orientation; second, it undermines the formation of a gay community out of which subjective experience might be formulated. The former is made clear in White's portrait of Bunny's lover Sean, who cannot accept his emerging relationship as a healthy alternative to heterosexual marriage. Instead, he sees the relationship as clear evidence of a loathed condition: "Sean didn't want to be gay, and waking up beside me was too much evidence for him that he was becoming homosexual" (209).

The latter problem emerges from the first, for the fragmented nature of the gay psyche that results from external oppression necessarily leads to objectification of the self and other homosexuals. A significant part of the novel is devoted to the narrator's sexual experiences in public toilets, and though these experiences are sometimes given a romantic aura of self-imposed exile from respectable society, White's narrator nonetheless acquiesces in the view that such encounters are criminal and unhealthy and that his fascination with them is obsessive: "Even though I was terrified of being arrested, I couldn't stop going to the toilets" (151). His remarkable confession makes clear that even though his action sums up his ostracization from society (his criminal deviance), he cannot choose but to embrace the danger that his status as outsider confers on him.

This is not to say that the narrator merely oppresses himself and is not the victim of external forces, but rather, that he cannot challenge those forces. Dangerous public sex remains for the narrator the only outlet in a society that denies him legitimate sexual and social outlets, and the novel suggests that the social forces that drive Bunny to the toilets make of him a metaphoric object confirming their own validity. In other words, his encounters in the toilets symbolize his willingness to embrace his status as outsider, for in their secrecy, they undermine the possibility of self-defining community. Because they are compelled, they deny the possibility of choice essential to establishing a subjective self.

At the heart of the novel, then, lies the narrator's ironic inability to envision the homosexual as anything other than alien. He tells us that he can understand the idea of a gay bar or a cruisey toilet, but not a gay restaurant: "The suggestion that gay men, like Negroes, might want to enjoy one another's company astounded me" (164). And later, he says, "The appeal of gay life for me was that it provided so many *glancing* contacts with other men" (201). Bunny sees gay men, gay life, and his gay self as narrow and unworthy of sustained interest. Moreover, he defines gay experience as limited in comparison to what he sees as the scope of heterosexual life. As a writer, he informs us, he wants to chronicle "marriage, birth, parental love, conjugal intimacy, the spicy anguish of adultery," that is, what he calls "the great occasions" (148). Bunny does not see that in defining the great occasions in exclusively heterosexual terms, he limits his own action and experience, reducing it to a shallow narcissism that is self-reflexive but not self-defining. In this way, he creates himself as the Other.

The climax of *The Beautiful Room Is Empty,* so different from the climax of *A Boy's Own Story,* makes perspicuous the connection between sexual politics and gay identity that is implicit throughout both works. The novel ends with the riot at the Stonewall Pub in New York on June 27, 1969. The incident, symbolically important to the gay community as the historical moment when it first constituted itself in opposition to an oppressive society, suggests to Bunny the possibility of change: "I caught myself foolishly imagining that gays might someday constitute a community rather than a diagnosis" (226). At the end of the novel, a community is promised that may lead to the establishment of a solid social identity, one not divided and compromised by the larger community. Significantly, Bunny's insight contrasts an old notion of the homosexual as Other, as illness to be diagnosed, to a new vision of homosexual as Self, a fellow in a community. And yet, the ultimate effect of this insight is compromised, for the world at large fails to respond to the initial glimpse of gay men's self-definition. Heady with anticipation, the narrator rushes out "to buy the morning papers to see how the Stonewall Uprising had been described. 'It's really our Bastille Day,' Lou said. But we couldn't find a single mention in the press of the turning point of our lives" (228).

At this point, it may seem odd to return to *Nocturnes for the King of Naples,* especially since it resists the political analysis that White himself has suggested may be appropriate to his works only after *States of Desire.* But the novel, White's second, is his first to deal explicitly with homosexuality, and even though it takes shape in the psychology rather than the sociology of character, when read in light of *A Boy's Own Story* and *The Beautiful Room Is Empty,* it reveals dimensions of gay identity that necessarily limit and define the gay man, placing him on the margins of society. *Nocturnes* is a series of poetic prose pieces about a betrayed lover addressed only as "you." Its explicit theme is desire and regret. As in the later novels, White's narrator is nameless, and, as do those novels, this one explores the problem of identity. This time, however, White dramatizes not the search for identity but the loss of it. And whereas the later novels explore the social and cultural factors that lead the gay man to define his homosexual self as Other, this novel examines the individual psychology of one man who behaves in ways that guarantee his exclusion from society.

Seen in one way, the narrator of *Nocturnes* finds himself in a position similar to that of the narrator at the end of *A Boy's Own Story* or to that of Sean in *The Beautiful Room.* He rejects a lover and his action suggests a rejection of self. Early in the novel, the narrator explains his longing to leave his older lover:

Now, years later, how easy it is to interpret that urge as a loveless boy's fear of a perfect love that came too late, but back then it seemed (my longing to get away) almost metaphysical. In fact I said to you, as we stood on the dock, "Doesn't it ever strike you as strange to be a man rather than a woman, to be here rather than," pointing toward the crown of candles, "there, for instance? Sometimes I want to explode into a million bits, all conscious, and shoot through space and then, I don't know, rain down on everything or, well, yeah, actually catch up with the light rays that bounced off people thousands of years ago." (1980a, 14)

The narrator's words apparently suggest his fear that a perfect love will somehow define him too precisely. His perfect love, he fears, will make him local in place and time and define him as his lover's accessory. The tension that results from his fear provides the surface meaning of the novel, and we find the narrator repeatedly trying to justify his rejection of a man who has extraordinary power over him. He tells us that his lover's celebrity, social standing, and love force him into a kind of submission that he feels compelled to flee, for he must try to amount to something on his own (84).

Ironically, however, the novel implies that in rejecting the lover, the narrator denies himself the possibility of transcendent experience as a self-defining subject. It becomes increasingly clear throughout the novel that the "you" addressed by the narrator can be more than an individual recalled in memory. He, in fact, becomes a semimythic figure that embodies the narrator's past, present, and future experience. Linking this figure with his own father and with the other men he has desired, the narrator sums up this sense of the lover when he apostrophizes him: "You are the song I wanted to sing, the god I wanted to celebrate or conjure. Before I knew you I loved you, now you've gone I find you everywhere, and for me you are my past, present and future, unchanged, equivalent only to yourself" (63). Significantly, the narrator tells us, he fashions the rejected lover out of the wreckage of adult passions (48–49), and the effort then to create the lover can be seen as an effort to define a sense of self in the form of another, to embody the whole history of individual experience in the figure of the beloved.

This situation is not exactly like the one in *A Boy's Own Story*, but a comparison with that novel reveals a similar ambivalence about the gay narrator's attempt to establish an identity. *Nocturnes* reveals the psychological impasse that results because the narrator cannot create himself as a subject identity. Both in theme and form, the novel insists on his perpetual status as Other. The narrator of *Nocturnes*, in fact, talks about himself as losing shape, form, and substance as he ages. He calls himself a "ghost" (32). But, more important, he notes that he has given up all possessions and all conversation. Only memory remains, and that memory is always of one person, "you," who the narrator tells us is found "everywhere, in foreign children, in my own childhood memories, in the bodies of hundreds of men I've ransacked" (87). On one level, then, the novel portrays a very complex action, for it seeks out and constructs a figure (the lost lover) who embodies the whole self of the narrator as Other at the same time that it tells the story of the narrator's fleeing that self.

In a less abstract sense, the novel suggests that the narrator's tragic limitation resides in his being objectified as an image. But though he imagines it is his ex-lover's vision of him that objectifies him, he knows, on a more profound level, that it is his own fabrication of the ex-lover that does so. At the end of the novel, the narrator describes himself by alluding to "the humiliated dignity of a Civil War soldier" who has been fixed in a photograph and who seems to cry out for pity (146–47). He reacts to the soldier in a way that sums up the similarity of the soldier's and his own condition:

But I have no pity to offer, since, I, too, am dying, and someone saw fit to play the same prank on me, imprisoning me within an antiquated tot's body, lacing me into a straightjacket that holds my arms folded in resignation before the maddening vision of a man or god who has died, gone away or never existed save in the tense, opaque presences of those things and people who, by virtue of claiming attention but denying the understanding, of demanding love at the cost of rewarding sympathy, must be addressed as "You." (147)

The narrator reveals that he has become an object like the soldier in the photograph because he is always perceived by the man or god he invented. And, more important, he identifies this man or god as the embodiment of those people and things that demand love and attention but then fail to return sympathy or understanding. His isolation and inactivity proceed from his absolute objectification within the world he inhabits as well as from the habit he has apparently learned from that world of objectifying himself in the gaze of a nonexistent, godlike lover.

Interestingly, *Nocturnes* is not a traditional narrative that might give shape—through conventional expectations—to an emerging persona. The novel exists only as a series of fragments that apparently represent the memories of the narrator as they merge into his consciousness of the lost lover. In essence, we know him only as we know the lover he fabricates, and so he never achieves independent selfhood as a character. The point of view of the novel contributes to this effect because as it is addressed to "you," it is necessarily addressed to the reader. The strategy, perhaps, prevents us from empathizing with the narrator, and it assures that he has constructed our gaze so that we perceive him as in a photograph, separate from us, an object. In short, we can never be "I" along with him.

Nocturnes for the King of Naples, then, might be said to be about the political reality of gender difference in gay life, though it explores that reality through the personal experience of one man. It is no accident that the novel opens and closes by evoking the rituals of promiscuous cruising—those fragments of gay life that seem most alien to outsiders and most typical—for they seemingly sum up the politics of marginalization. The narrator sees that upon the loss of his ideal lover he has been locked into a reality in which he searches perpetually for an unattainable Other that might allow him to define himself: "I could easily pick out," he tells us, "those expressionless, intriguing beauties I address as *you*" (148). But these intriguing beauties always and only manifest themselves as gods, as is made clear in the narrator's evoking the metaphor of a house of worship to describe the empty warehouses and docks where gay men cruise: "A moment before the barge's beam invaded the cathedral we were isolated men at prayer . . . ignoring everything in [our] search for the god among us" (4–5). The narrator seeks love in an ideal guise distinct from reality, but the returned gaze of that ideal figure necessarily reduces and objectifies. His habit of identifying himself through others keeps the gay man in collusion with a larger society that has, in fact, made of him the thing he would make of himself, an alien outsider, haunting the fringes of society, searching for a self in an ideal vision that threatens to negate his reality. His greatest fear is that he might lose himself in a homosexual Other. In reality, he is the homosexual Other, deprived of natural response and objectified as a subject photographed.

All three of White's novels that are explicitly about homosexuals and homosexuality dramatize a powerful stasis at the heart of gay identity. White's characters internalize a sense of themselves as Other that leads them away from the centers of their selves, away from society, and away from knowledge of what they might be. They never achieve a sense of being in its Sartrian meaning, and thus the novels provide something of a gloss upon the self-actualizing ethic of existentialism and its relevance to contemporary gay politics. The homosexual Other in White's work denies the possibility of Sartre's Saint Genet, who embraces his criminal Other self in his intention to be; rather, he remains the child Genet, "convinced that he is, in his very depth, *Another than Self*" (Sartre 1963, 35). And it is difficult to say of his characters that they therefore fail as self-authenticating characters, for they have been coerced into unauthentic postures. As Marilyn Frye points out, Sartre ignores the possibility that a person can be coerced into doing or not doing something against his or her will (1983, 54–55). The novels make clear that cultural control of ideas about the homosexual directs the individual gay man's control of himself. By internalizing his homosexual self as Other—and by internalizing this self in the language of the Other—the gay man denies himself the possibility of genuine subversion of his culture, at least in the sense that he demand it recognize his sexuality as a component of all sexuality.

If White's novels contribute anything to our thinking about gay identity, it may be the recognition that it is impossible to subvert the present cultural framework from within the discourses that define it. Though there are moments in *A Boy's Own Story* and *The Beautiful Room* when an apparently self-authenticating authorial voice breaks into the narrative to reflect ironically upon the thoughts and deeds of the narrator, the voice remains nothing more than that of the adult explaining the child. And though the ending of *The Beautiful Room* holds forth an apparent promise of liberation, neither that promise nor reality itself has solved the problem of the gay man's enforced separation from the society that creates and nurtures him. In a sense, then, the novel written before White's political conversion, *Nocturnes*, provides a sobering commentary on the political optimism of the last works. Its ghostlike narrator reminds us that beneath the rhetoric of liberation through self-defining community lies the complex and perhaps intractable problems of gay identity in post-Stonewall America. Seen in this light, the novels become powerful documents in our understanding of the roles gay men in America have been forced to play. Despite the freedom celebrated in gay polemic, White's novels reveal a still rocky landscape of gender relations.

Notes

1. The still-contested idea that homosexuality as we understand it did not exist until the eighteenth and nineteenth centuries is confirmed by Bray (1982) and Halpern (1990), among others.
2. Foucault and other post-structuralist thinkers would deny the possibility of self-defining choice that lies at the heart of Sartre's thought. It is not my purpose here to try to reconcile opposing points of view. Rather, I would suggest that although we might conceive the history of the homosexual as the history of his fabrication as a Subject, the vocabulary of existentialist philosophy provides a useful measure of the terms of the discourse that subjects him. As I will make clear in the conclusion, though Sartre's theory helps clarify White's work, these novels—in the long run—interrogate Sartre.

3. Much of the following material has been synthesized from Donovan 1985, Chapter 5, "Feminism and Existentialism."
4. Alan Hollinghurst, in reviewing the book for TLS (1983), made this observation but identified the magazine as the Edwardian *Boy's Own Paper*. Hollinghurst is apparently in error. *Boy's Own Magazine* was published under several titles in the 1860s and 1870s, but it never had the title Hollinghurst suggests.

Works Cited

Altman, Dennis. 1978. "The State and the New Homosexual." In *Coming Out in the Seventies,* 97–115. New York: St. Martin's P^ass 1978.

———. 1982. *The Homosexualization of America: The Americanization of the Homosexual.* New York: St. Martin's Press.

Beauvoir, Simone de. 1964. *The Second Sex.* Translated by H. M. Parshley. New York: Alfred A. Knopf.

Bray, Alan. 1982. *Homosexuality in Renaissance England.* London: Gay Men's Press.

Daly, Mary. 1978. *Gyn/Ecology: The Metaethics of Radical Feminism.* Boston: Beacon Press.

Donovan, Josephine. 1985. *Feminist Theory: The Intellectual Traditions of American Feminism.* New York: Frederick Ungar.

Foucault, Michel. 1978. *The History of Sexuality. Volume I: An Introduction.* Translated by Robert Hurley. New York: Vintage Books.

Frye, Marilyn. 1983. "In and Out of Harm's Way." In *The Politics of Reality: Essays in Feminist Theory,* 52–83. Trumansburg, N.Y.: Crossing Press.

Halpern, David M. 1990. *One Hundred Years of Homosexuality and Other Essays on Greek Love.* New York and London: Routledge.

Hollinghurst, Alan. 1983. "A Prince of Self-Approval." *Times Literary Supplement,* 19 August: 875.

Karlen, Arno. 1980. "Homosexuality in History." In *Homosexual Behavior: A Modern Reappraisal,* edited by Judd Marmor, 75–99. New York: Basic Books.

Sartre, Jean Paul. 1963. *Saint Genet: Actor and Martyr.* New York: New American Library.

Szasz, Thomas. 1970. *The Manufacture of Madness.* New York: Harper and Row.

Tax, Meredith. 1970. "Woman and Her Mind: The Story of an Everyday Life." In *Notes from the Second Year.* Unpublished manuscript.

White, Edmund. 1980a. *Nocturnes for the King of Naples.* New York: Penguin Books.

———. 1980b. *States of Desire: Travels in Gay America.* New York: E. P. Dutton.

———. 1982. *A Boy's Own Story.* New York: New American Library.

———. 1988. *The Beautiful Room Is Empty.* New York: Alfred A. Knopf.

Wittig, Monique. 1979. "Paradigm." In *Homosexualities and French Literature: Cultural Contexts/Critical Texts,* edited by George Stambolian and Elaine Marks, 114–21. Ithaca, N.Y.: Cornell University Press.

11. Female Athlete = Lesbian: A Myth Constructed from Gendex Role Expectations and Lesbiphobia

Karen Peper

Reflections

Growing up I yearned to play Little League, but in the pre-Title IX world of the early 1960s there was no opportunity for girls like me. The closest I came to realizing my dream was as the bat girl for my older brother's team. I never understood why girls weren't allowed to play. Excuses that we girls were weak or easily hurt were no excuse when I *knew* I could outhit, outrun, and outthrow the majority of my male peers. Why was it okay for me to join a swimming team but not a baseball team? It didn't make sense to my ten-year-old mind.

Into this confusion and disappointment I recall hearing the adult whisperings—playing "rough" (read: "team") sports made girls "that way." Now at ten I had no idea what "that way" was, but I certainly got the drift that it was not a good way to be! Nonetheless, the obvious injustice of the situation overrode my concern with being declared "that way" and I decided to petition my hometown Parks and Recreation Department to offer Little League for girls.

The male superintendent accepted the sheets of signatures collected in my one-person door-to-door neighborhood campaign. He thanked me and sent me on my way. I never got past the front desk on a follow-up visit. I decided it was going to be an uphill battle to find a spot on any organized ballfield.

In junior and senior high school I encountered a similar absence and resistance to athletic programs for girls. Petitioning the "powers that were" became a familiar process. These efforts met with partial success when the high school administration acquiesced to demonstrated student interest and offered tennis and track.

Even with enforcement of Title IX on the horizon, school officials held off to the last possible moment before incorporating a full-fledged athletic program for girls into our district's extracurricular program. As fate would have it, my graduation came a year too early to benefit from the Title IX mandates.

To this day, I am angered at the denial of athletic opportunity. I do believe, however, that I better understand the hesitancy of parents, teachers, recreation administrators, and school officials to allow young girls full athletic expression. I understand today what was unclear and hurtful as a ten-year-old. I know what the euphemism "that way" meant for the adults of the 1960s and probably for some folks today. It meant somehow that if little girls were allowed to be strong and powerful and gain self-confidence via participation in athletics they would not be "feminine," and therefore, they would be the only possible socially constructed opposite—"masculine" and *then* (so the illogic goes) they would be queer, inverse: in a word, dykes. I am convinced it was this unspoken fear and myth about lesbians that kept me from having the opportunity to express myself to my fullest athletic capacity.

The "logic" underlying this socially (mis)constructed mythology that female athletes are lesbians *and* that lesbians are somehow "masculine" has intrigued me ever since. The issue is a complex one and involves several *mis*constructions; namely, what it means to be "female," to be "athletic," and, most of all, to be a "lesbian." The terms and their socially constructed meanings continue to collide and produce misunderstanding even in the land of increased athletic opportunity for women and girls.

The purpose of this chapter is to take a look at how traditional "gendex" role expectations and lesbiphobia combine to produce a societal mythology that female athletes are lesbians, and how this mythology, by extension into nonathletic areas, is intended to undermine *all* attempts by women for self-definition outside the constraints of a misogynist, lesbiphobic patriarchy. The first section will explore how role expectations in general are (1) socially constructed, (2) psychologically balanced, and (3) linguistically and nonlinguistically communicated. The second section will focus specifically on the role construction and communication of "female," "athlete," and "lesbian" and demonstrate how these three roles have been misconstructed in such a way as to provide a "logical" connection to one another. This section will also include a discussion as to how these misconstructions are maintained despite society's apparently enlightened view of women as athletic. The third and final section will discuss how rooting construction of the female athlete role in misogynist and lesbiphobic attitudes serves to maintain patriarchal control over *all* women regardless of their affectional *or* athletic "preference."

Creating Our "Reality"

Construction of the "Self"

How do we come to understand and communicate our "reality"? From a constructivist perspective, this question is answerable by recognizing that individuals are *active* agents who construct their environment and their roles in that environment through "individually and socially constituted symbolic structures."[1] George Herbert Mead suggested that it is the *interaction* of these constructed symbolic structures that permits an individual to define her/his "self" and, thus, the role being played.[2]

According to Mead, the "self" consists of two interdependent components labeled "I" and "me." The "I" is the actor that behaves. The "me" incorporates the concept of societal "other"—the social mores, definitions, values, attitudes, and behavioral aspects. Based on this embodiment of the "other," the "me" provides "I" with direction and maintains control. Therefore, the individual is both acting and observing her/his actions at the same time. This means that an individual's behavior is part of an interpretative process rather than merely a response to a stimulus. Consequently, this process frees the individual to construct the experiences of the "self" and, therefore, to determine the "role" that the individual wishes to play. However, an important limitation to this construction of "self" is that the "me" typically restricts its concept of "other" to the societal context in which the individual is interacting. This shortcoming often serves to effectively limit the number and type of "roles" an individual may choose to construct.

Maintaining a Psychological Balance

An important component of "self-definition" and thereby of its byproduct, role construction, is that the "I" and the "me" seek *and* maintain a psychological balance. Should the "I" desire to behave in a manner conflicting with the "me"'s report of the "other," the "self" will be thrown into a state of psychological imbalance. According to the congruity principle as outlined by Osgood and Tannenbaum, humans seek a psychologically consistent view of the world. When presented with potentially conflicting information, individuals attempt to construct and maintain their sense of congruity by either ignoring the new information or interpreting it in such a way as to give a sense of psychological balance. In dealing with incongruity, an individual must rely on her/his previous frames of reference and, as Osgood and Tannenbaum note, these "judgmental frames of reference tend toward maximal simplicity" with an ensuing pressure to polarize along the evaluative dimension.[3] Therefore, as humans faced with psychological imbalance, we tend to seek the path of least resistance in restoring the comforting illusion of balance.

Employing Symbolic Structure Systems

Linguistic Types. The social construction and psychological balancing of the "self" and of the subsequent "roles" relies on the individual's use of symbolic structure systems, including both linguistic and nonlinguistic types. Linguistic systems include language's use of narrative myth and metaphor to construct an interpretation of "reality." Nonlinguistic systems include the actions and behaviors of those persons already assumed to be playing the "role" that an individual is in the process of socially constructing for her/his self.

Before proceeding with a discussion of metaphorical constructs as a linguistic device, it is important to briefly discuss how the term "myth" is being used in this article. Shirley Park Lowry suggests that myths are stories "whose vivid symbols render concrete a special perception about people and their world. . . . That they often embody the essence of our experience accounts for their power. . . . [A myth] guides our personal lives, supports or challenges a specific social order, makes our physical world a manageable place, or helps us accept life's mysteries . . . with serenity."[4]

Alan M. Olson, in his book *Myth, Symbol, and Reality,* writes, "It is difficult to think of a myth that does not either include symbols or *sustain itself upon symbolic or hidden meanings and inferences in one form or another*" (emphasis added).[5]

Myths have the power to be so apparently "real" that "until something happens to make returning to them impossible in a familiar way, one gives almost no thought [to them]."[6] Additionally, the "reality" that myths allow us to take for granted may be a reality based on a "highly limited and restricted vision."[7]

Myth making is enhanced through the use of metaphor—a linguistic device especially suited for connecting divergent ideas and, thereby, a device potentially responsible for establishing a relationship between those ideas which may represent a "limited and restricted vision." Metaphor is a device used to order and understand our "reality."

According to Eleanor Rosch, humans categorize in terms of prototypes and family resemblances.[8] Therefore, if a role, action, or object seems to have some resemblance to a particular prototype, humans will tend to group the activities or items together. This leads to a perceived connection/relationship between the activities/items. It is from this starting point of categorization that we then begin to support our ideas, our connections, by constructing arguments. As we do this, "we need to show the connections between things that are obvious—that we take for granted—and other things that are not obvious. We do this by putting ideas together [i.e., structuring metaphors]. These ideas constitute the content of the argument. The things we take for granted are the *starting point of the argument*" (emphasis added).[9]

A single concept may have several different metaphorical structurings that are not consistent with one another and therefore provide different interpretations and "starting points" for a discussion. Lakoff and Johnson acknowledge this dilemma: "In general, complete consistency across metaphors is rare; coherence, on the other hand, is typical. . . . A metaphor works when it satisfies a purpose, namely, understanding an *aspect* of the concept" (emphasis added).[10] Therefore, a particular role, action, or item may be "understood" differently simply by altering the metaphorical structuring.

The power of metaphors to help us "understand our reality" is evident. Perhaps, however, the most important aspect of metaphors is their capability to direct or "clue" us as to how we should conceive a particular role because "we act according to the way we conceive of things."[11] One ramification of this "acting" results in role playing.

Nonlinguistic Types. Role playing is an example of a nonlinguistic symbolic structure system. Erving Goffman asserts that life is basically a series of routines (roles) performed by individuals using appropriate "fronts." According to Goffman, there are two types of "fronts"—a personal front that involves an individual's presentation of their "self," and a social front in which the role is designated by an institution or by social custom.[12]

Based on the individual's interpretation of these two fronts, an individual constructs a role that she/he (1) wishes to portray, (2) is "expected" to portray, or (3) *thinks* that she/he is expected to portray. By combining the two "fronts" an individual is able to socially construct a role that may personally feel psychologically balanced despite being in apparent conflict with the explicit expectations as outlined by the social front. Thus, an individual may express a role in such a way as to either confirm or deny the societal *expectations* for the designated role.

Creating and Maintaining Our Mythology

Construction of the Role

What does a discussion about social construction of roles, human desire for psychological balance, and our use of linguistic and nonlinguistic symbolic structure systems have to do with female athletes often being assumed to be lesbians? What allows us to conceptualize this myth and make it part of our reality?

The answers to these two questions are tied to our understanding of how we *structure* our reality. It seems apparent that one of the most basic structures inherent in our culture is division by sex. The statement "boys will be boys and girls will be girls" is much more powerful than meets the eye. While factors such as age, socioeconomic status, ethnicity, and ability are also of concern to those attempting to understand the suprastructure of our society, it is on the basis of division by sex that we focus much of our scholarly work.

The recent historical studies of Bonnie Anderson and Judith Zinsser confirm that "women traditionally have been viewed first as women, a separate category of being."[13] These researchers confirm that division by sex seems to override "differences between eras, between classes, and between nations"[14] when it comes to historically examining the human condition.

This "female-or-male" focus seems logical enough since biological attributes make it apparently "easy" to label an individual as either of the female sex or the male sex regardless of age, race, or economic status. An extension of this biologically determined division is one of socially constructed concepts which we label "femininity" and "masculinity." These concepts are the psychological extensions of the initial biological division and are commonly discussed as "gender." Taken together, the biological and psychological divisions give rise to what I have chosen to label as "gendex" roles. In creating the term "gendex," my purpose is to linguistically illustrate the interconnectedness of sex and gender role construction. Putting "gender" first reminds us that roles are based *more* on socialized gender *constructs* than on biological sex *determinants*.

As a fundamental social construction, gendex roles and the attendant role expectations play a crucial part in determining how *all* roles are constructed and how psychological balance is maintained. The influence of gendex can readily be seen in the way in which words such as "female," "male," "feminine," and "masculine" are defined and also in the presence of a word such as "feminism" and the absence of its logical counterpart, "masculinism." The fact that there is no word to describe a "masculinist" role implies that this role is the hidden referent to which all other roles will be compared. This assumption is clearly born out when one peruses the lexicon.

The noun "female" is defined in *The American Heritage Dictionary* as "a woman or girl as distinguished from a man or boy," while the definition of "male" as a noun fails to include a parallel reference, i.e., a man or boy as distinguished from a woman or girl. Another interesting distinction is made when the dictionary lists synonyms for "feminine" and none for "masculine." Among the comments under synonyms for "feminine" one finds the following statements: "These adjectives describe what is of or appropriate to women. Often, as the opposite of 'masculine,' it [feminine] refers to things considered characteristic of women." In comparing the definitions of parallel terms, "womanish" and "mannish," a value judgment is certainly evident. "Womanish" refers to "qualities distinctive to but less admirable in women or with an unfavorable implication to such qualities in men,"[15] while "mannish" simply states "affectation of masculine traits or style by women."[16]

Another listed synonym for "feminine" is "effeminate." This word "is largely restricted in reference to men or things and implies lack of manliness or strength."[17] There is no similarly derogatory synonym for "masculine" that refers to women or things and implies a lack of womanliness or weakness.

In this "reality" of socially constructed polar opposite gendex roles, the implication is that an individual is either "female/feminine" or "male/masculine." When a "female" is "masculine" or a "male" is "feminine," both are demonstrating behavior that produces a sense of "psychological imbalance" for individuals taught to ascribe to a rigid definition of gendex roles. Naturally, these individuals seek to balance their perception of incongruity both in how they understand others who may appear to operate "outside" of traditional gendex roles and in how they may understand their *own* behaviors that may fall outside those same gendex role expectations.

How might this psychological balance between gendex role expectations and actual behavior be reinstated? Well, enter from stage right "lesbiphobia" and the attendant misconstruction of what it means to be a "lesbian." The misperception commonly taught and consequently held to be "true" by much of society is that to be a lesbian means desiring to be male-like. This perception, though erroneous, does provide the "perfect" (il)logical "solution" to the apparent imbalance produced when a female steps out of her prescribed gendex role. Thus, when a woman's biological sex and psychological gender are not paired along traditional (read: polarized) lines, she "*must*" be a lesbian.

Confusion and the implied (read: learned) psychological imbalance occurs most clearly when an individual engages in an activity that has been linguistically and nonlinguistically associated with the "other" biological sex. Even if a particular individual does not "buy into" this confusion, her membership in a society where such conflict and implied imbalance is "supposed" to exist probably indicates she is at least *aware* that her behavior either adheres to the gendex rules or is in opposition to them. In spite of a woman's *choice* to "break the rules," it seems unlikely she'd have no awareness of so doing. Subsequently, her understanding of what it means to "break the rules" would influence in some manner her self concept, her activity, and her attitude toward her chosen actions. In the case of athletic activity, it has been males who have been most often equated as engaging in athletics. Nonlinguistically, the individuals most often perceived as playing the role of "athlete" have been of the male sex, and linguistically, the term "athlete" is defined utilizing components that more readily line up with a "masculine" gendex role. The dictionary states: "Athlete: A person possessing the natural aptitudes for physical exercises and sports, as strength, agility, and endurance."[18]

While today's female may not experience the blatant sexism and discounting of her athleticism as did her foremothers, the societal *suggestion* that she feel somewhat "out of balance" with her dual roles of "female" and "athlete" is still present, albeit in much more subtle, indirect ways. Today's "athlete" that is "female" is still perceived as demonstrating behavior that is inconsistent with her *prescribed* gendex role, thus creating at least the *perception* of a socially constructed imbalance. She is, in effect, being perceived by others and may even perceive herself as being a deviant from her "appropriate" role as it relates to the male/masculine gendex role. As is always the case, psychological balance is sought. An individual who feels imbalanced either due to her awareness of others' perception of the role or due to her perception of a role she now finds herself playing, may choose to ignore the myth, discount/rationalize the myth, or embrace the myth. Whatever the individual's way of seeking balance, society itself must also reconcile that, as defined, the terms "athlete" and "female" are rooted in distinctly different gendex roles; a societal compromise must be made in order to achieve a *societal* perception of psychological balance.

Maintenance of the Role

Legislation and public pressure to conform to a late twentieth century notion of enlightenment and humanitarianism prevent most *overt* attempts to linguistically maintain the psychological imbalance of a female who participates in athletics. In fact, giving the *appearance* of accepting female athleticism is an important tool to a patriarchal society actually interested in maintaining the status quo of gendex roles. While appearing to have acquiesced to public pressure to halt sexist behavior, action, or attitudes toward athletic participation, in reality, gendex role expectations are alive and well. Ironically, a co-opting of egalitarian ideals has actually been utilized to maintain the status quo. One example: news coverage of adolescent athletic activities. A look at most of today's hometown newspapers reveals a sports section that includes stories on "girls' track and field" as well as "boys' track and field." On the surface, this practice appears to be evidence of "progress" in regard to respect for female participation in sports. Certainly, this approach is preferable to no coverage at all or to the former practice of stories on "girls track and field" and "track and field"—the latter implying, of course, that there was a distinction between *real* track and field and that done by Others (read: females). Despite the apparent "progress," there is a continued distinction based on gendex that indirectly supports a concept that the term "athlete" should be viewed differently depending on the gendex of the participant. *Overt* sexism has indeed been addressed. Yet a more insidious pressure remains in society's continued control over definition and construction of the "female athlete" role. These controls are powerful because they often masquerade as liberal, responsible attitudes toward female athletic participation.

For example, one way society attempts to maintain gendex roles while appearing to overcome them is to deny that the "female" is an "athlete"— a *real* athlete, that is! This "solution" has been implemented in various forms, including use of "girls' rules" and "boys' rules," wherein the "real" game is the boys' game and the girls play a modified, "feminized" version. This tactic is evident in the half-court, six-person version of girls' basketball as opposed to the whole-court, five-person "regular" (read: male) game *and* in bent knee (read: female) push-ups versus "regular" (read: male) push-ups *and* in the golf tees that are closer to the pin for the women. While all of these tactics masquerade as being supportive of female participation in sport, the effect is to impose a sense that women are not quite capable of being "fully athletic" (and therefore, fully male-like). This underlying, patronizing attitude "allows" (?) men to "allow" women the retention of their "femininity." Thus, the gendex role is assumed to be intact and the appearance of balance maintained.

Another method of heading off potential gendex confusion has been to deny females access to athletics by not providing financial or emotional support for their participation. While it is harder to overtly ignore female athletics today, discouragement from participation can take the form of providing inconvenient and inadequate access to facilities and equipment as well as overlap of sports "seasons" so that the females must make a choice as to what sport they will participate in.

A third method of heading *assumed* imbalance off at the pass is to allow females unlimited athletic expression *until* puberty. At this point, the emotional support is withdrawn and parental and peer pressure is exerted

on the female to move from participation as an athlete to supportive spectator of male athletes.

A fourth method for the female determined to continue being athletic is
to encourage her to participate in individual sports such as tennis, gymnas-
tics, or ice skating and avoid team sports such as softball, field hockey, or
basketball. A 1979 study found that females engaging in team sports were
perceived as having more "masculine" attributes than those in individual
sports.[19] These results were replicated in Guthrie's 1982 study wherein
women in physical education were perceived as significantly more "masculine" and "homosexual" than women college students in general and women
athletes participating in team sports were generally perceived as more
"homosexual" than those women athletes involved in individual sports.[20]

Societal control over definition and construction of the "female athlete"
role has been maintained utilizing a combination of these four methods.
Hence, there continues to be a subtle misrepresentation of athletic opportunity for women. Significantly, this misrepresentation of the terms "female
athlete" and "lesbian" has been further exploited due to an apparently tacit
agreement among athletes and athletic institutions to avoid direct discussion of this issue. This attitude is aptly expressed by Cheryl Miller, a
former standout college basketball player at Southern California who stated,
"Our goal at USC is to play like men on the court and behave like women
off the court."[21] This attitude and the ensuing silence surrounding the
mythology has allowed the role of the "female athlete" to continue to be
defined in patriarchal terms—with gender roles and lesbiphobia firmly
in place.

The Guthrie study is significant because it directly explored and statistically confirmed the presence of the predominantly "unspoken myth" that
females who insist on pursuing an athletic role are often assumed to be
lesbians. This study also brought to light the common misconception that
lesbians are women who wish to be like men. Guthrie found that the less
exposure her subjects had to "out" lesbians, the more they stereotyped
lesbians as being "masculine."[22]

Guthrie's study supports Rosch's theory of human categorization rooted
in terms of prototypes and family resemblances. Here is empirical evidence
that females participating in athletics are perceived as being more "masculine" than nonparticipating females, and by extension, the more "masculine"
they are, the more they are perceived as also being "lesbian." The prototype operating in both cases is the female who is stepping out of her rigidly

defined gendex role. The family resemblance allows individuals to construct a psychologically balanced scenario by linking the two perceived "deviant" gendex behaviors as connected to one another. Hence, the myth of female athlete as lesbian is created and psychological balance is restored.

The Merging of Myth and "Reality"

In all fairness, myths do not continue unless there is an element of truth in their construction. Such is the case with the "female athlete = lesbian" mythology. If Kinsey was correct in his numbers, one out of ten people is "exclusively homosexual." This suggests, then, that a conservative estimate is that one out of ten female athletes *is* a lesbian. However, the percentage of lesbians participating in athletics has been suggested at "30 to 60 percent, depending on who one listens to."[23] If this is indeed the case, an interesting question is raised—why might there be a higher ratio of lesbians participating in athletics than found in the general population?

One response to this might be found in Becker's assessment of "outsiders." He suggests that an "outsider" goes through several steps to becoming a member of an outsider group. In his description of behavior he lists five steps in the construction of a "deviant [*sic*] career."[24] Without much effort, one can see the parallels between a "female" labeled as an "outsider" to her gendex role because she participates in "athletics" and a "lesbian" labeled as an "outsider" because of her dismissal of a gendex role which prescribes a heterosexual form of intimacy. The five steps to constructing an "outsider" role are:

1. . . . the commission of a nonconforming act, an act that breaks some particular set of rules (participating in athletics/acknowledging one's lesbianism)
2. . . . the development of deviant [*sic*] motives and interests (*liking* participation in athletics/accepting and enjoying one's lesbianism)
3. . . . the experience of being caught and publicly being labeled as a deviant [*sic*] (being called a jock/being called a lesbian)
4. . . . the deviant [*sic*] identification becomes the controlling one (self-labeling primarily as an athlete/labeling oneself as a lesbian first and foremost)
5. . . . movement into an organized deviant [*sic*] group (joining a team or pursuing an athletic career/socialization revolves around the lesbian community)[25]

The "deviant" careers of the "female athlete" and of the "lesbian" seem to merge together as each identifies as an "outsider" from their gendex role. The "reputation" of athletics as a haven for lesbians may encourage women who are in the process of constructing their role as a "lesbian" to begin their search for role models on the fields and courts. Just as some women may avoid athletics because they perceive participation as posing a threat to their gendex role, other women may gravitate to athletics *because* they believe they will find support for their role construction as a lesbian.

The more important issue here is how the process of constructing the "female athlete" role represents a microcosm of a larger process—that of capitalizing on lesbiphobic attitudes to limit, suppress, and control *all* women regardless of their athletic performance *or* their affectional preference. The extensive patriarchically sponsored "negative" mythology and misunderstandings about womyn-loving-womyn creates a fertile atmosphere wherein the labeling of a woman as "lesbian" serves as a form of patriarchal control to keep women "in their place" via prescribed gendex roles. As the twentieth century draws to a close, the team sport playing female athlete, the "tomboy," is still the most blatant representation of woman stepping out of her ordained gendex role. She is often an "easy target" for lesbiphobic attacks. However, not far behind her is the "aggressive CEO," the "too-tough cop," the "assertive and independent professor," the "defiant single mother," the "questioning student." None of these women, regardless of their actual affectional preference, are immune from the lesbiphobic attacks. These attacks can come from external as well as internal sources. The sole intent is to keep women from feeling or being too powerful, too noticeable, too loud, too anything but slave to traditional female gendex roles.

The real importance of discussing the construction of the "female athlete = lesbian" mythology is to explode the silence still surrounding our discussion of the mechanisms underlying the limits imposed on women by traditional gendex role expectations and by the fear and misunderstanding of what it means to be a lesbian. Silence allows the lies about what it means to be a woman, to be a lesbian, to continue to function as a form of societal control. Silence allows women to remain divided from one another and keeps us confused and distracted from overcoming our learned misogynist attitudes. Silence keeps a woman from learning to love and appreciate other women as well as loving and appreciating herself.

Both unapologetic athletic participation and coming out as a strong, healthy lesbian encourages other women to expand their socially constructed gendex roles. Both processes focus on learning to achieve a psychological balance that is centered around "choice" rather than "pre-scription." Both processes confound the masculinist acceptance of polarities and limitations on human behavior. The acceptance of either role is per-ceived as a very real threat to the socially constructed worldview that attempts to convince women that they are "less than." Thus, both roles are often discussed in whispers and in terms of "deviancy." By not speaking out and correcting these misconstructions, women/athletes/lesbians inad-vertently allow a masculinist "norm" to continue to discount female experi-ence and strength.

Athletics has taught me many things, not the least important is that "growing up" really means reconstructing much of what was communicated to me as a female child. Today, as an adult in my thirties, I proudly reclaim myself as a womyn, as a lesbian, *and* as an athlete. I do so because I have a clear understanding that compliant participation with patriarchy is indeed a "game"—a very deadly one!

Notes

1. Jesse G. Delia, "Constructivism and the Study of Human Communication," *Quarterly Journal of Speech* 63 (February 1977), 69.
2. Anselm Strauss, ed., *George Herbert Mead on Social Psychology: Selected Papers,* revised ed. (Chicago: University of Chicago Press, 1972), xxi.
3. Charles E. Osgood and Percy H. Tannenbaum, "The Principle of Congruity in the Prediction of Attitude Change," *Psychological Review* 62, no. 1 (1955): 43.
4. Shirley Park Lowry, *Familiar Mysteries: The Truth in Myth* (New York: Oxford University Press, 1982), 3–4.
5. Alan M. Olson, *Myth, Symbol, and Reality* (Notre Dame, Ind.: University of Notre Dame Press, 1980), 1.
6. Ibid., 15.
7. Ibid., 4.
8. George Lakoff and Mark Johnson, *Metaphors We Live By* (Chicago: University of Chicago Press, 1980), 71.
9. Ibid., 97.
10. Ibid., 96–97.
11. Ibid., 5.
12. See Erving Goffman, *The Presentation of Self in Everyday Life* (Garden City, N.Y.: Doubleday-Anchor, 1959).
13. Bonnie S. Anderson and Judith P. Zinsser, *A History of Their Own: Women in*

Europe from Prehistory to the Present, vol. 1 (New York: Harper and Row, 1988), xv.

14. Ibid.
15. William Morris, ed., *The American Heritage Dictionary of the English Language,* 2d ed. (Boston: Houghton Mifflin, 1982), 496.
16. Ibid., 759.
17. Ibid., 496.
18. Ibid., 138.
19. Dianne Christine Jones, "The Relationship of Sex-Role Orientations to Stereotypes Held for Female Athletes in Selected Sports" (Ph.D. diss., Ohio State University, 1979), 165.
20. Sharon Ruth Guthrie, *Homophobia: Its Impact on Women in Sport and Physical Education,* Microfilm reproduction (Ann Arbor, Mich.: University Microfilms International, 1982), 169–70.
21. John McCormick, "A Heroine Who Plays Ball Like a Man," *Newsweek,* August 13, 1984, 27.
22. Guthrie, *Homophobia,* 169–70.
23. Linn ni Cobhan, "Lesbians in Physical Education and Sport," in *Lesbian Studies: Present and Future,* ed. Margaret Cruikshank (Old Westbury, N.Y.: Feminist Press, 1982), 182.
24. See Howard S. Becker, *Outsiders* (New York: Free Press, 1963).
25. Ibid., 25–39.

Bibliography

Anderson, Bonnie S., and Judith P. Zinsser. 1988. *A History of Their Own: Women in Europe from Prehistory to the Present.* Vol. 1. New York: Harper and Row.

Becker, Howard S. 1963. *Outsiders.* New York: Free Press.

Cruikshank, Margaret, ed. 1982. *Lesbian Studies: Present and Future.* Old Westbury, N.Y.: Feminist Press.

Delia, Jesse G. 1977. "Constructivism and the Study of Human Communication." *Quarterly Journal of Speech* 63 (February): 66–83.

Goffman, Erving. 1959. *The Presentation of Self in Everyday Life.* Garden City, N.Y.: Doubleday-Anchor.

Guthrie, Sharon Ruth. 1982. *Homophobia: Its Impact on Women in Sport and Physical Education.* Microfilm reproduction. Ann Arbor, Mich.: University Microfilms International.

Jones, Dianne Christine. 1979. "The Relationship of Sex-Role Orientations to Stereotypes Held for Female Athletes in Selected Sports." Ph.D. diss., Ohio State University.

Lakoff, George, and Mark Johnson. 1980. *Metaphors We Live By.* Chicago: University of Chicago Press.

Lowry, Shirley Park. 1982. *Familiar Mysteries: The Truth in Myth*. New York: Oxford University Press.

McCormick, John. 1984. "A Heroine Who Plays Ball Like a Man." *Newsweek*, August 13, 27.

Morris, William, ed. 1982. *The American Heritage Dictionary of the English Language*. 2d ed. Boston: Houghton Mifflin.

Olson, Alan M. 1980. *Myth, Symbol, and Reality*. Notre Dame, Ind.: University of Notre Dame Press.

Osgood, Charles E., and Percy H. Tannenbaum. 1955. "The Principle of Congruity in the Prediction of Attitude Change." *Psychological Review* 62, no. 1: 42–55.

Strauss, Anselm, ed. 1972. *George Herbert Mead on Social Psychology: Selected Papers*. Revised ed. Chicago: University of Chicago Press.

12. The Politics of Self and Other

Lynn C. Miller

In *Writing a Woman's Life,* Carolyn G. Heilbrun describes the power-lessness that befalls women when they are deprived access to the narratives of other women's lives by which they might model or imagine their own lives. If these narratives are not told or published, women are limited in the ways they can script or develop their own lives and are barred as contenders in the public sphere: "Power is the ability to take one's place in whatever discourse is essential to action and the right to have one's part matter."[1] When women do not play out the script demanded by those in power, that is, place marriage or another patriarchal institution (usually the church) at the center of their lives, the consequence of their suppression is that our entire culture has been deprived of the struggles and triumphs of women facing the challenges of a nontraditional life: the real story of the conflicts, anger, and joy of a marriage beyond the frame of romance or convention for example, or of the terrors, self-doubt and victories of an undisguised quest for achievement, or of a woman's love for other women. As Heilbrun states, "biographies of women, if they have been written at all, have been written under the constraints of acceptable discussion, of agreement about what can be left out."[2]

The denial of a rightful place in public (and private) discourse has affected the lives of gay men and lesbians for the same reason. The same society that automatically envisions women as "other" marginalizes homosexuals, minorities, and those with physical/mental/emotional differences, among others. As the recent and continuing struggle over canon formation and maintenance demonstrates, cultures are transmitted by narratives, and power in the culture belongs to those who control the writing, speaking, and dissemination of those narratives. The essays by Fuoss, Peper, and Radel demonstrate in various ways how the dominant heterosexual culture has restricted, suppressed, and distorted the narrative, stories, and lives of gay men and lesbians. Equally important, the essays discuss the difficulties of developing a healthy self-concept as a homosexual in a society where homophobia is such a pervasive part of the landscape that it is unconsciously internalized even by those of us who are homosexual. As Nicholas F. Radel states in discussing White's *A Boy's Own Story:* "The narrator, like all men, constitutes the homosexual as Other in his effort to legitimize the structures of privilege that empower him, and trouble results because the homosexual Other is himself."

It is significant that two of the three essays in this section, Radel's discussion of Edmund White's work and Fuoss's analysis of male homosexuality in young adult fiction, have the word "politics" in their titles, and that the third, concerned with the definitions of femaleness and femininity in the contexts of gender and sex roles, is inherently political as Peper delineates the marginalization of athletic women from the ranks of "normal" women. These writers rightly focus on two primary aspects: first, that the formation of an identity different from the norm, that is, the development of a self that configures characteristics of gender and sexual expression outside the bounds of traditional heterosexual masculinity and femininity, threatens traditional notions of the performance of gender; and second, that the expression, artistic or athletic or otherwise, of these identities and differences challenges societal norms. By creating pressure on and objecting to societal definitions of normative behavior and values, the homosexual by expressing himself/herself automatically enters the political arena, and the expression of homosexual behavior, whether through art, sports, or other endeavors, similarly raises political issues. The essays demonstrate the inseparability of politics and aesthetics. In the following sections, I will discuss the issues of silence, identity and self-concept, and performance of gender, all of which relate to the politics of exclusion raised by these three essays. In addition, I will consider implications of these essays and issues for communication studies and suggest possibilities for further research.

Silence and Self-Concept

In "Female Athlete = Lesbian," Karen Peper relates her confusion as a young girl with the assumption by adults that girls' participation in sports, particularly team sports, made girls "that way." The unspoken fear of adults, including school authorities, was that "if little girls were allowed to be strong and powerful and gain self-confidence via participation in athletics they would not be 'feminine' "—they would then be "masculine" and by extension, lesbian. The silence and subterfuge used in regard to this fear of lesbianism are important here. The pressures to conform to standards of "femininity" are strong, with the implication that those who don't conform are subject to terrible fates: for a woman to be unfeminine, and therefore masculine, makes her unattractive, unmarriageable, and worst, homosexual. Peper points out that psychological concepts of gender and biological divisions of sex combine in role formation; thus she creates the term "gendex," to "linguistically illustrate the interconnectedness of sex and gender role construction." Because of society's emphasis on feminine behavior for women, the woman athlete is perceived as an outsider. Both the female athlete and the lesbian are perceived as outsiders, and because of this convergence of the two in marginalized roles, Peper postulates that many women may gravitate toward athletics to find "support for their role construction as a lesbian."

Peper wishes to explode the myth that the powerful woman must be masculine and by implication lesbian; by exposing the myth, the silent underpinnings of the myth are exposed also. "Silence allows the lies about what it means to be a woman, to be a lesbian, to continue to function as a form of societal control. Silence allows women to remain divided from one another and keeps us confused and distracted from overcoming our learned misogynist attitudes."

The issue of silence also comes up in Kirk W. Fuoss's essay, "A Portrait of the Adolescent as a Young Gay." He revels that prior to 1969, homosexuality was absent in young adult fiction. With homosexuality unnamed, the dominant culture could see itself not as heterosexual culture but as culture itself: "As long as YA [young adult] fiction persisted in relegating homosexuality to the status of absence [of silence], it also persisted in perpetuating the myth that heterosexuality is the natural sexuality." Even now, the expression of homosexuality is muted in these novels, far more than depictions of violence against homosexuals. Fuoss goes on to say that "the texts published since then [1969] nevertheless exhibit a sustained resistance to the articulation, by a gay narrator, of his own story."

Silence denies the existence of difference and allows the dominant culture to believe that it is the only culture. It also, if chosen by a gay person, effectively denies the self. Silence in regard to homosexuality has been a major form of repression, both by homosexuals in choosing it and by the culture at large in denying homosexuality. In *Epistemology of the Closet,* Eve Kosofsky Sedgwick states, "The fact that silence is rendered as pointed and performative as speech, in relations around the closet, depends on and highlights more broadly the fact that ignorance is as potent and as multiple a thing there as is knowledge."[3] Our society has wielded this ignorance as a way to affirm itself, for when the silence is broken and homosexuality is recognized it is seen as deviant. As Nicholas Radel points out in his essay: "By defining the homosexual as ill, society can see itself as healthy."

All three authors point up the price of silence and denial in the development of the self-concept. Radel, in his exploration of White's works, places the struggle for identity and self at the heart of Edmund White's works: "[The novels] reveal the ways socially and culturally imposed restraints on gay freedoms necessarily deny gay subjectivity and isolate in gay men an idea of a homosexual self as Other that they themselves conceive as being separate from their apparently essential selves." The central act of betrayal by the narrator of his teacher Beattie in *A Boy's Own Story* expresses the warring impulses of sexual expression and social conformity: "The narrator's action brings into focus two conflicting desires, the desire for sexual fulfillment and the desire not to be a homosexual."

White himself sees the AIDS epidemic as having broken this silence, liberating many gay writers and introducing gay fiction to the larger society. In a recent essay in the *New York Times Magazine,* he writes, "The paradox is that AIDS, which destroyed so many of these distinguished writers, has also, as a phenomenon, made homosexuality a much more familiar part of the American landscape. The grotesque irony is that at the very moment so many writers are threatened with extinction gay literature is healthy and flourishing as never before."[4] He answers the skeptics who dismiss gay fiction as specialized or "ghettoized":

But those of us who write it are convinced that the potential audience for our work is no more circumscribed than it is for any other constituency. "It's no less universal than the writing of urban male Jews or black women," argues Michael Denneny of St. Martin's Press. "It's particularized—but so is all great fiction. . . . When reviewers say they're tired of reading about gay life, they're in the same position as Bill Moyers when he asked August Wilson if he ever got tired of talking about black life."[5]

Performance of Gender

Much of the objection to homosexuality in our culture lies in its expression. In other words, if the homosexual is silent, closeted, and acts "normal," the homosexual has some measure of acceptance because s/he is invisible. As Fuoss mentions in the relegating of gay characters to secondary status in young adult novels: "The implication seems to be that as far as authors of YA fiction are concerned, it's okay to talk about homosexuality as long as what you are 'really talking about' is something else." Some of this marginalization relates directly to performance of gender, to the normative demands of how people are expected to behave in fulfilling their gender and sex roles.

The homosexual often challenges the culture's definitions of masculine and feminine role behavior. And yet the very existence of rigid definitions of masculinity and femininity insures that there must be a scapegoat or an "other" who does not fulfill the role. Vito Russo states this clearly in *The Celluloid Closet:* "The idea that there was such a thing as a real man made the creation of the sissy inevitable. . . . Although at first there was no equation between sissyhood and actual homosexuality, the danger of gayness as the consequence of such behavior lurked always in the background."[6] This lurking fear that non-normative performance of gender will result in homosexuality is the same unspoken apprehension that Karen Peper describes as surrounding the female athlete: "Today's 'athlete' that is 'female' is still perceived as demonstrating behavior that is inconsistent with her *prescribed* gendex role, thus creating at least the *perception* of a socially constructed imbalance. She is, in effect, being perceived by others and may even perceive herself as being a deviant from her 'appropriate' role as it relates to the male/masculine gendex role." The woman athlete is in a double bind, for precisely the qualities that are rewarded in athletics—

aggression, independence, strength, power—are ascribed to masculinity in our culture. Thus for the female to succeed in sports, she must by her behavior "betray" her femininity, creating intense conflict for development of self and identity. She is automatically marginalized, because the definition of athlete, like the definitions of poet, artist, corporate executive, etc., is automatically male. The female athlete, like the female executive, the woman writer, is relegated to "other" status.

Female sexuality, both homosexual and heterosexual, is marginalized. The dearth of depictions in popular culture of lesbian expression indicates a continuing disinclination to take women seriously in a sexual way. Unless female sexuality is tied to men, through heterosexual intercourse or through relationship with a man, it is not represented. The only lesbian sexual behavior that is depicted is when the lesbian is obviously masculine, once again maintaining the standard of sexuality as being male. Furthermore, the vast variation of lesbian behavior, which is often not stereotypically masculine, is not portrayed in newspapers, magazines, film, television, or on the best-seller lists. Vito Russo points out the exotic qualities of the tomboy or the slightly masculine woman in early cinema: "Women did not merit the serious attention afforded male 'unnaturalness' because they did not betray the male myth by aspiring to male behavior; they simply mimicked it and lent it credibility."[7] Heterosexual male sexuality remains the standard for sexuality in our culture, against which all others, female heterosexual sexuality included, is compared. The performance of femininity, like the performance of effeminacy in male behavior, guarantees and sanctifies its polar opposite of masculinity. Androgyny as a construct is in many ways as threatening as effeminate men or masculine women, as it blurs the boundaries of gender role behavior that provides a safety net for those who need polarities to both reassure and define them. Binary oppositions like heterosexual/homosexual, good/evil, morality/immorality, white/black, healthy/sick, among others, create barriers against the always-lurking areas of ambiguity that many people would prefer to ignore.

Connections to Communication Studies and Research Directions

Many of the issues raised in these essays, particularly those of marginality, silence, and the performance of gender, have been central to feminist film and literary studies, gender studies, and communication studies for some time. Concerns of marginality fuel the multicultural debate and foster movements of political correctness across many college campuses. The treatment of gender by the authors discussed here has many possible extensions in communication-related research. Radel says of White's novels: "These novels about gay life both confirm and interrogate their historical milieu and its construction of sexual orientation as gender difference." This construction insures homosexual sexual orientation the same marginal position as femaleness, that of "other" and "object" outside of the realm of heterosexual maleness. Feminist Film critic Christine Gledhill states:

It has long been a commonplace of Feminist analysis that women are culturally located outside history—the world that is made and remade of the activity of real material men—and placed in an idealist sphere of nature, eternal values etc. It is also commonplace that women exist in cultural production as "the other," or the "eternal feminine," the necessary complement to the male, the opposite against which men struggle for self-definition and manhood.[8]

This same statement could be applied to homosexuality by replacing "women" with "homosexuals" and "men" with "male heterosexuals": homosexuals too have been located outside of history, their existence the necessary complement to heterosexuality, particularly to traditional manhood, the tradition of "real men" referred to above by Vito Russo.

The position of gender and homosexuality in our culture is something we in communication studies must continue to explore. Sedgwick maintains that "the charting of a space between something called 'sex' and something called 'gender' has been one of the most influential and successful undertakings of feminist thought."[9] She then goes on to say: "The second and perhaps even greater heuristic leap of feminism has been the recognition that categories of gender and, hence, oppressions of gender can have a structuring force for nodes of thought, for axes of cultural discrimination, whose thematic subject isn't explicitly gendered at all."[10] This recognition opens up many areas of culture, reading theory, and textual study to considerations of gender. In the gendering of culture, the polarities inherent in gender, those of masculine/feminine, dominant/submissive, powerful/weak, are mirrored. Obviously within heterosexual relationships these polarities exist, but they also exist in homosexual relationships as frequently within a couple, the more masculine partner is seen by society as more powerful. As communication scholars, we need to study how communication patterns evolve in these interactions and how power is gendered within all sorts of relationships, homosexual and heterosexual included, and all kinds of institutions, such as academia, the military, industry, government, and the family.

Just as feminist critics like Elizabeth Flynn and Patrocinio Schweickart[11] have commented that all of us in our androcentric culture learn to read like men, all of us have also learned to read like heterosexuals. Further study of the ways lesbian and gay writers and texts participate in filtering, masking, and unmasking this androcentrist and heterosexist reading and writing tradition would be fruitful. This inquiry can be extended into the ways in which language itself is used in terms of, for instance, choices of voice, persona, and style and how those choices influence and interact with readers in different ways.

As is the case in film and literature studies, issues of gender and performance occupy an increasingly central position in theater and performance studies. For example, Jeanie Forte considers the position of the female body as text in "Women's Performance Art: Feminism and Postmodernism," and Judith Butler looks at the social construction of the performance of gender in "Performative Acts and Gender Constitution: An Essay in Phenomenology and Feminist Theory"; both essays are found in a recent collection exploring aspects of feminist theory, gender and performance: *Performing Feminisms* edited by Sue-Ellen Case.[12] Female performance artists like Holly Hughes and Karen Finley challenge audience perceptions of "femininity," female sexuality, and gender politics.[13] Scholars in performance studies and theatre, like Jacqueline Taylor, Deanna Jent, Sande Zeig, and Donna Nudd, among others, look at gender conceptions and nonverbal enactments of gender in the classroom and in cross-gender performances.[14] An interesting examination of performance of gender in the visual arts can be found in Nancy J. Vickers's essay, "The Mistress in the Masterpiece,"[15] which explores the artist's use (and misuse) of the female body as inspiration, object, and text in Benvenuto Cellini's sculpture. As scholars of communication and performance, we need to continue to examine the work of artists inside and outside of academia as they work with gender and performance. Many teachers of performance routinely make cross-gender assignments in the classroom; more of the process and implications of this exercise, and of productions that feature nontraditional and cross-gender casting, need to be explored and analyzed. Cross-gender experiments in production expose the foundations of gender construction, illuminating our cultural preconceptions and biases toward our own performances of self and gender as well as our judgments of the performances of "others" around us.

The essays by Fuoss, Peper, and Radel, in their considerations of marginalization, individuation, and the politics of self and other, illuminate rich areas of inquiry for communication scholars. Increasing our understanding of the relationship between gender and power, an ongoing issue for homosexuals and heterosexuals alike, moves us toward integration and away from the cultural polarities that divide our society, toward greater participation in the public discourse.

Notes

1. Carolyn G. Heilbrun, *Writing a Woman's Life* (New York: Ballantine Books, 1988), 18.
2. Ibid., 30.
3. Eve Kosofsky Sedgwick, *Epistemology of the Closet* (Berkeley: University of California Press, 1990), 4.
4. Edmund White, "Out of the Closet, and Onto the Bookshelf," *New York Times Magazine*, June 16, 1991, 24.
5. Ibid., 24.
6. Vito Russo, *The Celluloid Closet: Homosexuality in the Movies* (New York: Harper and Row, 1981), 6.
7. Ibid., 13.
8. Christine Gledhill, "Recent Developments in Feminist Film Criticism," *Quarterly Review of Film Studies* 3, 4 (Fall 1978): 466.
9. Sedgwick, 27.
10. Ibid., 34.
11. Elizabeth A. Flynn and Patrocinio P. Schweickart, eds., *Gender and Reading: Essays on Readers, Texts, and Contexts* (Baltimore: Johns Hopkins University Press, 1986).
12. Sue-Ellen Case, ed., *Performing Feminisms: Feminist Critical Theory and Theatre* (Baltimore: Johns Hopkins University Press, 1990).
13. See Holly Hughes's script of "World without End" published in *Out from Under: Texts by Women Performance Artists*, edited by Lenora Champagne (New York: Theatre Communications Group, 1990); and Catherine Schuler's essay, "Spectator Response and Comprehension: The Problem of Karen Finley's *Constant State of Desire*," *Drama Review*, 34, 1 (Spring 1990): 131–45.
14. See Jacqueline Taylor, "Encoding and Decoding Nonverbal Gender Display in Cross-Gender Performances," *Women's Studies in Communication* 9 (Fall

1986): 76–88; Sande Zeig, "The Actor as Activator: Deconstructing Gender through Gesture," *Women and Performance* 2, 2 (1985): 12–16; Deanna Jent, "Sex Roles in Acting Class," *Theatre Studies* 35 (1990): 18–27; and Donna Nudd, "Establishing the Balance: Re-examining Students' Androcentric Readings of Katherine Anne Porter's 'Rope,' " *Communication Education* 40 (January 1991): 49–59.

15. Nancy J. Vickers, "The Mistress in the Masterpiece," *The Poetics of Gender,* ed. Nancy K. Miller (New York: Columbia University Press, 1986), 19–41.

PART FOUR

Interpersonal Communication in Gay and Lesbian Relationships

13. Self-Disclosure Behaviors of the Stigmatized: Strategies and Outcomes for the Revelation of Sexual Orientation

Timothy Edgar

Social scientists have become increasingly aware of the relational tensions and difficulties faced by individuals who possess traits or attributes that are potentially stigmatizing. In his insightful analysis, Erving Goffman argued that the particular interactional problems encountered by people vary according to the visibility of the attribute that makes them "different" or "less desirable"(3). For some individuals, like those who are physically handicapped, the trait is evident to the onlooker. Goffman referred to these persons as *discredited* (4). Because the discredited cannot hide their stigmatizing attributes, they must develop strategies for managing the tension that occurs in mixed contacts.[1]

Goffman offered a second classification for those individuals who assume that their "shortcomings" are "neither known about by those present nor immediately perceivable by them" (4). For this category of the stigmatized, Goffman used the label *discreditable*. For the discreditable, the issues related to interaction become more complex because a choice is involved. One can conceal the attribute or make it known. As Goffman stated, one must decide "to display or not to display, to tell or not to tell, to let on or not to let on, to lie or not to lie, and in each case to whom, how, when, and where" (42). If one chooses to continue concealment, then one must develop strategies for covering and for dealing with the anxiety of keeping the secret;[2] if one chooses to disclose, then one must face the possibility of rejection.[3]

Thus, the discreditable person often faces a serious dilemma. Disclosure can bring tremendous psychological and emotional rewards, but the individual runs the risk of driving others away (Coates and Winston, 230). Disclosure, then, is an omnipresent concern and consideration. Since so much is at stake for the discreditable with a disclosure decision, this is an issue that deserves attention.

This study examines the process of disclosure as it relates to one particular stigmatized group—gay men. Although the study focuses on a distinct group, the hope is that the experiences of gay men are similar enough to other discreditable persons that the derived information is useful to all stigmatized individuals.

Review of Literature

Self-disclosure has been singled out by many scholars as a central experience in the lives of gay men and others who possess discreditable characteristics.[4] In these studies, researchers identified strategies for concealment and strategies for tension reduction once the stigmatizing attribute is revealed. In both situations the ultimate goal of the discreditable person is to save face and reduce the risk of rejection. These types of strategies are important facets of the total disclosure picture for the stigmatized; however, they only account for part of the relevant communication processes that transpire. In general, researchers have failed to discuss *how* the information is revealed and the degree to which the actual disclosive message influences the reaction of the recipient of the potentially stigmatizing disclosure.

Erving Goffman and Barbara Ponse are two scholars who have suggested that stigmatized individuals utilize specific verbal strategies when revealing themselves to others. However, both of them provided only one example. Goffman claimed that disclosure by a stigmatized person sometimes occurs in a matter of fact manner. The person treats the disclosure as something not out of the ordinary, thus trapping the listener into responding in a way which is not extraordinary. For instance, one might interject into a conversation, "As someone who is gay, I can speak to that issue" (101). If the gay person treats this as nothing unusual, then the disclosee might feel uncomfortable for treating it differently.

Ponse found in a sample of lesbians that inference is a frequent choice for disclosure. Women in her study described how they make comments to others that imply their homosexuality without directly stating the fact. One woman said that in conversation she would make statements such as " 'She and I have done this' or 'She and I have done that' " (332). When the information is framed in this manner, the listener is not forced to respond to a direct statement.

Goffman and Ponse recognized the strategic nature of disclosing behavior, but they did not attempt to identify other important characteristics of a disclosive strategy beyond the directness or indirectness of the message. Also, they did not speculate about the success of such strategies.

One study that attempted to provide a wider range of information about disclosure strategies was conducted by Joel Wells and William Kline. They asked a sample of forty gay men and women to respond to the following question: How do you tell others that you are lesbian or gay? Like Goffman and Ponse, they found that strategies varied in degree of directness. In addition, they identified disclosures that prepared the receivers of the messages and disclosures that came as responses to questions (195). Unfortunately, Wells and Kline gave little detail about these categories and did not investigate how the recipients of the disclosures responded.

Joel Hencken has viewed this lack of information as a critical shortcoming of the literature on gay men and the stigmatized. He saw the deficiency as an unfortunate situation not only because the information would be intellectually appealing but also because it would be extremely beneficial to have in a pragmatic sense for those individuals who anticipate or who are experiencing the same situation (2–3). Hencken, a practicing clinical psychologist as well as a researcher, bemoaned the fact that clients who are hiding stigmatizing attributes, especially gay men, come to him and other clinicians for much needed advice on how to disclose with the least amount of pain or rejection. Hencken said that he and other clinicians are called upon to help but have been provided with no normative date to guide the clinical work. As a result, practitioners simply do not have many facts. He argued that if researchers could provide more insight into the strategic nature of this form of disclosure, then those in the helping professions "could gain some useful perspective on this complex psychosocial process, and free them-

selves of some of the misleading and even dangerous assumptions, ignorance, and misinformation of the past" (8).

Unfortunately, the general literature on self-disclosure has provided
little guidance on how to accomplish this task. Although hundreds of studies
related to disclosure have been published, there has been no systematic
effort to analyze the content of "real life" disclosive messages. The vast
majority of disclosure studies have relied on scaled questionnaires to determine a person's general predisposition to disclose. Those studies that have
focused on the actual event derived data from contrived laboratory settings
(Chelune, 24–26). These pursuits are informative but insufficient when
trying to illuminate the strategic nature of disclosures that are highly sensitive and potentially stigmatizing. Hencken suggested that alternate approaches be used (152). The present study attempted to do this by relying
on the retrospective accounts of gay men who have previously revealed
their sexual orientation to others.

Research Questions

To guide this study, two research questions were asked. The first related
to the construction of disclosive strategies; the second concerned outcome.

Q1: What are the characteristics of the strategies that gay men use when
disclosing their sexual orientation to others?

Q2: How do the strategies for the disclosure of sexual orientation relate to
the reaction of the recipient of the disclosure?

Method

Subjects

Whenever a sample is taken from a stigmatized population, inevitably a
problem exists with the external validity of the sample. Baseline population
figures do not exist. As a result, it is virtually impossible to meet the
normal requirements of probability sampling. Some suggest that this problem should not deter research on stigmatized groups because such samples, though inherently biased, "can be used to provide some important
information for purposes other than that of estimating population norms"

(Joseph et al., 1299). The aim of this project was to select a diverse sample of gay men from which theoretical and pragmatic insights would develop.

Subjects were recruited through Dignity, Inc. Dignity is a Roman Catholic–based gay organization not officially recognized by the Roman Catholic Church. At the time of data collection there were over 4,000 members of Dignity in the U.S. and Canada. According to James Bussen (personal communication, May 23, 1986), who was the national president of the organization, Dignity is comprised of a relatively heterogeneous group of gay individuals.

Five hundred survey packets were distributed to Dignity members through contact persons in eighteen chapters across the country. One hundred and forty-eight men responded. The subjects ranged in age from 17 to 68 with $M = 35.4$. The men also varied greatly in terms of demographic variables and life experiences.

Instrument

The questionnaire for this survey was designed to allow the subjects ample opportunity to describe in depth their experiences and strategies for disclosing information. The two most important questions concerned (1) specific strategies for disclosure; and (2) outcome of the episode.[5] More specifically, the subjects were asked to think of the one disclosure about their sexuality that they considered to be the most significant. They were then requested to describe in detail how they went about telling the other person that they are gay. Emphasis was to be placed on what was actually said during the disclosure.[6] To assess outcome, they were asked to give their impressions of the other person's reaction. All answers were anonymous.

Analyses

Q-Sort. In attempting to categorize the descriptions of the disclosure strategies the researcher decided that the answers were much too complex and varied to categorize simply into four or five areas. Instead, each response was viewed as a unique strategy, but for every individual strategy, specific dimensions to the disclosure were identified. The three most prevalent and significant dimensions were conceptualized along continua. These three dimensions were direct-indirect, initiated-noninitiated, and justified-nonjustified. The dimensions were derived by expanding upon the classification system created by Wells and Kline (194–95) and by searching for and using emergent themes found in an analysis of the complete data set.[7]

To classify each strategy along the three dimensions, a Q-sort was employed. This method is a useful tool for behavioral research in situations where a data set is composed of statements by individuals (Nunnally, 613). Responses are categorized along an integer scale in such a way that an approximate normal distribution of the data is "forced." Those responses that represent the most extreme examples of a particular variable end up on the outer regions of the distribution and the more neutral statements are placed or Q-sorted into the middle areas.

For this study, each response was sorted three times (once for each of the three dimensions) along a six-point scale. Points one and six each contained approximately eight percent of the responses; points two and five each accounted for 16 percent; and points three and four were composed of the remaining 52 percent of the disclosure accounts (26 percent for each). Of the 148 respondents who took part in the study, 30 of these were dropped from consideration for the analyses. These responses were eliminated for one of four reasons: (1) the subject did not respond to the question; (2) the response was illegible; (3) the response was nonsensical; or (4) the response did not directly answer the question.

To achieve a more reliable sort, the responses were coded for each of the three dimensions by three coders. The goal was to reach an intercoder reliability of .80.[8] Each coder was given three envelopes each containing 118 valid responses. Every individual response was on a separate piece of paper. A training session was held where I informed the coders about the details of the Q-sort technique. They were told to begin by dividing the responses according to the description of the particular dimension. For instance, when categorizing the answers along the direct-indirect dimension, they were to start by placing the 59 most direct responses in one pile and the 59 most indirect in the other stack. From there they were to divide the answers into piles of 9, 19, and 31 for each half. The slots with nine responses represented the extremes. Ties were to be broken at random. The disclosures that were the most direct, initiated, and nonjustified were categorized as six. The most indirect, noninitiated, and justified were classified in the one slot. Once reliability among the three coders was reached, the three scores for each dimension were summed and divided by three so that every subject would have one composite score for each of the three dimensions.

The three dimensions were intercorrelated to determine how independent they were. All of the correlations were low. The coefficients were direct-indirect with initiated-noninitiated ($r = .25$), direct-indirect with justified-nonjustified ($r = .07$), and initiated-noninitiated with justified-nonjustified ($r = -.18$). The results of these low correlations suggested that the dimensions tended to be independent and mutually exclusive.

Content Analysis. The perceptions of the disclosure recipients' reactions were coded into three categories. A *Positive* reaction was where the individual was accepting and supportive. A *Negative* reaction involved total rejection or emotional distance. The last category, *Mixed,* accounted for the middle range of the spectrum. This included such behaviors as an initial negative reaction coupled with a shift to positive relational growth (or vice versa), an ambiguous reaction, or an instance where the person disclosed to two people simultaneously (e.g., parents) and one accepted him and the other did not. Two coders were trained to categorize the responses. They achieved 93 percent agreement.

Statistical Analysis. In order to explore the relationship between disclosure strategies and outcome, a chi-square analysis was used. This procedure was performed three times, once for each of the three disclosure dimensions. Prior to the analysis, the rankings for each dimension were stratified into high, middle, and low divisions (approximately one-third in each). These divisions were cross-tabulated with the three outcome situations. Thus, three 3×3 matrices were produced for the analysis.

Results

Disclosure Dimensions

An important facet of this study was the identification of distinguishable characteristics of a disclosure event. Three dimensions of the disclosive act emerged from the literature and from the data: direct-indirect, initiated-noninitiated, and justified-nonjustified. In the following pages these dimensions are described in greater detail. Examples of the actual episodes as described by the subjects are used to illustrate the diversity in messages along the continua.[9]

Direct-Indirect. This dimensional characteristic closely resembled the disclosure strategies described by Goffman (101) and Ponse (331–32). Their examples, however, were limited in demonstrating the tremendous diversity that exists across this dimension. Within the present sample of gay men, descriptions of episodes ranged widely.

For many individuals, part of their strategy was to leave no room for ambiguity. There was no hesitancy and no long build-up or lead-in to the disclosure. Disclosure was precise and direct. One man told how even though the conversation itself was long and detailed, the actual disclosure had a very direct quality:

Generally, it was a very straightforward conversation. It occurred when we were alone at my house. I started by telling them that I was gay. We then spent an hour or so discussing how I knew, how long I'd known, was I seeing anyone, whether to tell our parents. . . . It was a good and supportive conversation.

On the other end of the spectrum were individuals who apparently either did not feel comfortable in being so straightforward or believed that the message would have a greater impact if it was communicated through more indirect means. In disclosing to a female friend, one subject asked the woman to read a passage from the Bible and draw her own conclusions:

I remember very clearly asking Barbara to look up a reference to homosexuality in Romans [the New Testament]. We had spoken before about religion and faith, so it was natural that I should proceed in this manner. She understood immediately, without my saying anything more—after a fitful cry on my part, we spoke until dawn.

Another man guided his father to understanding through a series of vague questions. The father was allowed to figure it out for himself and then the son confirmed the conclusion:

The strategy was to let him know who I was—but first pose it rhetorically and let him figure it out for himself later. He questioned me about being out all night with my openly gay friend, Steve. He said, "Does it bother you that Steve is gay?" I said no, that my roommate, Joe [in college] was gay and there was no problem.

(Silence.) I faltered and said, "Would it bother you if your son was gay?" (Dead silence.) "Well," I said, "I'm gay." He cried, pushed me away physically, and said, "Who did *this* to you?" I blew the strategy but gained a great deal of honest emotions. Some days I wonder if it is worth it, but it is always worth it.

Others tended to be slightly less vague but still maintained a degree of indirectness and ambiguity by failing to use exact terminology in their revelations. They described their feelings and actions in such a way that obvious inferences could be made about their true sexual nature, but the words "gay" or "homosexual" were never uttered. The following example illustrates the point well:

It was around Valentine's Day. She saw me writing a card and asked what the girl's name was. I said, "It's not a girl." Her teeth about hit the floor.

Finally, here is an example where the recipient of the disclosure played a role in the indirectness of the information. A young man, who was HIV positive, attempted to tell his parents that he was gay, but his mother turned the situation into a confrontation:

My mother was becoming frustrated with my illness (she was feeling very helpless that I was not getting any better). One morning early in November 1985 she presented her plan to get me better (prior to this I had told my family that I had hepatitis). I was sitting at the kitchen table taking my temperature while my mother was dogmatically outlining her plan. At that moment I felt almost like I was being backed into a corner (to me, her plan meant that she was going to be the Mother and I was going to be the Child; my independence had been obtained only after a long struggle and I felt it slowly slipping away). I took the thermometer out of my mouth and very calmly began, "I didn't want to tell you this, but . . . " My mother cut in immediately and shouted, "You have AIDS! Don't you! I knew it when I came in here in August! I knew about you (i.e., that I was gay) back on E. 33rd Street" (where I grew up as an adolescent). My father sat there very quietly and said, "Oh, boy."

Perhaps the most noteworthy aspect of this dimension was the indirect end of the continuum. Most of the self-disclosure research has suggested that disclosive messages are straightforward and literal. Little attention has been given to the potential inferential nature of a disclosive act. This type of message should be of special interest to those who study human relationships. When an important and risky message is revealed in this manner, the participants must truly *interact*. The recipient of the disclosure is forced to extend his/her interpretive powers and identify a trigger that provides him/her with an avenue for understanding. Indirect and inferential messages have been discussed in other contexts but virtually have been ignored with regard to self-disclosure.

Justified-Nonjustified. This dimension concerned the degree to which the person accounted for his disclosing behavior. The subjects described widely varying episodes of justifying the fact that they revealed this particular information. As part of their disclosures, many of the men also attempted to justify or explain their sexual orientation; however, the focus of the analysis for this dimension was the justification of the disclosive act itself. This concept of justification is similar to the description of accounts by Scott and Lyman except that they viewed an account as a response to a negative accusation (47). In the case of a potentially stigmatizing disclosure, the justification generally takes place before the recipient ever comments on the behavior. Thus, the justification tends to function as an anticipatory and preventive measure attached to the core message.

A number of the respondents did describe disclosures that contained no justifications at all. One man related a humorous story where he was playing cards with a female friend. Not only was it not necessary for him to justify his communicative actions, but the woman's response suggested that it was not necessary for him to disclose at all:

I was straight to the point—"Laurie, I'm gay." "Bernard, I've known that for a long time. So, what do you want, a cookie? Now deal the cards!"

Very detailed justifications were used by other people. As is the case with the following example, the justification often served as a preface to the actual disclosure:

I stated to her (my ex-fiance), "I can't stand seeing you hurt like this. . . . I think I'm hurting myself, too." Holding her hand while both of us were crying, I said, "I need for you to help me end this pain for both of us. I love you an awful lot, but I'm gay."

In many situations where the disclosure was highly justified, the ratio-nale was linked to the relationship with the other person. By using this strategy, the gay man may have tried to soften the blow through flattery. If the discloser indicated that his revelation was for the benefit of the other individual, then he counterbalanced the potential shocking information with a show of affection, concern, and positive regard. Stiles (257) has used a fever metaphor to describe how disclosure operates in this context. Just as a fever is simultaneously an indication of bodily disturbance and part of the restorative process, so can a sensitive disclosure function as both a sign of potential relational problems and an effort to repair any damage to the relationship. This example illustrates the point:

I prepared for months in advance, reading books, talking with friends, and even went to a counselor for several weeks before telling my parents in order to practice role playing the actual event. At dinner one night during Christmas break, I said, "There is something that I want to tell you two, and I want you to be an active part of my life, and feel that without telling, you won't be. It's that I'm gay." I then answered questions about when I knew, the causes of homosexuality, concerns about my career, etc. I believe that I said that I was tired of hiding, that their understanding of me hasn't been complete and that, while I valued their friendship, I had to be honest with them even if they couldn't accept or understand that honesty.

Although this data set indicated that justifications are employed to varying degrees, the results only give a preliminary picture of the different forms the justifications may take. Also, this data did not reveal the exact reasons why someone would not choose to provide justification-giving statements as part of the total disclosure picture. For example, do those gay men who feel less guilt about their sexuality perceive a lesser need to justify the disclosure? Does the degree of intimacy in the relationship account for variance in the level of justification? These are issues that future research should address more directly.

Initiated-Noninitiated. For this dimension, the focus was on the degree to which the discloser participated in the initiation of the disclosive interaction. Those revelations that were most highly initiated were thoughtfully planned and received no prompting from the recipient of the message. The discloser determined where, when, and how the information was revealed. The following case of disclosure to parents shows how this type of situation might transpire:

Once I decided to tell them I got out a calendar and chose a date on which to tell them. I gave myself a month to prepare. I then wrote to my uncle who I suspected was gay and told him about myself. He gave some advice. As it happens, my parents knew about him. On the planned day we were taking a ride to the shore. (I hadn't counted on that.) My aunt was also going along and I had no intention of telling her. The situation of the actual telling went this way. I managed to be alone in the car with my parents. They knew we were there together because I had something important to say.

Mom: Well, what is it?
Me: It's not easy to say.
Mom: Say a little prayer first.
Me: I guess I should just come out and say it. I'm gay.
Mom: You're only kidding, right?

One of the most intriguing findings was the discovery of people who played a minimal role in the initiation of the disclosure. This could have been because they were individuals who were just too frightened or apprehensive about disclosing and were only able to do so when the other person was in control of the situation. The desire to reveal may have been present for a long time, but they needed that extra push from the other individual to take the last step toward disclosure. This was indicated by the fact that many of the highly noninitiated scenarios were ones where the gay man could easily have lied or not responded in any way to the initiation on the part of the other, but they chose to avoid the easy way out. The example illustrates a response to a direct confrontation:

I was home visiting and my mother, brother, and I went grocery shopping. The store was very crowded and my brother was making "jokes" in very poor taste and very little humor about "queers." I became angry and told him to shut up. In turn he shot back angrily with, "Why? Are you queer?" I did not answer, at which point my mother asked, "Well, are you?" I answered, "Yes." The whole exchange was very tense and angry except for the part my mother played. Mom turned to me while we were doing dishes and from the blue said, "Jean [her best friend] seems to think you're gay. Are you?" (A long pause from me.) "Yes," I said.

Others were not put on the spot in such a direct manner but still took advantage of a situation where others initiated a conversation on a related topic. A context was provided and then the individuals seized the opportunity to segue into the desired disclosure. An emotional discussion between a son and his parents illustrates such a case:

Father had told me that he loved me and my mother (very difficult for him) and there were tears all around. It seemed like as good a time as any to tell him. I said, "Father, I think that it is possible that I'm gay." He said, "I know."

The data revealed the variability of the initiation of stigmatizing disclosure; however, further investigation is desirable. For instance, how does the degree of initiation relate to other variables such as locus of control and perceived power within relationships? By studying initiation of disclosure in conjunction with issues such as these, researchers can better understand the underlying motivations that lead gay men and other discreditable individuals to initiate a disclosive act or wait for the potential recipient to take the lead.

Outcome

The great majority of the subjects reported that the outcome of the disclosure episode was favorable (70 percent). Only 12 percent said that they received a negative response. And 17 percent claimed that the reaction was mixed. Surprisingly, the nature of the disclosure seemed to have little, if any, effect on the reaction of the recipient of the message. No significant results were found for any of the three chi-square analyses.

Discussion

The primary purpose of this research was to show that disclosures which contain potentially stigmatizing information are strategically formulated and enacted. The research is a departure from traditional self-disclosure studies where investigators have focused on the individual's general predisposition to reveal information about the self. Three dimensions of a disclosive act were identified: direct-indirect, initiated-noninitiated, and justified-nonjustified. I concede that this was an initial attempt at classification and there may be other important dimensions yet to be identified; however, this method of categorization does show that there is great variance in the strategies stigmatized people use.

This finding is an important one for general self-disclosure theory. The variability of the characteristics of highly risky and intimate messages emphasizes the interactive nature of the disclosure process. Too often in self-disclosure research, guiding models have been used that implicitly suggest that disclosure is a simple process which amounts to sending a message without regard for the receiver (Cline, 3). The complexity of the process frequently has been ignored. The findings in this study vividly illustrate the vital role the recipient of the disclosure plays in the formulation and the timing of the message. The results also are enlightening in regard to methodological issues. In the past, the vast majority of disclosure studies have relied on self-report scaled questionnaires and contrived laboratory experiments as the primary means of data collection. In this study, subjects were asked to describe their own real life disclosive experiences in great detail. Through this method, valuable information was gained that would not have been accessible through more traditional measures. Perhaps it would be difficult for individuals to recall clearly the details of a disclosive episode that is not as sensitive or threatening as the revelation of sexual orientation; however, self-disclosure researchers should continue to pursue strategies of data collection that allow for a closer look at the "insider's view" (Schneider and Conrad, 33) of his/her own experience.

The other goal of the study was more pragmatic in nature. Gay men and other discreditable individuals, for whom disclosure is a constant concern, could benefit greatly by knowing which strategies are most workable. That is, which form of disclosure will produce the most desirable outcome or reaction from the recipient of the message? Unfortunately, the results do not provide a conclusive answer to this question. The statistical analyses revealed no significant trends. This tentatively suggests that strategy choice has little if any impact on outcome. The finding may mean that disclosures of this sort are so sensitive and laden with emotion that the presentation of the actual message has little, if any, effect on the reception of the information. If the other person is predisposed not to be tolerant and accepting, then maybe no manner of disclosure will alter that mind set (at least initially). Perhaps the gay man should base strategy selection on personal comfort level rather than on the potential immediate reaction of the recipient.

This is a possible interpretation; however, for two reasons caution is urged in embracing this view. First, this was not a random sample of all gay men. The results provide insight, but they are not easily generalizable. Second, outcome was measured through the impressions of the people who disclosed. Their perceptions of the event may not coincide with what the recipients truly thought and felt. In order to examine this issue more fully, future investigations should sample from populations of individuals with different stigmatizing attributes and rely on data from both parties involved in the process.

Perhaps an even more important issue is the nature of the communication that occurs in the days, weeks, and months following the disclosure. The way in which the initial message is conveyed may not have a significant bearing on acceptance; however, the debriefing period and other future interactions could influence heavily the other person's attitude. The gay man may want to consider interactional alternatives to accommodate the other person's reaction. For example, the recipient of the disclosure may feel at first uncomfortable or confused. If so, the discloser could make the situation worse by trying to force acceptance. In this case, the other person may need some time to think and reflect upon the revelation before s/he completely understands his/her own feelings on the matter. Also, the gay man may want to consider the possible questions individuals might ask. This, too, could help them in reaching acceptance.

One of the men in the study wrote about the importance of post-disclosure support for the recipient. His comments eloquently summarize the complexity of the total process of stigmatizing disclosures:

Assuming that the object of the coming out process is someone that you care about, be prepared to help them deal with your revelation. It usually takes a gay person a long time to reach a point of disclosure. To dump that on someone and then leave them to deal with it alone is cruel. A gay person must take the steps necessary to help. Do not take your own emotional baggage and give it to someone else and think you role is done. Make the sharing of your gayness work for you as a way of cementing an already important relationship. Don't be scared off by negative reactions. We are all in this together and only when "coming out" is no longer necessary will those negative reactions go away.

Notes

1. A mixed contact is an interactional episode between the possessor of the stigmatizing attribute and the normal. Thompson and Seibold define the "normal" as the individual "who does not bear the stigma at issue and who finds the attribute discrediting" (231).
2. For a discussion about the anxiety and stress related to hiding a stigmatizing trait, see Ehrlich (130–41); Ellenberger (29–42); and Schneider and Conrad (36–39).
3. Many researchers have cited instances of rejection suffered by discreditable persons after they disclose. See Ponse (330–31) and Schneider and Conrad (36) for vivid examples.

4. In addition to the studies that have discussed gay individuals (Cass, 219–35; Coleman, 31–43; Dank, 180–95; de Monteflores and Schultz, 59–72; Lee, 49–78; Ponse, 313–38; Wells and Kline, 191–97), there also are those which have focused on people with epilepsy (Kleck, 1239–48; Schneider and Conrad, 32–44; Scambler and Hopkins, 26–43), alcoholics and drug addicts (Gary and Hammond, 142–43), women with unwanted sexual experiences (Mims and Chang, 7–14), and infertile couples (Miall, 268–82).

5. This study was done in conjunction with an investigation of the communication problems of people in high risk groups due to AIDS. Thus, there were several questions on the survey that did not directly relate to disclosure issues.

6. The researcher was initially concerned that the subjects would not be able to recall the event with enough precision. A pilot study showed that these events were so significant for these men that they were able to remember the episodes in great detail.

7. For an example of how this procedure has been used in other research on the stigmatized, see Schneider and Conrad (33). A copy of the complete coding instructions is available from the author.

8. Reliability was computed by intercorrelating the ratings of all three coders. The three correlations were then averaged. The .80 criterion was achieved for two of the three dimensions. The reliability for the initiated-noninitiated dimension was .79. The researcher considered this to be acceptable because of the exploratory nature of the project. Krippendorff has viewed this as an acceptable practice under these circumstances (147).

9. For all descriptions of disclosure episodes, the names of individuals and places were changed.

Works Cited

Cass, Vivienne C. 1979. "Homosexual Identity Formation: A Theoretical Model." *Journal of Homosexuality* 4: 219–35.

Chelune, Gordon J. 1979. "Measuring Openness in Interpersonal Communication." In *Self-Disclosure,* edited by Gordon J. Chelune, 1–27. San Francisco: Jossey-Bass.

Cline, Rebecca. 1982. "Revealing and Relating: A Review of Self-Disclosure Theory and Research." Paper delivered at the meeting of the International Communication Association, Boston.

Coates, Dan, and Tina Winston. 1987. "The Dilemma of Stress Disclosure." In *Self-Disclosure: Theory, Research, and Therapy,* edited by Valerian J. Derlega and John H. Berg, 229–55. New York: Plenum Press.

Coleman, Eli. 1982. "Developmental Stages of the Coming Out Process." *Journal of Homosexuality* 3: 31–43.

Dank, Barry M. 1971. "Coming Out in the Gay World." *Psychiatry* 34: 180–95.

de Monteflores, Carmen, and Stephen J. Schultz. 1978. "Coming Out: Similarities and Differences for Lesbians and Gay Men." *Journal of Social Issues* 34: 59–72.

Ehrlich, Larry G. 1981. "The Pathogenic Secret." In *Gayspeak,* edited by James Chesebro, 130–41. New York: Pilgrim Press.

Ellenberger, Henri R. 1966. "The Pathogenic Secret and Its Therapeutics." *Journal of History of the Behavioral Sciences* 2: 29–42.

Gary, A. L., and R. Hammond. 1970. "Self-Disclosure of Alcoholics and Drug Addicts." *Psychotherapy: Theory, Research, and Practice* 7: 142–43.

Goffman, Erving. 1963. *Stigma: Notes on the Management of Spoiled Identity.* Englewood Cliffs, N.J.: Prentice-Hall.

Hencken, Joel David. 1984. *Sexual-Orientation Self-Disclosure.* Ph.D. diss., University of Michigan. Ann Arbor, Mich.: University Microfilms.

Joseph, Jill G., Carol-Ann Emmons, Ronald C. Kessler, Camille B. Wortman, Keith O'Brien, William T. Hocker, and Catherine Schaefer. 1984. "Coping with the Threat of AIDS: An Approach to Psychosocial Assessment." *American Psychologist* 39: 1297–1302.

Kleck, Robert E. 1968. "Self-Disclosure of the Nonobviously Stigmatized." *Psychological Reports* 28: 1239–48.

Krippendorff, Klaus. 1980. *Content Analysis: An Introduction to Its Methodology.* Beverly Hills, Cal.: Sage Publications.

Lee, John Alan. 1977. "Going Public: A Study in the Sociology of Homosexual Liberation." *Journal of Homosexuality* 3: 49–78.

Miall, Charlene E. 1986. "The Stigma of Involuntary Childlessness." *Social Problems* 33: 268–82.

Mims, Fern H., and Audrey S. Chang. 1984. "Unwanted Sexual Experiences of Young Women." *Journal of Psychosocial Nursing and Mental Health* 22: 7–14.

Nunnally, Jum C. 1978. *Psychometric Theory.* 2d ed. New York: McGraw-Hill.

Ponse, Barbara. 1976. "Secrecy in the Lesbian World." *Urban Life* 5: 313–38.

Scambler, Graham, and Anthony Hopkins. 1986. "Being Epileptic: Coming to Terms with Stigma." *Sociology of Health Illness* 8: 26–43.

Schneider, Joseph W., and Peter Conrad. 1980. "In the Closet with Illness: Epilepsy, Stigma Potential, and Information Control." *Social Problems* 28: 32–44.

Scott, Marvin B., and Stanford M. Lyman. 1968. "Accounts." *American Psychological Review* 33: 46–62.

Stiles, William B. 1987. " 'I Have to Talk to Somebody': A Fever Model of Disclosure." In *Self-Disclosure: Theory, Research, and Therapy,* edited by Valerian J. Derlega and John H. Berg, 257–82. New York: Plenum Press.

Thompson, Teresa L., and David R. Seibold. 1978. "Stigma Management in *Normal*-Stigmatized Interactions: Hypothesis and a Model of Stigma Acceptance." *Human Communication Research* 3: 231–42.

Wells, Joel W., and William B. Kline. 1987. "Self-Disclosure of Homosexual Orientation." *Journal of Social Psychology* 127: 191–97.

14. Gender and Relationship Crises: Contrasting Reasons, Responses, and Relational Orientations

Julia T. Wood

Apart from our relationships with other people, there would be no moral necessity.

—Piaget, 1932

This study contributes to the understanding of how people conceive and manage problems in serious romantic relationships. Prior scholarship has identified two orientations toward relationships.[1] Characterized by theme and associated consistently with gender (not biological sex), these two orientations reflect different conceptions of morality and lead to distinct codes of interpersonal conduct. They represent, wrote Gilligan, "two modes of describing the relationship between other and self."[2] Exploring how these themes illuminate gay men and lesbian's management of relational stress is the focus of this chapter.

Prior Scholarship

Research on Relationship Stress

Work by Duck[3] and Baxter,[4] among others, has crystallized major reasons for ending relationships. Hill et al. found common reasons for break-ups to

238

be boredom, divergent interests, and one or both partners' preference for independence.[5] Similarly, Cody reported the reasons heterosexuals most often cited for break-ups were personality faults in partners, an unwillingness to compromise, and a feeling of being restricted by a relationship.[6] Baxter, too, found relationships may end to allow greater autonomy.[7]

Research on Gender Differences in Break-Ups

Of the sundry factors implicated in relational stress, gender has emerged as especially salient. It appears linked to how discontent is defined; how dissatisfaction is expressed, managed, and resolved; and how conflict is regarded by partners. Bell argues gender is the single most significant social factor in understanding relationships.[8] Understanding of gender's influence on relationship process was enriched by Gilligan's findings on gender-associated moral voices.[9] Drawing upon earlier work by scholars such as Lever[10] and Chodorow,[11] Gilligan argued that there are two orientations or "voices" which are typically but neither necessarily nor invariably associated with the two genders. The masculine voice esteems equality of individual rights and fairness from which evolves an interpersonal orientation based on hierarchy, adherence to abstract principles, and separateness of humans. In contrast is the feminine voice that emphasizes equity and caring and regards relationships as webs of processual, overlapping connections and responsibilities.

Substantial scholarship indicates there are pronounced, systematic differences between masculine and feminine modes of creating and expressing closeness.[12] In general, men interact behaviorally and seek to preserve some distance within relationships. Women generally prioritize communication and use it to increase closeness and interdependence. These findings are consistent with Gilligan's findings that the morality of rights emphasizes separation over connection, while the morality of caring accords proportionately greater weight to interconnection than to independence. In turn, these differences in relational orientation promote distinct interpersonal attitudes and actions. Most notably, women tend to attend closely to interaction as a barometer of relational health, while men seem generally less aware of interpersonal dynamics.[13] Women's communication is typically more disclosive, expressive, and affective than men's,[14] and women are usually more conversationally responsive than men.[15] Existing research further suggests women are inclined to address problems, while men tend to deny or avoid them.[16] Support for this difference came from Wood's finding that women respond to crises by communicating, encouraging mutual involvement, and preserving potential for future contact. Men, in contrast, were more likely to promote self-interest and adhere to external principles.[17] Rusbult's program of research has consistently found women voice problems and/or are loyal to relationships in times of stress, while men are more likely to respond with passive neglect and/or withdrawal.[18] These findings are consistent with the basic distinction between men's tendency to view humans as separate and women's conception of individuals as complexly connected.[19]

The overwhelming bulk of research on romantic relationships has focused on heterosexuals, despite repeated findings that homosexuals do not differ in many respects from heterosexuals.[20] Redressing this exclusion, the study reported here focused on gays and lesbians to increase the inclusiveness of the existing understanding of relationships and to provide findings that might assist counselors who work with gay and lesbian couples.[21]

From the limited research that has been conducted on homosexual relationships, several findings emerge. First, the central values in enduring lesbian bonds appear to be development, companionship, affection, and open communication,[22] and sustaining emotional closeness seems to work in tandem with preserving each partner's autonomy and an egalitarian power structure for the bond.[23] Seeking closeness is consistent with western sex role expectations of women while valuing autonomy and egalitarianism reflects feminist ideology.

Orientations toward power and money seem particularly prominent as distinctions between gay and lesbian couples. According to Blumstein and Schwartz, "Money establishes the balance of power in relationships except among lesbians."[24] Elaborating this, they noted "in gay male couples income is an extremely important force in determining which partner will be dominant"[25] and "lesbians do not use income to establish dominance . . . they use it to avoid having one woman dependent on the other."[26] Echoing findings on heterosexual male-female differences, they also reported that "lesbians cannot seem to find enough time together . . . while gay men are more satisfied with the amount of time they do have. . . . Lesbian couples tend to be relationship centered."[27]

Finally, directly relevant to the present research was Rusbult and Iwaniszek's report that males, both heterosexual and gay, are more likely than females to respond to relational dissatisfaction and stress by exiting the relationship or avoiding discussion of problems. Females of both sexual orientations are more likely to respond to interpersonal stresses with loyalty and active efforts to identify, discuss, and resolve problems.[28]

The foregoing research suggests lesbian and gay relationships may be contexts that intensify male and female orientations. It could be argued that within traditional society women's desire for emotional intimacy with partners has been possible only at the cost of personal autonomy, a particularly high tariff since this leaves women unprepared to take charge of their own lives. Not constrained by an opposite-sex partner, lesbian couples may resolve this tension by using autonomy to make intimacy safe by, in Raymond's words, ensuring that a "friend does not lose her Self in the heightened awareness of and attachment to another woman."[29] Existing research encourages a parallel interpretation of gay bonds. Since both partners are male, there is little to attenuate socialized masculine qualities such as competitiveness, self-interest, and power guarding. It could be argued that male-male intimacy heightens men's inclination to see and guard power and to maintain considerable autonomy since each partner is prone to compete for power and its concomitants.

Based on prior research, three research questions guided the study reported here:

1. What reasons for crises in serious romantic relationships are identified by gays and lesbians, and do the reasons differ between the two groups?
2. How do lesbians and gays describe their thoughts and actions during times of relational crisis, and are there differences between their descriptions?
3. To what extent is there correspondence between lesbian and female relational orientations and between gay and male relational orientations?

Methods and Procedures

This study employed an interpretive methodology,[30] which attempts to understand individuals in their own terms, rather than those imposed by researchers.

Analysis of Data

For this study, I examined gay men and lesbians' retrospective accounts of crises in romantic relationships. An assessment of this form of data may be found in Lloyd and Cate.[31] Gay and lesbian friends requested volunteers, and I provided stamped envelopes so that responses could be returned anonymously. Each participant wrote a three-page response to explain what she or he considered the causes and issues of a severe crisis in a committed relationship and how she or he felt and acted during the period of stress.

Of the 65 questionnaires distributed, a total of 43 complete and usable ones were returned: 23 from lesbians and 20 from gays; thus, there was a 66.15 percent return rate. Respondents were nonstudents from the south, west, and north-central United States. Mean age was 25.23 for lesbians and 29.70 for gay men.

Based on my prior work,[32] I analyzed respondents' accounts to discover patterns in their language and thinking about relationship crises. To establish the reliability of patterns I discerned, a second researcher also read and analyzed responses. Reliability between our interpretations was high, averaging 86.75 percent agreement between us. We resolved areas of disagreement so that all responses could be used.

Prior research indicates that concerns with self, other, and the relationship generally distinguish between male and female orientations toward crises. Those concerns also emerged in the accounts of gays and lesbians, yet a modification was warranted. Gay and lesbian relationship comments were sufficiently distinct to require separating the category "relationship" into two categories: process and avoidance, which respectively captured lesbians and gay men's general orientation toward their distressed relationships. This revision in the initial categories supports prior findings on generalizable differences between women's and men's modes of dealing with interpersonal conflict.

To better understand individuals' experiences, I studied each account in depth by functioning as a critic whose focus is how people use language to define and connect values, motives, and courses of action. In what follows I report themes in accounts.

To allow readers themselves to appreciate gay and lesbian voices, I intersperse generous excerpts into my discussion of themes in the ac-

Table 1
Reported Reasons for Crises

Reason	% gay men	% lesbians	% total
Relationship Dynamics	9.09	36.51	27.08
Communication	—	22.22	
Fit with web	—	14.29	
Trust/effort/no talk	9.09		
Personal Autonomy	27.27	34.92	32.29
Restrictions on self	27.27	23.81	
Need to discover self	—	11.11	
Problems in Partner	63.63	22.12	36.46
Emotional dependency	30.30	9.54	
Incompatibility	21.21	12.58	
Financial irresponsibility	12.12	—	
Other	—	6.35	6.35
Intercoder Reliability	87.79	87.30	87.50

Note: Since gay men and lesbians cited different reasons for crises, their responses are reported in terms of percentage of comments for each group of respondents. There were 96 reasons stated in the entire data: 33 from gay men and 63 from lesbians.

counts. My interpretation was read by two gay and two lesbians academics to place themes I discerned within the context of gay and lesbian culture.

Definition of Relationship Crises

There were striking and consistent differences between the weight assigned by gay men and lesbians to the three categories of reasons for crises. The men's accounts gave greatest weight to problems in partners, followed by needs for autonomy and relationship dynamics. The women described their reasons, in descending order, as relationship dynamics, need for autonomy and self-knowledge, and problems in partners.

Gay Men's Definitions of Crises

The two major sources of relationship crises cited by men, problems in partners and autonomy, seemed interrelated. A third reason, relationship dynamics, was far less salient in accounts.

Problems in Partners. Seventeen of 20 gay men cited problems in partners as reasons for relationship crisis, and this accounted for 63.63 percent of reasons reported. Three types of problems were identified: emotional needs, personality conflict, and finances.

The most often named partner problem was emotional needs, which respondents described as burdens:

He began to rely on me to take charge of his life or at least to be more involved in it than I thought was fair. My partner suffered an emotional breakdown after his parents disowned him. He needed too much emotional support from me. This man and I had been together for four years when his life fell apart [death of brother, emergency surgery, unemployment]. Partner's need for support outstripped what I thought I should have to invest.

I was very tired and getting physically and emotionally worn. I realized I didn't get much in return.

I tried to be supportive for awhile, but after a month I felt he was expecting too much from me.

My partner tried to make up [for my loans of money] by doing more of the cooking and cleaning, but I still thought it was unfair.

It didn't seem right, just not fair.

These descriptions reflect a concern with equality of rights between separate individuals. Respondents' language suggests they perceived a built-in limit to support they should provide an intimate and kept track of investments and payoffs. A partner who exceeds that limit for whatever reasons is a burden. Accounts further implied investments in intimacy, as in the world of commerce, were made in at least tacit anticipation of returns.

These accounts reflect the writers' detachment from partners, an independence between self and other. This stance has been captured in Gilligan and Wiggins's distinction between sympathy (feeling for) and compassion (feeling with). The former entails distance between the sympathizer and the object of sympathy, which is consistent with conceiving self as independent of others and with protecting self from intrusions by others.[33] This emerged as the central theme running through gay men's accounts.

A second type of partner problem consisted of personality incompatibilities. Included in this category were poor self-concept, aggressiveness, selfishness, depression, and smoking. Respondents' tendency not to elaborate these problems suggests they regarded them as self-evident reasons for dissatisfaction.

A final category of partner problems was financial irresponsibility. Mentioned by over one-third of respondents, this emerged as a salient point of contention in many relationships:

He didn't pay his half of the bills. His financial problems made him dependent [and it was] necessary for me to preserve my independence and financial status.

I couldn't have lived with someone who couldn't pay his bills on time. My financial security was at stake.

I don't want to be involved with someone who couldn't [*sic*] handle money.

My partner expected me to help him out financially when he ran out of money. [Despite his consistent repayment each month] I was being used . . . financially exploited. Partner must be able to take care of himself *in all respects*—self-sufficient, especially about money!

Apparently money does talk and loudly in gay relationships. The salience of money supports Blumstein and Schwartz's (1983) finding that income is a pivotal force in gay bonds. As with other problems described by gay men, a partner's financial troubles are a burden if they affect the self. Consistent across gays' descriptions was the view that partners are not entitled to unreciprocated time, support, or money.

Personal Autonomy. Needs for personal freedom appeared in 9 of the 20 men's accounts, and they comprised roughly one-quarter of all reasons cited for crises. Consistent with viewing people as separate, my respondents expressed a pronounced conflict between extensive togetherness and autonomy:

We had become too much alike. I was losing my individuality. After several months my partner wanted to join me for movies with other friends, to have dinners together, etc. I felt stifled.

I was feeling "trapped." I couldn't really develop my own personality. We started doing everything together all the time. . . . I had no life of my own.

Gay men's descriptions of partner problems suggest a relational orientation consistent with existing knowledge of sex roles: males tend to regard others' needs as impingements on their autonomy; and, if needs conflict, priority goes to self. The morality of rights relies on rules for what is fair, equal, or earned rather than what is needed.

Relationship Dynamics. Only three men mentioned this reason and each cited a single, distinct issue: lack of trust, too much work required to keep the relationship intact, and no communication. Most striking is this category's low salience. Inattention to this dimension of relationships suggests the gay respondents were unaware of the critical role of communication in interpersonal relationships and/or lacked vocabulary and socialization that encourage discussing interpersonal dynamics.

Lesbians' Descriptions of Crises

In their accounts of crises, lesbian respondents accorded approximately equal importance to relationship dynamics and autonomy; less salient were problems in partners.

Relationship Dynamics. Most often mentioned as a reason for crisis was relationship dynamics, which accounted for just over one-third of all reasons cited by lesbians and which appeared in 20 of the 23 accounts. Comprising this category were two distinct issues: communication difficulties and tension between the relationship and other aspects of respondents' lives. Cited by 14 women, the theme of communication problems is well captured in these excerpts:

Our problem was lack of communication. She wouldn't talk about what was bothering her or about her feelings about our relationship. I wasn't sure where I stood because she wouldn't let me in.

Together our inability to confront ourselves and each other in a constructive way. My lack of confidence. Her inability to express needs. Both partners' dynamics. The relationship itself was at stake. The issue was communication. I really just wanted her to talk more about . . . how she was feeling in general and about me.

These descriptions exemplify Gilligan's finding that women conceive self and other within the context of relationships.[34] An awareness of the relationship frames and makes meaningful individual feelings, needs, and acts.

The second problem in relational dynamics concerned a lack of fit between the bond and writers' overall lives. Discussed by 9 women, this issue reflected women's conception of relationships as a web of interacting, overlapping connections among themselves and others. Just as self and other are not conceived apart from a relationship, neither is a particular relationship isolated from a larger network. Thus, crisis may result when one commitment does not cohere with other aspects of a woman's life:

Her inability or unwillingness to accept or befriend any of my other friends. Although I was madly in love with her, I loved my friends too.
    We just weren't part of each other's lives and didn't know each other's friends and became disconnected.
    I didn't share enough of my other life with her—the nonsexual part.
    The problem was insularity. She had her world with her friends. I had mine, and we didn't fit in each other's. The strain of living in separate worlds [in a long distance relationship] was just too much—it was fragmenting my life and my sense of self.

The fact that this theme has not been previously noted may reflect its rootedness in women's relational orientation. Prior research's restriction to heterosexual relationships may have obscured interpersonal issues distinctive of the female voice, which is muted by the entrenched power differential in mixed-sex bonds. Women often end relationships that do not support a primary commitment with a man, and they may also suppress dissatisfaction with the couple network just as they have been shown to subordinate other preferences. This issue's prominence in my data supports other findings that lesbian relationships do not require subordination to maintain dyadic harmony.

Personal Autonomy and Self-Knowledge. Roughly equal to relational dynamics as a reason for crises was concern that commitment constrained personal development. Two issues defined this category: conflict between identity and responsibilities of commitment, and dissatisfaction with current self-knowledge. Nearly all respondents mentioned one of these issues.
    Concern that a relationship constricted the self was reported by 15 women, who focused on balancing relationship responsibilities and personal needs. Exemplifying this is an account from a forty-one-year-old:

The problem was being pressured to change in a way that I was not comfortable with. . . . At risk were my sense of self worth and confusion because while wanting and trying to be accommodating, I was ignoring my own needs and wants.

Experience mediated by reflection gave this woman a clear sense of what endangered her. While she wanted to accommodate her partner, neglecting or violating her own identity was too great a cost to incur. Other responses reiterated this theme:

I didn't want a part-time relationship in which I wouldn't have an equal voice in the circumstances of our time.

I wondered if I would ever get my need for conversation/analysis met with her and I knew I couldn't live without this in a lover relationship.

The relationship was destructive for me. I'd been in self-destructive relationships before, and I learned from them what harms me.

You get out because you find you cannot be yourself, and this is never acceptable for either person.

Reflecting a less developed version of this issue was the second theme, which involved incomplete self-understanding that was an issue for 7 women:

[The problem was] my lack of knowledge regarding my own needs of an intimate. . . . Because I couldn't recognize my own needs, I couldn't tell them to her.

Youth—the need to . . . learn what I value. [I] hadn't had enough experience with other women to be sure of any long-term commitment.

There were too many unexplored corners of the world. I had to try these to discover which ones fit with me.

These comments reflect twin beliefs that understanding self is intrinsically important and that only with a settled knowledge of self can one make an honest, informed commitment to another. Without such knowledge, the first writer explained, one cannot collaborate effectively to create a mutually satisfying bond.

Problems in Partners. Less emphasized than relational dynamics and personal knowledge, problems in partners were cited by 14 respondents. Two types of problems were a partner's lack of self-knowledge and value incompatibilities between partners.

The first type mirrored the need for self-knowledge just discussed. Respondents recognized partners' needs to find themselves despite what that implied about ending a valued bond:

My partner tended to lean on me. . . . It made her less than she could be. Her personal growth was impeded.

My lover was 11 years younger. She had not realized her own potential. It became necessary for her to strike out on her own in order to put her life into perspective.

My lover had not been lovers with a man before and needed to figure that out.

My partner . . . loved me but hadn't had enough experience. I knew she needed to learn about herself before she could know what she needed in a long-term relationship.

Particularly interesting is the contrast between lesbian and gay accounts of problems in partners. The women did not express resentment or blame when a partner's needs threatened the bond. In fact, they actively supported partners, even when doing so was painful. Contrary to this were men's inclinations to view partners' needs as burdensome.

The second set of partner problems described by female respondents, incompatibilities in attitudes and values, was reported straightforwardly and requires little interpretation:

I perceived her as controlling.
The sexual problems were unsolvable.
Her need to be superior. Mine to be equal.

These reasons extend the identity issues discussed earlier. If a woman knows herself well enough to realize what she needs and can give to a partner, then certain issues can be identified as irreconcilable, in which case negotiation would be moot. So both gays and lesbians regarded some issues as self-evident reasons to terminate bonds.

The reasons evident in accounts create a coherent picture of issues that precipitate crises in lesbian romantic relationships. The relationship forms the frame. Within that context self and other's needs are seen as legitimate and interwoven, a stance that reflects the interconnectedness of self and other found to be characteristic of the female orientation toward relationships.

Responding to Crises

Paralleling differences in definitions of relationship crises were equally pronounced differences in responses to problems. During crises gay men avoided partners and affirmed their own needs and rights. Lesbians, in contrast, collaborated with partners, reviewed personal needs, and consid-

Table 2
Reported Responses to Crises

Response	% gay men	% lesbians	% total
Relationship Process		49.11	28.00
Discussed with partner	—	21.05	
Maintained connection	—	15.78	
Sought counselling	—	12.28	
Avoiding/Exiting	53.49	—	24.00
Unilateral decision	37.21	—	
Confrontation	9.30	—	
Talked with friends	6.98	—	
Took Care of Self	41.86	24.56	32.00
Questioned self	—	12.28	
Affirmed/honored self	18.60	12.28	
Calculated returns	23.26	—	
Considered Partner	2.33	26.32	16.00
Took partner's perspective	2.33	14.04	
Accommodated partner	—	12.28	
Intercoder Reliability	86.04	85.96	86.00

Note: Percentages are for comments made. Of the 100 coded responses, 57 were from lesbians and 43 were from gay men.

ered partners' perspectives. These differences, like those in definitions of crises, cohere with research on gender socialization.

Gay Responses to Crises

Gay men reported their primary ways of dealing with crises were to exclude partners from decision making (cited by 17 men) and to assure themselves their decisions were fair (cited by 18).

Exclusion of Partner. Fully 85 percent of the men reported avoiding communicating with partners, and only one man mentioned talking with his partner during a crisis. Accounts identified three excluding strategies: unilateral decision making, confrontation, and going to outsiders for personal support.

The most often reported form of excluding partners was refusal to talk until a unilateral decision had been reached:

I didn't talk to him until I'd made up my mind.
   I denied any problems when Mike asked if something was wrong. . . . Then I left and left a terse note.
   After I thought it through I told him of my decision.
   One day I just told my partner I'd found someone else. Then I packed and left.
   I explained how I felt. He did not feel the same way. . . . I told him it was too late.

Evident in these accounts is the view of people as separate, which promotes belief that one is entitled to make unilateral decisions. In turn, this legitimizes excluding partners and withholding perceptions of problems that affect both people. Men who did talk with partners gravitated toward confrontational communication, which precluded problem solving and mutual involvement. Often this took the form of an "announcement" that a relationship was over:

I confronted him and he got angry. I suppose I was insensitive (yelled at him quite a bit and treated him like an inferior child).
   I just exploded. I was pretty insulting and ugly. He left when I told him I didn't want him anymore.
   I did confront him and told him . . . we were through.

These excerpts extend the principle of unilateral decision making to highlight power as an issue. Common to insults, insensitivity, ultimatums, and confrontations is presumption of a power differential that entitles one partner to make and impose decisions affecting both. This hierarchy-bound stance confirms themes in male socialization[35] as well as in Blumstein and Schwartz's finding that the issue of power achieves maximum salience in gay relationships.[36]
   Gay men also reported securing support for their decisions by talking with outsiders predisposed to their viewpoints:

I talked with several friends who would understand how I felt.
   I discussed the relationship with a brother and a friend.
   I couldn't talk with him [partner].
   I talked with friends who supported what I felt.

Seeking counsel with others likely to agree with one's position both excludes partners and protects self-interest. These tendencies were further evident in the second major category of gays' responses to crises.

Self-Interest and Self-Affirmation. Putting self first was mentioned by nearly all gay men and comprised 41.86 percent of their responses. Within this category were two strategies that seemed sequentially related: calculating the balance between rewards and investments and affirming personal rights and decisions.

Ten accounts described computations of exchange, which underlined the independence of partners and reliance on abstract principles to evaluate relationships:

I considered my needs and how much I was having to invest in our relationship. It didn't seem fair because I was putting in more than I was getting.

I weighed out the pros and cons of the relationship and saw the balance was to my disadvantage.

I thought about how much time and energy I was spending propping him up and how much that was taking from me and how little I was getting back.

Weighed the pros (+) and cons (-) of this. Only one (-) and many (+) attributes outweighed it.

I realized I didn't get much in return. It wasn't fair.

These accounts evidence characteristics linked consistently to sex-role socialization. Each account assumes the legitimacy of analyzing a relationship by an abstract formula (e.g., pros and cons, amounts given and gotten) and judging the result of the calculation by an abstract, generalized standard (e.g., fairness, equality of investment and reward). Each account further assumes detachment between the evaluator and the object of evaluation and thus, independence between self and judgment rendered.[37] Gays' conclusions that "it didn't seem fair," "the balance was to my disadvantage," it required more than "I should have to invest" suggest the writers defined themselves as simply implementing standards that existed independent of them. This reflects detachment from the relationship as well as its fate, i.e., judgments follow logically from external standards.

Consistent with the theoretical framework advanced by Gilligan and expanded by Wood, these accounts reveal a relational orientation that regards individuals as separate from others, even intimates, and grounds moral judgments on abstract principles for which fairness is the cornerstone. Equally consistent with research on sex roles and with interpretations previously presented in this study is the unilateral exercise of power assumed by gays in evaluating relationships. Gay men in this study indicated neither efforts to take the role of the other nor recognition of partners' stake in the process and outcome of managing relational stress.

The second strategy in this category, self-affirmation, appeared to grow out of the calculation process—a kind of post-hoc bolstering of a decision that ratified putting their needs first:

I respected my needs and myself. I didn't retreat.
I protected myself and my interests.
I fought for my own needs and values.
I was firm. I respected my rights. I stood my ground.
I did not let my needs and goals get subordinated.
When it came down to it, I needed to help me.

The gay men then affirmed the rightness of their decisions and, thus, the integrity of a unilateral decision-making process:

I was correct in feeling like he should get his finances in order before we lived together.
My decision was right, so it was fair to both of us.
The decision was the correct one.
I was fair in considering both pros and cons of the relationship, so my decision was the only one.

And they celebrated their self-sufficiency:

I realized my personal happiness and well-being were not tied to one relationship.
I had pass [*sic*] the test in that my happiness in life was not dependent on someone else.
I realized how much I loved myself. I was OK in myself.

These accounts award clear priority to the respondents' needs, interests, and rights: when partners' needs conflict, one's own are honored. This hierarchical view of relationships is reflected in the competitive, even combative tone pervading the accounts. Language choices such as "stood my ground," "didn't retreat," and "fought for" suggest respondents conceived crises as competitions in which one person wins at another's expense: battle lines were drawn.

Conceiving relationships hierarchically has been cogently critiqued by Bellah and his colleagues, who expressed concern that the traditional view of love as commitment has been eclipsed by a view that values freedom from obligation to others and self-gratification.[38] Within the morality of rights, responsibility to self is primary, and separation rather than connection is sought.[39] This theoretical explanation provides a coherent view of gay men's responses to relationship crises in this study.

Lesbians' Responses to Crises

Three strategies comprised lesbians' responses to crises: emphasizing the relationship and interaction processes, reflecting on personal identity, and recognizing partners' perspectives. The substantial attention accorded to each supports my prior finding that women seek to balance responsibilities to self, other, and the relationship that connects them.[40]

Emphasizing Relationship and Interaction Processes. In direct contrast to gays' responses to crises, lesbians accorded top priority—both temporal and conceptual—to relationships and the processes that define them. Mentioned by 21 lesbians, this accounted for 49.12 percent of their responses. Comprising this category were three foci: talking with partners, maintaining a connection with partners, and engaging in counseling.

Talking with partners was explicitly cited by 12 women and implied in 8 additional accounts. (Only explicit references were coded.) Typical comments were these:

We tried to talk and work things out.
    We talked together. . . . We're still working on this after two years, but we've come a long way!
    We talked and kept talking until we both felt satisfied with our understandings of each other and what we should do.
    My initial way of dealing with the problem was to avoid seeing [partner]. I felt inadequate and fearful. Still, I knew we should talk and decide together so we did talk a lot and for a long time and we ultimately arrived at a joint resolution—without the extended conversations, painful though it [*sic*] was, we couldn't have achieved this.
    We talked openly with each other so that we each felt we'd been honest and we felt more closure on our relationship.
    Ann and I talked often as we kept trying to make it work—sort of like progress

checks to see how each other was. . . . We finally did split, but we were both glad we worked it through/talked it through together.

Language choices suggest lesbian respondents regarded communication as a responsibility, not merely a prerogative, of intimacy. Reverberating through these accounts is a commitment to mutuality, as underlined by terms such as "we," "until we both felt satisfied," "joint resolution," and "what we should do."

Women also demonstrated high regard for the *process* of communication as a primary means of constructing a joint decision, rather than a forum for announcing a *fait accompli* as it was for some gay men. This supports Rusbult's report that women tend to "voice" problems in an "an attempt to rescue something of value that is in danger of being damaged."[41] The women's criteria for both decisions and sufficiency of talk did not exist *a priori*, but evolved through the process of communicating. For lesbians, adequate talk and satisfactory decisions are collaborative and respectful of communication processes. A second reported means of attending to relationships was efforts to retain a connection with partners. Not necessarily equivalent to continuing the romance, this response focused on maintaining some connection with partners. Emphases on communication and maintaining connections suggest lesbians intrinsically value individuals and relationships rather than regarding them as static and category specific, for example, romance.

Given this, it is not surprising that only 7 did not explicitly mention a continuing relationship with the partner while 5 preserved the romance, and 9 forged friendships after ending the romance. This pattern reinforces the previously noted finding that women conceive themselves within a web of human connections that coheres by continually incorporating new and redefined relationships as it evolves. Lesbian women's accounts affirmed this commitment to relationships:

Anne and I had a history and we had responsibilities to each other, especially not to give up or take the easy out when the going got rough.

By trying to make it work despite all of the problems, we felt we'd been true to our commitment to each other and we'd given the relationship every chance before ending. Only then could we separate with peace and mutual sureness.

We didn't give up just because there was a problem. We both expressed a desire to find ways of making it work.

I was scared, unsure that S and I could work it out, but it surely seemed worth the effort.

We tried to work things out instead of just throwing in the towel when we hit rough times—that wouldn't have been right after we'd been such intimates for so long.

We had helped each other grow in many ways and I thought we could grow from helping each other through this time [of separating] too.

We both believed that a commitment to another is serious and not to be abandoned casually or even with good reason until we (1) understood why we weren't good together anymore and (2) whether that could be changed.

These comments echo the mutuality that characterizes other portions of women's accounts. Respondents' language emphasizes a view of relationships and partners as interdependent: "we had responsibilities to each other," "we'd given the relationship every chance," "we'd been true to our commitment," "mutual sureness," and "we both believed."

A third means of attending to relationships was counseling, which 7 women reported. In describing the value of counseling, respondents indicated understanding relationships is intrinsically important; its value is not contingent on outcome. This buttresses the long-standing finding that women generally adopt a processual, fluid view of interaction and relationships, which fosters a keen awareness of what is happening between people. Men tend to adopt a more instrumental, categorical view of relationships, which subordinates understanding and processual engagement to goal achievement and which defines relationships within relatively exclusive and nonfluid compartments.[42] Thus, if a romance ends, men tend to define the relationship as ended while women seek to redefine the nature of the connection.

Reflection on Personal Identity. Fourteen lesbians reported that self-reflection was one of their responses to intimate crisis. Comprising this category were two complementary themes: self-criticism and recognizing responsibilities to self.

Seven respondents reported confronting personal expectations and shortcomings. An especially articulate thirty-two-year-old woman wrote of her struggle to "realize that, for whatever reason, at any moment I could find myself alone. By wrestling with that fear and incorporating it into my psyche, I have [learned] . . . to juggle the unromantic, scary notion of being alone with the romantic, necessary ability to compromise." Such critical self-scrutiny was reported by other lesbians:

I thought about my feelings and her needs and tried to decide whether I was being unrealistic. . . .
   I sought councelling [*sic*] to understand myself.
   It [the relationship problem] made me seek help and perhaps opened me to really looking at myself honestly.
   I knew I had to help treat the silence and barriers between us.
   I had to acknowledge my own needs, while "okay," were a bit excessive at times.

Respondents insisted on understanding their own feelings and needs, examining their own faults, and—when appropriate—trying to alter their attitudes and actions. Believing that relationship problems result from both partners, lesbians regarded responding to problems as a mutual responsibility. Women's capacity to be self-critical, however, did not entail subordinating self to others. Complementing the focus on critical self-examination was legitimation of personal needs:

To have self-respect, want a relationship that is relatively harmonious and peaceful and mutually other and self-accepting is something I deserve.
   I finally realized that I had certain needs that were important too.
   At the same time [as seeing partner's needs] I had to claim my own feelings and needs. I couldn't just set them aside.

Respondents' dual respect for their own needs and those of others exemplifies Gilligan's argument that as women mature morally they realize that principles of honoring human needs and showing care should not exclude the self. Thus, as women evolve morally, they reconcile the apparent conflict between caring for others and self into a synthetic moral principle that mandates honoring the needs of all humans. Respondents' maturity (mean age of 25.23) enhances the plausibility that many had achieved this stage of development. The third response reported by women further supports this interpretation.

Recognizing Partners' Perspectives and Needs. Cited by 12 lesbians, this response entailed efforts to understand a partner's needs, requests, and view of the situation; and attempts to accommodate a partner by adjusting personal expectations, behaviors, and attitudes.

Eight women reported that understanding their partners' views was essential to their overall response to the crisis. A thirty-nine-year-old woman's account provides a rich example of this:

First I tried to recognize that the fact she didn't talk to me in ways I wanted did *not* mean she didn't care about me and my needs. Second, I tried to give her credit for the changes she *had* made.

This writer first distinguishes clearly the "fact" of unsatisfying communication from inferences about her partner's motives or affection. Adopting a perspective outside of her own, she tolerated the ambiguity of according legitimacy to two divergent definitions of a situation of intense personal salience. Further awareness of her partner's perspective is demonstrated by the second sentence, which acts as a reminder of what the partner has done to accommodate the writer. To make sense of the situation, the writer incorporates her partner's perspective into her own thinking, illustrating lesbians' consistent emphasis on mutuality, prominent throughout the accounts.

I tried to see both sides of the situation, not just say it was S's fault.
 I didn't engage in blaming—focused on understanding both of our feelings without trying to label one right and the other wrong. I claimed my own feelings while respecting hers. I thought a lot first about her needs and problems and my own I stood up for mine while serving hers. It wasn't a zero-sum situation because we wouldn't let it be.

Extending this, a number of women reported efforts to accommodate partners. Illustrative is this response from a thirty-eight-year-old woman who believed in monogamy and whose partner did not:

I had to decide to stop punishing her for hurting me. . . . I decided to stay with her—to see if nonmonogamy were possible. For me it wasn't.

By trying an open relationship, the writer honored her partner's values and the larger value of allowing relationships to evolve and change without *a priori* constraints on the form they may take. Yet the ultimate decision, that nonmonogamy was unacceptable, reveals the writer's refusal to forsake her own now-tested needs and values in deference to those of another. To honor another may require reviewing one's own values, but it does not call for abandoning them. This demonstrates the highest level of women's moral development at which responsibilities to self and other are balanced.

I tried to give her space to figure out she wasn't heterosexual, even though that was painful for me to do. I tried to accept an open relationship, but I couldn't do it. After several months of this trial we split. I thought that I should consider having some of [my] needs met in other relationships with friends. S shouldn't have to provide everything.

Considered in concert, lesbians' responses to crises in close relationships form a coherent picture consistent with Gilligan's theory of the feminine moral stance. The relationship itself is the context within which considerations of self and other are embedded. This reflects a relational orientation in which partners are understood as interdependent and thus responsible to both self and other. Such interdependency entails opening oneself to a far more profound influence from the other than is likely in relationships premised on independence.

Conclusions and Suggestions for Future Research

This study of gay men's and lesbians' accounts of intimate crises yielded six preliminary findings that merit further investigation.

1. Three inductively derived categories of reasons describe crises in gay and lesbian romantic relationships: relational dynamics, need for/threats to autonomy, and problems in partners.
2. Lesbians gave approximately equal value to relational dynamics and autonomy and less to problems in partners.
3. For gays, problems in partners predominated while personal autonomy was moderately important and relational dynamics were only minimally noted.
4. In responding to crises, lesbians reported giving primary attention to the relationship and interaction processes that maximize mutual involvement and understanding. Approximately half as much emphasis was placed on each of the other two responses cited by lesbians: honoring responsibilities to self and showing consideration to partners.
5. The predominant way gay men reported responding to crisis was to

avoid interaction with partners. Gays also described substantial efforts
to protect self-interest.
6. The differences between gay and lesbian accounts represent intensified
versions of well-established gender-based distinctions. Since same-sex
relationships approximate "pure forms" of gender cultures, unique features of each gender's orientation should be more visible than in heterosexual relationships, where each orientation is mitigated by the presence of and accommodations to an alternate orientation.

Strong consistency between my data and studies with larger samples
suggests my findings are more generalizable than sample size alone justi-
fies. Differences between gay men and lesbians' definitions of and responses to crises echo prior findings about distinctions between gay men
and lesbians and between men and women. The coherence between the
data reported here and extant scholarship enhances the weight we may
reasonably attach to both.

My preliminary findings support and extend knowledge about homosexual relationships and gender-linked distinctions in attitude and action. Consistent with Blumstein and Schwartz's report,[43] this investigation found
power to be highly salient in gay relationships but not in lesbian ones.
Equally consistent was the prominence of financial issues in gays' accounts
and their nonsalience in lesbians' accounts. Gay men associated both money
and power with independence, which they valued highly.

Lesbians' construals of and responses to crises echoed Ramsay et al.'s[44]
findings that lesbians' relationship priorities are development, companionship, affection, and open communication. The dual emphases on emotional
closeness and autonomy of each partner support Peplau et al.'s conclusion
that enduring lesbian marriages are characterized by a harmonious blend of
two distinct values: dyadic attachment and autonomy.[45] The data of this
study further intimate, as suggested by Raymond,[46] that these two values
interact: autonomy provides a personal strength that renders attachment to
another nonthreatening to the integrity of self.

This study also adds to the understanding of gender-based distinctions
in how actors define and act within close relationships. Consistent with
Gilligan's theory of divergent paths of male and female moral development,
my respondents embodied two distinct orientations toward relationships.
The approach characteristic of males in this and other studies awards
primacy to individuals rather than relationships, separateness rather than

interdependence, and rules to determine fairness rather than flexible criteria processually derived through the process of a given relationship. In contrast is a second orientation, typical of women in this study and in prior research. Within this view, primacy is accorded to relationships, individuals are considered within that context, interdependence of partners is assumed, and particular relationships provide the basis for deriving criteria to guide interaction and resolution in a mutual, flexible manner characterized by the ethics of care and compassion.

This analysis coheres with Rusbult's findings that males rely on exiting and neglect as responses to crises while females favor loyalty and giving voice to problems.[47] Support was also found for Rusbult and Iwaniszek's finding that males—both heterosexual and homosexual—tend to respond to relational problems by avoiding communication and by leaving, while females—both heterosexual and homosexual—tend to respond with commitment and active efforts to deal with problems.[48]

The consistent and strong findings of distinction suggest relational orientation is a concept with substantial heuristic, integrative, and explanatory power. In addition to its association with gender, relational orientation may be linked to issues such as investments in relationships,[49] role-taking ability,[50] long-term consequences for individual and dyadic health,[51] and styles of loving.[52]

Another issue important to our roles as scholars, teachers, and clinicians is how to present the differences in relational orientations in ways that broaden individuals' understandings and perspectives on human experience. Thus, a priority of scholarship, pedagogy, and counseling is developing vocabularies that as much as possible avoid attaching hierarchical values to different relational orientations and that enhance the possibilities of understanding and appreciating the distinct logic and legitimacy of each.

Notes

1. C. Gilligan, *In a Different Voice: Psychological Theory and Women's Development* (Cambridge, Mass.: Harvard University Press, 1982).
2. Ibid., 1.
3. S. W. Duck, "A Topography of Relationship Disengagement and Dissolution," in *Personal Relationships 4: Dissolving Personal Relationships,* ed. S. W. Duck, 1–30 (New York: Academic Press, 1982).
4. L. A. Baxter, "Strategies for Ending Relationships: Two Studies," *Western*

Journal of Speech Communication 46 (1982): 223–41; L. A. Baxter, "Trajectories of Relationship Disengagement," *Journal of Social and Personal Relationships* 1 (1984): 29–48; L. A. Baxter and J. Philpott, "Attribution-based Strategies for Initiating and Terminating Relationships," *Communication Quarterly* 30 (1982): 217–24.

5. C. T. Hill, Z. Rubin, and L. A. Peplau, "Breakups before Marriage: The End of 103 Affairs," *Journal of Social Issues* 32 (1976): 147–68.

6. M. Cody, "A Typology of Disengagement Strategies and an Examination of the Role Intimacy, Reactions to Inequity, and Relational Problems Play in Strategy Selection," *Communication Monographs* 49 (1982): 148–70.

7. L. A. Baxter, "Gender Differences in Heterosexual Rules Embedded in Breakup Accounts," *Journal of Social and Personal Relationships* 3 (1986): 289–306.

8. R. Bell, *Worlds of Friendship* (Beverly Hills, Cal.: Sage Publications, 1981).

9. Gilligan 1982.

10. J. Lever, "Sex Differences in Games Children Play," *Social Problems* 43 (1976): 478–87; J. Lever, "Sex Differences in the Complexity of Children's Play and Games," *American Sociological Review* 43 (1978): 471–83.

11. N. Chodorow, *The Reproduction of Motherhood* (Berkeley: University of California Press, 1978).

12. J. T. Wood, "Different Voices in Relationship Crises: An Extension of Gilligan's Theory," *American Behavioral Scientist* 29 (1986): 273–301; J. T. Wood, "Engendered Relationships: Interaction, Caring, Responsibility, and Power in Close Relationships," in *Relationship Processes 3: Contexts of Close Relationships,* ed. S. W. Duck (London: Sage, forthcoming); J. T. Wood, "Engendered Identities: Shaping Voice and Mind through Gender," in *Intrapersonal Communication: Different Voices, Different Minds,* ed. D. Vocate (Hillsdale, N.J.: Lawrence Erlbaum, forthcoming).

13. L. A. Baxter and W. Wilmot, "Taboo Topics in Close Relationships," *Journal of Social and Personal Relationships* 2 (1985): 253–69; Z. Rubin, L. A. Peplau, and C. T. Hill, "Loving and Leaving: Sex Differences in Romantic Attachments," *Sex Roles* 7 (1981): 821–35.

14. J. D. Balswick and C. W. Peek, "The Inexpressive Male: A Tragedy of American Society," *Family Coordinator* 20 (1971): 363–68; J. L. Fischer and L. R. Narus, Jr., "Sex Roles and Intimacy in Same Sex and Other Sex Relationships," *Psychology of Women Quarterly* 5 (1981): 444–55.

15. P. Fishman, "Interaction: The Work Women Do," *Social Problems* 25 (1978): 397–406.

16. H. H. Kelley, J. D. Cunningham, J. A. Grisham, L. M. Lefebvre, C. R. Sink, and G. Yablon, "Sex Differences in Comments Made during Conflict within Close Heterosexual Pairs," *Sex Roles* 4 (1978): 473–91.

17. Wood 1986.

18. C. E. Rusbult, "Responses to Dissatisfaction in Close Relationships: The Exit-Voice-Loyalty-Neglect Model," in *Intimate Relationships: Development, Dynamics, and Deterioration,* ed. D. Pereleman and S. Duck (London: Sage, 1987), 209–38.

19. Gilligan 1982; C. Gilligan and G. Wiggins, "The Origins of Morality in Early Childhood Relationships," paper presented at the 1986 Philosophy Colloquium at the University of North Carolina, Chapel Hill.

20. M. Freedman, *Homosexuality and Psychological Functioning* (Belmont, Cal.: Brooks/Cole, 1971); J. Hopkins, "The Lesbian Personality," *British Journal of Psychiatry* 115 (1969): 1433–36; A. K. Oberstone and H. Sukoneck, "Psychological Adjustment and Lifestyle of Single Lesbians and Single Heterosexual Women," *Psychology of Women Quarterly* 1 (1976): 172–88; N. Thompson, R. McCandless, and B. Strickland, "Personal Adjustment of Male and Female Homosexuals and Heterosexuals," *Journal of Abnormal Psychology* 78 (1971): 237–40.

21. K. Mannion, "Psychology and the Lesbian: A Critical Review of the Research," in *Female Psychology: The Emerging Self,* ed. S. Cox (New York: St. Martin's Press, 1981).

22. J. Ramsay, J. D. Latham, and C. U. Lindquist, "Long-term Same-Sex Relationships: Correlates of Adjustment," paper presented at the American Psychological Association Convention, Toronto, Canada, 1978.

23. L. A. Peplau, S. Cochran, K. Rook, and C. Desky, "Loving Women: Attraction and Autonomy in Lesbian Relationships," *Journal of Social Issues* 34 (1978): 29–47.

24. P. Blumstein and P. Schwartz, *American Couples: Money, Work, Sex* (New York: Simon and Schuster, 1985), 53.

25. Ibid., 59.

26. Ibid., 60.

27. Ibid., 179.

28. C. E. Rusbult and J. Iwaniszek, "Problem-solving in Male and Female Homosexual and Heterosexual Relationships," unpublished manuscript, University of Kentucky, Lexington, n.d.

29. J. Raymond, *A Passion for Friends* (Boston: Beacon Press, 1986), 225.

30. C. Geertz, "Blurred Genres: The Refiguration of Social Thought," *American Scholar* 49 (1980): 167.

31. S. Lloyd and R. Cate, "The Developmental Course of Conflict in Dissolution of Premarital Relationships," *Journal of Social and Personal Relationships* 2 (1985): 179–94.

32. Wood 1986.

33. Gilligan and Wiggins 1986.

34. Gilligan 1982: 29–33.

35. J. Lever 1976, 1978; D. Maltz and R. Borker, "A Cultural Approach to Male-Female Communication," in *Language and Social Identity,* ed. J. J. Gumperz (New York: Columbia University Press, 1982).

36. Blumstein and Schwartz 1985.

37. Gilligan 1982.

38. R. N. Bellah, R. Madsen, W. M. Sullivan, A. Swidler, and S. M. Tipton, *Habits of the Heart: Individualism and Commitment in American Life* (Berkeley: University of California Press, 1985).

39. Gilligan 1982: 12–19.
40. Wood 1986.
41. Rusbult 1987: 227.
42. Rubin et al. 1981; A. W. Schaef, *Women's Reality: An Emerging Female System in White Male Society* (Minneapolis: Winston, 1981).
43. Blumstein and Schwartz 1985.
44. Ramsay et al. 1978.
45. Peplau et al. 1978.
46. Raymond 1986.
47. Rusbult 1987.
48. Ibid.; Rusbult and Iwaniszek n.d.
49. M. Lund, "The Development of Investment and Commitment Scales for Predicting Continuity of Personal Relationships," *Journal of Social and Personal Relationships* 2 (1985): 3–23.
50. Gilligan and Wiggins 1986; Wood 1986.
51. Rusbult 1987.
52. C. Hendrick, S. Hendrick, F. Foote, and M. Slapion-Foote, "Do Men and Women Love Differently?" *Journal of Social and Personal Relationships* 1 (1984): 177–95.

15. Gay and Lesbian Couple Relationships

Mary Anne Fitzpatrick, Fred E. Jandt,
Fred L. Myrick, and Timothy Edgar

The study of personal and social relationships blossomed during the eighties. Scholars in a variety of disciplines studied the factors that lead to the initiation, maintenance, and deterioration of the relationships we have with others. Many investigators concluded that it is the communication between partners that accounts for the stability and satisfaction experienced in the relationship (Fitzpatrick 1988; Gottman 1979).

Within the field of communication, the study of communication in relationships has had three main traditions: Relational topoi, relational communication, and relational typology. Relational topoi work has concentrated on examining how different types of relationships manifest different affect, power, and involvement states (Burgoon and Hale 1984). Relational communication work has examined dialogues between partners for what these dialogues say about the essential power relations between them (Rogers-Millar and Millar 1979). And relational typological work has discriminated communication patterns and sequences in types of couples based on their levels of interdependence, ideology, and expressivity (Fitzpatrick 1988).

In this chapter, we adopt the relational typological approach because it subsumes the other two perspectives. The relational typology has been able to predict patterns of relational control in couples (Best 1979; Williamson and Fitzpatrick 1985) as well as patterns of conversational involvement, affect, and self-disclosure (Fitzpatrick 1988). Although we argue for the theoretical inclusiveness of the typological approach, this approach suffers from the same major limitation of the other two traditions. That is, all three have limited their application to ongoing heterosexual relationships. The purpose of this paper is to report the first in a series of typological investigations designed to uncover patterns of communication in ongoing homosexual relationships.

The study of homosexual relationships is important for both conceptual and pragmatic reasons. Society does not provide support for gay couples (e.g., recognized marriages, joint income tax, and so forth). Yet even without these supports, significant numbers of gay men and lesbians have entered into and established ongoing, healthy, functioning relationships. How they have done so, and the varieties of relationships they have maintained, can enrich our understanding of social and personal relationships. In addition to the conceptual richness afforded by studying homosexual relationships, understanding the factors that hold couples together as well as those that drive them apart may help in dealing with the AIDS crisis. Although AIDS represents a serious medical problem, successful interventions require an understanding of relationships.

We review and critique the recent research conducted on homosexual relationships and then present the strategy we employed to study ongoing homosexual relationships.

The Nature of Homosexual Relationships

Although scholars throughout the twentieth century have pursued the study of heterosexual marriages, interest in the investigation of homosexual couples did not begin until the late 1970s. Research with gay men and lesbians was limited because of the difficulty in securing research samples. Many individuals feared participation in research because of concerns about confidentiality. Consequently, many studies sampled only openly gay populations who frequented gay bars (Tuller 1978).

Although sexual activity is only one of several factors that accounts for the development and maintenance of homosexual relationships (Peplau 1982), the most popular means of classifying homosexual couples has been through sexual exclusivity. That is, to what degree are partners sexually faithful to one another? Primarily, researchers have used this variable to create a dichotomous typology. Couples were categorized as either *open* (not sexually exclusive) or *closed* (sexually exclusive). Bell and Weinberg (1978) used the open-closed dichotomy to explain a number of individual differences. For instance, gay males in closed relationships reported higher degrees of self-acceptance. Those in open relationships were significantly more depressed and tense than their counterparts in closed relationships. In terms of relational variables, Blasband and Peplau (1985) found no differences between open and closed couples in their level of satisfaction with, or commitment to, the relationship.

In sum, gay male couples who were sampled in research showed little evidence of relational exclusivity (Harry 1982; McWhirter and Mattison 1984; Tuller 1978), yet clearly had committed relationships (Lewis et al. 1981; Peplau and Cochran 1981). Indeed, Kurdek and Schmitt (1986a) found that both sexually open and closed couples appear to have negotiated satisfying relationships. What appeared to matter was the degree of agreement between partners about sexual exclusivity.

In addition to sexual exclusivity, other relational variables have been examined. For instance, researchers have measured relational cohesion and role adaptability (Zacks, Green, and Marrow 1988), commitment (Lewis et al. 1981), autonomy and attraction (Peplau and Cochran 1981), adjustment (Dailey 1979; Kurdek 1987), relational quality (Kurdek and Schmitt 1986a; Kurdek 1989), satisfaction (Duffy and Rusbult 1986; Kurdek 1988; Kurdek and Schmitt 1986b), and equalitarian decision making (Harry 1982). Similar variable have also been used as a basis for comparing individual differences within homosexual populations (e.g., McWhirter and Mattison 1984) and for comparing heterosexual to homosexual couples (e.g., Blumstein and Schwartz 1983) and lesbian to gay male couples (e.g., Tuller 1978).

Despite the information generated from these studies, much of the research has been limited to exploring only one or two variables. And few papers explore gay male and lesbian relationships with the same framework. To expand our understanding of homosexual relationships, we adopt a polythetic classification approach. Such an approach begins with the assumption that within any sample of couples, a few discrete types exist. And these types of couples communicate in different ways with different outcomes.

A Typology of Marriage

Relational typologies constitute a major breakthrough for therapists/counselors based on the advantages (conceptually and methodologically) of integrating clinical practice, research, and theory. By focusing on couples defined along multidimensional criteria rather than on one or two variables, researchers identify more meaningful and stable relationships between variables. These results can be more easily translated into clinical interventions. Despite the utility of the construct of a marital or family typology, however, many of these typologies are not as helpful because they tend to be intuitively rather than empirically derived (Fitzpatrick 1984). A decade of research by Fitzpatrick (1976, 1977, 1981, 1983, 1984, 1988) has established empirically a typology for characterizing heterosexual couples. (For a comprehensive discussion of the typology's development and validation, see Fitzpatrick 1988.) Briefly, the procedures followed by Fitzpatrick in the typology's development were: (a) identifying significant conceptual areas in marital and family life, (b) developing measures that delineated dimensions of marital life, and (c) comparing spouses' relational definitions to determine types.

The Relational Dimensions Instrument (RDI) identified three dimensions of married life: ideology (e.g., relational beliefs, values, and standards), interdependence (e.g., degree of connectedness), and conflict (e.g., behaviors of avoidance/ engagement). By comparing spouses' responses to the RDI, couple types were characterized as traditional, independent, separate, or mixed. If both spouses agree independently on their relational definition, they are categorized as pure types (i.e., traditional, independent, or separate), whereas husbands and wives who diverge in their perspectives of marriage are classified as mixed couple types.

Traditional couples hold conventional ideological values about relationships (e.g., wives change their last names, infidelity is unacceptable), demonstrate interdependence (e.g., share time, space, companionship), and describe their communication as nonassertive but engage in rather than avoid marital conflicts. By contrast, independents espouse nonconventional values about relational and family life (e.g., relationships should not constrain individual freedom), exhibit a high degree of sharing and companionship that qualitatively differs from traditional couples in that independents maintain separate physical space (e.g., bathrooms, offices), and do not keep regular time schedules yet tend to engage in rather than avoid conflict. Finally, couples who define themselves as separates are conventional on marital and family issues yet at the same time uphold the value of individual freedom over relational maintenance, have significantly less companionship and sharing (e.g., maintain psychological distance, reflect autonomy in use of space), and describe their communication as persuasive and assertive, but avoid open marital conflicts.

Mixed couple types include spouses who define marital life differently according to ideology, interdependence, and communication. Approximately forty percent of couples surveyed fall into one of the mixed types and no one mixed type predominates numerically (Fitzpatrick 1988).

The delineation of a typology of marriage through the use of a carefully constructed and thoroughly tested self-report device that questions spouses about important dimensions of relationships would scarcely be worthy of notice without the variety of methods that have been employed to explore its ramifications. In particular, direct observations have been made of conflict, control, and disclosure processes within marriages of the various types. Expectations about marriage reflected in the typology can help to describe the communication behaviors of the traditional, independents, separates, and mixed couple types during conflicts. The following picture of the various couples emerges from the research on conflict interactions.

Traditionals tend to avoid conflict more than they realize, but in general are cooperative and conciliatory. For these couples, conflicts are somewhat easier to resolve because traditionals tend to argue about content rather than relational issues. Traditionals value parenting, spending time with each other in close proximity, and place marriage (duality) over independence. Of particular note is that although the husband in this marriage is very sextyped in his interpersonal behaviors, this husband is able to self-disclose to his wife.

Independents are constantly renegotiating relational roles and each spouse resents a partner's attempt to avoid conflict by withdrawing. Independents value their careers, coworkers, and friends outside the relationship and need their own personal space. These couples can disclose both positive and negative feelings to their spouses. The downside for independents is that because of their high expressivity, they experience serious conflicts with each other.

Separates touch base with partners regularly but maintain both psychological and spatial distance. Most separates seek emotional support/reinforcement outside the relationship. Overall separates experience little direct conflict in their marriage, for two reasons. First, since separate couples agree with one another on a number of basic family issues, they have less potential for disagreements. Second, separates appear unable to coordinate their interaction effectively enough to engage in a direct open discussion of disagreements. A separate spouse may display outright hostility but quickly retreat if a partner disagrees. In other words, separates rarely discuss conflict and withdraw immediately when spouses introduce stressful topics.

The conflict patterns of the mixed couple types depend on the particular combination of relational definitions under scrutiny. Separate/traditionals rarely argue and when they do the burden of attempting to pen the field for the discussion of difficult issues falls to the wife. In the traditional/independent pairing, the wife is more likely to engage the conflicts and the traditional husband more likely to be conciliatory and prone to compromise.

The mere presence of marital conflict, however, is not an unconditional sign of relational dysfunction. As Fitzpatrick (1988) has shown, many couples (e.g., up to one-third of large research samples) not only agree to disagree, but actually look to their conflict as an important indication that their individual identities have not been subsumed in the relationship. The difference between the conflict-tolerant independent couples and the more conflict-avoidant traditional couples for whom conflict is problematic is one of meaning. Independent couples have established a shared understanding that within their relationship conflict equals success, or at a minimum, conflict is unrelated to love and relational satisfaction.

A Typological Study of Relationships

We began our examination of communication and conflict in homosexual relationships by attempting to categorize a sample of gay male and lesbian couples with the Relational Dimensions Instrument. We believe that in any sample of couples we will find traditional, independent, and separate relational definitions.

In this study, we wanted to examine how the distribution of the relational definitions in a homosexual sample compares to a major random sample of heterosexual couples (Fitzpatrick and Indvik 1982). And we considered differences across the various types of couples on a number of factors such as demographics, sexual exclusivity, and so forth.

Participants for this study were contacted through Couples National Network, an organization formed for purposes of providing social, educational, and humanitarian outreach services to individuals participating in homosexual relationships. With no religious or political affiliation, this organization has chapters in Atlanta, Dallas, Houston, Long Beach, Los Angeles, Phoenix, San Bernardino/Riverside, San Diego, and Tucson. In October 1989, packets were sent to each chapter chair. Each packet contained two questionnaires, two postage-paid return envelopes, and a cover letter explaining the study and asking each person to complete the questionnaire without help from the partner. To ensure complete anonymity, chapter chairs addressed the packets to their members.

In addition to the anonymity assurances, newsletters of the various associations contained requests to participate in the study and an endorsement of the study by the National Network. Packets were provided for about three hundred members. Of these, 163 participants completed our mailed questionnaire. A majority of our respondents were white (92 percent) and middle class (63 percent).

Participants completed the Relational Dimensions Instrument. Using the statistical procedures discussed by Fitzpatrick (1988), 85 participants were categorized as traditionals (51 percent); 33 as independents (20 percent); and 47 as separates (29 percent). How do these percentages compare to a major random sample of heterosexual couples? For gay males, there are approximately the *same* proportion of traditionals, yet significantly *fewer* independents and *more* separates than in the random, heterosexual sample. For lesbians, there were significantly *more* traditionals, *fewer* independents, and *fewer* separates than in the random, heterosexual sample. As we expected, the same three basic definitions of relationship occur in both the homosexual and heterosexual samples. Differences between the two samples occur in the number of traditionals. There are more traditional individuals in the homosexual than in the heterosexual sample.

Of the 163 participants, 15 partners did not respond, leaving us with 74 couples to compute couple type. This sample has the 60 percent agreement rate (i.e., both members assign the relationship to the same type) we find in other samples, indicating that the couples did not compare responses before returning them to us. Of our 74 couples, 28 are traditional, 6 are independents and 10 are separates. The rest are evenly split among the mixed couples (e.g., traditional/independent). Again, in comparison to the random sample of heterosexual couples, traditionals predominate and there are statistically fewer independent couples.

We compared the various types of couples on a variety of sociodemographic factors and found no differences on how long the couple had been together, how they met, age, race, social class, or educational background. Across the couple types, there were no differences in political orientations, in religious faith, in locus of decision control, or in income. Traditional couples were, however, more likely to share their incomes entirely with one another in contrast to the other types. The few sociodemographic differences among the couple types parallel those of the major random sample of relationships. Couple type is a description of the psychological interior of a relationship and is not a measure of social status or demographic factors.

The majority of these couples have a life-long commitment and a high degree of relational satisfaction. Interestingly, however, when there are differences among the couples, the traditionals have somewhat less commitment and relational satisfaction than do the couples with other relationship styles. In other work, the traditionals have the highest level of commitment and satisfaction (Fitzpatrick 1988). In another sharp contrast with previous work, the separates spend significantly more leisure time with one another (91 percent) than do couples in any type of traditional arrangement (58 percent).

Although there were no significant differences by couple type, the majority of individuals we sampled had experienced significant discrimination in reference to family related issues as a consequence of their homosexuality. The majority of our respondents felt discrimination related to hospital visitation rights, adoption, employment benefits for partners, and so forth.

Sexual Issues

There are significant differences across the couple type as to views on monogamy (chi-square = 18.51; df = 10; p < .05). Sixty-eight percent of the total sample are monogamous, although 25 percent of the sample are monogamous with agreed exceptions. Traditionals and traditional/independents have the highest percentage of agreements about nonmonogamy (66 percent and 50 percent).

Our previous comparisons across couple types have grouped the lesbian and gay male couples. We have no theoretical reason to hypothesize, for example, that traditional lesbian couples will be significantly different than gay male couples on the degree of happiness or satisfaction they experience in their relationship. On issues related to sexuality and AIDS, however, we have examined both couple type and sex differences. Notably, for example, a significantly higher proportion of lesbian couples are monogamous (94 percent) in contrast to gay male couples (64 percent).

There are no differences across the couple types as to how many times the partner has broken the monogamy agreement in the relationship, although there are differences among the types concerning how many times the respondent admits to breaking the agreement on monogamy (chi-square $= 36.26$; df $= 15$; $p < .05$). Seventy-two percent of the individuals say they never break their monogamy agreement, although 38 percent of the independents sometimes or occasionally break their agreement. As for sex differences, 70 percent of the gay males and 80 percent of the lesbians have never broken their monogamy agreements. Data from surveys of heterosexual unions indicate that approximately 50 percent of heterosexual couples have broken the monogamy agreement. Thus we could argue that this sample of homosexuals is significantly more conservative about sexuality than similar samples of heterosexuals.

There are differences in the amount of sexual satisfaction experienced in the couple types (chi-square $= 42.01$; df $= 20$; $p < .03$). Only 5 percent of the separates rate their sexual relationship as unsatisfactory, whereas 75 percent of the separate/traditionals see their sexual relationship negatively. There are strong sex differences in discussing levels of sexual satisfaction in the relationship. First, 74 percent of the lesbians rate their sexual relationship as excellent, whereas only 33 percent of the gay males consider their sexual relationship to be excellent. Fourteen percent of the gay men see their relationship as unsatisfactory, compared to 6 percent of the lesbians.

AIDS and Relationships

Although none of the couples were more likely than others to see AIDS as having an effect on the formation of the relationship, there were significant differences across the types as to the effect that AIDS had on intentions to stay together (chi-square $= 23.30$; df $= 15$; $p < .08$). Sixty percent of the couples say that AIDS had no effect on their intention to stay together. The data also suggest that traditionals are more likely to assign AIDS a major role in their intention to stay together. For lesbians, AIDS appears to play little role in either forming (86 percent say none) or maintaining their relationship (89 percent say none). In contrast, about 33 percent of the gay men ascribe to AIDS some role in establishing their relationship and almost 50 percent say that the disease has some role in maintaining their current relationship.

In general, AIDS is of little concern for lesbians in this sample. Overall, 77 percent of the sample is not at risk, although 8 percent rate themselves or their partners as HIV positive or with ARC/AIDS complex. There are significant differences by couple type concerning self risk (chi-square = 24.84; df = 15; p < .05) and partner risk (chi-square = 27.10; df = 15; p < .03). A majority of traditionals (50 percent) and traditional/independents (66 percent) see themselves as at risk.

Sixty-six percent of the subjects had no sex outside of their primary relationship this year, and 63 percent believe this is true for the partner, although 13 percent say they do not know whether or not their partner has had sex with another person in the past year. Only 1 percent say they have had unsafe sex, and less than 1 percent of the respondents believe that their partners have had unsafe sex.

There are significant differences across the couple types in reports of practicing safe sex outside the relationship (chi-square = 32.15; df = 15; p < .006) and perceptions of the partner's practice of safer sex (chi-square = 38.92; df = 20; p < .007). Fifty percent of the traditionals and 50 percent of the traditional/separates have had safer sex outside their relationship within the past year. Sixty-six percent of traditionals say their partners have had safe sex outside their relationship in the past year.

Discussion

There has been little effort to examine homosexual couples by applying typological frameworks developed within the literature on heterosexual couples. Our initial investigation is very promising. First, we have been able to clearly and unambiguously categorize couples using the RDI. Second, this categorization has discriminated couples on specific sexual and relational variables although not on the sociodemographic ones. This pattern of findings is in line with our previous work on heterosexual couples. That is, couple type measures different states of relationship and not a couple's place in the demographic strata.

The homosexual sample differs from previous samples in that there are significantly fewer independent couples in the homosexual sample than in previous heterosexual samples. Since our sample was not a random one, what can account for this difference?

One explanation may be that our respondents were significantly more likely to be integrated into the homosexual community. Since we contacted these individuals through an organization that supports positive aspects of relationships, we may have tapped a sample of individuals with close network ties. In a classic study, Harry and Lovely (1979) found that individuals who were most integrated into the gay community were in relationships that were more "marriage-like." That is, they tended to live more often with their lovers and had monogamous arrangements and more emotional intimacy. Their social lives were also more likely to include relationships with other homosexual couples.

Within the terms of the typology, such individuals are more likely to have traditional orientations toward relationships. Some of those will pair this traditional orientation with a close interdependent bond (i.e., traditionals) and others will pair that ideology with a less connected bond (i.e., separates).

Alternatively, in the absence of socially provided supports for relationships, homosexuals may be more likely to "act out" traditional understandings of ongoing relationships. Rather than define new relationship patterns for same-sex couples, homosexual couples may be more likely to "act out" their understanding of a stable relationship first presented to them in their birth family. Same-sex couples may have discovered that relationship stability is facilitated by traditional patterns. Thus it is not surprising that traditionals report the greatest role that AIDS has in maintaining their relationship. The threat may reinforce the need to maintain the relationship pattern.

It is particularly pointed, then, that the areas of reported discrimination are in the areas of traditional "family" rights (i.e., hospital visitation, adoption and employment benefits). Society may have become more accepting of individual gay men and lesbians, but it may ironically still reject gay couples who are more likely to be traditional in values and roles than heterosexual couples.

The research discussed in this chapter was supported in part by a Vilas Professorship awarded to the first author. Postage and printing were provided by a grant from the Office of Academic Resources, California State University, San Bernardino. The authors would like to thank Couples National Network, Inc., for distributing questionnaires to their members and also the Newsletter for Gay and Lesbian Couples for their permission to adopt a version of their national survey of lesbian and gay couples.

Works Cited

Bell, A. P., and M. Weinberg. 1978. *Homosexualities: A Study of Diversity among Men and Women.* New York: Simon and Schuster.

Best, P. 1979. "Relational control in marriage." Master's thesis, University of Wisconsin, Milwaukee.

Blasband, D., and L. A. Peplau. 1985. "Sexual exclusivity versus openness in gay male couples." *Archives of Sexual Behavior* 14: 395–412.

Blumstein, P., and P. Schwartz. 1983. *American Couples.* New York: William Morrow.

Burgoon, J. K., and J. L. Hale. 1984. "The fundamental topoi of relational communication." *Communication Monographs* 51: 193–214.

Dailey, D. M. 1979. "Adjustment of heterosexual and homosexual couples in pairing relationships: An exploratory study." *Journal of Sex Research* 15: 143–57.

Duffy, S. M., and C. A. Rusbult. 1986. "Satisfaction and commitment in homosexual and heterosexual relationships." *Journal of Homosexuality* 12: 1–23.

Fitzpatrick, M. A. 1976. "A typological examination of communication in enduring relationships." Ph.D. diss., Temple University.

———. 1977. "A typological approach to communication in relationships." In *Communication Yearbook* 1, ed. B. Rubin, 263–75. Rutgers: Transaction.

———. 1981. "A typological approach to enduring relationships: Children as audience to the parental relationships." *Journal of Comparative Family Studies* 12: 81–94.

———. 1983. "Predicting couples' communication from couples' self-reports." In *Communication Yearbook* 7, ed. R. N. Bostrom and B. H. Westley, 49–82. Beverly Hills, Calif.: Sage.

———. 1984. "A typological approach to marital interaction: Recent theory and research." In *Advances in Experimental Social Psychology,* vol. 18, ed. L. Berkowitz, 1–47. Orlando, Fla.: Academic Press.

———. 1988. *Between Husbands and Wives.* Newbury Park, Calif.: Sage.

Fitzpatrick, M. A., and J. Indvik. 1982. "The instrumental and expressive domains of marital communication." *Human Communication Research* 8: 195–213.

Gottman, M. M. 1979. *Marital Interaction: Experimental Investigations*. New York: Academic Press.

Harry, J. 1982. "Decision making and age differences among gay male couples." *Journal of Homosexuality* 8: 9–21.

Harry, J., and R. Lovely. 1979. "Gay marriages and communities of sexual orientation." *Alternative Lifestyles* 2: 177–200.

Kurdek, L. A. 1987. "Sex role self schema and psychological adjustment in coupled homosexual and heterosexual men and women." *Sex Roles* 17: 549–62.

———. 1988. "Relationship quality of gay and lesbian cohabitating couples." *Journal of Homosexuality* 16: 91–115.

———. 1989. "Relationship quality in gay and lesbian cohabitating couples: A 1-year follow-up study." *Journal of Social and Personal Relationships* 6: 39–59.

Kurdek, L. A., and J. P. Schmitt. 1986a. "Relationship quality of gay men in closed or open relationships." *Journal of Homosexuality* 12: 85–99.

———. 1986b. "Relationship quality of partners in heterosexual married, heterosexual cohabitating, and gay and lesbian relationships." *Journal of Personality and Social Psychology* 51: 711–20.

Lewis, R. A., E. B. Kozac, R. M. Milardo, and W. A. Grosnick. 1981. "Commitment in same-sex love relationships." *Alternative Lifestyles* 4: 22–42.

McWhirter, D. P., and A. M. Mattison. 1984. *The Male Couple: How Relationships Develop*. Englewood Cliffs, N.J.: Prentice-Hall.

Peplau, L. A. 1982. "Research on homosexual couples: An overview." *Journal of Homosexuality* 8: 3–8.

Peplau, L. A., and S. D. Cochran. 1981. "Value orientations in the intimate relationships of gay men." *Journal of Homosexuality* 6: 1–9.

Rogers-Millar, L. E., and F. E. Millar. 1979. "Domineeringness and dominance: A transactional view." *Human Communication Research* 5: 238–46.

Tuller, N. R. 1978. "Couples: The hidden segment of the gay world." *Journal of Homosexuality* 3: 331–43.

Williamson, R. N., and M. A. Fitzpatrick. 1985. "Two approaches to marital interaction: Relational control patterns in marital types." *Communication Monographs* 52: 236–52.

Zacks, E., R. J. Green, and J. Marrow. 1988. "Comparing lesbians and heterosexual couples on the circumplex model: An initial investigation." *Family Process* 27: 471–84.

16. Reflections on Interpersonal Communication in Gay and Lesbian Relationships

Dorothy S. Painter

Providing commentary for a section as broad as this one on interpersonal communication is a task both maddeningly complex and also delightfully challenging. The methodologies significantly differ, the perspectives and assumptions concerning what one does and how one measures assumed-to-exist factors such as intention and impact differ, and the results bear little resemblance to one another in either form or structure. Clearly, these collective authors are different people, studying different things, using different methods, and professing different assumptions all leading to different interpretations of the things they call results. An interesting experiment might be to have each of the sets of authors interpret one another's results for the differing conclusions that might be drawn. What is is not what is, after all; what is is how what is is interpreted. Hence, the interpretative process is the underlying sense behind all interpersonal communication as it attempts to investigate how people communicate with one another and the strategies they employ. The cautious reader will always read insight-professing social science research with an eye toward questioning the underlying assumptions and their necessary influence on both the questions asked and the responses constructed and offered as answers.

All three of the articles in this section build both their questions and their answers from their theoretical assumptions, and all three are quite clear in this regard. The piece by Edgar is well grounded in the literature of self-disclosure research and not only follows the pattern of such research — although in a more qualitative style than some of the cited articles — but also uses three primary dimensions for analysis that are derived utilizing concepts previously developed in self-disclosure research in conjunction with the current study's data. Disclosure strategies can then be scaled on three dimensions: direct-indirect, initiated-noninitiated, and justified-nonjustified. By building within the self-disclosure framework of research, Edgar can then demonstrate how the communication patterns of gay men in self-disclosure situations fit or do not fit with what is known within the discipline, as well as add to the knowledge base of that particular area of communication research. Edgar further enhances understanding in the self-disclosure field by focusing on actual events and avoiding the artificial atmosphere of the research laboratory.

Although beginning her study by laying some groundwork in traditional communication research that focuses on relationship/couple communication, Wood leads her readers further and further into the psychological theories of Carol Gilligan until it is clear that Gilligan's work forms the basic underlying assumptions of Wood's research. Whether readers derive useful information from Wood's article depends largely upon their dedication to the inherent interdisciplinary nature of the social sciences and their understanding and acceptance of Gilligan's work. If a reader loves Gilligan, she will enjoy this piece for the concrete support it can be seen as providing; if a reader disagrees with Gilligan, she will probably question many of Wood's interpretations and conclusions. Also a qualitative piece, Wood uses percentages of responses coded as fitting within particular psychologically derived categories to discuss different communication strategies used by gay men and lesbian women for dealing with self-defined crisis in a primary relationship. Interestingly, the crises the respondents chose to report upon (and Wood chose to share with her readers) are almost all focused on relationship termination, rather than crisis resolution that produces other outcomes. Although Wood does not discuss this, it may well speak quite loudly about how we, as gays and lesbians, define crisis in our lives and what we expect as the outcome of such an event. That is, we may define a crisis as conflict within a primary relationship of sufficient magnitude to result in relationship termination.

If this is so, then Wood's results could be reinterpreted as strategies for relationship termination rather than crisis management (when crisis is used in a broader sense as it is in much of communication research). If the men and women in Wood's study are really doing the same thing (ending a primary relationship), the interest, then, is not so much on the strategies they employ but the *way they talk about it.* Rather than support the notion that women and men are vastly different in their styles of communication (which is seen as flowing from the inherent differences in the value systems and moral development of women and men), one could reinterpret the respondents' self reports to examine how men and women talk about the same type of event differently and how they talk about their talk reflexively.

The gay and lesbian couple relationship article by Fitzpatrick, Jandt, Myrick, and Edgar begins with a strong grounding within the area of relational topology much the same way that Edgar's piece alone is clearly grounded within its traditional communication genre. Of benefit to the reader, the distinctions among relational topoi, relational communication, and relational topology are explicated well. Also similar to an assumption made by Edgar that a finite number of identifiable communication dimensions exist, the study produced by Fitzpatrick, Jandt, Myrick, and Edgar assumes that a finite number of discrete relationship types exist that can be identified. Further, the authors assume that different relationship types contain different communication styles and strategies that produce different outcomes. Also, much as Edgar's work utilizes previous research in the area to generate communication dimensions, this study relies on previously developed and tested dimensions of "married life" to construct different types of relationships: traditional, independent, separate, or mixed. The Fitzpatrick, Jandt, Myrick, and Edgar research examines both lesbians and gays, as does the article by Wood. Further, it compares the results from the lesbian and gay subjects to results found in previously sampled heterosexual populations.

In reading these three articles, two issues of justification are particularly striking. First, all three articles claim or strongly imply that part of the importance of their research is that it can be used to increase knowledge of *all* people, both homosexual and heterosexual. In Wood's article, she talks about differing female and male forms or styles of communication and proposes that past studies utilizing presumed-to-be heterosexual subjects in mixed-sex dyads confounds the forms or styles somewhat, as individuals work to accommodate the differing style of the opposite sex partner. In lesbian and gay partnerships, however, she states that one may see a more pure form of the sex-specific communication strategies that flow from the differing underlying value systems that Gilligan suggests. If this is so, then one must take a rather essentialistic view of communication style with women and men having innate forms that can be more easily seen when not confounded through opposite-sex interaction. Of course, a more social constructionist view would have subjects interacting very differently in same-sex and opposite-sex interactions with the bulk of the work being done to accommodate and make sense of the interaction as ongoing process.

The article by Edgar speaks of the communication strategies employed by gay men to self-disclose their sexual orientation as perhaps providing information generalizable to other stigmatized groups and their patterns of self-disclosure. The underlying assumption of stigmatization, as described by Erving Goffman, and the effect of a "spoiled" identity, suggests that certain communication strategies may be inherent to the management of a socially discredited identity; and that through the study of groups such as gay men, we may come to learn more about the ways in which members of other socially stigmatized groups publicly manage their identities as well.

The Fitzpatrick, Jandt, Myrick, and Edgar piece is straightforward in its grounding in research of both heterosexual couples and gay male couples, with little reported about lesbian couples research. Their research seems to function for two purposes: to utilize a relational topological approach previously applied to only heterosexual couples such that the results may be compared across sexual orientations, and to broaden the understanding of personal relationship communication as a general field of study. Hence, although the area of gay and lesbian communication is enhanced by their study, the authors emphasize the broader applicability by tying it to the body of research using heterosexual couples.

That all three articles in some way tie the importance of their results to heterosexuals as either a comparison to heterosexuals, a more pure understanding of a phenomenon accomplished by heterosexuals, or an aid to heterosexual clinicians in understanding their gay clients raises questions concerning how we feel we must justify the study of our own population by claiming benefit to the heterosexual majority. Of course, most studies hint at some broader applicability than the specific limitations of the study itself, and some come right out and suggest generalizability. However, perhaps due to the heterosexual as norm phenomenon, when we (lesbian and gay researchers) do studies of gay and lesbian populations, there is a tendency to specifically name and attempt to show specific relevance to the hetero-sexual majority.

This is not meant as a criticism of these authors, but merely an observa-tion that this phenomenon is embedded in much of our research, and we need to be aware of what we are telling our readers and ourselves about who and what is important. What is important is clearly what is powerful, and within the field of communication (and other scholarly disciplines and indeed all of society), the power is still held firmly by a predominantly assumed-to-be heterosexual majority. The question then becomes, does this majority (or the few powerful individuals who drive this majority) care enough about what they can learn about themselves through our research to justify our embedding their importance in the work that we do? Will they benefit us enough (through accepting our research as "legitimate") to justify the ever-present message that we study ourselves not just to study ourselves but to benefit the majority (who are constantly being studied and written about) as well? Without falling back upon undefined psychological terms, how do these messages affect our sense of self-value and self-worth? What message does it send to young gay and lesbian researchers and what does it tell the heterosexual majority about how much we value ourselves? My attempt here is not to demonstrate political naivety, but to call into question this important issue such that each individual writing a study of lesbian and gay people must consciously decide what type of rationale to include instead of following what seems to be generally prac-ticed.

One other striking feature in the rationales of these works is the degree to which they are in some way tied to the expanding field of applied communication. Once seen as a less than charming reason for doing re-search, applied communication has become more respectable in recent years, as can be seen in the newly released official journal of the Speech Communication Association, *Journal of Applied Communication Research.* The applied nature of the rationales is related to members of the gay and lesbian community acting as service consumers primarily in areas of counseling or human services. Edgar talks about the need of clinical psychologists and other similar professionals to gain insightful information to help them inform their patients concerning how to disclose potentially painful information; Wood states that professional counselors need informa-tion to help them work with lesbian and gay couples; and the article by

Fitzpatrick, Jandt, Myrick, and Edgar suggests that the information provided about couples can be used by professionals in dealing with the AIDS crisis.

On one level it seems critical that we provide this information for lesbian, gay, and straight professionals who work in sensitive areas with members of the lesbian and gay community. Clearly, this type of applied research is of benefit to all of us if it is utilized by community service providers. However, as we spend our limited energy and resources providing this information to an assumed-to-be largely heterosexual group, we must continue to ask ourselves what work is *not* being done because of the emphasis placed on this work, who primarily benefits from our work, and when professionals are going to accept the responsibility of educating themselves instead of expecting us to do it for them. If we are treated badly by the professional clinician due to her or his ignorance concerning gay men and lesbian women, is it our fault as professionals for not providing enough easily accessible information, or does the responsibility lie squarely with the professional to seek out his or her own education? This does not mean that it would be desirable to have heterosexuals determining the assumed-to-be norms of the lesbian and gay communities. It does, however, suggest that gay and lesbian researchers should be able to balance their research agendas to investigate the lesbian and gay communities for their own sake and not always as a benefit for some other group.

All three of the articles presented here raise important issues for the gay and lesbian communities, and all three point to areas of future research through both what they discuss and what they indirectly, and perhaps unintentionally, suggest. Edgar suggests the most complex model of communication that hints strongly at multiple registers of meaning embedded in subjects' utterances. How one goes about *talking as normal* as a member of a specific speech community reflects how skilled one is at managing various levels of reality simultaneously. Artful self-disclosure may be conceived more as how one talks about a subject than what one says. Following this line of reasoning leads one in two separate directions. First, it suggests that professionals need to realize that they cannot provide answers to clients' questions if those questions are asking "what" oriented questions; they need to know more about artful communication practices for an extremely complex communicative group. Second, it points to a need for future studies that examine in depth how various aspects of meaning are accomplished by gay and lesbian speakers. Since identity is often a key element in "reading" the meaning of an utterance of a given speaker, we need to be concerned with how the hiding or shading of this identity complicates the sense-making process. As such, statements that self-disclose information about one's identity serve to potentially change the interpreted meaning of all utterances including the self-disclosure message itself. How gay and lesbian speakers artfully accomplish the management of identity and meaning simultaneously both within and outside of their communities is a research area that can be broken down into numerous specific studies, each focusing on one particular aspect of lesbian and gay talk.

Wood provides fascinating examples of responses from her subjects, and the richness of this talk and the detail it provides suggest a number of issues for the lesbian and gay communities and further research topics. All of Wood's subjects report a dissatisfaction within a primary relationship caused by a weakness or flaw in their partner, not themselves. None of them said that they lacked money or social skills or the ability to emotionally care for themselves. The closest any of them got to discussing personal vulnerability was to report an unwillingness or inability to constantly give to an overly demanding partner. None of the subjects reported a personal inability to maintain autonomy within a relationship. I kept wondering, where are all the "weak" partners and why don't they ever get in studies? What Wood suggests to us is that relationships get talked about in some very specific ways that upon analysis might tell us many things about the underlying assumptions and values we share within our communities about the partnerships we form and the ways in which we interact with one another. Through an analysis of the talk provided, one might begin to unravel the complex set of assumptions concerning how we structure our families, how we constitute them, and how we verbally maintain a sense of their reality in a society that not only provides no social supports or recognitions for them, but openly denies the legitimacy of gay and lesbian partnerships.

The article by Fitzpatrick, Jandt, Myrick, and Edgar also speaks to the subject of gay and lesbian partnerships in terms of their internal structure and the external denial of, or at least lack of support for, gay and lesbian relationships on the part of society. How members of the lesbian and gay communities respond to events and crises within their communities and lives given the lack of societal support structures is a subject that permits examination of how the very nature of the concept of "community" is constituted and maintained. Areas of lesbian and gay people's lives usually made invisible by the lack of societal recognition and legitimacy may be made apparent through the study of communicative data generated from within the communities. Two primary categories of life events are those celebratory ones that lack recognition (including family maintenance) and those involved with loss that lack support (such as loss of a long-term partner and the bereavement process).

Returning to the Edgar article for a moment, it would be interesting to ask how the general self-disclosure patterns utilized by gay men to disclose orientation to noncommunity members compare to self-disclosure strategies used both within the community among members and outside the community to self-disclose other types of stigmatized identity such as HIV status. Do common patterns exist or are different strategies employed? More specifically, does the type of information potentially disclosed determine the strategy employed and are some strategies employed with only certain types of information?

Overall, the study of gay and lesbian interpersonal communication allows us to explore and illustrate the very nature of how we do who we are. Lesbian and gay individuals are unique as members of a stigmatized group, inasmuch as other stigmatized groups are either a lifelong identity with a biological family group and membership identity begun in childhood (race, religion), or not an identity one uses as a basis for the formation of community (ex-convicts, ex-mental patients, epileptics). Aided by the lack of societal support for the gay and lesbian communities that often camouflages the tentative nature of taken-for-granted structures, it is possible to see how communication works on a constitutive level to actually do the interpretative meaning of our sense of reality. The complexity and fluidity of lesbian and gay communication demand highly skilled and artful practices; and through the study of these practices, communication scholars may gain a more comprehensive and in-depth understanding of the very nature and process of interpersonal communication.

PART FIVE

Coming Out in the Classroom

17. Performing the (Lesbian) Self: Teacher as Text

Jacqueline Taylor

College teaching is not new for me; I have been teaching full-time for more than twelve years. The stagefright I experienced in the first few terms now seems a distant memory. So why is it that when the work in question is authored by Adrienne Rich, May Sarton, Olga Broumas, Elizabeth Bishop, or Gertrude Stein, my palms grow sweaty and my heart starts to pound? What's a seasoned teacher like me, one who has stood in front of hundreds of students to talk about literature and performance, doing with performance anxiety? The answer is that my anxiety is a particular species of performance anxiety, anxiety about what part of myself to reveal to the class as I, a lesbian feminist teacher, teach the works of these lesbian authors. What persona shall I assume as we discuss these works?

The act of teaching any subject is an act of performance. We assume the persona we believe will best facilitate learning. We make decisions about what aspects of ourselves to reveal as we explore various aspects of literature. But when the literature and the teacher are both lesbian, the issues involved in this performance of the self are particularly loaded.

Back in the good old prefeminist, prestructuralist, and pre-Stonewall days, the answer to this question of what persona to assume must have been more clear-cut. One simply did not deal with sexual orientation in the classroom. I graduated from college in 1973 (I realize that this date is not, strictly speaking, prefeminist, prestructuralist, and pre-Stonewall, but at the small college I attended in Kentucky, and I suspect at many large metropolitan institutions as well, it might as well have been) with an English major without having heard it whispered that Walt Whitman, Virginia Woolf, and Willa Cather were anything other than heterosexual. If my professors knew differently, they weren't telling. If the author's sexual orientation was not considered in the classroom, the teacher's sexual orientation was an even more profoundly forbidden topic, except, of course, in the sort of speculative gossip we all participated in about our teachers but never like to imagine ourselves the subject of.

Well, times have changed. It is no longer unusual to bring information about the sexual orientation of lesbian and gay authors into classroom discussions of these writers' works. Judy Grahn traces a lesbian poetic tradition in *The Highest Apple* (1985). Bonnie Zimmerman's interpretive volume, *The Safe Sea of Women: Lesbian Fiction 1969–1989* (1990), like-wise posits a lesbian tradition. Mark Lilly's anthology, *Lesbian and Gay Writing* (1990), assumes the significance of the writer's sexual orientation. Gay studies, lesbian studies, and/or queer studies receive regular mention in academic writing, university press catalogues, and papers at academic conferences, if somewhat less frequently in many curricula. And women's studies has moved from the early calls for the inclusion of women authors in literature courses to an increasingly sophisticated body of feminist theory, including theories about feminist pedagogy.

Feminist pedagogy, solidly grounded in feminist theory, does the fol-lowing:

1. Actively resists sexism and the network of interlocking systems of oppression that help to keep it in place, including racism, classism, ageism, anti-Semitism, and of course, heterosexism.
2. Explodes the myth of objectivity. There is no neutral position. Every-body, by definition, has a point of view.
3. Asks for a multiplicity of speaking subjects to describe their subjective truths. We have some hope of knowing what the whole looks like if all the different parts explain themselves.
4. Values the personal as a means of knowing. Freed from the tyranny of the objective fallacy, we can begin to acknowledge the power of personal experience as a source of knowledge. This is, of course, what "the personal is political" means.

5. Critiques hierarchical structures including the teacher-student hierarchy.

Performance of literature, the subspecialty of communication within which I teach literature, is well-positioned to take advantage of feminist and post-structuralist insights. Well before feminism and post-structuralism had an impact on the academy, performance studies proponents maintained that in entering into the particular voice of an other we can break down egocentrism and solipsism.[1] All we who teach performance know that our students are engaged in a particularly personal kind of self-disclosure, even as they struggle to take on the persona of another self. So now we have feminist pedagogy and principles of performance all in support of a lesbian voice at the head of the class. Yet the issue remains complex.

Performance lives in the body. And my body tells me that feminist teaching in general, and teaching lesbian literature in particular, is both vital and dangerous for me. Not to cover these topics, to participate in the construction of the silence that surrounds lesbian lives, is not neutral but is an act of homophobia. It helps to keep prejudice against lesbians and gay men intact. But even to teach as a feminist makes one a lesbian suspect.[2] To teach about lesbians makes one more so. I fear the loss of my credibility, fear that once my students pigeonhole me as a lesbian, they can readily dismiss anything else I might have to say. As one professor expressed it, "It's as if there's this sort of screen: No matter what you talk about, it's coming from a lesbian."[3]

And although I tell myself that these worries are paranoid, the fact remains that I could lose my job. I am teaching, after all, at a Catholic university. A Catholic university whose president withdrew a speaking invitation to Eleanor Smeal a few years back because of her association with the National Organization for Women's stand on abortion.[4] A Catholic university that prides itself on its tolerance and even valuing of diversity, but one where a rather eminent lesbian feminist philosopher was denied tenure a few years ago. According to the oral tradition, it is a good place to be a gay or lesbian faculty member, but when I look around at my gay and lesbian colleagues, I come to the conclusion that that means it's OK to be out to your peers, but keep quiet about it around the students. And with all but your closest friends among the faculty or those you know to be gay, keep quiet about it as well. According to the oral tradition, a gay male professor came out to the vice president and dean of faculties a few years ago. She assured him that she had known he was gay all along, and that DePaul did not care what he did with his personal life as long as he behaved professionally. But I do not know what phrases like that mean. If it means keep your hands off your students, I have nothing to worry about. If it means, be a well-rounded scholar, teacher, committee member, I think I'm OK. But if it means, as I strongly suspect it might, that your sexuality is your own private business and as long as it stays private, as long as you do not mention it in the classroom, we will not object, then I have reason to worry.

When I teach narrative, I talk about the way the author selects a selected self from the total complex of human qualities she or he possesses a selected self as the authorial presence, the implied author, of the text. To illustrate the concept, I talk about the teacher persona I draw on in the classroom and her distinction from the persona who writes letters to my mother who is further distinct from the persona who visits my best friend in California.

I realize that we select aspects of ourselves to present in different situations and that certain kinds of personal information do not belong in the classroom. Part of the problem, though, is the heterosexist notion that one's sexual orientation (preference, it is usually called, as if I ended up a lesbian by thumbing through a lifestyle catalogue and deciding that although many of the options were nice, my personal preference was for women) is a private matter. This notion derives, I believe, from the assumption that my lesbianism can be reduced to the fact that I have sex with a woman. What we do in bed, people in our culture agree, is a private matter and certainly not appropriate for the classroom. In point of fact, however, being a lesbian is a much more profound and encompassing identity than this reductionist conception admits. When I became a lesbian, I did not merely turn to another page in the sexual preference menu. I experienced an ontological shift. And as is the nature of ontological shifts, when the earth stopped moving, nothing in my world looked the same as it had looked before. In a profound way, as a lesbian-feminist in a heterosexist world, I view dominant culture from the margins. It is a marginality that I find extraordinarily productive, for it has made starkly clear to me the limitations of any single view of the world and has in a personal way exploded the myth of objectivity. I am not interested in a debate about whether the insights I have gained in this way are unavailable by any other means. The important point is that if I am to adequately account for how I see things from where I stand, I have to account for that in a lesbian voice. And teaching in a lesbian voice (the only authentic teaching voice I possess) while remaining partially closeted in the classroom is an exercise in schizophrenia.

Faced with this dilemma, I have tried to teach in a way that makes me visible to those students who need to know that I am a lesbian while allowing those who need to ignore it to do so. Here is how I do it: I am entirely out to my colleagues—bringing my partner to school functions, serving as moderator for a gay and lesbian student group, and even presenting a workshop for faculty on the gay and lesbian community in Chicago. In the classroom my approach is more guarded. I take a strong stand against homophobia and heterosexism. In literary texts, this means that if a text is heterosexist in its values, we talk about it. It means that homophobic remarks by students are challenged just as racist and sexist remarks are challenged. In discussions I allow for the possibility that not all relationships are heterosexual. I make lesbians and gay men visible, by talking about them whenever they would logically come up in class discussions if we were not all under pressure all the time to engage in a conspiracy of silence. When I am talking about heterosexuals, I *say* heterosexuals. In a less heterosexist world, these behaviors would not be taken as evidence of my lesbianism. Heterosexual teachers need to join gay and lesbian teachers in avoiding heterosexual presumption. Unfortunately, it is a rare heterosexual teacher who teaches as if there were gay men and lesbians in the world.

What I usually do not do is say "we." And I do not talk about my partner or my family in ways that reveal my membership in a lesbian household. Consequently I obscure and deny one of my own sources of insight into and information about lesbian texts, heterosexist literature, and what it means to be marginalized and alienated. When the topic is human communication, I also obscure one of my sources of insight into human communication, gender relationships, and human relationships. If this does not seem peculiar to you, then try to imagine an African-American instructor teaching James Baldwin or Richard Wright or Nikki Giovanni or Toni Morrison and talking about African Americans as "they." Try to imagine a performance class in which this African-American instructor talked about African Americans as if they were separate from herself. Try to imagine her never bringing her personal experience of having black skin in racist white America to bear on the discussion.

Is my approach working? By some measures, it is working well. I have my job, I have tenure, I have the respect and trust of my colleagues to the extent that they have elected me to a college-level personnel committee and the faculty council, and I chair my department. Lesbians and gay men recognize me and come to me outside class to talk about themselves or about what it means to them to have a visible lesbian teacher. Students whose parents are gay or lesbian drop in and talk about the difference they feel from other students and their struggles to "come out" about their family members. Young women and men struggling to come to grips with their sexual orientation also recognize me, and these too occasionally come to talk about their fears that they might be lesbian or gay. I suspect there are many others who never have the nerve to broach the subject, but who take courage from the knowledge that they are not the only ones who find themselves at odds with a heterosexual world. These young people desperately need role models who can counter the stereotype of the lonely, bitter gay man or lesbian doomed to a life of isolation, or even visible evidence that the silence about the lives of lesbians and gay men is a lie. Many of the heterosexual students recognize me as a lesbian as well, and perhaps in some cases knowing me makes it a little more difficult for them to hold on to the heterosexist prejudices so common in our culture.

One male student reported to me a conversation with another young man in his performance of literature class: "She's a good teacher," my friend was told, "but she's a lesbian." "Yes, I know," my friend replied. "That's one of the things I like about her. We have something in common." It is a fun story, but it makes absolutely clear where on the balance sheet my lesbianism lies for many students—if I am a good teacher, they reason, it is in spite of the fact, not because, I am a lesbian.

On the whole, I think my approach is working. But it is costly. In all honesty, it is costly in both directions. On the one hand it is frightening to be as out as I am in the classroom. On the other hand, it is costly to dissemble at all, to say "they" when I mean "we," to keep silent about experience that is absolutely germane to our discussion. I have identified in this essay much of what I believe to be at stake when I choose my teaching persona: my credibility, my job, feminist principles, the fullest possible reading of the literature, nonheterosexist teaching, visibility of lesbian and gay role models, breaking down homophobic stereotypes. Most crucially, though, what is at stake is my integrity. If I am to have the power of my own voice, I must acknowledge that it is a lesbian voice. Anything less than that is death to the spirit.

Notes

1. The work of Wallace Bacon is strongly identified with this argument. See, for instance, his textbook, *The Art of Interpretation*. New York: Holt, Rinehart, and Winston, 1979.
2. For a personal account of one heterosexual teacher's struggle with this conflation of feminist and lesbian, see Linda Bamber, "Class Struggle," *Women's Review of Books* 7, no. 5 (February 1990): 20–21.
3. Carolyn J. Mooney, "Homosexuals in Academe: Fear of Backlash Clouds Reactions to Increased Tolerance," *Chronicle of Higher Education,* September 23, 1992, A17.
4. She was eventually reinvited after a great deal of uproar from faculty and students, but I was left with a very shaky feeling about the risks of teaching as a lesbian.

Works Cited

Beck, Evelyn Torten. 1983. "Self-Disclosure and the Commitment to Social Change." In *Learning Our Way: Essays in Feminist Education,* edited by Charlotte Bunch and Sandra Pollack, 285–91. Trumansburg, N.Y.: Crossing Press.

Cruikshank, Margaret. 1982. *Lesbian Studies: Present and Future.* Old Westbury, N.Y.: Feminist Press.

McDaniel, Judith. 1985. "Is There Room for Me in the Closet? Or, My Life as the Only Lesbian Professor." In *Gendered Subjects,* edited by Margo Culley and Catherine Portuges, 130–35. Boston: Routledge and Kegan Paul.

Mooney, Carolyn J. 1992. "Homosexuals in Academe: Fear of Backlash Clouds Reactions to Increased Tolerance." *Chronicle of Higher Education,* September 23, A17.

18. Coming Out to Students: Notes from the College Classroom

Elenie Opffer

Since the Stonewall Rebellion of 1969, lesbian, gay, and bisexual people have been building a solid presence in both separate communities and within mainstream institutions. By coming out to families, friends, and colleagues as well as the media, we have brought lesbian, gay, and bisexual issues and lifestyles to the forefront of the American consciousness. Many Americans have changed their views toward homosexuality in a positive direction, with the majority supporting gay civil rights in the areas of employment. However, many of the same people who support nondiscrimination in employment oppose homosexual marriage and adoption. Even worse, the right wing has been targeting gays with referendum campaigns and antigay legislation. Gays have become the most hated minority group and have experienced the greatest increase in hate violence. The combination of support, ambivalence, and complete intolerance have moved us from "the love that dare not speak its name" to a locus of national policy debate (Hatfield 1989; Smith 1989; and Turque et al. 1992).

One of the arenas in which this debate continues is within our institutions of higher learning. While traditionally considered a bastion of liberal thinking and open-mindedness, several studies have uncovered a large percentage of homophobic sentiment on college campuses (American Council of Education and UCLA 1979; Crew 1978a; Norris 1992). Confirming these reports, a number of college instructors have written of their personal experiences

296

with homophobia on campus (Beck 1982; Bennett 1982; Brogan 1978; Gurko 1980; Manahan 1982; McDaniel 1980; and McNaron 1982). What the literature to date reveals is that homophobia on the part of students, faculty, and administration functions to suppress meaningful research and analysis of lesbian and gay subject matter as well as personal expression of lesbian and gay individuals in the academic community (Crew 1978a; Cruikshank 1982; Harbeck 1992).

Given the controversy over lesbian, gay, and bisexual existence, coming out remains an issue for many lesbian, gay, and bisexual college instructors. On the one hand we have mainstream psychologists, educators, educational researchers, and human rights advocates with compelling arguments for open expression. On the other hand, we have a myriad of fears and obstacles, from negative teaching evaluations from homophobic students to denial of promotion and tenure by antigay department heads. As Brogan has stated, "Who is to say the pendulum won't swing back to the 'dark ages' of mysterious and secret firings?" (Brogan 1978, 155).

Despite the chilly climate, many college instructors have chosen to come out. Research on lesbian, gay, and bisexual issues in a variety of disciplines has evolved into the field of lesbian, gay, and bisexual studies. Anthologies reflect first person experiences of the brave souls, yet no systematic analysis of reasons, methods and challenges to coming out as a college instructor exist. This essay will address this need by exploring the motivation, strategies, and challenges of college teachers who come out to students.

Background Discussion

In examining the literature, I found no studies on the coming out process of lesbian and gay college instructors. However, I did find information in psychology, educational research, and in several anthologies of essays by lesbian and gay teachers who reflected on their own coming out experience on campus that was relevant to this study.

Psychologists proclaim a need for self-disclosure, personal authenticity, and self-acceptance for optimal mental health (Fromm 1955; Rogers 1959; Jourard 1964) and for developing and sustaining satisfying interpersonal relationships (Horney 1937; Fromm 1939; Rogers 1951; Jourard 1968). Educational researchers have found self-acceptance and self-disclosure particularly relevant to the teaching profession (Rogers 1983; Shui 1983). College teaching evaluators have found these factors important at the college level (McKeachie 1970; Thielens 1971; Wilson et al. 1975). In fact, some of the research has shown that student-faculty relationships comprise one of the most significant aspects of college education (Wilson et al. 1975). Many instructors have taken a firm stand on academia's responsibility to address gay and lesbian issues and expose the hidden truths about our lives (Davenport 1982; DeVito 1981; Fontaine 1982; McNaron 1982; Rich 1986). DeVito (1981) also stated that students need openly gay and lesbian teachers as positive role models to counter the negative stereotypes. Jandt and Darsey (1981) identified the importance of access to accurate information on lesbian and gay existence to the coming out process. Harbeck and Uribe (1992) stressed the importance of this information to lesbian and gay students for effective life functioning and survival. Harbeck (1992) points out that the Department of Health and Human Services estimates that of the 5,000 annual suicides of youths between the ages of fifteen and twenty-four, up to 30 percent may be attributed to sexual preference issues and societal disapproval of homosexuality.

In his anthology of articles on gay academics, Crew (1978b) discovered many contributors who felt that their lesbian and gay identity and politics could not be separated from their academic teaching and research. Their reasons ranged from and often combined personal, professional, and social or political concerns.

From the personal realm, several teachers reported a need to come out to retain their sanity and feel like integrated human beings. McDaniel (1980) and McNaron (1982) both reported the severe depressions and loss of self-esteem involved in remaining closeted. Bennett (1982) compared closeted life to living in a void, while Rich (1986) evoked an image of looking in a mirror and seeing nothing. Bennett (1982) explained that in trying to pass as straight, even the simple events of everyday life get twisted. Hiding her lesbianism, she felt hypocritical, fearful, and complicit in perpetuating her own oppression.

While quite a few instructors stressed the personal impetus to come out, others emphasized the need to come out to maximize their teaching potential and remain consistent with their pedagogical methodologies. Several teachers in the social sciences and humanities used a personal approach to teaching about problems in personal and social identity (Beck 1982;

Brogan 1978; Davenport 1982; Fontaine 1982; McDaniel 1980). They found a need to model reflection and disclosure for the class to learn to do the same. DeVito (1981) and Brogan (1978) found that their own openness promoted intrapersonal, interpersonal, and intercultural understanding in the classroom.

The ways in which teachers reported coming out varied as much as their motives. For many, coming out to students was a developmental process in which they started with individuals, then came out to some classes, and eventually to all classes. Segrest (1982) came out to individual students outside the classroom exclusively. Others began with an individual approach as an interim strategy until they could find greater job security (i.e., tenure), or more courage to address the entire class (Beck 1982; Fontaine 1982; Gurko 1982; McDaniel 1980; and McNaron 1982). Beck attempted coming out by using nonverbal signs to cue her students in the classroom, such as wearing a labrys to class. McDaniel wore a ring with a double women's symbol. Both these teachers note that only other lesbian students who were somewhat familiar with the lesbian subculture understood the significance of the jewelry.

Several teachers came out by integrating lesbian and gay material into their curriculum. The bolder presented the material themselves, and identified themselves as lesbians and gay men (Brogan 1978; Manahan 1982; McDaniel 1980; McNaron 1982; Rich 1986). McNaron stated that she scheduled a group presentation by members of the outside community to come in and talk about lesbian experience before coming out to students on her own.

Most of the teachers reported positive experiences in revealing their lesbian or gay identities. Brogan (1978) and McNaron (1982) felt empowered and creatively inspired. Brogan got a burst of energy in creating his gay literature class while McNaron's writing and publishing became prolific. Coming out boosted the self-esteem of McNaron and McDaniel (1980) and allowed them to end self-destructive behaviors. Brogan, Manahan, and McDaniel felt personal and classroom tensions cease.

Davenport (1982) experienced hostile responses from students, but attributed it largely to her political perspective. As a result, she constantly fought a personal sense of alienation and isolation on campus. McDaniel (1980) describes coming out as equally "liberating and terrifying" to students. Those students unsure of their own sexuality tended to feel threatened while closeted lesbians felt pressured to come out. However, she felt that the stress offered a unique opportunity for growth that would otherwise not have existed.

Some teachers were so motivated by their own positive experience that they moved on to become activists to facilitate other instructors and students to come out and/or learn about lesbian and gay existence. McNaron (1982) got involved in the lesbian caucus within her national professional association and became involved with others pressing for the inclusion of lesbian materials in the public school curriculum. Gearhart led her colleagues to form the Lesbian and Gay Caucus in the Speech Communication Association (Chesebro 1981). The Gay Academic Union boasts of hundreds of individuals attending their regional meetings (Crew 1978b). Regardless of accompanying stress and strain, lesbian and gay academics have been coming out successfully and having an impact on both students and the academic environment.

Given the claims of psychologists, educators and educational researchers, and lesbian and gay liberationists, lesbian and gay college instructors face a genuine and compelling cause to come out to their students. Coming out is essential to the mental health of teachers and students, can enhance both teaching and learning, can facilitate interpersonal and intercultural understanding, as well as provide accurate information and counter negative stereotypes. By coming out, lesbian and gay teachers can serve as positive role models and provide experientially based knowledge about lesbian and gay culture. As more questions concerning public policy and laws on homosexuality face the population, citizens desperately need accurate information.

Methodology

As an open member of the lesbian and gay community, I was surprised with the difficulty of finding willing participants for my study. I resorted to a networking technique described by McCall and Simmons (1969) as snowball sampling. With each interview I attempted to elicit referrals to other informants. My criteria for selection was self-identification as lesbians or gay men to at least one class or to current students on campus outside the classroom. I interviewed a total of seventeen college instructors in the San Francisco Bay Area.

I obtained topical life histories in private, face-to-face, intensive interviews. The interviews were taped and transcribed. The data was analyzed, catalogued, and described to provide a cursory overview of the strategies lesbian and gay teachers use to come out and the effects they perceive this has on their teaching, their students, and their academic work and careers. All the names have been changed to assure the informants of complete anonymity.

Demographic Description and Background of the Participants

Seventeen individuals participated in the study, ranging in age from twenty-seven to fifty-two years old. The majority of the participants were caucasian, with one Asian and one who was part Native American. Twelve were women and five were men. All of them were born and raised in the United States as either Catholic, Protestant, or Jewish.

The participants had a minimum of two years teaching experience, with a maximum of twenty-nine years. The majority had between five and twenty years of teaching experience. Six of the participants were tenured professors or assistant professors, four were full-time lecturers with the remaining seven holding the rank of part-time lecturer.

Findings

What Made You Decide to Come Out to Your Students?

Teachers proposed a variety of reasons for coming out to their students, including educational, professional, personal, and sociopolitical concerns. The categories tended to overlap rather than maintain distinct boundaries.

The primary reason teachers reported coming out was to serve learning needs. These needs broke down into cognitive and affective domains. Sixteen subjects reported a desire to educate students on lesbian and gay issues and culture, serving a cognitive function. Twelve teachers stated they wanted to serve as a role model, which also provided students with cognitive learning. For many students, their "out" instructor may be the first open lesbian or gay man who is a healthy, productive professional. The openness of the instructor may also serve an affective need. The openness of the instructor frequently creates a safer climate for students, gay or straight, to disclose personal information and improve their writing, increase their participation in classroom discussions, or improve their interpersonal effectiveness. Lesbian and gay students may feel support for being gay or pursuing academic research in lesbian or gay areas. Finally, an open lesbian or gay man may serve as an academic advisor to gay students, which serves an affective as well as cognitive need.

Lorna: It's important for students to know that a lesbian doesn't have two horns and green eyes.

Christine: It's a supportive function. I want them to know they have an ally . . . that there's someone else in the world like them. That it's OK. . . . I am a role model for them. If they see that people with jobs and everything can be homosexual, then maybe they'll think they're OK.

Monica: I feel like it's an academic deficiency not to address gay and lesbian issues . . . the opposite of the view that you're stretching the personal thing.

   I remember teaching a class way back in 1974 in sex discrimination at the law school. Two women students approached me about not talking about lesbians. I said yeah, we should, but I don't think I did any kind of a decent job on the subject. That was regrettable because there were lesbian mother custody cases that were going on at the time that were interesting. So when we neglect homosexuality in almost everything we teach, we neglect minds along with sexuality. . . . It's taken me a while to get there. But now it's affected the subject matter of what I teach.

John: I just think it's a part of them knowing me and me knowing them, and part of bringing them out as writers is allowing them to write about anything they want, their sexual identity, their relationships. Very often in class there's a period in their life they would like to do an autobiographical paper on. They would hold back unless they knew the teacher is receptive to that kind of art form.

Skip: Students have a lot of problems. . . . They don't know who to talk to, who to have help them get the kind of medical or psychological or social attention they need while they're confronting these problems. . . . I can provide both an academic and a social resource. . . . An open gay who is willing to talk to them . . . there is a need for it, the same way there is a need for ethnic people on campus.

Twelve teachers emphasized professional reasons for coming out. Coming out increased effectiveness in a variety of ways. First of all, it freed teachers from worries that students would discover they were gay and lose respect for them. The energy that gets wasted on passing strategies would then be directed into teaching methods and attention to students. Subjects also reported that the integration of their personal and professional identities released their creativity and increased their productivity as teachers and writers.

Penny: Overall, I think that teaching is a relationship. . . . I really don't think a relationship has much potential if I'm in the closet. And it frees me to be a better teacher, to be more comfortable and be more myself, from the practical level of being able to deal with something homophobic that comes up and have them know I'm a lesbian dealing with it and not pretend I'm a liberal dealing with it, to being able to use the materials I want to use to just being able to be myself.

Kerry: I come out more to help people understand lesbianism as an oppression by talking about its connections to other oppressions and to introduce who I am. It's not just standing out by itself. It represents my whole political beliefs. And women's studies is just integrated, and it comes up all the time as it should.

James: Gay studies has actually been the thing that's worked best for me in terms of emotional gratification. I write, I get known. The satisfying thing of being politically active . . . [is that] the gay stuff is me. A lot of my intellectualism is fed by my intuitive experience. . . . I would also teach economics differently next time. . . . I would try to find a way to develop the personal dimension of it. So in some ways, the gay [studies] class has sort of made me think what I'd try to do about that.

Several teachers perceived that coming out increased their credibility. First of all, it allowed students to perceive them as honest, forthright people. Second, it gave students the impression that they were trustworthy and respected by the teacher. Finally, it increased teachers' credibility on lesbian and gay subjects.

Some of the teachers reported more personal reasons for coming out in class. Eight revealed their belief that they simply had a high tendency to disclose personal information. Four maintained that they needed to address some homophobic remarks that came up in class from a personal perspective. Five found themselves moved to come out after witnessing other teachers or individuals coming out to a group, after listening to speeches about coming out, or after participating in or witnessing gay rights rallies or riots. Eight subjects stated they felt a need to be honest while one emphasized ethical reasons for coming out. Six people expressed a need to feel fully integrated as human beings. Several expressed a combination of the above reasons.

James: I belong to a tell-all generation. I talk about myself easily, and a lot, and I don't have much discomfort in doing it. But it's something I learned through gay liberation.

John: I think it's been a gradual process that as far as one can come out as a teacher and more and more to my friends—this sense of not being integrated. You don't want to have a compartmentalized life. You want to put it all together. And I just hated carrying around a secret. One of the remnants I have from being Catholic is a penchant for confession. I don't like to go around with people not knowing things that I consider me, or basically positive.

Skip: It was in reaction to a statement that had been made and instead of challenging it in an impersonal way, I simply said that as a gay I find that totally intolerable and then I realized what I'd said. Well, my foot's in my mouth and the fat's in the fire so just go through with it. I was very disappointed because nobody threw rocks, or got upset or anything else. We had a very lively discussion after that.

Monica: I began to realize that going public was valuable. That there were things that could be accomplished out of it, in terms of personal strength and personal reward and in terms of other people. The more I thought about it, the more I thought how different and in some ways how much less painful my life would have been had there been visible lesbians in the university and more out. This is not to say they weren't out, but they weren't visible to me. So it became partly a question of ethics to try to return some good out of an experience that had been mixed.

Sociopolitical concerns overlapped most significantly with other reasons for coming out. Twelve participants stated their desire to bring about social change through education. These teachers wanted to build support for lesbian and gay civil rights by familiarizing gay and straight students with information about lesbian and gay issues and culture. Teachers reported lecturing as well as providing a forum for discussion, supporting research and providing resources on lesbian and gay subjects. Three teachers professed a desire to see more lesbian and gay teachers hold power positions in academia as a gay rights strategy.

How Did You Choose to Come Out?

The previous section on reasons for coming out to students underscores the instructors' strong commitment to teaching excellence. Given the possible negative consequences of revealing homosexuality in a homophobic society, most of the teachers gave serious thought to ways they could come out. Even the three instructors who came out inadvertently the first time have thought about coming out since that initial experience.

While some teachers reported consistent and deliberate ways of coming out, most stated that coming out differed from class to class and year to year. It appears that instructors developed a repertoire of coming out methods. After experimenting with a few approaches, they reported that coming out was situational, or context-bound. Their perceptions of the class members combined with the course subject matter, learning objectives, and teaching philosophy and methods shaped the instructors' choices. The following section will present the approaches identified.

While teaching a course on foreign affairs does not necessarily mean that the instructor is a foreigner, the instructors reported that students assumed that a teacher of gay or lesbian subjects is gay. Seven teachers had taught lesbian or gay courses, i.e., "Sociology of Homosexuality" or "Lesbian Literature." Teaching in lesbian and gay studies is a way of coming out. None of these teachers taught gay or lesbian studies courses exclusively. Hence, they had other ways of coming out in other courses.

Ten instructors stated that their coming out inevitably arose from teaching lesbian or gay subject matter. These teachers planned and integrated lesbian and/or gay material into other courses in the social sciences, arts, or humanities. Unlike the automatic assumption found in courses that focused exclusively on gay and lesbian subjects, these teachers made coming out statements. They came out more directly because they could not refer to lesbians and gay men as "they." Hence, using the personal pronoun revealed their own sexual identity. The means of integrating lesbian and gay material included lectures, discussions, group projects done by students, guest panelists, and readings.

Six teachers came out spontaneously when prompted by unplanned discussions in the classroom. These teachers came out by using examples from their own life that revealed their intimate relationships, or discussed lesbian or gay issues and culture from a personal perspective. Discussions on communication, relationships, philosophy, contemporary events, or social issues sparked a need to express ideas from personal experience.

Three of the teachers who disclosed personal information to illustrate points in classroom discussions reported coming out inadvertently the first time.

Marjorie: It was a slip of the tongue. I wanted to tell the class about some interesting ideas about a partner relationship . . . so I started saying, "We were talking about this, and I said this, and she said this," and it was obvious that my lover was a she. That was out, that I had a woman lover. It wasn't that I felt compelled or even a desire to tell them I had a woman lover. I wanted to give them this insight about working through a love relationship.

Sarah: We were discussing women's rights, and Stacey made some statement about people jumping on her lesbian separatist point of view. But I'm not a separatist. So I made some statements that weren't as radical as hers, just a lesbian point of view, and stated that I was saying this as a lesbian, and it just happened. Coming out was secondary to what we were discussing. Afterwards, I realized that I had, but see, I don't consciously come out. I speak from who I am no matter what we're talking about. And the act of coming out is secondary to what I'm saying.

Several teachers had written articles on lesbian or gay subjects that they used in class. One had written a "confessional" autobiographical novel in which he explores his own life as a gay man. Another shared her lesbian poetry. These teachers used their writings as assignments or optional readings in their classes.

Five participants reported coming out through nonverbal symbols. They reported that clothing, jewelry, buttons, and hairstyles indicate membership in the lesbian or gay community. Nonverbal behavior, including posture, voice pitch, and stress patterns may also communicate sexual identity.

Three instructors stated that they came out to individual students during private meetings outside of class. While serving as advisers in private meetings, these teachers explained they came out in response to needs they perceived in the students. Christine and Skip came out to gay students seemingly at odds with their own sexual identity. Julie came out to students who came to her for research direction on lesbian and gay issues. She noted that students frequently research areas they themselves are dealing with, and feels her coming out serves an affective as well as academic function.

Six participants reported conscious planning and timing of their coming out to students. Four teachers revealed a strategy of building a rapport with their students, and coming out when they felt they were liked and respected, and had developed a safe, supportive climate in the classroom.

Rhonda related the most detailed plan for coming out. She begins by group building in the class as a whole and by spending some time outside of class with students. In establishing interpersonal relationships, she identifies the lesbian students in the class and comes out to them exclusively. She then offers them the opportunity to participate in a panel on lesbianism in her classes. With the support of the other lesbians in the class, she comes out with her fellow panelists.

Rhonda: I feel that if I came out the first day of class I wouldn't end up with as many allies. People come to trust me come to find out I'm a lesbian . . . so they already feel some kind of closeness to me and with other people in the class, and then we come out.

Monica: Because of the heightened sensitivity on my end to the sort of delicacy of sexual identification among people who are say, eighteen years old—I was respectful of some degree of preparation for them. . . . I would give them more time with me. The modus operandi is they know you're a nice person, right, so . . . there is this whole progression. It's superstitious too, because people are gonna like you, or they're not.

Christine: They already knew me at my best, my very best, and they loved me, they publicly acclaimed their affection for me. I had them over a barrel, there was nothing they could do. They couldn't say, "That weirdo, we knew it all the time."

Judy: My style is to let them know and trust me as a human being, then find out I'm a lesbian and maybe something will click—that, "Oh my God, if she's a lesbian, maybe lot's of other women whom I like are lesbians."

In contrast to the deliberately delayed method, three participants reported direct, immediate coming out approaches. These individuals usually announce their lesbian or gay identities during introductions, the first or second day of class. Serena wanted to make her lesbian identity very overt. In her experience, just announcing she worked in the gay movement did not clue all students into her lesbian identity. Kerry stated that she incorporated it into her list of other facets of her identity, such as being Jewish and being a mother. These three individuals were gay or women's liberation activists, and felt a need to come out in all situations in their lives.

Several teachers expressed a desire to approach coming out in a more direct fashion, but did not feel it was right for them. One had tried it for three years, and decided to come out more gradually.

Judy: My first way of doing it was to announce it on the first day of class. . . . About two or three years later, I stopped doing that. It seemed a little counterproductive, and I decided that a better way to do it is to wait and let people get to know me without a label because too many people balk behind the label.

How Did You Feel about Coming Out?

For most of the subjects, the first coming out experience in class was a dramatic event. They reported clear images and sense memories. Five participants reported high levels of communication apprehension during their first, and sometimes subsequent, coming out experiences. For example, one woman stated she "practically whispered it" while another admitted she "sort of mumbled it" her first time. The following stories revealed the feelings of excitement and fear.

Judy: I remember my heart beating very hard and my face flushing very red at the end of the women's block course at the end of Spring '73 when I said I had a woman lover, and it was pretty much like that in lessening degrees as I got used to it. The first time I said it in class my heart was pounding and I was nervous, but I was sure I wanted to do it and it got consecutively easier to do. It became less of an issue. But even now there's a distinct rise in my blood pressure. I feel it. It's a risk. I know it will have an impact. It's still taboo. So my body reacts to that, and my heart pounds faster and I still have all those symptoms just to a lesser degree. I'm a little scared is what I'm saying. I don't really know how it will come out, and I have to gird my loins a little bit every time.

Skip: I could have cut my throat. Because all of a sudden I was doing something very uncharacteristic of me, and that was just simply going into totally new territory without reading the guidebooks first. This time I just launched out on my own and did something, and I then had this feeling that I needed to be very cautious, to close back up again. To be more tentative, so for about a week, I wavered back and forth with all sorts of weird feelings. And all of a sudden, it became very comfortable.

Julie: I think I was probably somewhat antsy. I remember being antsy about publicly coming out opposed to the Briggs Initiative in the classroom, rather than as an issue that one should examine, which is kind of a neutral thing.

Susan: I remember the first time I did, I just went by it so fast, right, that I remember later a couple of women students asked me, "Did you say that?" Because they weren't sure, right? So I thought to myself, I must have speeded by that so quick, you know.

Christine: My theoretical preparation just dissolved and my heart started beating very fast. I turned six shades of purple, stopped breathing, and sort of sunk very low in my chair. I was stalling for time. I said, "Well, I'm not sure if I should tell you, I've never told any students before." And they said, "Well, you can tell us." And we really did have such a good rapport in this class. I knew it was true that I could. And I was up for it anyway, I was feeling feisty. So I said that it [my lover] was a woman. I mean, I couldn't even tell the reactions. I wasn't even looking at them. I was just totally going, [screams] "What am I doing!"

While some respondents felt fear and apprehension, some others felt exhilaration and relief.

What Allows You to Come Out?

The participants reported that several factors made coming out easier. Starting the list was teaching a gay or lesbian class. With a lesbian or gay course, the teacher knows that enrolled students come to class with an open mind regarding homosexuality, either because they are lesbian or gay themselves, or because they want to learn more about homosexual issues and culture. In these cases, being a lesbian or gay man increases one's credibility. Individuals who focused much of their teaching and research interests on lesbian and gay issues reported the most ease in coming out.

Another major factor consisted of job security. Such assurance took the form of university, departmental, or student support. Eight of the subjects stated that they worked in a liberal department and university, in which they felt safe to come out. Two individuals waited until they had tenure to assure themselves of university backing. One instructor felt it was safer once she had received favorable results on a formal teaching effectiveness evaluation. Three instructors felt that developing rapport in the classroom gave them the confidence to come out.

Experience with teaching and coming out also played significant roles in giving teachers the self-confidence to come out.

Julie: I think I'm a lot more comfortable as a teacher and knowing the kinds of things I can do and the kind of stuff I can fall back on. Just being at ease in the classroom makes a hell of a difference.

Serena: Before coming out to that class in the East Bay, I rehearsed forty times. . . . I had three friends go over the role play in my coming out with my mother . . . but once I was really out in public, it was just like saying, you know, I come from New York.

A commitment to values, whether political, educational, or personal, also facilitated coming out for many individuals.

Monica: It felt very compelling as a process. I mean, I feel like there is a righteous struggle to be fought about many people. So that brought out the best in me.

Susan: I really believe that what helps people come out is politics. A real belief in certain oppressions and inequalities in society and real understanding of how it needs to be changed. And the only way you can do it is by speaking out and taking a stand. I think that's it. There's a slogan that Clara Frasier had; she wanted to have a button that said, "Free Speech. Use It or Lose It."

John: If you're going to be yourself and be respected by other people, then this is a fundamental thing they need to know about you. It's not the only thing, but if they don't know it, it's an awful big part of you that's missing. Or, there's an error about their concept of you. I think the urge to integrity, openness, and to really want to communicate with people and understand where other people are coming from will all help.

For many people, resolving coming out issues in other contexts and developing a positive self-concept and sense of independence paved the way for coming out to students and larger groups.

Judy: It was a real step-wise process. I came out to my friendship network and then my family in the first phase. Then I came out at the school level by announcing myself in class as a second phase. I finally got to the point where if I made public appearances, like out in the community or on TV or something, I was capable of saying I was a lesbian.

Penny: Part of it has to do with where you're at with your process of self-acceptance about being a lesbian. . . . You have to start out feeling like I'm OK, even if these thirty students drop my class, I still know it's OK that I'm a lesbian . . . and I guess the ability to be objective enough to look at the way people react and not personalize it.

Terry: I think that just general independence is the most important thing for coming out, and that's been one of the reasons it's been easier for me. Not just to assume that everybody liked me but if they don't, it's OK. I'm capable of setting my own standards, making my own decisions, and going against the flow if I think it's right.

Several people perceived personal qualities, abilities, and growth as facilitative factors. Given the different degrees of public disclosure, individuals frequently felt their coming out failed to measure up to the degree of disclosure of extremely public activists and accounted for the difference. Others reflected on their own situations.

Lorna: I think if you have a really strong suit of armor, that would make it easier to come out. One of my problems is that I worry too much about what other people think of me. I'm trying to get away from that. . . . I just come out because I talk about what concerns me. I'm not real closemouthed. I tend to relate to people interpersonally, so it would be hard to conceal it. My personality is pretty open. And since I wasn't raised in a real repressive situation, I didn't develop that paranoia. So I tend to think it's going to be alright, and that's a great advantage. More times than not, if you think it's going to be OK, they're going to go along with you. My general optimism, outgoingness and having come to this area, have helped a lot.

Marjorie: I think self-love, self-respect, and self-knowing. I don't think it's character traits as much as ways of being. Those are essential ingredients to being exactly who you are.

Christine: I think someone who is really outgoing, like a political activist or radical lesbian or something . . . loves to shock people or at least get them to think. . . . I think one of the things that makes me more likely to come out than other people is that I'm really insistent. I mean, I don't tend to have too many masks. I'm fairly transparent. And fairly committed to truth, I mean I don't play a lot of games. So I'm more likely to come out than some people because I can't stand any kind of dishonesty. It bothers me a lot. I'm less likely than other people because I can't stand conflict as much as other people who seek it out.

Serena: From an extrovert-introvert point of view, I think it's harder for an extrovert to keep quiet about it. It's easier for a person who's self-contained not to feel the strictures quite so much. But somebody who discloses all over the landscape every hour of the day, it's hard not to disclose that.

How Have Your Students Responded to Your Coming Out?

The majority of the individuals evaluated their coming out experiences in the classroom positively. A few teachers who reported positive results took a long range perspective. The immediate effects included resistance and hostility. However, the discussions that ensued as people had time to adjust and absorb new information resulted in learning, and decreased homophobia.

Serena: Short range, it's sort of a matter of perception. Like nonverbally picking up those stunned looks, or sort of frozen looks. . . . On the long range, that has to do with the texture of my professional life. Things have happened, and now I can sit back and speculate. I think I've determined it by feedback that has come to me, both positive and negative, but mainly positive, and the way I dealt with that and the motivation I have had because I continue to be open. And that of course snowballs, because I get more positive feedback, so then I do more openness, and get more positive feedback, so it really escalates in a good way.

Monica: Some react to your saying to them I'm a lesbian by "huuuh?" Then they come back a week later with more receptivity to you as a person, and with a better ability to listen to what you have to say. The main thing and the key is getting past the fear. Getting people past the stage of "Oh God, this is all too weird, I can't stand this stage."

For some teachers, the classroom climate improved immediately. They felt trust increased, which increased participation in discussions as well as increasing the level of personal disclosure. For others, coming out led to lively discussions in which they felt significant learning took place. The open gay or lesbian teacher could address questions, provide information, and thus change incorrect perceptions and stereotypes. Individuals stated that they measured effects by looking at the class dynamics.

Christine: Later on the repercussions in that class [were] that the class got even better than it was before. . . . There's something that convinces the student that the teacher's a human being and they loosen up a lot.

Rhonda: They become much more informal after that. Much more personal. Like in any relationship, you're hiding a part of yourself before you tell. Once you tell, you feel closer. And it's had this side effect of creating a much closer thing for the whole class.

Julie: [The students] were way ahead of me. They were real supportive. In fact, a couple of lesbians came up and said how pleased they were that I had taken a stand. I didn't get any negative stuff at all. I think my concerns were greater than reality.

Two instructors believed that one or two students may have dropped their class as a result of witnessing their teacher come out. These instructors expressed a belief that since so many others benefitted from the process, the gains far outweighed the losses.

Several instructors reported some hostility in classes that focused on gay issues or topics. Bob felt attacked by upper middle class lesbian and gay men. Attributing it to classism, he felt his image was inconsistent with upper middle class expectations of what a college professor should be like. He explained the problem as follows:

Bob: We get into a bigotry of human types where there are politically correct types of people. And I mean often the people who are expressive of those casual types of bigotries are unaware that they are bigotries directed at a class characteristic. I look and act like a working-class Irish guy from the docks. That's where it comes from, you know, so I have a broken nose and gnarled hands, and that's why I talk a little gruffly and I'm a little more assertive and loud perhaps. I think my problem is I don't quite fit academia.

Penny experienced three types of negative responses. The first she characterized as a homophobic response, although the antigay sentiments were masked by attacking the standards of the writing presented in class rather than directly objecting to the lesbian content. She reported the event as follows:

Penny: She came in and said, just because something is written by a member of a minority group does not necessarily make it good writing. . . . She was convinced that this writing was trash, and that I had just decided that because it was lesbian, and I was a lesbian, I didn't have proper standards because my thinking was skewed toward my sexual persuasion.

The second type of negative response she characterized as a more tolerable homophobic response. She felt the inquiries came from a "larger lack of consciousness."

Penny: I felt that desire to learn underneath their stupid questions. They asked things like, "Don't you worry if you write lesbian material that others won't understand it?" or "Why can't you do something about your writing so that nonlesbians can get it too?"

Penny reported a third type of negative response. She believed that "lesbians who I don't think have their shit together use me to dump on." She felt that lesbians who had not completed their coming out processes were threatened by her openness and used her to vent their anger and frustration.

Different political perspectives formed the final point of contention in Penny's classes. For some lesbian separatists, Penny was not separatist enough, while other students accused her of being too separatist.

Six other teachers mirrored Penny's experience of finding conflict in the area of political perspectives. With classes that are not expressly lesbian or gay-oriented, introduction of gay or lesbian material into the curriculum was attacked as biased or political rather than academic. In classes that were focused on lesbian or gay themes, students would attack the political perspectives presented. It appeared that some students feared that their own experience would not be reflected in the course content.

Terry had reflected upon this problem and gave a careful analysis.

Terry: Well, it sounds like because there are no [gay] courses, and because there have been historically no [gay] courses, then when a course comes along, then it's expected to be everything to everybody. A person expects it to reflect their reality because they are homosexuals. If it doesn't meet their expectations, they get angry at this point.

Hence, many students make emotional investments in classes with a focus on lesbian and issues. This commitment leads to high expectations and can result in conflicts and confrontations when expectations aren't met.

The effect on individual students mirrored the classroom responses, but was reflected in students' individual work. Students felt safe to disclose more personal information in their writing, particularly if they were lesbians or gay men. Students also felt freer to research lesbian and gay subjects and raise lesbian and gay topics in class.

Several teachers noted that their coming out prompted the Johari window effect to take place in their office: Students felt safe to come in during office hours and talk about their personal concerns as well as their grades.

James: They would come to my office hours and hang out. . . . They worried about their grades and stuff. And then, I don't know, we were just talking, and they would start pouring their hearts out.

Skip: Anyone can come in and talk to me.

Do You Think Coming Out Has Affected Your Career?

Over one half of the participants reported that news of their coming out spreads through student networks. Three individuals stated that they didn't even need to come out anymore because the majority of their students come to class aware of the teacher's sexual preference. Six teachers believed that their open lesbian or gay male identity may be part of the criteria students used to pick the course. One-third of the instructors reported that once they came out, they were perceived as experts on gay and lesbian subjects and sought by colleagues and students for information. These teachers stated that students frequently sought them to supervise research on lesbian and gay subjects as well.

Several instructors complained of labeling. They felt that some heterosexuals stereotyped them, made assumptions or drew political battle lines on the basis of their sexual preference. They feared that their colleagues as well as students may only see them as experts on homosexuality rather than perceive the homosexual identity and expertise as one aspect of a multidimensional person.

Four individuals chose to incorporate lesbian activism into their careers as teachers. Despite the fact that they chose to merge their professional and sexual identities, they sometimes regretted the limitations.

Serena: When I first came to State, I couldn't say anything except I'm a lesbian, I realized that my total identity was wrapped up in being a lesbian and that I had something else beside that. I lost my whole career with my being a lesbian thing.

So since 1971, it's been a process of regaining my professional life in the face of my being open about who I am.

The fear of having people limit their perceptions of out teachers as only lesbians or gay men was echoed by most of the subjects. However, only one person felt that coming out hurt his career. Three participants noted that they might not be able to land jobs at more conservative universities. Ten of the instructors attributed the lack of effect on their careers to the liberal attitudes at their schools. They felt that had they been at more conservative institutions, they either would not have come out, or they would have lost their jobs for doing so.

Discussion

This study represents an attempt to describe and categorize how university instructors come out to students. At the time of data collection, no studies of the coming out process within this context had been done.

In fact, with the exception of Jandt and Darsey (1981), this author found no studies of coming out as a communication process. Hence, I undertook an exploration of methods, strategies, and effects as experienced in face-to-face interaction as well as the reasoning behind these processes.

The approaches to coming out varied from very direct, deliberate, and immediate announcements included in introductory remarks to delayed, strategically timed statements incorporated in lessons or discussions. Some individuals came out inadvertently during unplanned discussions. Others came out in subtler ways by implying it verbally or nonverbally. A few came out primarily to individual students outside of class.

The teachers who waited until later in the semester felt a need to develop a rapport before disclosing possibly discrediting information. By creating a positive relationship with students first, students were seen to experience cognitive dissonance or an inability to negate the positive attributes of the teacher. These strategic instructors felt they helped to eliminate homophobia by changing attitudes and breaking stereotypes.

For some individuals, a solo coming out presentation felt too threatening. These teachers developed support among other lesbian, gay, or bisexual students before exposing their own sexual preference to the entire class. Such an approach was made possible by the symbols such as clothing, jewelry, dress, buttons, and hairstyles that can indicate membership in the lesbian, gay, or bisexual community. Nonverbal behavior, including posture, voice pitch, and intonation patterns may also communicate sexual identity. The inexplicitness of this form of communication allows for an ambiguous interpretation. On the one hand, individuals who are members of the gay community can use these symbols to signal fellow members, while leaving the nongay community completely unaware or keeping them guessing. Hence a teacher who uses any of these symbols can allow herself to be identified by fellow gays while passing for straight amongst heterosexuals. On the other hand, ambiguity can also allow for stereotyping or incorrect assumptions. For example, a heterosexual student of mine complained that many fellow students assumed she was a lesbian because she wore a leather jacket. While gay men used to subtly communicate their identities by piercing one ear, straight men now find it stylish to pierce one ear. Hence, nonverbal symbols can obfuscate, confuse, or allow for incorrect interpretations.

The reasons for coming out included educational, professional, personal, and sociopolitical concerns. On an educational level, teachers expressed a need to present accurate information about lesbians and gay men and personal and academic support for lesbian and gay students. Professional concerns revolved around teaching effectiveness. Many instructors felt they could focus more on teaching if they weren't juggling passing strategies and "dancing around pronouns" in their interactions with students. These individuals also expressed a belief in honesty as a necessary condition for an effective teacher-student relationship.

Many of the teachers who spoke of the need for honesty also perceived this as important from a personal perspective. The personal dimension also revealed a high measure of personal disclosure as part of the out-professor's communication style. On the sociopolitical level, instructors maintained a desire to change people's attitudes toward lesbians and gays. Several felt that they accomplished this by presenting information and serving as a positive role model. A few teachers felt they could create heterosexual allies for the lesbian and gay movement. Others were more concerned with supporting their lesbian and gay students personally and academically to bring about social change.

The factors that facilitated coming out in class included finding support from students, colleagues, or administrators. Comfort and practice with one's sexual identity and teaching also played a significant role in easing public disclosure. Finally, individuals with strong convictions on the necessity of coming out found the process easier.

The participants reported personal and social effects to coming out. Many confessed they experienced a high degree of communication apprehension when coming out, yet found the experience exhilarating and liberating. Several found it improved their teaching.

In the classroom, coming out frequently caused a stir, or put students into mild shock. Most teachers perceived that the process led their students to learn more about lesbians, gay men, or bisexuals, and contend that it decreased their students' homophobia. Several individuals felt that it improved the classroom climate, led to increased participation and openness in discussions, and inspired lesbian, gay, or bisexual students to come out.

Most teachers found that coming out brought them closer to their students on an individual basis as well. Students would see teachers outside the classroom and seek counseling or consulting on personal as well as academic matters. Several teachers felt they were serving important needs, particularly to lesbian, gay, and bisexual students.

The long-term effects included developing a reputation on campus as an open lesbian, gay, or bisexual person. Positively framed, these teachers saw themselves as campus lesbian, gay, and bisexual resources. The negative aspect consisted of reductionist labeling, stereotyping, and assumptions on the part of homophobic colleagues. A few individuals expressed some resentment on the limitations by themselves or others when their professional and sexual identities completely merged. Others enjoyed the opportunity to focus their careers on lesbian, gay, or bisexual matters.

Implications for Future Research

Communication researchers and theorists have given little attention to the coming out process in interpersonal or group interaction. Most of the current theoretical literature deals with etiological concerns. This study has sought to explore what goes on in face-to-face interactions as perceived by the participants.

Several factors limit the results of this study. First of all, the snowball sampling resulted in a fairly homogeneous group, indicating a need to get a more representative sample. Given the sensitivity of the subject matter and impossibility of a random sample, a quota sampling method may generate a more representative group.

A second constraint consisted of the geographic boundaries of this researcher. Most of the subjects interviewed taught in the greater San Francisco Bay Area, a location known for more liberal attitudes than other regions of the country. The interviews were conducted on a one-time basis. The changes in approach and attitudes revealed by older, more experienced individuals indicate the value of conducting a longitudinal study.

The notes on effects of coming out to students were strictly the observations of the teachers who came out. As noted by the participants themselves, their perception was colored by their intense emotions. Some form of triangulation could be built into the study to get a broader perspective on interaction processes. Some possibilities include interviewing students and observing the process in the classroom.

Despite the limitations, this study revealed the following insights into coming out in the classroom setting: (1) coming out in class usually involves serious thought and consideration of the effects; (2) most teachers who came out expressed a commitment to teaching excellence, personal integrity, and/or lesbian, gay, and bisexual rights; (3) most instructors experienced coming out as a dramatic event, at least initially, and gradually became more and more accustomed to the experience over time; (4) teachers' coming out approaches depend on their perceptions of the students, their teaching objectives, methods, and philosophy, as well as unplanned circumstances; and (5) coming out repeatedly often leads to a reputation as a lesbian, gay, or bisexual advocate.

Works Cited

American Council on Education and UCLA. 1979. *The American Freshman: National Norms for Fall 1979.*

Beck, E. T. 1982. "Teaching about Jewish Lesbians in Literature: From Zeitl and Rickel to the Tree of Begets." In *Lesbian Studies, Present and Future,* ed. M. Cruikshank, 81–87. New York: Feminist Press.

Bennett, P. 1982. "Dyke in Academe." In *Lesbian Studies, Present and Future,* ed. M. Cruikshank, 3–8. New York: Feminist Press.

Brogan, J. E. 1978. "Teaching Gay Literature in San Francisco." In *The Gay Academic,* ed. L. Crew, 152–63. Palm Springs, Calif.: ETC Publications.

Chesebro, J. W. 1981. "Introduction." In *Gayspeak: Gay Male and Lesbian Communication,* ix–xvi. New York: Pilgrim Press.

Crew, L. 1978a. "Before Emancipation: Gay Persons as Viewed by Chairpersons in English." In *The Gay Academic,* 3–48. Palm Springs, Calif.: ETC Publications.

———. 1978b. "Introduction: An Antidote to Hemlock." In *The Gay Academic,* xvii–xix. Palm Springs, Calif.: ETC Publications.

Cruikshank, M., ed. 1981. *The Lesbian Path.* Tallahassee, Fla.: Naiad Press.

———. 1982. *Lesbian Studies: Present and Future.* New York: Feminist Press.

Davenport, D. 1982. "Black Lesbians in Academia: Visible Invisibility." In *Lesbian Studies, Present and Future,* ed. M. Cruikshank, 9–11. New York: Feminist Press.

DeVito, J. A. 1981. "Educational Responsibilities to Gay Male and Lesbian Students." In *Gayspeak: Gay Male and Lesbian Communication,* ed. J. W. Chesebro, 197–208. New York: Pilgrim Press.

Fontaine, C. 1982. "Teaching the Psychology of Women: A Lesbian Feminist Perspective." In *Lesbian Studies, Present and Future,* ed. M. Cruikshank, 70–80. New York: Feminist Press.

Fromm, E. 1939. "Selfishness and Self-Love." *Psychiatry* 2: 507–23.

———. 1955. *The Sane Society.* New York: Holt, Rinehart, and Winston.

Gurko, J. 1980. "Coming Out in Berkeley in 1967." In *The Lesbian Path,* ed. M. Cruikshank, 43–50. Tallahassee, Fla.: Naiad Press.

———. 1982. "Sexual Energy in the Classroom." In *Lesbian Studies, Present and Future,* ed. M. Cruikshank, 25–31. New York: Feminist Press.

Harbeck, K. M. 1992. "Introduction." In *Coming Out of the Classroom Closet: Gay and Lesbian Students, Teachers and Curricula,* 1–7. New York: Harrington Park Press.

Harbeck, K. M., and V. Uribe. 1992. "Addressing the Needs of Lesbian, Gay and Bisexual Youth." In *Coming Out of the Classroom Closet: Gay and Lesbian Students, Teachers and Curricula,* ed. K. M. Harbeck, 9–28. New York: Harrington Park Press.

Hatfield, L. D. 1989. "New Poll: How the U.S. Views Gays." *San Francisco Examiner,* 5 June, A19.

Horney, K. 1937. *The Neurotic Personality of Our Time.* New York: Norton Press.

Jandt, F., and J. Darsey. 1981. "Coming Out as a Communicative Process." In *Gayspeak: Gay Male and Lesbian Communication,* ed. J. W. Chesebro, 12–27. New York: Pilgrim Press.

Jourard, S. 1964. *The Transparent Self.* New York: Van Nostrand.

———. 1968. "Healthy Personality and Self-Disclosure." In *The Self in Social Interaction,* Vol. 1, ed. C. Gordon and K. J. Gergen, 423–34. New York: John Wiley and Sons.

Lewis, S. G. 1979. *Sunday's Women: A Report on Lesbian Life Today.* Boston: Beacon Press.

McCall, G. J., and J. L. Simmons. 1969. *Issues in Participant Observation.* Reading, Mass.: Addison-Wesley.

McDaniel, J. 1980. "My Life as the Only Lesbian Professor." In *The Lesbian Path,* ed. M. Cruikshank, 160–65. Tallahassee, Fla.: Naiad Press.

McKeachie, W. J. 1970. "Research on College Teaching: A Review." Washington, D.C.: Educational Resources Information Center.

McNaron, T. A. H. 1982. " 'Out' at the University: Myth and Reality." In *Lesbian Studies, Present and Future,* ed. M. Cruikshank, 12–15. New York: Feminist Press.

Manahan, N. 1982. "Homophobia in the Classroom." In *Lesbian Studies, Present and Future,* ed. M. Cruikshank, 66–69. New York: Feminist Press.

Norris, William P. 1992. "Liberal Attitudes, Homophobic Acts: The Paradoxes of the Homosexual Experience in a Liberal Institution." In *Coming Out of the Classroom Closet: Gay and Lesbian Students, Teachers, and Curricula,* ed. K. M. Harbeck. New York: Hayworth Press.

Rich, A. 1986. "Invisibility in Academe." In *Blood, Poetry and Roses: Selected Prose 1979–1985,* 198–201. New York: W. W. Norton.

Rogers, C. R. 1951. *Client-Centered Therapy.* Boston: Houghton, Mifflin.

———. 1959. "A Theory of Therapy, Personality, and Interpersonal Relationships, as Developed in the Client-Centered Framework." In *Psychology: A Study of Science,* Vol. 3, ed. S. Koch, 184–256. New York: McGraw-Hill.

———. 1983. "Research in Person-Centered Issues in Education." In *Freedom to Learn for the 80's.* Columbus, Ohio: Charles E. Merrill.

Segrest, M. 1982. "I Lead Two Lives: Confessions of a Closet Baptist." In *Lesbian Studies, Present and Future,* ed. M. Cruikshank, 16–19. New York: Feminist Press.

Shui, L. K. 1983. *Psychology for Teaching and Caring.* Toronto: Kensington Educational.

Smith, J. 1989. "A Gay Basher Asks : Why?" *San Francisco Examiner,* 7 June, A11.

Thielens, W., Jr. 1971. "The Teacher-Student Interaction in Higher Education: Student Viewpoint." In *Encyclopedia of Education,* ed. L. Deighton, vol. 9, 54–63. New York: Macmillan and the Free Press.

Turque, B., C. Friday, J. Jordan, D. Glick, P. Annin, F. Chideya, A. Duignan-Calabra, P. Rogers, C. Haessly. 1992. "Gays Under Fire." *Newsweek,* 14 September, 34–40.

Wilson, R. C., J. G. Gaff, E. Dienst, L. Wood, and L. J. Barry. 1975. *College Professors and Their Impact on Students.* New York: John Wiley and Sons.

19. Coming Out in the Classroom: Faculty Disclosures of Sexuality

R. Jeffrey Ringer

The Caucus for Gay and Lesbian Concerns of the Speech Communication Association (SCA) organizes conference sessions for the Association's annual meeting. At its business meeting each year caucus members discuss potential topics for the coming year's conference. One of the most frequently requested session topics has been "coming out in the classroom." Members continuously want to discuss whether or not they should come out in their classes, if others are coming out, what the consequences and implications of coming out would be, how to do it, when to do it, and other related questions. Indeed, the sessions during which we discuss such topics are among our most well attended.

The discussions often focus on the teacher's desire to be honest and open with their students. Although some caucus members feel no desire to discuss their private lives in the classroom, others feel compelled to do so. But they are unsure of how others will react to their disclosure. They know of colleagues who have not been hired because of their sexual orientation and they suspect that some have been fired because of it.

If the results of a report by the Task Force on Homosexuality of the American Sociological Association are typical of other departments, discrimination may be rampant in academia. The 1982 report indicated that 63 percent of the sociology departments surveyed said that hiring a known homosexual would pose serious difficulties, and 84 percent held serious reservations about hiring a gay activist. Similar attitudes were found among the chairs of English departments (Crew 1987, 47). Although both of these reports are dated, there is little evidence to suggest gay and lesbian faculty are receiving more support on our campuses. The courts are reluctant to support gay faculty members who have been fired unless the first amendment is involved (D'Emilio 1987b).

Some argue that gay and lesbian teachers should come out in their classes to help educate others and to weaken stereotypes. John D'Emilio (1987a) argues: "The ideals of our profession demand that we come out. The teachers we all remember best and cherish most are the ones who were models of integrity in the classroom and in their lives, the ones for whom the search for justice and truth did not represent empty words. If we decline to take up this challenge, we will be failing our students and ourselves." Yet given a climate identified by the surveys cited above, coming out may still be dangerous for one's career. It would be useful, therefore, to learn more about whether or not one's colleagues are coming out in their classes.

The Caucus on Gay and Lesbian Concerns of SCA has previously expressed an interest in gay and lesbian issues. DeVito (1981) outlined the responsibilities that teachers have to their gay and lesbian students. Specifically, he recommended that teachers recognize the gay and lesbian existence, avoid stereotypes, avoid heterosexual presumption, and recognize the influence of affectional preference on communication (201–5). But we have not addressed coming out in the classroom. We do not know if our colleagues are coming out in their classes. We do not know how those who are are doing it. The answers to these questions will provide gay and lesbian faculty members with insight into the feelings of their colleagues about coming out.

This study was designed to investigate these issues. A questionnaire was distributed to the members of the Caucus on Gay and Lesbian Concerns of the SCA. The questionnaire was guided by the following research questions:

R1: To what degree do members of the caucus discuss homosexuality in their classes and what is the context of these discussions?

R2: To what extent do members of the caucus reveal their sexuality and what is the context of these discussions?

R3: What issues are important to consider when deciding whether or not to reveal one's sexuality in class?

Questionnaires were sent to the membership of the caucus as an insert to a newsletter. The questionnaire contained ten questions. Twenty-seven (20.7 percent) questionnaires were returned. The responses to these questionnaires are presented not to represent a statistical sample from which to generalize about the caucus, but as a means of identifying important issues and concerns.

The questionnaire contained ten questions. The first question asked the respondent if they had ever discussed homosexuality in any of their classes. If the answer was yes, they were asked to identify which classes and the context of the discussion; if the answer was no, they were asked why they had not. The second question asked if they had ever revealed their sexuality in any of their classes. If the answer was yes, they were asked what they revealed and what the context of the discussion was; if no, they were asked why they had not. The third question asked if they had ever brought a gay or lesbian person into any of their classes to discuss homosexuality. If yes, they were asked who they brought and what the context of the discussion was; if no, they were asked why they had not. The fourth question asked if they felt it was appropriate for gay and lesbian faculty members to discuss their sexuality in their classes. They were to respond on a scale that had five response choices: never, rarely, sometimes, usually, and always. The fifth question asked what issues they felt needed to be considered when faculty members discussed their sexuality in their classes. Questions six through ten addressed demographic issues.

Of the twenty-seven respondents, twenty were male, six were female, and one individual circled both male and female, claiming that gender is constructed and that the question was inappropriate for this type of questionnaire. Seventeen of the respondents held tenured positions, four held tenure-track positions, five held nontenure-track positions, and one individual was a teaching assistant. The respondents are associated with institutions with an average student population of 10,721 (both mean and median), with a range of 750 to 30,000. The departments represented included Speech, Communications/Theatre/TV-Film, Speech and Theatre Arts, Communication, Classics, English/Speech Communication, Technical Communication, Theatre, English/Physical Education, Social Studies, Women's Studies, Humanities, and Rhetoric and Communication Studies. Twenty-three of the respondents identified themselves as homosexual (including both gay men and lesbians), two as bisexual, one as heterosexual, and one as other. One man indicated he has a homosexual orientation but is behaviorally asexual. Another individual indicated that he is both asexual and multisexual.

The responses to questions one through five were summarized and tallied. All responses will be presented and discussed.

The first research question asked to what degree members of the caucus discuss homosexuality in their classes and what the context of these discussions is. This question was addressed through the first survey question that asked if the respondent had ever discussed homosexuality in any classes. Twenty-four said yes and three said no. The classes most often cited were:

Public Speaking	6
Interpersonal Communication	4
Fundamentals or Principles of Communication	3
Intercultural Communication	3
Debate	3
Group Dynamics	3
Theatre	2
Women's Studies	2
Writing/Research Writing	2

The discussions occurred in a variety of contexts. For the Public Speaking course the contexts included:

- panel discussion topics
- attitude-belief change exercise
- speech topics and discussions
- examples of arguments

For Interpersonal Communication the contexts included:

- differences between heterosexual and homosexual relationships
- language and sublanguage
- consistency needs
- semantics

- gay slang
- sexuality
- responses to a joke about a person with AIDS

For the Fundamentals course the contexts included:

- understanding others
- bias
- prejudice
- responses to remarks made by other students

For Intercultural Communication courses the contexts included:

- communication between dominant and out-of-power groups

For the Debate courses the contexts included:

- debate proposals written by the National Forensic League
- an essay on AIDS to examine logical fallacies
- the proposition: should gay males-lesbians be allowed to adopt children?

For Group Dynamics the context was a discussion topic. For Theatre the context was gay characters in plays. For Women's Studies the contexts were sexuality and lesbianism. For Writing the contexts included examples of arguments or subcultures. For the remaining classes the contexts included:

- counseling
- gay relationships
- gay families
- networks
- invasion of privacy
- discussions of current topics

Clearly, homosexuality is addressed in a variety of classes in relationship to a variety of concepts.

The third survey question also related to the first research question. This question asked if respondents had ever brought a gay or lesbian person into their classes to discuss homosexuality. Six individuals indicated that they had. One person had brought in a Metropolitan Community Church Minister, an AIDS Activist, and a Lesbian/Feminist. Another brought the copresidents of the Gay and Lesbian Club into a Human Communication class because the students had indicated on a survey that they would have a hard time listening to a homosexual. A Theatre instructor brought gay persons into two classes to give insight into gay characters. Another brought speakers into the Cross Cultural Communication class to discuss homosexuals as a culture.

The negative responses to the guest speaker question fell into six categories. The most often cited was related to course content and context. Nine people indicated that homosexuality was not relevant or necessary for their course content. Three individuals said they do not use outside speakers. Two said they never considered it. One said teachers must present two sides to every issue. One said they would only bring in such a speaker if they had done research in gay/lesbian communication. One said there is an abundance of literature on gays and lesbians so assigned readings will expose students to the necessary issues.

The second research question asked, to what extent do members of the caucus reveal their sexuality and what is the context of these discussions? This was addressed through the second survey question. The question asked if the respondents ever revealed their sexuality in any of their classes. If yes, they were asked to indicate what they revealed and the context of the discussion. If no, they were asked why not. Five individuals indicated that they revealed their sexuality in the classroom. One individual indirectly revealed his sexuality. Twenty-one said they have never revealed their sexuality in their classes.

Of the affirmative responses, two indicated that they revealed their lesbianism in women's studies classes. The contexts were homophobia and lesbian contribution to culture. One of these indicated that she revealed her lesbianism by referring to lesbians as "we," not "they." One person revealed her homosexuality after students in the class made reference to "queer bait" jokes. This woman asked the students how many of them knew someone who was gay and about half raised their hands. She told them that they all knew someone who was gay and it was she. One woman who is married commented in class that she thought a particular woman was beautiful and received negative comments on class evaluations months later. Another person revealed his homosexuality during a person-perception exercise in which students talk about their self-image and compare it to how others see them. This person also spoke about his homosexuality in sociology classes.

One response was classified as indirect. This individual indicated that he may reveal it indirectly by his speech patterns or gestures, but he never made an in-class announcement of it. This individual also indicated that he has informed small groups of students outside of the classroom.

The remaining twenty-one had not revealed their sexuality in their classes. The reasons given by these individuals have been classified into eight categories. The two most often cited reasons were that sexuality is personal and not appropriate for class discussion and that the information is not useful in class. Five individuals referred to each of these reasons. Three said they had never been asked. Two indicated each of the following reasons: the department/school is not supportive; a need to maintain emotional distance; interference with learning/listening; and the issue is indirectly known, and so it is not necessary to make the statement. One person said it never seemed necessary.

The third research question asked what issues are important to consider when deciding whether or not to reveal one's sexuality in class. This research question was addressed by survey questions four and five. Survey question four asked if it is appropriate for gay and lesbian faculty members to discuss their sexuality in their classes. The responses are identified below:

Never appropriate	2
Rarely appropriate	9
Sometimes appropriate	12
Usually appropriate	3
Always appropriate	0

Question five asked what issues needed to be considered when discussing one's sexuality in class. These responses were classified into six categories. The most often cited response was relevance. Seventeen respondents said relevance to course context or content was an important consideration. Nine respondents said the motivation or purpose of the disclosure was an important consideration. This category included both personal and academic purposes. Included in the personal purposes were: grandslamming, catharsis, and expected outcome (e.g., role model). Five said job security. Four said the effect on learning. These responses implied that the disclosure might serve as a distraction to learning and listening in the class. Three said teacher credibility. These included such statements as "teachers should use objective rather than subjective reasonings," "arguments may be diluted because of personal prejudices," and "teachers should present equitable presentations of issues." The last category was "other," into which eight responses fell. These included providing support for other gays and lesbians; ways to do it so it is relevant; is sexuality a public or private concern; will the benefits outweigh the disadvantages; level of sophistication of the students; degree of explicitness; will disclosure evoke strong emotional reactions; and relationship with the class.

The purpose of this questionnaire was to identify the issues and concerns that caucus members have about coming out in the classroom. If we know how other members of the caucus approach homosexuality in the classroom, whether they disclose their sexuality in their classes, and what issues they feel are important to be considered when deciding whether or not to disclose, we can make a more informed decision about coming out ourselves. Although the number of respondents in this study probably does not constitute a large enough sample to generalize about the entire caucus, the responses do provide us insight into the issue. The results of the present research suggest homosexuality is discussed in a variety of different speech communication and related classes and in a variety of different concepts/topics. The concepts empathy, bias, prejudice, slang, semantics, sublanguages, and communication between dominant and out-of-power groups are currently illustrated through discussions that relate to homosexuality.

Few of the respondents come out in their classes, but many indicate that it is sometimes appropriate to do so. The methods of disclosure identified by these respondents (including both direct and indirect) may be of use to other teachers.

This study also identifies the many different issues that are sometimes considered by faculty members who are considering coming out in their classes. These include the relevance of such disclosure to course content, the purpose or motivation behind such disclosure, job security, the disclosure's effect on learning, and the effect such disclosure will have on the teacher's credibility. This list of issues may be of help to others who are considering coming out.

This research project was limited by several factors, particularly the sample. The questionnaire was distributed to members of the Caucus on Gay and Lesbian Concerns. There are undoubtedly many gay and lesbian speech communication teachers who are not members of this caucus. These individuals were not reached by this survey. A second limitation concerns the questions themselves. Many of the respondents indicated that the topic of homosexuality was not relevant to their course content but they did not indicate what courses they taught and the questionnaire did not extract that information. This information would have been valuable. Certainly, coming out in a parliamentary procedure class is not as relevant as coming out in an interpersonal communication class.

Overall this study informs us about how some individuals come out in the classroom and considerations they make when doing so. Future research should consider the impact such disclosure might have on learning. This could be examined in a variety of ways. The students of teachers who have come out in the classroom could be interviewed to determine the impact the disclosure had on them. Experimentally this question could be addressed by creating scenarios that described teachers coming out in the classroom and assessed students' reactions and attitudes toward such behavior.

The question of "coming out in the classroom" is an important one for teachers of communication (as evidenced by the interest in the topic among caucus members and the number of respondents in this survey indicating that it is sometimes appropriate in classes). If self-disclosure is an appropriate tool to enhance learning (as suggested by Downs, Javidi, and Nussbaum 1988; Nussbaum and Scott 1979; and Nussbaum and Scott 1980), we need to know how coming out would influence learning. Intuitively, one would expect that honest and open discussions in classes focusing on human communication would be respected, admired, and encouraged. However, the myths and stereotypes that prevail in our society may not permit such respect, admiration, and encouragement. If we determine when and how coming out will be appropriate and effective, we will enhance the learning experience for both teacher and student.

Works Cited

Crew, Louie. 1987. "Before Emancipation: Gay Persons as Viewed by Chairpersons in English." In *The Gay Academic,* 3–48. Palm Springs, Cal.: ETC Publications.

D'Emilio, John. 1987a. "Homosexual Professors Owe It to Their Students to Come Out." *Chronicle of Higher Education,* 28 October: 52.

———. 1987b. "The Issue of Sexual Preference on College Campuses: Retrospect and Prospect." In *Educating Men and Women Together: Coeducation in a Changing World,* edited by C. Lasser, 142–54. Urbana, Ill.: University of Illinois Press.

DeVito, Joseph A. 1981. "Educational Responsibilities to Gay Male and Lesbian Students." In *Gayspeak: Gay Male and Lesbian Communication,* edited by James Chesebro, 197–207. New York: Pilgrim Press.

Downs, Valerie C., Manoochehr Javidi, and Jon F. Nussbaum. 1988. "An Analysis of Teachers' Verbal Communication within the College Classroom: Use of Humor, Self-Disclosure, and Narratives." *Communication Education* 37: 127–41.

Nussbaum, Jon F., and Michael D. Scott. 1979. "The Relationship among Communicator Style, Perceived Self-Disclosure, and Classroom Learning." In *Communication Yearbook* 3, edited by Dan Nimmo, 561–84. New Brunswick, N.J.: Transaction Books.

———. 1980. "Student Learning as a Relational Outcome of Teacher-Student Interaction." In *Communication Yearbook* 4, edited by Dan Nimmo, 533–52. New Brunswick, N.J.: Transaction Books.

20. Ways of Coming Out in the Classroom

Mercilee M. Jenkins

Coming out in the classroom is a striking example of the personal, political, and professional all coming together in one moment. As such it demonstrates the power and importance of studying lesbian, gay, and bisexual communication. Various features of communication are highlighted by different groups and contexts. Being gay, lesbian, or bisexual accentuates the processes of self-disclosure in a unique way. A stigmatized sexual identity creates the interpersonal dilemma of whether or not to come out. That is something heterosexuals don't ever have to think about. And yet it is a dilemma that we all face to some degree and in some way. All of us have aspects of our selves that we fear disclosing to others. Therefore, we have the opportunity to look at self-disclosure from a fresh perspective by studying how gay men, lesbians, and bisexuals manage their sexual identities. But more importantly, by looking at coming out in the classroom we bring the issue home where we can fully explore the ramifications of being authentic and a teacher and queer. In other words, can we practice what we teach?

Ringer's survey of twenty-seven (twenty males, six females and one undeclared) members of the SCA Caucus on Gay and Lesbian Concerns asks the basic questions. Do you discuss lesbian and gay issues in the classroom? Most do. Do you come out in the classroom? Most don't. Those who did not reveal their own sexuality acknowledged that it might be appropriate at times for gay and lesbian faculty members to do so, but they considered their own sexuality personal and not appropriate for class discussion. Thus, they seemed to see the value of coming out in the classroom on a theoretical level, but were not implementing these ideas in their own classes.

The good news is provided by Opffer, who interviewed seventeen faculty members who did come out in a variety of ways. The twelve women and five men she talked with generally had positive experiences coming out in the classroom. In most cases, coming out was directly relevant to the content of their courses. Thus, they felt that coming out increased their effectiveness as teachers, enhanced students' learning, and provided a positive example for all students of what a gay or lesbian person was like. This study demonstrates the variety of ways there are to come out and that how one comes out is very situational or context-bound. The major limitation of this study is that it was done in the San Francisco Bay Area, which is noted for its more liberal attitudes.

Taylor's paper provides the balance regionally and practically. She offers a personal view of what it means to be a lesbian professor at a midwestern Catholic university. She has chosen to acknowledge her views on gay and lesbian literature without always coming out directly. This is as far as she can go and she acknowledges the limitations and ironies of this stance by comparing her position to that of an African-American teacher being asked to teach African-American literature without personally acknowledging his or her heritage. Taylor's paper points up the hard choices and compromises we make everyday and their impact on our teaching effectiveness and our sense of ourselves.

These three papers raise some intriguing questions for future research. The majority of Opffer's informants were full-time or part-time female lecturers, in contrast to Ringer's respondents who were mostly tenured men. This makes me wonder if we are seeing the effects of age, gender, political climate, or political consciousness on their contrasting findings. Are female faculty more self-disclosing than male faculty? How much of a factor is job security in choosing to come out? How has the political consciousness of lesbians and gay men changed over the last ten or twenty years? What about bisexuals? Both studies include them demographically without acknowledging them in the title of the paper or the discussion. This is typical of most studies done on homosexuals.

As a bisexual feminist, I feel we are a group whose existence needs to be acknowledged by the gay and lesbian academic community. We are a very rich source of data on all the topics covered in *Queer Words, Queer Images*. We face coming out in gay and straight contexts with little support and often open hostility accompanied by denial of our identity—"it's just a phase."

My own experience of coming out in the classroom spans the spectrum of experiences represented in these chapters. In my eighteen years of teaching, I have not come out, come out indirectly, and come out directly in a variety of courses related to interpersonal communication, gender and communication, and, most recently, sexual identity and communication. My experiences with coming out directly have been more positive than my experiences coming out indirectly, but then I do teach at San Francisco State University. I have found that when students speculate on my sexual preference their attitudes are more negative toward me. Over the last two years, I have come out permanently because I teach a class in lesbian, gay, and bisexual studies and I wrote an autobiographical play about the twenty-year off-and-on relationship between a gay man and a bisexual woman. In case there had been any doubts, I put it in the program that I was a bisexual feminist who believed in doing things differently. I hope that's what we continue to do: put it in the program, at national conventions, in our curriculum, in our research, and in our classrooms. We go on record as who we are, knowing this is an educational experience for students and teachers that is as important as anything else to be learned at college.

Contributors

JAMES W. CHESEBRO (Ph.D., University of Minnesota, 1972) is Chair and Professor of Communication at Indiana State University.

JAMES DARSEY (Ph.D., University of Wisconsin, 1985) is Assistant Professor of Communication at the Ohio State University.

JOSEPH A. DEVITO (Ph.D., University of Illinois, 1964) is Professor of Communications at Hunter College of the City University of New York.

TIMOTHY EDGAR (Ph.D., Purdue University, 1986) is Assistant Professor of Speech Communication at the University of Maryland.

MARY ANNE FITZPATRICK (Ph.D., Temple University, 1976) is Professor and Director of the Center for Communication Research at the University of Wisconsin.

KAREN A. FOSS (Ph.D., University of Iowa, 1976) is Associate Professor of Communication and Journalism at the University of New Mexico.

KIRK FUOSS (M.A., University of North Carolina, 1985) is Assistant Professor in the Department of Speech and Theatre Arts at St. Lawrence University.

LARRY GROSS (Ph.D., Columbia University, 1968) is Professor of Communication at the Annenberg School at the University of Pennsylvania.

DARLENE M. HANTZIS (Ph.D., Louisiana State University, 1988) is Director of the Women's Studies Program and Assistant Professor in the Communication Department at Indiana State University.

FRED E. JANDT (Ph.D., Bowling Green State University, 1970) is Professor of Communication at California State University, San Bernardino.

MERCILEE M. JENKINS (Ph.D., University of Illinois, 1983) is Professor of Speech and Communication at San Francisco State University.

VALERIE LEHR (Ph.D., University of Maryland, 1990) is Assistant Professor of Government and Coordinator of Gender Studies at St. Lawrence University.

LYNN C. MILLER (Ph.D., University of Southern California, 1980) is Associate Professor of Performance Studies at the University of Texas.

MARGUERITE J. MORITZ (Ph.D., Northwestern University, 1985) is Associate Professor of Journalism and Mass Communication, University of Colorado, Boulder.

FRED L. MYRICK (Ph.D., University of Texas, 1972) is Associate Professor of Marketing at Spring Hill College.

EMILE C. NETZHAMMER (Ph.D., University of Utah, 1987) is Chair and Associate Professor of Communication at Buffalo State College, Buffalo, New York.

ELENIE OPFFER (M.A., San Francisco State University, 1990) is a communication educator and consultant to nonprofit agencies and public schools in the San Francisco Bay Area.

DOROTHY S. PAINTER (Ph.D., Ohio State University, 1978) is Academic Counselor and Staff Assistant in the Colleges of the Arts and Sciences, and is Adjunct Assistant Professor of Women's Studies, both at the Ohio State University.

KAREN PEPER (Ph.D., Wayne State University, 1988) is a writer and psychotherapist in private practice.

NICHOLAS F. RADEL (Ph.D., Indiana University, 1982) is Associate Professor of English at Furman University.

R. JEFFREY RINGER (Ph.D., Ohio University, 1987) is Associate Professor of Speech Communication at St. Cloud State University.

SCOTT A. SHAMP (Ph.D., University of Utah, 1988) is Assistant Professor in the Henry W. Grady College of Journalism and Mass Communication at the University of Georgia.

PAUL SIEGEL (Ph.D., Northwestern University, 1982) is Associate Professor of Communication Arts at Gallaudet University.

JACQUELINE TAYLOR (Ph.D., University of Texas, 1980) is Professor and Chair of the Department of Communication at DePaul University.

JULIA T. WOOD (Ph.D., Penn State University, 1975) is Professor of Speech Communication at the University of North Carolina, Chapel Hill.

Name Index

Subject Index